INSIGHT GUIDE
Venice

APA PUBLICATIONS
Part of the Langenscheidt Publishing Group

ABOUT THIS BOOK

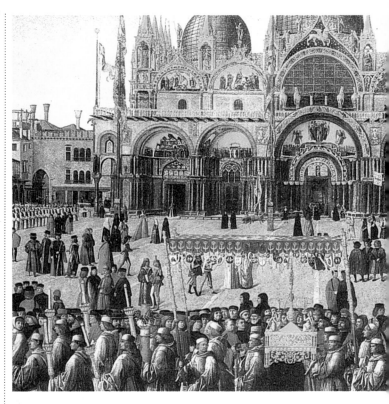

Editorial

Project Editor
Lisa Gerard-Sharp
Managing Editor
Roger Williams
Editorial Director
Brian Bell

Distribution

UK & Ireland
GeoCenter International Ltd
The Viables Centre , Harrow Way
Basingstoke, Hants RG22 4BJ
Fax: (44) 1256-817988

United States
Langenscheidt Publishers, Inc.
46–35 54th Road, Maspeth, NY 11378
Fax: (718) 784-0640

Australia & New Zealand
Hema Maps Pty. Ltd.
24 Allgas Street, Slacks Creek 4127
Brisbane, Australia
Tel: (61) 7 3290 0322
Fax: (61) 7 3290 0478

Worldwide
**APA Publications GmbH & Co.
Verlag KG (Singapore branch)**
38 Joo Koon Road, Singapore 628990
Tel: (65) 865-1600
Fax: (65) 861-6438

Printing

Insight Print Services (Pte) Ltd
38 Joo Koon Road, Singapore 628990
Tel: (65) 865-1600
Fax: (65) 861-6438

©1999 Apa Publications GmbH & Co
Verlag KG (Singapore branch).
All Rights Reserved
First Edition 1988
Third Edition 1998

CONTACTING THE EDITORS
Although every effort is made to
provide accurate information in
this publication, we live in a
fast-changing world and would
appreciate it if readers would
call our attention to any errors or
outdated information that may
occur by writing to us at:
**Insight Guides, P.O. Box 7910,
London SE1 8ZB, England.
Fax: (44 171) 620-1074.
e-mail:
insight@apaguide.demon.co.uk**

This guidebook combines the interests and enthusiasms of two of the world's best known information providers: Insight Guides, whose titles have set the standard for visual travel guides since 1970, and Discovery Channel, the world's premier source of nonfiction television programming.

The editors of Insight Guides provide both practical advice and general understanding about a destination's history, culture and people. Discovery Channel and its Web site, www.discovery.com, help millions of viewers explore their world from the comfort of their own home and also encourage them to explore it firsthand.

How to use this book

This book is carefully structured both to convey an understanding of the city and its culture and to guide readers around its myriad sights and along its enchanting canals.

◆ We introduce the city with a look at the **People** who live there, followed by **History** and **Features** sections which cover the city's glorious past, vivid personalities and great artistic achievements.

◆ The main **Places** section provides a full run-down of all the sights worth seeing. The principal places of interest are co-ordinated by number with full-colour maps.

EXPLORE YOUR WORLD
Discovery
CHANNEL

Bellini's *Procession in San Marco.*

◆ The **Travel Tips** listings section provides a convenient point of reference for information on travelling around the city, hotels, restaurants, shopping and festivals. Information may be located quickly by referring to the back cover flap – and the flaps serve as bookmarks.

◆ **Photographs** are chosen both to illustrate attractions and geography but also to convey the many moods of Venice and the rhythm of life of the people who live there.

The author
Insight Guides have a reputation for calling on a variety of authoritative experts to provide essays and information. This new edition of *Insight Guide: Venice,* however, is an exception. **Lisa Gerard-Sharp**, a gifted writer and major contributor to the series' Italian titles, took on the whole book. Although a writer and broadcaster with a special interest in Italy, she was wary of tackling Venice, a reluctance shared by most Italians. In foreign eyes, Venice may be a dream city we have all visited, if only in our imaginations. However, in Italian eyes, the slithery nature of the lagoon, coupled with the indomitable Venetian spirit, provoke admiration rather than affection. Historically, the Republic was feared, rarely loved or understood.

Like many visitors, Gerard-Sharp was first drawn to the glistening surface of Venice, a carnivalesque stage-set for idle posing and romantic shenanigans. "In time, this deepened into an appreciation of the deliciously sinister nature of Venice in winter, with its undertow of decadence," she says. While living in Italy, she worked as a film editor, documentary-maker and language specialist. Recently, she has reported on the changing Venetian political scene. "However, the joy of Venice is that the city is supple enough to become a landscape of the senses and a cypher for almost anything," she says.

Other contributors
Much of the photography for this new edition was provided by **Bill Wassman**, another regular Insight Guides contributor, and **Ross Miller**, photographer for the *Insight Compact Guide to Venice*. Sub-editing and proof reading was by **Christopher Catling**, picture research was by **Hilary Genin** and the editor was **Roger Williams**.

Map Legend

✈	Airport
🚌	Bus Station
P	Parking
🛈	Tourist Information
✉	Post Office
✝ ♂	Church/Ruins
🛉	Statue/Monument
★	Place of Interest

The main places of interest in the Places section are coordinated by number with a full-colour map (e.g. ❶), and a symbol at the top of every right-hand page tells you where to find the map.

CONTENTS

Maps

Interior plans of
the Doge's Palace and
the Basilica di San Marco
face the inside back cover.

A Central Venice map is
inside the front flap.
A Venice Transport Network
map is inside the back flap.

Introduction

History

Features

**Welcome
to the city**

Travel Tips

Insight on...

Information panels

Places

Art trails

THE VENETIANS

They're often characterised as being cold and contradictory, but the Venetians do have a surprisingly hedonistic streak

The character of the city "is old, conservative and resistant to change. Here in the historic centre we lack the capacity for renewal, or even the numbers required to effect a change." Massimo Cacciari, the philosopher Mayor of Venice, speaks as ponderously and lugubriously as ever.

Certainly, the population is ageing and in decline, with the number of visitors far exceeding the resident population. Yet the elusive Venetian spirit transcends such truisms, defies the simple arithmetic of the doom-mongers, and refuses to be confined by the straight-jacket of tourism.

In a city defined by the sea, there can be no fortress mentality, only ebb and flow. In short, the slippery lagoon-dwellers retain their distinctiveness, or as much of it as they ever had. The decline is in numbers but not in spirit.

The key to understanding

The survival of the local dialect, *Venessian*, forms a strong bond with the Venetians who have moved to the mainland *di là dall'acqua*, "over the water". The dialect, incomprehensible to most visitors, is also a way of keeping in touch with Venetian values and of preserving privacy.

Not that the Venetians wish to be unfriendly to visitors: they are naturally sociable, and happy to share their home with like-minded spirits. Nor do they wish to live in a museum, but in a living city. To this end, they are courteous and tolerant, as befits a cosmopolitan people who have come to terms with the loss of empire. Their philosophical detachment is often mistaken for aloofness, with their calm and sanguine air likened to Anglo-Saxon aplomb.

The outside view of Venetians has not always been so charitable. Indeed, Italians from else-

PRECEDING PAGES: San Giorgio by night; golden palaces of the Grand Canal; the geometry of gondolas; Palazzo Pesaro (Fortuny Museum) during an exhibition.
LEFT: a gondolier's trade is traditionally passed down from father to son. **RIGHT:** chic fashion designer.

where in the country still harbour a vague antipathy to the city, fuelled by historical grievances. The Republic was feared and respected but not much loved. Venetian justice was severe and far-reaching, with cruel deaths reserved for traitors to the Republic. Widespread fear was engendered by the Venetians' skill at spying.

Within Venice, post-boxes for secret denunciations, known as *bocche di leoni* ("lion's mouths") were placed along the walls of public buildings. Yet rivals envied the autonomous approach and the mercantile spirit of a great trading empire, as well as their shrewd mastery of foreign affairs and good governance of the Republic at home.

Today, the lingering image of the Venetians is that of a cool and closed people, cosmopolitan, canny and conservative, but, behind that, concealing a sinister heart. Yet there is a lighter side to the Venetians: a satirical, playful nature sustained by pageantry, carnivals and masked balls. The Venetians were always prone to social ostentation, lavish expenditure and a love of finery. This hedonistic reputation was acquired in the 18th-century during a period of decadence. In theory, strict sumptuary laws and dress codes restricted the use of luxury fabrics. Yet the greater the decline, the sharper the sense of fun. This risqué, pleasure-seeking image was matched by morals which were every bit as slippery and mercurial as the lagoon itself.

City of Casanova and illicit liaisons

From medieval times onwards, Venice was famed for its courtesans and enjoyed a risqué image that persists to the present. Situated midway between seductiveness and salaciousness, Venice still relishes its reputation as a place for mistresses and illicit assignations – even if yesterday's unofficial contract of convenience is now swathed in frothy, commercial romance. In the 15th century, prostitution in the Frezzeria quarter near San Marco was officially sanctioned. This was supposedly to help preserve the honour of Venetian ladies. Brothels also flourished in the banking district of the Rialto, the commercial hub of the Republic, which was soon to become equally famous for its fleshpots. A 16th-century survey noted that the city boasted 3,000 noblewomen but over 11,000 prostitutes. Yet in a city graced by gondolas,

dreamy mists and Casanova, seduction was raised to a fine art.

A well-deserved reputation for pleasure-seeking should not obscure the Venetians' more refined tastes. Their pronounced aesthetic sense is evident in both art and architecture. In painting, there is a penchant for colour and sensuality, and a poetic sensibility, rather than for more rational, monumental forms. As for architecture, while the Florentine *palazzo* is austere and unadorned, the Venetian equivalent is opulent, ostentatious, and decorative almost to the point of gaudiness. In music, too, the population is discerning, with a love of composition predat-

ing Monteverdi (1567–1643), Vivaldi (1678–1741) and the foundation of the city's first opera house (1637).

The Venetians are also noted for their curiosity and spirit of intellectual enquiry, a disposition that led to great empire-building. Yet this lofty outlook is tempered by a profound indifference to matters beyond the lagoon. It is a characteristic personified by Marco Polo, the legendary explorer, who remained a home-town boy: "Every time I describe a city, I am saying something about Venice." If this sounds contradictory, bear in mind the words of writer J.G. Links: "Consistency is not a virtue held very high by Venetians."

Labyrinthine Venice

Like Marco Polo, the Venetians are victims of classic Italian *campanilismo*, a firm attachment to their roots. They tend to travel widely but, wherever they go, nostalgia follows. This can partly be explained by the physical uniqueness of Venice: the mercurial climate, the shimmering light, the slow pace of life, and the watery chimera of the city are reasons enough for loving the place. Only in the *calli* and *campi* of Venice, far from the traffic's roar, can Venetians

distinct neighbourhoods dotted with numerous parishes. Every parish has its main church, *campo* (square), bar and *alimentari* (food shop) where you can often get *vino sfuso* (draught wine). Although the distinctiveness of individual parishes is being eroded, certain districts retain a clear character. Cannaregio, in particular, is the last bastion for working-class Venetians who have not moved to the mainland. As in the remoter parts of Castello, the washing-bedecked alleys are home to children and cats. Around the

be themselves, and fully express their open, sociable nature.

Venice is a labyrinth, even with a map. A Venetian, when asked the way, says: "*sempre diritto, cinque minuti*" (straight ahead, five minutes), but "straight ahead" is as the crow flies and a Venetian can get a long way in five minutes by using all the short cuts (*andar per le sconte*). In the words of J.G. Links: "If he does not answer *sempre diritto,* he is not a Venetian and his directions must be treated with caution".

The city is divided into six *sestieri* (districts),

LEFT: sweet dreams in San Cassiano parish.
ABOVE: Venice rivals Paris as a honeymoon destination.

Rialto lies a surprisingly humble slice of Venetian life, with squalid alleys, but also a popular market, one of the few places where you will only hear Italian or the guttural sing-song of Venetian dialect. But throughout Venice, the *campo* or *campiello* (tiny square) is at the heart of community life. Further away from San Marco, Sunday is still spent streaming from church to a *trattoria* for lunch.

One foot in the grave

Venetians tend to be elderly: there are almost three times as many pensioners as children under fourteen. Churches such as San Zulian are under threat of closure, with an average of 30 parishioners who attend Mass, all elderly. By contrast, Venice's 4,000 children seem to lead a charmed life, despite the lack of facilities. Although they play in the Giardini Pubblici, the main park, most prefer their home *campo*, the parish square. Although teenagers fare less well, there is a vibrant university quarter around Ca' Foscari in Dorsoduro. To outsiders, the quirkiness of studious Venice, and especially working Venice, holds a rarified, undeniable charm.

Working on water

"Pronti!" cries the garbage man *(spazzin)* in the early morning. On collection day, he goes call-ing and whistling from door to door; the heaped sacks he leaves on the canal bank are carried away by ship to be burnt. During high water, the same team sees to the laying of duck-boards over key routes, but major tidal flooding means the suspension of refuse collection as the boats cannot pass under bridges.

"Posta!" shouts the mailman. *"Siora Maria na letera de so fio."* (Signora Maria, a letter from your son). An upstairs window opens, Signora Maria lets down a basket on a string and pulls it up with her letter. This saves a trip up and down the stairs; there are few lifts in the tall thin *palazzi* of Venice.

NOBLESSE OBLIGE

The cosmopolitan socialite Princess Ira von Fursten-berg was brought up in Venice and has a home there still (her mother was a member of the Agnelli dynasty, still Italy's leading entrepreneurial firm). As a child growing up in the 1940s, Ira led a magical existence, roaming through the San Marco *sestiere* (district) on foot or by boat. "I knew every corner and *calle* (alley) ... every day was an enchantment."

As a pampered princess, Ira lived with her family and servants in the *piano nobile* (aristocratic apartments) of the Palazzo Mocenigo on the Grand Canal. This was a privileged yet ritualised Venice of convent school, Sunday finery, dancing classes and amateur dramat-ics. She remembers performing impromptu plays for the servants while her parents attended a première at La Fenice opera house or dined in glittering style else-where on the Grand Canal.

On Sunday, Ira accompanied her parents to Mass in San Marco, after which her elders set off to sip martinis at the celebrated Harry's Bar while she indulged in romantic longings. Today Ira considers St Mark's Square to have become tarnished by 20th-century mass tourism, and the city "too fragile and too small" to cope with the teeming hordes of visitors. Yet Venice remains for her "a frozen expression of beauty", as well as being her enchanted childhood playground.

Indispensable *carretti,* or push carts, trundle through the alleyways. *"Attenzione!"* (Look out!) is the warning cry of the delivery boys who navigate the crowded streets. The Venetians scatter at once, while tourists remain stubbornly standing in the way and are often run over. It is an amusing sight to see the delivery boys carrying stacks of lighter loads on their backs, or anything from flower pots to leaning towers of pizzas balanced on their heads. Many Venetians have their own push-carts and, since water taxis are costly, the locals push the *carretto* to the family car in its garage and bring home trunks and suitcases this way.

In practice, few boats keep to the speed limit – hence the controversy over the dangerous wash from motor boats. The *gondolieri* often demonstrate vociferously in front of the city hall, but so far in vain.

In Venetian dialect, gondoliers are known as *"Papa"*, which is what one shouts when wanting to cross the Grand Canal. When used simply as a crossing service, this comfortable and cheap gondola ferry is called a *traghetto.* Venetians stand during short trips but anyone with a poor sense of balance is advised to sit down. When the gondolier has pleasant passengers and the sirocco hasn't blown him into a bad mood,

Vaporetti and gondolas

Venetians are well-served by the *vaporetti,* with line 1 the work-horse of water-buses, the slowest and most popular since it stops at every mooring place on the Grand Canal. Only the police, fire and ambulance services are allowed to break the speed limit of 5 miles an hour (8 kph). In emergencies, the water ambulance speeds along with blue lights flashing, rocking any passing gondola in its wake. (The sick are transported in carrying chairs since there are no stretchers.)

LEFT: catering for every taste.
ABOVE: studying the city's architecture.

he may even sing a spontaneous burst of *"La biondina in gondoeta"*.

The sirocco is a warm, humid wind that oppresses everyone in summer. Women keep cool with the aid of an elegant fan, while men flap rolled up newspapers. When stormy sirocco winds blow in winter, the high-water siren sounds, provoking a chain reaction. Shop-keepers pile their wares on higher shelves; walkers quickly don gumboots; narrow duck-boards are put down in the main alleys and campi. Off these safe routes, non-Venetians are clearly distinguished by their inability to divine the different levels of pavements, to comical effect, by turn sinking leadenly into deep water and squelching like a duck on dry land. Anybody who can do so makes for home. Normally no-one lives on the ground floor in Venice – otherwise it would mean taking a gondola to reach the bedroom during high water (*acqua alta*).

The Venetian philosophy

Walking slowly echoes the languid pace of city life; such is the Venetian philosophy. There is always time to greet friends, gossip, choose between the grand Caffè Florian and a cosy neighbourhood bar. Venetians love stretching out a social greeting into a leisurely chat. Friends can't lose touch in Venice; you hear the

talk of the town every day. Standing at a bar counter, the locals sip an *ombretta*, a small glass of wine, and choose a *ciccheto*, a savoury snack of meat balls, baby squid, cheese or *crostini* (toasted rounds of bread spread with liver paste, capers and anchovies). A Venetian has no post-BSE qualms about tucking into *nervetti*, ox nerves boiled in onions.

Window-shopping

Affluent Venetians may browse in the glittering Mercerie, the main shopping street since the Middle Ages. But the designer silks, fine linens and exclusive jewellery shops around Piazza San Marco are beyond the purse of many Venetians. Instead, ordinary shoppers head for the humdrum Lista di Spagna, near the station, for their household supplies, or to La Strada Nuova, towards the Rialto. Locals love shopping at the Erberie, the exuberant morning fruit and vegetable market at the Rialto, and at the adjoining Pescheria, the fish market which is situated by the Grand Canal.

A stranger watching this scene might dismiss Venice as provincial. Far from it: Venice is a cosmopolitan city where virtues and vices are visible for all to see. Nothing is hidden; one strolls along, steps onto the stage to see and be seen, just for the fun of it. Apart from summer strollers, the city is relatively quiet at night. High rents have forced many ordinary Venetians to abandon the city at nightfall, returning to their homes on Mestre. Venice is then left to the tourists (and those servicing the tourist industry) as well as to wealthier Venetians or working-class residents committed to the city. Nightlife is suitably restrained, restricted to cafés, concerts and a few clubs.

A Venetian élite may still meet to strains of Vivaldi at the fireside of a freshly gilded salon. However, most Venetians prefer a prosaic stroll and a meal out, knowing that a "prosaic" stroll around the canal sides can encompass more magic and drama than is available in any of the city's formal theatres.

The cultural choice

However, Venetian culture-vultures are well catered for. The Goldoni Theatre stages plays by the eponymous playwright (1707–93), author of delightful comedies in Venetian dialect. Classical concerts are held in St Mark's as well as in Santo Stefano, San Rocco and La Pietà, once Vivaldi's home church. Since the recent destruction of La Fenice, the glorious opera house has been ignominiously relocated to the Palafenice, a tented affair on the island of Tronchetto, also the site of the city car park. Apart from the opera season, the Film Festival, the Biennale and Carnival are the highlights of the Venetian social calendar.

Venetian youngsters tend to congregate at fashionable *gelaterie* (ice-cream parlours) and *pizzerie*. One popular meeting-place is the bronze monument to Carlo Goldoni on Campo San Bartolomeo near the Rialto. Every evening talkative students stream along in jeans and trainers; their demands for discotheques and sports centres fall on deaf ears. Goldoni, on his pedestal, allows himself a sardonic smile in recognition of these sparky descendants of his Harlequins and Columbines.

On summer weekends, adventurous students may head for the clubs at Jesolo, the garish coastal resort which lies just to the south of Venice. Gamblers, on the other hand, will flock to the Casino, sited at the Lido in summer and in the Palazzo Vendramin-Calergi, on the Grand Canal, in winter.

Water playground

At the first hint of summer, Venetian nobles fled the city for the Palladian villas of the Brenta Canal, a practice that still prevails on a small scale. Today's Venetians are vigorous outdoors folk, on the water in summer and on the ski slopes in winter. Thanks to its unique location, Venice has much to offer. The seaside resort on the city's doorstep is the Lido, that elegant bathing beach which becomes a second home to Venetians in summer. On sweltering Sundays, the resort's manicured beaches are packed and the brash amusement arcades overflowing. Active youngsters cycle along the Lido's Lungomare (Esplanade), from the quays on the lagoon to the Adriatic sea walls. Known as the lagoon run, it is probably the most poetic ride in the world.

The lagoons provide contemplation for fishermen and bird-watchers in all seasons. Venetian families also enjoy leisurely days out on terra firma: the lovely hills near Asolo or Conegliano are inviting spots for a stroll to see villas or visit rustic wine taverns. Winter means mountains and the prospect of good skiing: the Dolomites are only an hour away by car and are a popular destination for the traditional New Year's *settimana bianca* ("white week"), a short skiing break. Indeed, many Venetians keep a winter place in Cortina d'Ampezzo, Italy's top ski resort.

A true Venetian family owns a car and a boat. Since the "green revolution", however, citizens have declared war on motorboats (*motoscafi*): their choppy wake, noise and smell should be eliminated. Rowing and sailing regattas are all the rage nowadays. One has to learn to row standing up, so beginners often fall into the water. (However, a course with Bucintoro or Querini, the famous rowing clubs, soon solves the problem.)

The water city's festivals radiate the pomp of days gone by. However, even minor festivals, such as the Cat Festival, reveal aspects of the Venetian character. The spotlight is not on pampered pure-breds but on "*il gatto di laguna*" the alley cat. During the event, Micio and Micia, as they are called, are given extra rations and, bizarrely, a round of applause. The Venetians are great cat-lovers: over 200,000 cats roam free, at least two per person. Surviving on restaurant scraps, or regularly fed by old

women, the cats are so content that they don't hunt rats any more.

Cool, independent Venetians, though reluctant to be compared with alley cats, are nothing if not survivors. Mayor Cacciari is sanguine about the future of his fellow-citizens and beloved city: "If Venice has any vitality left, it will seize the moment. If it is dead in human terms, it will die. After all, Babylon, Alexandria and Rome have all died." While at odds with the Venetians' positive approach to life, this view can be taken to represent the city's classic philosophical detachment. As such, the Mayor shows himself to be a contradictory character, and that is the mark of a true Venetian. ❑

LEFT: Venetians, both postmen and poseurs.
RIGHT: city children are spoilt for choice.

Decisive Dates

AD 337 First record of a lagoon settlement.
453: Barbarian invasions cause flight to the lagoon.
421: Legendary foundation of Venice on 25 March, conveniently the Feast Day of St Mark.
452: Attila the Hun plunders the Veneto.
453: Aquilea sacked by Attila, prompting an exodus of refugees towards Venetian lagoon.
568: Mass migrations from the mainland to Venice.
639: Island of Torcello colonised and cathedral founded.

1000: Venice controls the Adriatic coast. The Marriage to the Sea ceremony is inaugurated in honour of Doge Pietro Orseolo II's defeat of Dalmatian pirates in the Adriatic.
1096-9: Venice joins the Crusades, providing ships and supplies for the First Crusade to liberate the Holy Land.
1104: The foundation of the Arsenale.
1128: First street lighting in Venice.
1171: The six districts *(sestieri)* founded.
1173: First Rialto Bridge begun.
1202–4: The Fourth Crusade; the Sack of Constantinople and the Venetian conquest of Byzantium provides the springboard for the

697: According to Venetian legend, the election of Paoluccio Anafesta, the first Doge.
726: Election of Orso Ipato, the first recorded Doge, who rules the lagoon from the now-vanished colony of Heraclea.
800: Charlemagne crowned Holy Roman Emperor.
814: The population moves to *Rivo Alto* (Rialto), a more hospitable and easily defended island. Venetian coins first minted. Work begins on the first Doge's Palace.
828: Theft of St Mark's body, removed from Alexandria to Venice.
834: First Basilica San Marco completed.
840: Tacit independence from Byzantium.

growth of the Venetian empire.
1200–70: Venice emerges as a world power.
1271–95: Marco Polo's epic journeys to China.
1284: Gold ducats first minted in Venice.
1297: Establishment of a patrician autocracy.
1348–9: Plague kills half the population.
1309: Work begins on present Doge's Palace.
1310: Council of Ten established as a check on individual power and to monitor security.
1325: The names of Venetian noble families first inscribed in the *Libro d'Oro*, the Golden Book, or aristocratic register.
1355: Doge Faliero (Falier) is beheaded for treason against the Venetian Republic.
1373: A Jewish community first established.

1379–80: War of Chioggia and decisive defeat of the Genoese.

1403–5: Acquisition of Belluno, Padua, Verona.

1453: Constantinople falls to Turks; zenith of Venetian empire: Treviso, Bergamo, Ravenna, Friuli, Udine and Istria are conquered.

1454: Acquisition of Treviso, Friuli, Bergamo, Ravenna.

1457: The powerful Doge Foscari deposed.

1489: Cyprus ceded to Venice by Queen Caterina Cornaro (Corner).

1506: Names of ruling families are fixed in the Golden Book: no new entries allowed.

1508: League of Cambrai unites Europe against Venice. Titian's *Assumption* hung in the Frari church, Venice. Birth of Palladio, architect from the Veneto.

1516: Jews confined to the Venetian Ghetto.

1519: Birth of Tintoretto, the Venetian Mannerist painter.

1528: Birth of the painter Paolo Veronese.

1570: Loss of Cyprus to the Turks.

1571: Battle of Lepanto, decisive naval victory against the Turks.

1577: Palladio designs Il Redentore (The Redeemer) church.

1567: Birth of the composer Monteverdi.

1580: Birth of the Baroque architect Longhena.

1630: Venice again struck by the plague.

1669: Loss of Crete to Turks, last major Venetian colony.

1693: Birth of Tiepolo, the Rococo artist.

1703: Vivaldi made musical director, La Pietà.

1708: A severe winter freezes the lagoon allowing Venetians to walk to the mainland.

1718: Venice surrenders Morea (Peloponnese) to the Turks signalling the loss of the Venetian maritime empire; Venice left with the Ionian islands and the Dalmatian coast.

1720: The opening of Florian's café.

1752: Completion of the sea walls.

1755: Casanova imprisoned in Doge's Palace.

1757: Canova, the neo-classical sculptor, born.

1790: Opening of La Fenice opera house.

1797: Fall of the 1,000-year-old Venetian Republic. Doge Lodovico Manin abdicates. Napoleon grants Venice and its territories to Austria in return for Lombardy.

1800: Papal conclave in Venice to elect Pope.

1805–14: Venice under Napoleonic rule.

1815–66: Venice ceded to Austria under the terms of the Congress of Vienna; Austrian occupation.

1846: Venice joined to mainland by railway causeway.

1848: Failed Venetian uprising against the Austrians.

1861: Vittorio Emanuele crowned King of Italy.

1866: Venice annexed to Kingdom of Italy.

1885: First Biennale art exhibition.

1902: Campanile (belltower) in Piazza San Marco collapses.

1926: Porto Marghera industrial zone built.

1931: Road causeway built to the mainland.

1932: First Venice Film Festival.

1945: British liberate city from Nazi forces.

1960: Construction of Marco Polo airport.

1966: Worst flood in Venetian history.

1979: Venice Carnival revived.

1985: Centenary of Biennale art exhibition.

1988: First stage of flood barrier complete.

1995: Gianni de Michelis, former city mayor and foreign minister, imprisoned for corruption.

1996: Burning down of La Fenice. The worst floods and *acqua alta* (high tides) since 1966.

1997: Separatists briefly capture St Mark's belltower.

1997–2000: Planned rebuilding of La Fenice.

PRECEDING PAGE: the Rialto district in the 17th century.
LEFT: the lion of St Mark, symbol of Venice.
RIGHT: Harlequin, from the *commedia dell'arte*.

CITY IN THE LAGOON

It had an unpromising start, founded by refugees among stagnant marshes on the shores of the Adriatic. Yet Venice became the most powerful city in the west

Venice as a city "was a foundling, floating upon the waters like Moses in a basket among the bulrushes. It was therefore obliged to be inventive, to steal and to improvise." Writer Mary McCarthy sets the scene for the city's mythic status. The legendary foundation of Venice was in AD 421, on 25 March, a

"Who in their senses would build more than a fishing hut on the malarial, malodorous shoals and sandbanks of the Venetian lagoon?" The historian John Julius Norwich answers his own question: "Those who had no choice." The Barbarians swept through Italy in the 5th and 6th centuries, leaving a trail of devastation. The

date conveniently coinciding with the feast of the city's patron saint, St Mark. Venice readily spun itself a romantic tapestry that has hoodwinked many a historian. Unlike its mainland rivals, Venice had been born free and Christian but without a golden Roman past. To make amends, the city claimed descent from ancient Troy and cultivated the mystique of Byzantium, its one and only master. Early settlers to Venice brought Roman souvenirs salvaged from their ruined homes on the mainland. This city without antiquity also looked east for its aesthetic identity, with Constantinople (modern Istanbul) the unwitting provider of purloined memorials to a fabricated golden age.

refugees, driven from the remnants of a glorious Roman past, found themselves washed up on these inhospitable islands.

Escape from Atilla the Hun

Conventional wisdom has it that Venice was founded by migrants from the mainland fleeing to safety in the lagoon. However, it is conceivable the Lagoon was already home to a fishing community. The first exodus was prompted by the arrival of Attila the Hun bearing down on northern Italy. Mass migrations began in 568 after a wave of Goths swept through the Veneto, terrorising the populations of Padua, Altino and Aquileia. The fugitives fled to the marshy coast

HOW THE BUILDING BEGAN

The city is not built on the water but in the water, a subtle distinction. In fact, Venice is not built on piles and stakes but on mud flats and tiny sand banks divided by canals and swept by the ebb and flow of tides. The instability of the terrain led the Venetians to devise a complex system that would give the buildings lightness and elasticity without sacrificing stability. The construction methods were ingenious and have lasted a millennium in some cases. The piling system was highly effective, with closely packed piles not rotting in the waterlogged soil. (The absence of free oxygen prevented the presence of microbes and therefore decay.)

Even so, the early masons could not have foreseen the present problems: building supports weakened by corrosion and by the wash of powerful boats, and the deepening of canals. Likewise, the leaning belltowers often do so because of the compaction of the subsoil.

To make marshy pockets suitable as building land, the early city government permitted the dumping of ballast and rafts of firewood; this caused silting and the formation of mud banks. However, the instability of the terrain meant that the city needed to rest on deep foundations. The subsoil is alternately hard and soft, with layers of soft mud, firm clay, springy peat, sandy clay and watery sand, with *caranto* (compressed clay and sand) at the bottom of the lagoon. To cope with this instability, buildings were supported by a forest of timber piles (*pali*) driven deep into the subsoil. The oak piles came from the Lido and were later supplemented by oak, larch and pine from the Alps and Dalmatia (modern-day Croatia), a Venetian territory. Working from the outside in, concentric circles of piles were driven through the unstable lagoon floor to the bedrock of compacted clay. The number and thickness of the piles depended on the weight of the building: La Salute church, for instance, is supported by over a million piles.

The piles provided the base for a platform of horizontal beams, the *zatterone*, a raft-like structure made of larchwood, cemented in place with a mixture of stone and brick. The floor was then reinforced with Istrian stone; this marble-like stone, resistant to salt erosion, helped create damp-proof foundations. Oak beams and boards were placed on top, often finished by a traditional light marble floor.

and lagoon islands, settling in Chioggia, Malamocco, Torcello, Murano and Burano. The island of Torcello was colonised in 639 AD and remained the leading Venetian lagoon city, site of a magnificent cathedral, until the population's definitive move to the Rialto in 814 AD.

As a vassal of Byzantium, the Eastern Roman Empire, Torcello acted as an effective trading post with Constantinople. Unlike many mainland cities, Venice was never feudal but born mercantile. A keen commercial spirit was bolstered by protectionism and monopolies. The shortage of land and the exposed position in the lagoon turned the island dwellers into skilful

traders. The medium of exchange was salt and salted fish, called "edible money" by the chronicler Cassiodorus. Yet even in the 8th century Venetian traders visited the Lombard capital of Pavia laden down with velvets and silks, peacock feathers and prized furs.

Astride two worlds

Venice bordered two worlds: the Byzantine and Moslem East and the Latin-Germanic West. As

LEFT: early settlements in the lagoon, a 16th-century drawing by Sabbadino.
ABOVE: arrival of the relics of St Mark, a 13th-century mosaic on the west facade of Basilica di San Marco.

the gateway to the East, the city traded Levantine incense, silks and spices for northern staples, including salt and wheat. Venice was helped by its command of the river mouths leading into northern Italy. The city conveniently lay at the crossing of rival trading routes: the Byzantine sway over Mediterranean trade was challenged by Moslem commercial routes, a consequence of the Arab conquest of Syria, North Africa and Spain. By the 9th century, slaves were the mainstay of Venetian trade, along with salt, fish and timber. Slaves were mainly Slavs but Greek Orthodox and Anglo-Saxon captives were not unknown.

When the population moved to the relative safety of the Rivo Alto (literally the "high bank", the site of today's Rialto markets), the Venice we know today was born. The election of the first Doge in 726 AD paved the way for the oligarchy that founded Venice's fortune. Work on the Doge's first fortress-palace commenced in 814 AD, laying the foundations for the present palace. The institution of the Doge was a marker in Venetian independence, a confident identity crowned by the patronage of St Mark. Venice was only nominally under Byzantine rule but its independence was tacitly acknowledged in 840 AD when the city signed a treaty with the Holy Roman Emperor without seeking permission from Constantinople.

The mystique of St Mark

The theft of St Mark's relics from Alexandria in 828 AD showed the Venetian gift for improvisation and myth-making: the deed granted the city instant status, mystique and the presumed protection of St Mark. The Venetian triumph was marked by the decision to build St Mark's Basilica the following year. Under the protection of St Mark, Venice could equate material gain with spiritual riches. Trade was turned into a means of glorifying the fledgling city; Christian duty later sanctioned the Crusades against the infidels (and entitled the victors to spoils). If Venice enjoyed a reputation as a virtuous state, it was a reflection of its perceived stability rather than its morals. Yet this continuity was the product of a singular government.

LEFT: the Arsenal in an old engraving.
RIGHT: "The Sack of Byzantium" by Tintoretto.

THE LION OF SAINT MARK

On feast days, the banner of the winged lion flies before St Mark's Basilica. It represents St Mark, the symbol of Venice and the spirit of the city. Venice proudly proclaimed itself the Republic of St Mark; coins were minted bearing his image; his patronage transformed these lagoon-dwellers into a chosen people, gave wings to their aspirations and achievements. The inventive Venetians turned the Byzantine chimera into the winged lion, while the emperor became a saint. To this day, the Venetians hold their patron saint in high esteem.

The mummified body of the city's patron saint was stolen from Alexandria, cunningly hidden in a consignment of pork which, being an abomination to Muslims was unlikely to be searched. Once safely in Venice, the relics were destined for display in a new basilica, built in honour of the saint. For 700 years, the relics remained in the crypt, but in 1811 they were moved to rest under the high altar.

St Mark's Basilica can still be read as a tribute to the saint, with sacred lions present on the mosaics and portals of the facade; sometimes the lion bears an open Gospel with the legend *Pax tibi Marce* (Peace be with you, Mark). A walk through Venice reveals a veritable safari park, with lions watching over most major monuments.

By AD 1000, Venice controlled the Adriatic coast, having eliminated piracy, although piracy still existed on the Aegean and Ionian seas. The conquest of Dalmatia (Croatia) was achieved under the leadership of Doge Pietro Orseolo (991–1009). His diplomatic skills were even greater than his military prowess, and he successfully juggled the powers of East and West. Ready supplies of timber, iron and hemp provided a stimulus to the Venetian ship-building industry. The Venetians were soon the leading ship operators in the Mediterranean. Nonetheless, from the 11th century Venice faced naval challenges from the merchant republics of Pisa and Genoa. The Venetians defeated the Pisans off Rhodes in 1099, signalling the despatch of a former maritime power. From then onwards, the main threat was posed by the Genoese and the Turks.

Spoils from the crusades

The Crusades were launched by Pope Urban II in 1095 to protect Byzantium and free the Holy Land. Venice eagerly participated, shamelessly exploiting both sides. Not only did the Venetian fleet returned laden with booty in 1100, but the episode acted as a spur to their maritime ambitions. Venice extended its foothold in the

BOOTY FROM BYZANTIUM

As the chief link between Byzantium and Western Europe, Venice received Byzantine art in a more concentrated form. The Treasury of St Mark's contains a number of works that reached Venice from Byzantium, especially after the Sack of Constantinople in 1204. The mosaics, brought back as booty were incorporated into great buildings or copied by local Greek masters. The mosaics are symbolic rather than realistic, studded with archaic allusions and bathed in radiant colours. The mosaics represent a fusion of the decorative and the descriptive. Close to the scenes are legible, but from afar the pattern predominates, with courtly refinement and idealised figures blending into a tapestry of gold.

The Byzantine sensibility also informed Venetian architecture and local art forms well into the Renaissance. As the art critic John Steer writes: "Bellini's late works bring Venetian painting back to its central concerns: colour, texture and surface pattern. These things are part of the Venetian tradition, going back to the mosaics and enamels in San Marco, where each *tessera* (tile) is at the same time as beautiful as a material in itself, part of a total surface pattern, and a fragment of the image for which it stands".

Aegean, Syria and the Black Sea. In 1122 the Venetians defeated the Egyptian fleet that was besieging Jaffa and then went on to sack Byzantine ports in the Aegean and the Adriatic. Trade in the Levant increased with ships sailing to Haifa, Jaffa and Tyre.

The Fourth Crusade (1201–4) marked a turning point in Venetian history, the spur to their formation of a maritime empire, commander of the Adriatic and eastern Mediterranean. During the Crusades, the Venetians traded with both sides as well as profiting from the transport of pilgrims; since the Venetians supplied the fleet, pilgrims who failed to pay were sold as slaves.

The Crusades reached a climax in the Sack of Constantinople, led by the blind but charismatic 90-year-old Doge Enrico Dandolo. A French chronicler was duly impressed: "The Doge was standing armed at the bow of his galley and had before him the banner of St Mark. He called out to his sailors to put him ashore quickly or he would do justice to their bodies". The Venetians were skilled at siege operations and returned in 1204 for a successful assault on a city that, as the seat of the Byzantine Eastern Empire, had never fallen. Venice was rewarded with the lion's share of the new Latin empire.

The Venetian victory is regarded as a shameful episode, with the invaders charged with wanton destruction and desecration as well as the deposing of the Greek Emperor. In addition to receiving three-eighths of the empire, vital trading ports, Constantinople's arsenal and docks, the Venetians looted the city. Booty, now in St Mark's, included the rearing Roman horses from the stadium in Constantinople and the Madonna Nicopeia, a sacred icon which acted as the Byzantine battle standard. The orgy of looting enriched Venice but did irreparable harm to East-West relations. Yet although the Venetians were responsible for deposing the Greeks, they saw themselves not as usurpers but as the true heirs of Constantine, the Catholic restorers of the rightful empire.

The Sea State

The emergence of the Sea State (*stato da mar*) showed that dominion of the seas was paramount to Venetian policy. However, mainland conquests in Padua, Treviso and Ferrara were also welcome. The period from 1260 until 1380 reflected the transition from Byzantine rule to the Venetian Imperial age. With Genoese help, the deposed Byzantine emperors recovered Constantinople in 1261 and Venice lost a number of privileges. However, underlying the conflict was the Venetians' great rivalry with the Genoese, which continued into the next century.

The 1379–80 War of Chioggia was sparked by the Venetian claim to control the Dardanelles. In response, the Genoese mounted a naval blockade at Chioggia. The Genoese penetrated the Lagoon, but they failed to challenge the city of Venice, a waterbound maze without gates, walls or escape routes. The result was a decisive Venetian victory and the once-great naval power of Genoa no longer posed a threat.

Much more troubling was the devastation caused by the Black Death. The plague of 1348 reached Venice from the East and decimated the populous city by three-fifths. In the 14th century, Venice boasted 160,000 inhabitants at a time when a city of 20,000 was considered large; west of Italy, only Paris approached Venice, with a population of 100,000. It took the city almost 200 years to return to the same size. However, for all the tribulations of this period, it also marked the emergence of the Republic's unique system of government. ❑

Marco Polo

In the West, Marco Polo is lauded as the first famous explorer, while in China he has cult status, posthumously celebrated as the first "friend of China". Modern scholars are divided as to whether Marco Polo's epic journeys into Asia are wondrous fact or glorious fabrication. Some critics feel that he strayed no further than Persia, although his uncles, Niccolo and Maffei, went into Asia. Supporters prefer to see Polo as the first explorer and chronicler of China, a talented merchant and administrator who found favour with Kublai Khan.

Like many Venetian merchant families, the Polo clan maintained trading houses abroad, at Constantinople and in the Crimea. The family home was in Cannaregio in Venice, where the atmospheric courtyard, Corte del Milion, still stands. Tradition has it that there were two journeys, the first in 1265 ending in the East, and the second in 1271–95, which centred on an extended stay in China. On the first voyage, Niccolo and Maffei Polo traded a cargo of Venetian goods in Constantinople before sailing on to the Black Sea. There, merchandise was bartered for Russian and Turkish goods before the final thrust into the East. This journey is accepted by most historians, but the second, involving Marco Polo and his uncles, is more controversial. This was essentially an overland expedition into the heart of China. After a three-year journey through Baghdad, Persia and central Asia, they reached Peking in 1275. There Marco Polo claimed to have met Kublai Khan, the Mongol Emperor, and to have been appointed governor of the Yangzhou region.

There have been attempts to debunk the Marco Polo story, but some facts are beyond dispute. He was imprisoned in 1298 by the Genoese, and he recounted his adventures to a fellow-prisoner, with whom he recorded his exploits in *Il Milione*, known as *The Travels of Marco Polo*. Yet there are no references to him in Chinese records and we have scant information on his linguistic skills. Polo did not mention the cruel custom of foot-binding, the Great Wall of China escaped his attention and he failed to notice tea ceremonies despite visiting such tea-growing centres as Hangzhou and Fujian.

The case for Marco Polo rests on the fact that he was a merchant, not an historian, primarily interested in the East for the purposes of trade. His defenders argue that women with bound feet would be closeted at home; that he probably had interpreters; and if Chinese records fail to mention the Venetian, he was mere wallpaper in the splendid court of Kublai, the Great Mongol Khan at Shangdu.

Polo chronicled everything from the system of taxation and administration to the abundance of cotton and silk, sugar, spices and especially pepper. A convincing detail was the fabulous amount of pepper used in a single day. Chinese novelties Polo recorded include the practice of coal mining and the Chinese skill at making porcelain. He was the first European to report the use of paper money. Polo has also been credited with introducing ice

cream and noodles to Italy though these were introduced to Sicily centuries earlier by the Arabs.

The harshest critics claim that Marco Polo based his book on his uncles' genuine forays into the East, interwoven with tales told by other merchants and information plagiarised from Persian guidebooks. Even on Polo's return to Venice in 1295, contemporaries found his tales hard to believe. Few could accept a description of Hangzhou which, with a population of 2 million, was the biggest city in the world. Most historians admit that Marco Polo was prone to exaggeration but not a fantasist. Whatever the veracity of his accounts of the "lands of spices", their geography and the sea-routes, he fascinated and influenced generations of seafarers, including the Genoese, Christopher Columbus. ❏

RIGHT: a woodcut of Marco Polo from the German edition of his book of travels.

SUPREME STATESMEN

The Venetian Empire was sustained by an aristocratic yet egalitarian society in which patriotism was the paramount virtue

Machiavelli, the great political thinker, praised the city's statecraft as "deserving to be celebrated above any principality in Italy". He was impressed by the Venetians' imperialist ambitions, their skill at diplomacy, and a name which "spread terror over the seas". The State's reputation for ruthlessness was merited. When Doge Vitale Michiel was assassinated in 1172 his murderers sought refuge by San Zaccaria.

As a punishment, neighbouring houses were razed to the ground and a ban imposed upon building in stone, one that survived until this century. Treason was always punishable by death. Antonio Foscarini, a 17th-century ambassador to France and England, was falsely condemned as a spy and hanged by his foot in the Piazzetta, a common Venetian end.

This successful, if sinister, state was run by a closed circle, with its workings inscrutable, not merely to outsiders but to many of its participants, as well.

Unique system of government

In 1516 a proud Venetian announced to the Great Council: "The Greek republics did not last more than 450 years, the Roman 700, and this one has lasted more than 1,000." Although this was an exaggeration, the constitution did remain virtually unchanged from 1310 to the fall of the Republic in 1797.

Despite the ebb and flow of political events, Venetian grandeur was built on the bedrock of a unique system of government. The State was governed according to an extraordinary combination of monarchical, patrician and democratic principles. Its stability was guaranteed by a sophisticated system of checks and balances, preventing any one family or individual from seizing power.

Not that the system was immune to abuse.

LEFT: Bellini's painting of Doge Loredan, the great diplomat, who ruled for 20 years from 1501.
RIGHT: a *bocca di leone*, or "mouth of truth" letterbox, in the Doge's Palace.

One aspect suggests that the Italian propensity for political corruption has a Venetian origin. Before a major vote, members of the Great Council gathered in front of the Doge's Palace and the richer members tried to buy the votes of the impoverished nobles, the *barnabotti*. (Named the *broglio,* after the area in front of the

palace, this practice has also bequeathed us the term "imbroglio".)

As the bedrock of the Republic, the *Maggior Consiglio* (Great Council) confirmed political appointments and passed laws. Although it could not propose laws, it had the power of veto. One of its major functions was to elect the Doge, the leader of the Republic. The Council sat in the Doge's Palace, with the Doge in the centre, on the bench of St Mark, and the nobles ranged around him. Designed to represent the whole city, in time the Council became an elite corps of the Venetian nobility.

In 1297 a reform known as the "Closure of the Great Council" increased membership to

1,000, with all noblemen over the age of 26 obliged to serve; by 1323 membership was for life and by the 16th century there were several thousand members, representing various branches of 150 families. In effect, every nobleman was a servant of the state.

The onerous nature of this service is clear in the weekly Sunday sittings and numerous unpaid duties. In session, secret notes were circulated with the common plea: "Don't elect me! Don't see me!"

The Senate proposed and debated legislation as well as providing the administrative class. Created in about 1250, it comprised about 60

members chosen from the Grand Council and elected for a year, although this could be extended by re-election. Senators had to be over the age of 40, although the age limit was eventually lowered to 30.

They were helped by more than 100 *ex officio* members who had no voting rights. The Council of Ten, established in 1310, was designed to safeguard the constitutional institutions of the Republic. Presided over by the Doge, it comprised 10 Senators and six "sages". In time it acquired a sinister reputation, thanks to the pervasiveness and brutal efficiency of the Venetian secret police.

The Council also responded to the anony-

mous denunciations which were posted in *bocche di leoni* (lion's heads) placed along the walls of public buildings. In addition, the Republic was underpinned by myriad other councils and consultative bodies.

A patrician and patriotic society

Venice was a city-state run along republican lines by an aristocracy. The *Libro d'Oro* (Golden Book), first formalised in 1506, was the register of the Venetian nobility. Only those inscribed therein could seek high office. Exceptional services to the State could make a citizen eligible for membership. Occasionally wealthy commoners could buy their way in, but it took generations for the family to become accepted.

In this seemingly egalitarian society, patricians did not use titles and palaces were known as houses, (*case*, abbreviated to *Ca'*). To curb the development of powerful clans, the Republic even forbade patricians from acting as godfathers to other nobles' children. Yet certain elements of egalitarianism prevailed: there was no elite district; the nobility and populace lived cheek by jowl; patrician children played contentedly with retainers' children. However, after the fall of the Republic, egalitarianism didn't prevent the nobles, opportunists to a man, accepting their new Austrian titles with alacrity.

In terms of finances and freedom of movement, the merchant classes often fared better than the patricians. In the charmed but circumscribed circle of the oligarchy, nobility entailed obligations: foreign visits required authorisation from the State; gifts to officials had to be declared and relinquished; even an ambassadorship had to be funded by the ambassador himself.

As the writer Jan Morris remarked: "Beneath the patrician crust, the merchant classes and working men had carefully defined rights of their own." The merchant classes were allowed to set up trading posts in the empire while the elite of the citizen class provided civil servants and even the Chancellor of the Republic.

Both the merchant and citizen classes were sustained by countless privileges and powerful confraternities. Devotion to the Republic transcended class, with all citizens fed on a diet of elaborate state ceremonial and sumptuous art, the mirror of the times.   ❑

LEFT: the torture chamber in the Doge's Palace.

The Doge

O f the first 25 Doges, according to the chroniclers, three were murdered, one was executed for treason, three were judicially blinded, four were deposed, one was exiled, four abdicated, one became a saint and one was killed in a battle with pirates. Yet the time-honoured institution, the monopoly of old men, functioned well. As the mystical standard-bearer of St Mark and the symbol of Republican Venice, the Doge had no equal in grandeur amongst the Italian princes. Indeed, the Dogeship enjoyed an aura of Papal or Imperial majesty. Resplendent in gold and white, the Doge stood out from the red-clad Senators and sombrely-dressed patricians. His head was crowned with a *corno*, a bejewelled peaked cap. Yet behind the pomp and ceremony lay the cornerstone of the Republic, an institution dating back to AD 726, or to AD 697 if one accepts local lore. Enlightened for its day, the system effectively prevented the rise of family factions or the emergence of a despot.

Although the Doge was an elected office from the 9th century, complicated balloting procedures came into force in the 12th century. For the final ballot, a boy was picked out of the crowd; his job was to distribute and add up the canvas counters used in the vote; his reward was lifetime service with the Doge. Despite such care, the names of the same families had a habit of recurring: the Mocenigo clan furnished seven Doges alone and the Contarini eight. "They kill not with blood but with ballots" was an outsider's sharp verdict on Venetian machinations. Even so, the system of State paternalism served its purpose, producing stability without stagnation, and strong government without despotism. The last in a line of 120 Doges was elected the year the French Revolution broke out: an oligarchy masquerading as a Republic was challenged by newly Republican France. Lodovico Manin, the unfortunate last Doge, reputedly responded to news of his own election by bursting into tears and fainting.

The Doge was elected for life by patrician members of the Great Council. The archetypal Doge was a wealthy, 72-year-old elder statesman from a prominent family. To control family cliques, the Doge's immediate relations were banned from high office and any commercial enterprise. From the 16th century onwards the Dogaressa, his wife, was

RIGHT: the Doge, like the Pope, was elected for life, but bitter politics could make that life short.

no longer crowned. The Doge himself was watched closely; he was forbidden private contact with ambassadors and always accompanied by councillors on foreign missions. The Doge's immediate family were forbidden from leaving the city without the express agreement of the Great Council. Such was the scrutiny that the Doge's correspondence was censored. His income was strictly controlled and he was not allowed to accept any gifts except flowers and fragrant herbs.

The Doge presided over the Signoria, an inner Cabinet comprising three heads of the judiciary and six councillors, representing each of the city districts (*sestieri*). Their consent was required in all decisions.

The Republic's myriad advisory bodies, and the complex rotation of offices, ensured that dictatorship was impossible and conspiracies quickly nipped in the bud. The much-feared Council of Ten policed the patrician order and kept a check on the Doge's power.

In a system hallowed by tradition, the Doge was addressed as the "most serene prince". Several Doges succumbed to princely pomposity, an approach typified by Doge Agostino Barbarigo's addition of a princely staircase to the Doge's Palace. Yet despite the restrictions on his power, the Doge should not be portrayed as a figurehead, the proverbial bird in a gilded cage. In truth, he was a leading statesman who could work the checks and balances of the Constitution. ❑

QUEEN OF THE SEAS

*Deploying devious diplomacy, Venice consolidated its power and became
an exotic marketplace linking the eastern and western worlds*

As the supreme naval power of the age, Venice was truly the Queen of the Seas. While Tuscan and Genoese wealth depended on banking and industry, the Venetian Republic prospered on foreign trade alone. Although patrician, the governing class were merchants rather than feudal barons or rentiers.

From the start, Venice had imperial ambitions only insofar as they secured maritime trade; conquest was secondary. As the historian D.S. Chambers remarked: "Empire is better understood as dominion and administration, and for Venice the flag followed trade to a greater extent than it did to any other Mediterranean city." Nor did the emerging Venetian empire ever lose touch with its mercantile roots. Yet this quest for supremacy would never have been successful without the city's clear sense of identity, a self-confidence verging on vanity. The "soldiers of the seas" cultivated the spirit of a chosen island race, one set apart by its social cohesion and glorious constitution. Writer Jan Morris even compared Venice with England, "another maritime oligarchy" in which, Venetians considered themselves "not rich men or poor men, privileged or powerless, but citizens of Venice".

Seeds of empire

At home, the State had a monopoly on salt and grain, stored in imposing warehouses on the Grand Canal. Local trades included tanning, silk weaving and glass-blowing, with ship-building and textiles significant by the 16th century. However, real wealth rested on international commerce. The great trade routes out of Turkestan, Persia, Arabia and Afghanistan all converged on the sea-ports of the Levant. These were the shipping lanes that kept the Republic rich. Egypt, Beirut and Byzantium were key trading partners but Venetian outposts were strung along the shores of the Mediterranean and Middle East.

Yet in the 15th century the pattern of trade

LEFT: "The Bucintoro", the Doge's barge, by Canaletto.
RIGHT: Venetian cog, 15th-century engraving.

shifted westwards, with the route to the Black Sea becoming less important. This was an import-export economy on a vast scale, including the transport of slaves and pilgrims as well as freight. Consuls, customs officials, administrators and ambassadors were despatched overseas in the company of merchants and armed

convoys. The empire was highly organised, with bonded warehouses and customs offices imposing levies on all goods passing through its jurisdiction. The winged lion, the symbol of Venetian ascendancy, flew over countless territories and trading posts throughout the city's expanding empire.

The spice trade

Spices had been a valuable commodity since Roman times but the Crusades marked the expansion of the trade, one the Venetians monopolised until the 16th century. The outlandish use of spices which soldiers and pilgrims had learnt in the Orient now found its way into European kitchens. Exotic seasonings were prized for their pungency, preservative powers and the flavour of fabled lands. Venetian warehouses were filled with pepper, cinnamon, cloves, ginger, turmeric, nutmeg and cardamom. Spices were only a part of the Venetian imports from the East; other luxury goods included silk, furs, velvets, precious stones, perfumes and pearls. The Venetians operated a salt and grain cartel in the Adriatic; they traded in wine and wheat from Apulia, jewels from Asia, hides and silver from the Balkan hinterland, furs and slaves from the Black Sea, and wax, honey, wheat, oil and wine from the Greek Islands.

the Arsenal, the largest industrial complex of medieval Europe. Sea voyages were nevertheless a dangerous undertaking, with the risk of pirate attacks, stormy weather and poor navigation. It was not until the end of the 13th century that accurate charts and compasses assisted navigation, with ships no longer at the mercy of bad weather or forced to seek nightly anchorage. Improved ship-building techniques resulted in greater speed and cargo space. Two types of ship were used in international trade: the long galley, complete with sails and oars, and cogs, roomy sailing ships. The galleys, essentially ships of war, benefited from considerable speed

Such Mediterranean goods were traded for Flemish cloth and English wool. Cotton and sugar were shipped from plantations in Cyprus and Egypt while metalwork and precious cloth came from Greece and the Levant in general. From the late 15th century, Venetian state galleys were routed to the Catalan coast and to North Africa where spices from either Alexandria or Syria could be bartered for local honey, wax and leather.

A seafaring city

Oriental goods first reached Venice in Byzantine ships but soon the Venetians developed a large merchant marine fleet. Ships were built in

and fighting power. They controlled the trade in luxury goods and served on trade routes with regular timetables.

Maritime ventures

At the beginning of the 15th century, 3,000 trading vessels sailed under the Venetian flag. Most were in the coastal trade, delivering wood, stone or grain, or formed part of the fishing fleet. Overseas trade was carried out by 300 ships which sailed alone or in heavily armed State convoys, a system which survived until the mid-16th century. The costs of safe passage and cargo space acted as an incentive for private ship-owners to travel at their own risk and reap the rewards. A way of offsetting the business risk of the perilous voyage was to form a partnership, or *colleganza*. This agreement stipulated that one party remained in Venice and provided three-quarters of the capital while the other, who went on the voyage, put up the remaining quarter. The profit was divided between the two.

The slave trade

The Venetians signed a treaty with the Turks and traded in "goods forbidden to Christians" such as arms, ship-building materials and even slaves. Although the slave trade had been for-

the return fare, a donkey ride to Jerusalem and the various customs duties imposed upon Christians in the Holy Land.

Portuguese challenge

The Portuguese voyages of exploration posed the greatest threat to the Republic's monopoly of the spice trade. In 1498 Vasco da Gama rounded the Cape of Good Hope to India, opening up the sea route to the East. His success traditionally marks the decline of Venetian trade but this is not wholly accurate. Of all the spices, the Portuguese were only pre-eminent in pepper; even here, their transport costs were high

bidden since the 9th century, it was nonetheless still a good source of income. The slaves were mostly obtained from the Black Sea where the convoys sailed on from Byzantium. Greek-Orthodox Georgians, for instance, who were resold in Egypt and North Africa, could be traded in good faith as "non-Christians" because they were non-Catholics; nor was trade with heathen slaves forbidden. Pilgrimages represented a profitable sideline for the Venetians: pilgrims were offered a package tour, including

and the quality inferior. By the mid-1560s, Venice was re-exporting even greater quantities of pepper and cotton.

A colonial power

The empire was divided into overseas dominions (*stato da mar*) and mainland teritories (*stato da terrafirma*), with the former originally more important. As early as the 14th century the Adriatic was known as the Gulf of Venice, such was their trading monopoly. Their sway over the Adriatic led to treaties with Slav-controlled ports and then domination of Dalmatia (Croatia). The Greek islands were an attractive prize, yielding wine and corn from Crete, raisins from

LEFT: the Arsenal under foreign yoke: the French and Austrians alternated rule.
ABOVE: "The Battle of Lepanto", from the Doge's Palace.

Zante, olive oil and wine from Corfu. Dominion over key Greek territories had been established in the 13th century, from Mykonos and Corfu (and, for several years, Athens) to Crete, the most valuable colony. The Albanian coast also presented conquests, as did the Greek mainland: Morea (the Peloponnese) was prized for its wine and wheat. To secure the Gulf of Corinth, Lepanto was acquired in 1407, with Cyprus gained in 1489.

The 15th century saw a systematic pursuit of the *stato da terrafirma*, Italian mainland teritories. By 1405, Vicenza, Verona and Padua had come under Venetian sway. A century later,

Venetian territory encompassed the modern regions of the Veneto and Friuli-Venezia Giulia, as well as the Istrian peninsula. The mainland territories were not a poor substitute for overseas dominions but part of the Venetians' plans for consolidation. However, the Italian lands later compensated for losses in the East. Under Doge Francesco Foscari, Venice pursued an expansionist policy in mainland Italy: between 1432–54, conquests around Brescia in Lombardy were followed by control of the entire area up to the river Adda, just east of Milan. However, at the same time the Ottomans were battering the doors of Constantinople.

In 1453 Constantinople fell to the Turks, leav-

ing Venice the leading Christian city in the Mediterranean. Ottoman expansion was initially a spur to Venice since many dominions sought Venetian protection. Moreover, the Turks were more interested in slaves and tributes than in disrupting trade. For Venetians, religion was not allowed to interfere with commerce. Pope Pius II berated the Venetians for their lack of belligerence: "Too much intercourse with the Turks has made you the friend of Mohammedans." But Venetian merchants had always traded as readily with Egyptian and Syrian Moslems as with Greek Christians in Byzantium.

The Turkish threat

By the late 15th century the Turks were in a position to challenge the Republic's maritime empire but relatively few Venetian possessions were lost. Venetian policy in the 16th century was designed to keep its possessions intact in the face of Turkish expansion and the ambitions of the European powers. The League of Cambrai in 1508 was an attempt by the European powers and the Italian city-states to check Venetian expansion. However, by devious diplomacy Venice regained and consolidated its lost possessions. A policy of appeasement with Istanbul (Constantinople) was carried out to protect Venetian trade, helped by the fact that the Turks depended upon Venice for access to European markets. Yet Venice was ready to resist Ottoman expansion: to these ends, great fortresses were erected in Corfu, Crete, Cyprus, on the Greek mainland, and in Dalmatia.

In 1570 the Turks brutally captured Cyprus, a Venetian possession, provoking the Christian world to respond to the "infidels". In 1571 the Holy League of Venice, Spain and the Papacy engaged the enemy off Lepanto, a Hellenic port. Although outnumbered, the Christians inflicted a crushing defeat on the Turks in one of the greatest Mediterranean naval battles. During combat, 30,000 Turks were killed or captured, with 9,000 Christian casualties. However, the victory did little to stifle Ottoman expansion and, in retrospect, it can be seen as the high watermark of the Venetian empire. At home, the Serene Republic still flourished, but forces were at work that would lead to its decline. ❏

LEFT: detail from Titian's Pesaro altarpiece in the Frari church. **RIGHT:** Carpaccio's paintings perfectly capture everyday life in 15th-century Venice.

HEYDAY OF THE VENETIAN REPUBLIC

At its zenith, the Venetian Republic was a political heavyweight, queen of the Adriatic and an effective power player in world affairs

"Many a subject land looked at the winged lion's marble piles, where Venice sat in state, throned on her hundred isles", wrote Lord Byron as he reflected on the glory that was La Serenissima. He was writing of the Venetian heyday, between the 14th and 16th centuries, the age of empire, a golden age of conquest abroad and patriotic display at home. Citizens declared themselves "Venetians first, Christians afterwards", implying a greater duty to State and empire than to God. "Redeem us, O Christ", sang the choir in St Mark's, to which the response was distinctly unorthodox: "to the Most Serene and Excellent Doge, Health, Honour and Victory Perpetual". Paradoxically, the Republic's strength lay in its perceived weakness, in the belief that Venice was always alone in the world, forced to fend for herself and shun the shifting sands of political allegiances. In turn, rivals envied the Venetians' autonomous approach and the mercantile spirit of a great trading empire – not to mention their shrewd mastery of foreign affairs and good governance of the Republic at home.

OSTENTATION AND PURITANISM

La Serenissima's role as a Mediterranean power was perfectly captured by Venetian artists, both for patrons and posterity. The Republic was fed on a diet of pomp, with sumptuous receptions and lay and religious feasts; some of these are celebrated in the paintings of Bellini and Carpaccio. However, the Venetian taste for portraying pageantry went beyond the dictates of patrons. Moreover, despite a reputation for extravagance, the Republic harboured a puritanical streak. The prominence of black costumes in 16th-century Venice led a modern historian to liken the scene to "a Swiss Sunday". Yet in this authoritarian, regimented and censorious city, some nobles lived so lavishly that the State imposed laws governing dress codes and the gilding of gondolas.

▷ **AWARDS FOR THE FAVOURED**
On special occasions, the Doge would distribute medals, such as this 17th-century silver *osella*, to the Gran Consiglio, the council of nobles which had elected him.

△ **SEALED LIPS**
Secret denunciations could be posted in a *bocca di leone* ("lion's mouth" letter box). The boxes were placed in various locations across the city.

▷ **WEDDED TO THE SEA**
The Bucintoro, the Doge's barge, was lavishly decorated with gilded carvings and used for important state visits. On Ascension Day, it carried the Doge to the Lido, where he would perform the ceremony of Venice's Marriage with the Sea, a famous city tradition captured on canvas by Canaletto (1657–1768).

△ **SEAT OF THE SENATE**
An 18th-century painting by by Gabriele Bella shows the room where the Doge would consult his 200 Senators.

Today, visitors to the Doge's Palace (below) can still admire Tintoretto's decoration of the Sala del Senato, which dates from 1574.

OUTPOSTS OF EMPIRE

Military towers, citadels and lighthouses on the Croatian coast, Cyprus and Crete *(above)* attest to the reach of the Venetian empire. Such imperial power was born of patriotism, geography and trading supremacy. Venice bordered two worlds, the Byzantine and Moslem East and the Latin-Germanic West. As gateway to the East, the city traded incense, precious metals, slaves, silks and spices for northern staples, including salt and wheat. The purpose of Venetian imperialistic ambitions was to preserve trade routes and consolidate commercial opportunities. As a result, Venice became a melting pot for "Jews, Turks, Armenians, Persians, Moors, Greeks and Slavs ... negotiating in this great emporium, which is always crowded with strangers" (John Evelyn).

The conquest of Croatia was achieved in the 10th century, and Venice soon developed trading posts in the Aegean, Black Sea and Syria. The Sack of Constantinople in 1204 gave Venice "one quarter and half a quarter" of the Roman Empire. Valour was expected in the name of Venetian glory: blind Doge Dandolo stormed Constantinople at the age of 90.

◁ NAVAL POWER

Venetian naval power was second to none. Here Holy Roman Emperor Frederick I Barbarossa, who was in conflict with the Pope and the Lombard League, surrenders to Doge Ziani in 1176.

▽ DOGE'S FINERY

Doges wore distinctive hats, made of embroidered silk and adorned with precious stones, such as this *corno* worn by Doge Barbarigo (1485–1501).

SUNSET ON THE SERENE SOCIETY

It was all too good to last. In a final blaze of colour and glory, the mighty
Republic was forced to bow to the fresh winds of change

Any view of Venice in the 17th century is of an eclipsed empire and a city tainted by terminal decline. Yet only hindsight provides such certainty. To the Venetians themselves, it was a vibrant age which ended in the dazzle and display of 18th-century art. The sunset was pleasurable yet poignant, particularly for the patrician class. In the face of hostility from the great powers, Venice opted for armed neutrality. Thanks to this, and the sure-footedness of its institutions, the Republic became a byword for stability in a troubled Europe.

Storm clouds at sea

Objectively, the 17th century brought the Venetians little good fortune. The once flourishing maritime empire was on the wane. The Hapsburgs developed the harbour of Trieste and encouraged piratical raids on Venetian ships. Long-running disputes with the Papacy also came to a head. Venice had always taken a stand as an independent sovereign state: *Siamo veneziani, poi cristiani* (We are first Venetians, then Christians). While professing faith in the Pope as supreme spiritual leader, the Venetians insisted that the Doge and his officers were the masters of temporal affairs.

The Papacy believed that the Republic treated Protestants too liberally and rejected the assumption that Rome should routinely rubber-stamp the Venetian candidate for Patriarch of Venice. After Venice refused to hand over two clerics to Roman ecclesiastical courts, the whole city was excommunicated. The Venetians were unbowed and the interdict was removed a year later, with much loss of face to the Papacy.

Swings and roundabouts

The plague of 1630 confirmed the waning powers of Venice, compounded by changing patterns of world trade. The decline was signalled

by the circumnavigation of Africa and the subsequent by-passing of the Mediterranean with the development of northern and transatlantic routes. The commercial axis shifted towards the North Sea, favouring Dutch and English ports to the detriment of Venice. However, the eclipse of Venice was also hastened by Turkish naval

supremacy in the eastern Mediterranean and by the loss of the colonial empire to the Ottomans. Yet the picture was less bleak than has often been painted. After a protracted struggle, Venice lost Crete in 1669 but this was mitigated by the preservation of Dalmatia and the gain of Morea (1684–8) in a campaign led by Doge Francesco Morosini. Although the decline was irreversible, some trade and banking business survived and Venice remained a wealthy and exotic city.

A cosmopolitan city

Venice was termed "the metropolis of all Italy" by delighted visitors. The diarist John Evelyn (1620–1706) was surprised by the Venetian

LEFT: "The Dancing Lesson" by Pietro Longhi, which can be seen in the Accademia.
RIGHT: Carpaccio's "Venetian Ladies" (1507), mistakenly thought to be courtesans.

melting pot: "Jews, Turks, Armenians, Persians, Moors, Greeks, Dalmatians all in their native fashions, negotiating in this famous emporium." The far-flung empire in the Levant had turned Venice into the most cosmopolitan of cities, where East and West mingled. The Greeks, the longest established foreign community, had their own church, school and liturgical centre (*see page 189*). The Armenians, ensconced since the 12th century, enjoyed a similarly privileged position, first with their own church and later with a private island granted by the Doge. The Albanians and Dalmatians (Croatians) were established enough to have their own confrater-nity houses. A Jewish community had resided in Venice since the 14th century, acting as traditional money-lenders. The glittering emporium of Venice also attracted German and Turkish traders who were granted magnificent warehouses and bases on the Grand Canal.

The end of an era

The 18th century was a time in which Venice withdrew from the world stage. The wars against the Turks had cost the Republic dearly; armed neutrality became the new objective, with a refusal to become involved in the wars of the French, Spanish and Austrian succession.

THE SUMPTUARY LAWS

The Venetian State interfered in the lives of its citizens to an extraordinary degree. Only the overriding patriotism of the Venetian nobility, their pride in the Republic and their solidarity with their fellow citizens enabled the State to pass highly restrictive laws without revolt. In one particular area, the State acted as a grim guardian of its own wealth, banning public lavishness.

The Sumptuary Laws were restrictions on the conspicuous display of wealth, designed to avoid profligacy and curb the patricians' overweaning pride. Established in 1562, these checks on patrician spending governed everything from dowries, jewellery and costumes to boats and building regulations. Not that rich Venetians were slow to circumvent such controls. Although the Great Council decreed that gondolas should be painted black, the nobles simply draped the boats in costly Eastern carpets and glittering brocades.

Likewise, noblewomen took to wearing pattens, bizarre tottering shoes, which allowed them to bend the rules governing the length of trains. The laws were riddled with loopholes: while only a limited quantity of silver and gold plate could be displayed, there were no restrictions on the amount a family could actually possess.

The Rialto was no longer a centre of overseas trade; the great clearing houses were now Genoa, Livorno, Trieste and northern Europe. However, as commentator Francis Russell says: "Visible wealth, historic ceremonial and a lingering memory of the triumphal defence of Corfu against the Ottoman Turks in 1716 ensured that the city remained far more than a mere magnet for the tourist." But Morea and the Aegean possessions were finally lost in 1718 at the Peace of Passarowitz, a treaty concluded without Venetian participation. The loss signalled the end of the mighty maritime empire and the confirmation of Austrian power.

ing age of elegance, indulgence and *dolce vita*. The spectacle of Venetian demise held its own fascination, with the 18th-century dying in a blaze of artistic glory. The illusionistic effects of Tiepolo (*see page 170*), Italy's last grandscale imaginative painter, trumpeted the greatest illusion: that Venice was still serene and splendid, gloriously in control of its own destiny.

Fall of the Republic

In 1789, the year that Lodovico Manin was elected as Doge, the French Revolution broke out. Napoleon, soon embroiled in conflict with Austria, was determined to destroy the Venet-

All that remained of Venice was its Republican dignity. According to critic Michael Levey, "Its grandeur and gravity, embodied by red-clad senators, were almost anachronistic, and there was some piquancy in a Europe of monarchs and princes in the tremendous, impersonal dignity of a state that continued to be a republic." Attempts to democratise the archaic government were stifled by the conservative elite. Yet for the patrician class, this was an inward-look-

LEFT: "The Opera Rehearsal" (detail) by Mario Ricci gives a glimpse of salon life.
ABOVE: Carpaccio's "The Lion of St Mark", showing the Doge's Palace in the background, where it is hung.

ian oligarchy. He provoked a quarrel with the Venetians over a frigate and declared: "I want no more Inquisitors, no more Senate, I shall be an Attila to the Venetian State." In 1796 he marched into the Veneto without encountering any resistance. In 1797 the last in the line of 120 Doges abdicated in recognition of the *fait accompli* of Napoleon's victories in northern Italy. In a tumultuous sitting, the Great Council declared the death of the Republic. Laying down the *cufieta*, the linen cap worn under the Doge's crown, Lodovico Manin turned to his valet and declared with great dignity: "Take it away; I shall not be needing it again."

A provisional government was soon installed

but the arrival of French troops spelt disaster for the city. Although Venice was consigned to Austria in 1797, French rule was reinstated between 1805–15 and imposed its Empire style on the city's architecture.

Even though historians have treated the French rather lightly, their actions were far more destructive than Austrian rule. Carrying off the spoils of war to the Louvre in Paris was unremarkable; after all, the Venetians themselves returned with booty after the Sack of Constantinople. It was the destruction of churches, convents, palaces and shipyards that made a lasting impact. The monasteries were also suppressed

and their treasures dispersed. The creation of the Giardini Pubblici (public gardens) entailed the demolition of a church, a cluster of historic buildings and medieval granaries next to the Mint. French building schemes were suitably grandiose: in Piazza San Marco, a wing was added to enclose the square.

Austrian rule

Delivered into Austrian hands by Napoleon in 1798, Venice became an appendage of the Austrian empire. The new rulers occupied the city three times, finally leaving in 1866 when Venice voted to join the United Kingdom of Italy. William Dean Howells, the American Consul in

Venice, spoke of "a nation in mourning", noting the disappearance of 'that public gaiety and private hospitality for which the city was once famous'. He failed to note any meeting of minds between victors and vanquished. While the Venetians were a mercurial people: "like the tide, six hours up and six hours down", the Austrians were regarded as "slow and dull-witted".

Yet coming under the Austrian yoke was providential in some respects. Although the Austrians were loathed as an occupying power and resented for their burdensome bureaucracy, they governed justly and liberally, at least until the 1848 Revolution. The outcome was a provisional Venetian Republic set up under the heroic Daniele Manin, but this fell in 1849.

An island no longer

The Austrians had a practical bent, building bridges, funding questionable restoration projects and filling in insalubrious canals. In 1846 they built the historic causeway linking Venice to the mainland, and the railway system – Venice was an island no more. However, the city was virtually destitute during Austrian rule: there were no more government jobs, Trieste became the favoured Adriatic port, shipbuilding dwindled and tourism was negligible. The legacy of the Austrians' 58-year rule was restricted to bridge-building and the introduction of the apple strudel.

During the Austrian era, Howells noted that there was "inevitably some international lovemaking". Indeed, many Austrian administrators married impoverished patricians and settled in Venice. While conquest rankled with the nobility, it was the loss of former glory that saved Venice for future generations. The local aristocracy and bourgeoisie were reduced to poverty and could not indulge in the ambitious building programmes that scarred many European cities. Few palaces were redecorated in grandiose 19th-century taste and so remain as a testament to the glory days of the Republic. Venetian luck also held out in modern times: during the Second World War, when so many other historic cities were being bombed to rubble, Venice was saved because, reputedly, it was the first city to be protected on both the German and the Allied heritage lists. ❏

LEFT: Giuseppe Garibaldi, revolutionary leader.
RIGHT: collapse of the San Marco Campanile in 1902.

SAVING THE CITY

Severe floods in 1966 galvanised the world into taking action

to preserve Venice from the ravages of the sea

Oh Venice! Venice! When thy marble walls
Are level with the waters there shall be
A cry of nations o'er thy sunken halls
A loud lament along the sweeping sea!

In his epic, *Childe Harold*, Lord Byron sounded the city's death knell. But in truth Venice has been in peril since the first foolhardy settlers sank the first stakes into the lagoon. Reports of the dowager's death may be exaggerated but the politicians still need to protect the fragile eco-system of the lagoon and solve the intractable problems between historic Venice and the modern mainland. "It has become a classic case of the collision of warring interests: ecologists versus industrialists, city planners versus regional planners, developers versus preservationists". Dora Jane Hamblin's analysis from the 1970s remains valid, despite the valiant efforts of local government.

Separatist siege

In 1997 armed commandos staged a bizarre independence bid to mark the 200th anniversary of the fall of the Republic. After occupying St Mark's belltower and unfurling the Lion of St Mark, the Separatists declared: "Attention, the Most Serene Venetian government has occupied the belltower of St Mark's. Long live the Serenissima."

The protest was foiled by *carabinieri* (armed police) who scaled the tower with a telescopic ladder and caught the commandos by surprise. Separatist sentiment has been spurred by corruption and resentment at high taxes, Roman rule and state bureaucracy. The Northern League, the Separatist party, had only won 10 per cent of the national vote and was smarting from defeats in local elections. "Our problems will not be solved by this kind of behaviour,"

LEFT: Grand Canal rally of the Northern League in 1996 to proclaim the self-styled Republic of Padania. Supporters of Padania, with its capital as Venice, flew the Venetian red-and-yellow banner of St Mark.
RIGHT: the Murazzi, the city's colossal sea walls.

shrugged a waiter in St Mark's Square, "We are more worried about subsidence and rising water levels." It was a similar story a year earlier. In 1996 the leader of the League, Umberto Bossi, launched his "march on the river Po" and proclaimed Venice the capital of Padania, his make-believe kingdom. The Mayor of Venice rejected Bossi's view of his city as a mythical northern Italian state. Fellow Venetians dismissed such protests as an irrelevance: Arrigo Cipriani, the owner of Harry's Bar, was more forthright: "Bossi belongs in an asylum with people who think they are Napoleon."

Murky waters

Venetian politics are rarely dull: the former Mayor, the disco-loving Gianni de Michelis, was imprisoned for corruption in 1995. As the proponent of a misguided plan to drain the Lagoon for the site of Expo 2000, he should be released just in time to celebrate the millennium in a more ecologically sound fashion. By contrast, Mayor Cacciari is the antithesis of the proverbially corrupt professional politician. When first invited to enter politics in the 1980s, he roundly snubbed de Michelis with the quip: "No thanks, my family's got plenty of money already." Since then, his left-wing administration has faced huge obstacles, from an arson attack on the opera house to perilous floods, from continuing pollution to the problems of a dying community.

The greatest threats to Venice are seen as the ecological balance of the Lagoon and the preservation of Venice as a living community in the face of a declining population. Resolving

cil, and a certain nostalgia, but that is all. While the mainland is industrial, entrepreneurial and left-wing, the historic centre is elderly, conservative, tourism-led and ecologically minded. In a recent referendum, the two parts of the city voted to remain together. However, the benefits of this are rather one-sided: the mainland gains from the lustre of historic Venice, while the Lagoon city remains shackled to its bullying younger brother.

Exodus

Yet despite the undoubted tensions, the picture is muddied by economic interdependence and

such problems is made all the more difficult by the many petty vested interests.

Divided city

The old city motto used to be: "Drink in the culture of Venice – find inner serenity in the Serenissima." Today's citizens are a little short of serenity. Venice is the capital of the Veneto, one of the richest regions in Italy, yet the city struggles to survive. Venice, along with the islands of the Lido, Murano, Burano and Torcello, forms the natural "floating world" of the Lagoon. But over the causeway lies Mestre, both the missing half of Venice and another world. The two communities share a city coun-

family ties. In the past 20 years there has been a flight from the islands to the mainland, *al di là dall'acqua* (over the water). When people leave, a precious slice of Venetian life is lost. The population has halved since 1945: only 70,000 people live in historic Venice, with a further 45,000 on outlying islands and 190,000 on the mainland. Yet over 30,000 people commute daily; others come to their home city as tourists. Managers from the mainland visit Venice to entertain a business partner or to battle with red tape. Historic Venice mainly offers jobs in tourism and public administration. Tourism employs over a third of the population, processing up to 12 million visitors a year, with the majority only spending their days in the city. At the end of the day, convoys of tourists wend their way through the narrow alleys to the railway station, and from there to cheaper lodgings on the mainland. Venetians who don't want to live on the city's glorious memories also move to the mainland. They are joined by young families or entrepreneurs frustrated from starting businesses in the historic centre.

The new face of Venice
In recent years there has been a realisation that Venice should not have to swing between the twin poles of tourism and industrialisation.

for the conference trade. To this end, a Palladian convent has already been converted into a conference centre, and the huge neo-Gothic flour mill, called the Mulino Stucky, is being turned into a mixture of housing, hotel accommodation and conference centre in the near future.

Crafts revival
Venice has enjoyed a solid crafts base since the 16th century but this has been allowed to decline, with bookbinders and master-gilders turning into mask sellers. The craft base runs deeper than Burano lace and Murano glassware yet even these have achieved world fame:

While tourism will always be important, industry divides the city: in simplistic terms, residents in the historic centre fear industrial pollution while citizens "over the water" need the jobs that industry brings. However, alternatives are in the pipeline. Venice will always be a costly place for commercial ventures, so added value economics is a logical path to follow: this entails developing the fledgling computing sector, reviving the crafts tradition and competing

LEFT: daily delivery of fruit and vegetables to the Rialto market beside the Grand Canal.
ABOVE: the traditional and painstaking process of making lace on the island of Burano.

Venetian chandeliers adorn the President's Oval Office in the White House. Traditional crafts include textile design and decorative metalwork. Craftsmen still turn out exquisite mirrors and Venetian marble floors. The restoration sector is thriving, with work for sculptors and stonemasons and lacquer-workers, mosaicists and master-carpenters, furniture-makers and picture-restorers. At the fashionable end of the scale are the antique dealers, interior decorators, jewellery designers and genuine mask-makers.

Housing trap
There is a premium to pay for living in Venice, with the cost of city housing now beyond many

families. Even without the problem of an inflated property market and the preponderance of second homes, the absence of an affordable rental sector and the sheer upkeep of Venetian homes is daunting enough. "Suggestions by Venice in Peril that the poor should be encouraged back into the old city have about them a touch of guilt. Tourism has helped to empty the city and now tourists want the poor returned to give more authenticity to the street scene." Journalist Simon Jenkins makes a rather harsh judgement since the city is making genuine, if belated, attempts to stem the flight to the mainland. Some see the political solution to the city

are both an ever-present danger and a safeguard from stagnation. The Lagoon is dependent on the cleansing tides, a process already harmed by the diversion of rivers and the creation of solid land from mudflats. Yet the same protective tidal waters threaten silting and catastrophic flooding. Human interference and pollution also play a part: the sight of oil tankers bearing down on the Doge's Palace may be just a bad memory but cruise ships and hulking naval ships are not.

Early sea defences

The lagoon city has always faced the contradictory dangers of death by drowning and death by

problems as a special statute for Venice, with the creation of a unified authority similar to the Vatican. Optimists would expect this to lead to economic privileges, such as housing grants, and business and tax incentives, as well as unique environmental laws.

The endangered ecosystem

The city's population problems are matched by equally precarious environmental issues. If Venice is not to be doomed to a watery grave, the unique Lagoon world must be protected. The elements conspire to form a three-pronged attack on the city, from the air, land and sea, with water posing the gravest threat. The tides

suffocation: the encroaching sea had to be tamed and the silting sands held at bay. To stop the silt from clogging the entire lagoon, the Venetians buttressed the mud banks to protect the city, originally with wooden palisades and later with stone walls. They also closed some of the gaps between the sand bars (*lidi*), leaving only three entrances. Then as now, these served to strengthen the city defences and channel the cleansing tides. From the 15th century, major drainage schemes took place, including breakwaters. The Murazzi sea walls, built of Istrian stone in 1741, were one of the Republic's greatest feats of civil engineering. The legendary Magistracy of the Waters still exists to supervise the Lagoon's precarious ebb and flow. Sea walls and dykes are maintained, with narrow canals and wide shipping lanes dredged to prevent silting. After decades of neglect, the canals are benefiting from a dredging programme, in place since the 1990s. Although the damage was hidden below the surface, many household pipes were blocked and the canals clogged.

Mainland moans

No matter how welcome these improvements, many of Venice's ecological problems can be traced back to the mainland. The industrial port of Marghera is blamed for many of Venice's ills, reclaimed land and the exodus from historic Venice was unstoppable. The attraction of easily heated homes with damp-free ground floors and properly functioning bathrooms played no small part in helping people decide.

Pollution problems

With hindsight, many of the ensuing problems were predictable. Over the years, the Mestre-Marghera industrial complex has dumped tons of pollutants into the Lagoon. The culprits include Montedison and Enichem, as well as Enel, the state energy authority. Closing the petro-chemical complex is the obvious solution

from water and air pollution to subsidence and flooding. Yet like historic Venice, it too was born from necessity. The Arsenal was closed during World War I, to the despair of the 8,000-strong workforce. To save the citizens from ruin, local benefactors and patriots created a modern industrial centre on the mainland. Porto Marghera was born, built over the mud flats. It was served by the dormitory suburb of Mestre, developed in the 1920s. After World War II, a second industrial zone was built over more

---

LEFT: an ocean liner, bringing a fresh batch of tourists, sweeps into the fragile Lagoon.
ABOVE: pollution on mainland Mestre and Marghera.

but too harmful to the economy for politicians to contemplate. Instead, the proposed solution is to lay huge pipelines to take the waste out to the open sea: a kind gift from Venice to tourism on the Adriatic.

Toxic fumes from the port are also damaging Venice's fragile buildings and statuary. Sulphur-based emissions are produced by industrial and domestic smoke as well as from the natural decay of vegetation on the Lagoon mud flats. Sulphur dioxide combines with the salty air to form a toxic cocktail that damages the city fabric. Still, the conversion of heating systems from oil to gas has cut down on the sulphur dioxide in the atmosphere. In addition, industrial filtration systems have reduced pollution from Marghera, with the remaining fumes mostly swept inland. In the 1960s, the city realised that glass furnaces in Murano were also responsible for churning out sulphuric acid, so action was eventually taken.

No longer sinking

Venice officially stopped sinking in 1983 after the extraction of underground water was forbidden. The drawing of millions of gallons of water from artesian wells in Marghera had led to a sharp fall in the water table and threatened subsidence. In the 1970s aqueducts were built

them. In fact, the occasional foul smells are more likely to come from rotting algae and vegetable matter than from chemicals. As for the canals, the wash from the *vaporetti* (water buses) causes erosion, eating away at the stonework of Grand Canal palaces. Salt and damp are causing the collapse of palaces as fine as Ca' Foscari (*see page 173*). The harm caused by motor boats has prompted the city council to press for design changes to reduce the wash.

On a positive note, there is a proposal to turn the Venetian Lagoon into a marine park stretching from the Lido to Chioggia. More modest initiatives are already under way, with Green

to pipe water from inland rivers to the industrial zone. However, Venetian subsidence is partly caused by the weight of the city, with many monuments under threat. St Mark's belltower collapsed in 1902 while among today's 170 belltowers, few are perpendicular.

The detergents problem

Nor is Venice itself blameless. While domestic sewage is treated, baths and sinks still drain into the canals. As a result, phosphate-enriched household detergents have been banned. It is essential to decrease the quantity of phosphates in the Lagoon given that plant and marine life are being suffocated by the algae that thrive on

groups striving to publicise the Lagoon as well as protect it. In one scheme, city children from Venetian families on the mainland are introduced to the wonders of the Lagoon. Since many know little of their heritage, the idea is to educate them in ecology and encourage the émigrés to return. The mainland families would be satisfied with secure jobs and homes on either side of the water. The Mayor is sanguine about the fate of his beloved city: "If Venice has any vitality left, it will seize the moment. If it is dead in human terms, it will die." ❑

ABOVE: although the city officially stopped sinking in 1983, Piazza San Marco is frequently submerged.

Restoration

Venice's privileged position has ensured that the world's eye is always upon the city, with the protection of the international community not far behind. The 19th century witnessed several debatable restoration projects, notably the Fondaco dei Turchi. However, in the 1860s, the art historian John Ruskin led a successful campaign to stop the controversial remodelling of St Mark's Basilica. Since then, the British, and latterly the Americans, have been at the forefront of foreign restoration projects. In the 1950s the deterioration of both buildings and art treasures became apparent but the international community was finally galvanised into action by the great flood of 1966. Ever since, Venice has had myriad rescuers or would-be saviours, including over 30 international bodies. Prominent among them are UNESCO, the British Venice in Peril Fund and the American Save Venice Committee. Every year, the international community pledges over a million dollars to restoration in Venice, a sum easily matched by the Italian government and the European Union.

It is agreed policy to employ local craftsmen, led by an Italian team of expert restorers and overseen by the state heritage and conservation bodies. State and private sponsorship play a part, with vast funds contributed by the Italian government. Whether restoration is subsidised by a private company or an international charity, the "adopt a building" approach is common, with one site restored by one body, except for major projects. Despite the dead hand of Italian bureaucracy, in recent years the city has been effective in tapping a pool of local craftsmen, with a craft centre created on the island of San Servolo. Complementing this is the restoration centre for paintings based in the former church of San Gregorio, near La Salute.

Apart from San Marco, the city's most prestigious restoration project has been La Fenice, destroyed by fire in 1996. The decision was taken to rebuild the opera house before the year 2000, *com'era, dov'era* (as it was, where it was). Since the late 1990s several major museums or galleries have been partially or fully closed for radical restoration. The Fondaco dei Turchi, housing the Natural History Museum, is again closed for restoration, as is the Museo Fortuny, the Museum of Textile Design. Although the Ca d'Oro art gallery is freshly restored, visits to Ca' Rezzonico, its Grand Canal

sister, are restricted to one floor. In Ca' Pesaro, the Oriental Museum is open but the Modern Art Museum is under wraps until the year 2000. As for palaces, particularly the prestigious ones on the Grand Canal, restoration is a never-ending process. Ca' Foscari, the grand seat of the university, is swathed in scaffolding.

Churches are in a slightly healthier position as much has already been done. Venice in Peril, for instance, has restored Madonna dell'Orto, San Nicolò dei Mendicoli and Santa Maria Materdomini, as well as helping restore Torcello Cathedral. In neighbouring Murano, the facade of Santa Maria Donato, the island's finest Byzantine church, is

shrouded under scaffolding. In Cannaregio, the delightful Santa Maria dei Miracoli is being restored after the disastrous effects of the previous attempt revealed the corrosive effects of salt; this was destroying the fabric from inside and depositing white encrustations on the precious marble surfaces. However, if churches are closed, the cause may simply be "lack of personnel" or deconsecration. Le Zitelle is a case in point, a Palladian church and convent on the Giudecca, recently converted into a conference centre. After decades of neglect, Mulino Stucky, the neo-Gothic industrial mill on the Giudecca, is also being converted into a conference centre, hotel and affordable housing, a project to be ready for the millennium. ❑

RIGHT: San Marco under wraps.

ARCHITECTURAL STYLE

The Venetian architectural style is an eclectic and inspired blend

of Byzantine, Gothic and Renaissance influences

A rchitects call Venice an artificial city, "a city born adult". It was never a blank slate but built from remnants of ruined cities: Venice salvaged Roman bricks from Adriatic villas and recycled arches and statuary from churches and palaces in the romantic colony of Torcello. As the gateway to the East, Venice raided Byzantium for booty to adorn its noble facades. From marbles to mosaics, the eastern colonies provided precious materials to transform the inhospitable lagoon islands into an imperial capital.

Oriental allure

Architecturally, the city succumbed to the spell of the East, with a Byzantine spirit poured into a Gothic mould; only reluctantly was Venice lured into the Renaissance. The palace is the classic unit of Venetian architecture, a form influenced by the Roman country villa and by Byzantine buildings in Ravenna and Constantinople. Characterised by colour, decoration and eclecticism, the result is a synthesis of styles simply known as Venetian. Plaques and roundels created chiaroscuro effects and offset the flatness of the facade; the vivid marbles also reflected the local love of colour.

Although many of the frescoed facades have not survived the ravages of time and humidity, some have been sympathetically recreated on the Grand Canal. Yet the vernacular Venetian style is a hybrid. A typical cluster of buildings may show influences from East and West, sport Moorish windows, a Gothic structure, Veneto-Byzantine decoration and Renaissance or Baroque flourishes.

Materials were shipped to Venice with great difficulty: piling and timber came from the Lido, from alpine forests and from the Balkans; carved stones and friezes were raided from Greek and Roman classical temples; white Istrian stone was used for facings, arcading and windows; small, flat Roman bricks served as

building blocks, salvaged from villas destroyed by the Barbarian hordes; red Verona marble provided flooring; exotic marble came from Greece, with semi-precious stones from Constantinople; only glass was home-made in Murano, although brick was later made from local clay.

Venice is a city of brick rather than stone: at most a stone-clad city; pink-hued bricks predominate, with cool stone restricted to finishings. According to the writer Mary McCarthy, the city's beauty comes from "the thin marble veneers with which the brick surface is coated". Its sheer weight made stone unsuitable as the prime building material, at least until piling techniques became sophisticated enough to cope with such structures as La Salute church, supported by a million piles.

Since Venice began as a satellite of Byzantium, the Oriental legacy is tangible. Craftsmen from Constantinople worked on the oldest buildings, as did Greek mosaicists. In Venice,

LEFT: courtyard of the glorious Gothic Ca' d'Oro.
RIGHT: the Palazzo Loredan, on the Grand Canal.

Byzantine religious architecture is far more impressive than the civil equivalent. To appreciate the early city settlement, there is no substitute for visiting the remote island of Torcello. The basilica feels deeply Byzantine, founded in AD 639 and modified between the 9th and 11th centuries. Inspired by Ravenna, its centrepiece is the Byzantine mosaic-studded apse.

Next door, the domed church of Santa Fosca is the perfect expression of the Byzantine notion of space. The Greek cross plan is complemented by small Oriental apses; outside, an octagonal portico rests on Veneto-Byzantine capitals. This stilted portico is considered to have been the prototype for arcades on traditional Venetian palaces. Here, as elsewhere in the church, Romanesque austerity is shot through with Byzantine decorative motifs.

In central Venice, the majority of Byzantine buildings lie around the Rialto, the oldest section of the city, or close to San Marco. San Giacomo di Rialto is considered to be the oldest church, and it displays the Byzantine Greek cross design. The austere San Nicolò dei Mendicoli, built for the poor, also retains its 7th-century basilican plan and small double-mullioned windows. However, San Marco remains the supreme example of Byzantine architecture, an

WELL-HEADS

Carved well-heads are a familiar feature of Venice, from the drum-shaped Roman well-head outside the Basilica in Torcello to a trio of delightful wells situated on Campo Santa Maria Formosa. The well-heads mask a complex and costly system below, acting as an outlet for an underground chain of storage tanks which often run the length of the *campo*. The rainwater was collected through apertures in the *campo* floor, purified through sand-filters and channelled into cisterns. Since the late 19th century, however, the city's water has come from artesian wells on the mainland.

elongated version of the five-domed Greek cross design, based on the Church of the Apostles in Constantinople.

Veneto-Byzantine style

Given the Venetian talent for fusion, the emergence of a unique Veneto-Byzantine style was a matter of course. Popular from the 11th to 13th centuries, this was an Oriental, flowery form, with ornate capitals, pediments and niches and Byzantine arches. Slender columns (cushion or basket capitals) and stilted arches gave way to Moorish design, especially the horseshoe arch and the inflected arch, resembling a quivering flame. A taste for crenellations was acquired from the Muslim world though most crenellated parapets have long gone. The Byzantine legacy is a love of voluptuous materials, from inlaid marble to porphyry and jasper. Facades were adorned with *paterae*, decorative stone or marble plaques, often bearing symbolic foliage and animal motifs: gryphons, eagles, lions, and peacocks symbolising eternal life through baptism, or vine leaves representing the "true vine" of St John's Gospel.

The Ca' da Mosto on the Grand Canal is one of the best-preserved Veneto-Byzantine palaces. This 12th-century residence has an elegant loggia on the first floor, with arches adorned by fine

was the *casa-fondaco*, combining the roles of commercial office and family home. The house followed a three-tiered plan that became the pattern for centuries to come. In the Veneto-Byzantine merchant's house an arcade ran along the ground floor with a loggia running across the floor above. Side turrets or parapets *(torreselle)* were a reminder of the days of defensive fortifications. The top floor could have a covered loggia *(liagò)*, a feature of 13th and 14th-century Venetian houses.

The Fondaco dei Tedeschi on the Grand Canal is a monumental square structure, previously a warehouse and residence for German

paterae. The Ca' Loredan, which is also on the Grand Canal, retains ground-floor arcading surmounted by an open gallery. The original marble plaques and 12th-century capitals remain.

In Cannaregio, Veneto-Byzantine friezes and roundels adorn the courtyard of the Corte del Milion, where Marco Polo's family reputedly lived.

Merchant homes

This eclectic Venetian style has left its mark on palaces and warehouses *(fondaci)*. The model

merchants. The arcade at water level made for easy unloading; above is a bare facade which was frescoed by Giorgione and finished by Titian; poetic fragments remain in the Ca' d'Oro museum. The inner courtyard is framed by a loggia and porticoed facades, which were once frescoed by Titian.

The nearby Fondaco dei Turchi has been radically restored but remains close to its original form if not spirit. As an emporium for Turkish merchants, the crenellated building was practical yet decorative, with waterside loading bays below a Romanesque portico.

The aesthete John Ruskin believed that Venetian post-Gothic architecture was a dese-

LEFT: octagonal portico of Santa Fosca, Torcello.
ABOVE: Basilica of Santi Maria e Donato, Murano.

cration. While this is blind prejudice, it is the Gothic palaces of the 13th to 15th centuries that are one of the city's chief glories. Gothic is the most common city style and also the loveliest. The great Venetian building boom of this period coincided with the expansion of the Ottoman empire. Although this meant the relinquishing of Venice's eastern colonies and retrenchment abroad, the city architecture benefited from the recall of resources and master-craftsmen.

Noble Gothic palaces

Compared with its Byzantine predecessor, the Gothic palace was a nobler yet more ostenta-

tious creation. The pure curve of a Byzantine arch progressed to a pointed Moorish arch and then to a Gothic ogival arch. The Byzantine continuous loggia evolved into a fully-fledged loggia with cusped arches and quatrefoil (four-leaf) motifs. Glorious windows were framed by filigree stonework, with brick and stucco used in delicate two-tone colour combinations. Yet Venetian Gothic is as idiosyncratic as the city: trade with the Levant in the period ensured palaces bore an Islamic and Byzantine stamp.

The Venetian love of *paterae* to embellish facades was extremely resilient and survived until Renaissance times. By the same token, facades continued to be studded with classical

THE CAMPO

More than any great work of art, the homely *campo* (square) encapsulates the distinctiveness of Venice. The quintessential *campo* is probably a lopsided space containing a church, a cluster of decrepit palaces, russet pantiled roofs, the odd warehouse, a bridge, a gondoliers' station, a carved well-head sprouting weeds, and an alleycat lurking in a smelly *sottoportego*. Beneath a facade with a chipped lion's head, a mangey dog suns himself by a flower stall while his master plays cards or chess with a friend from the news-stand next-door. They greet a parishioner going into church, at ease with the ritual of prayer.

As a mosaic of small islands, the Venetian urban pattern is traced with bridges and narrow alleys which unexpectedly lead to a spacious, sun-drenched square. The *campo* is at the heart of the community, enclosing the parish church and lined with patrician palaces, concealing more modest houses behind. Major *campi* contain a monastery or an oratory as well as a *scuola*, a confraternity which acted as the hub of social life for the bourgeoisie. These squares were originally paved in a herringbone brick pattern but this was replaced by hardy flint flagstones in the 18th century. Each *campo* was designed to have at least one cistern and well. The *campo* is often the product of piecemeal development, of demolition and rebuilding, creating a warren of buildings to fill the space. As the writer Jonathan Keates says, "Even St Mark's, which looks harmonious enough today, was flung together piecemeal."

San Marco is the only square in Venice to be called a *piazza:* every other square is either a *campo* or a tinier *campiello*. Each has its own individual charm, from stately Campo Santo Stefano, the place for a chic aperitif in stylish Dorsoduro, to huge Campo San Polo, once the stage for popular fairs and bullfights but now a lively square overrun by boisterous children. Particularly in summer, certain squares are taken over by posing students, notably Campo Sant'Angelo, Campo San Luca, Campo San Barnaba and Campo San Bartolomeo. The tiny *campi* and *campielli* in the Castello district are worth exploring at any time of day, representing the cheery underside of working-class Venice. The *campo* is often one's lasting visual memory of the city.

Greek sculpture or Byzantine carvings copied from Constantinople.

The Ca d'Oro is perhaps the finest Gothic palace, with detail as delicate as an Oriental carpet. Decorated in a Venetian interpretation of Flamboyant Gothic style, the palace's stone tracery becomes lighter and more fragile as it reaches the top, creating a sensation of giddy space. This clever inversion of space and solids is a feature of Venetian vernacular.

The Doge's Palace began life as a 9th-century castle but it was transformed into an undisputed masterpiece of graceful High Gothic style. Seeming to float on air, the loggia and portico ship's keel ceilings, as in Santo Stefano, San Polo and San Giovanni in Bragora.

Renaissance splendour

The end of the 15th century was a golden age for all Venetian art forms, a flowering which was Renaissance Venice. Yet although palaces acquired a classical air, native conservatism prevailed and a hybrid of Venetian Gothic survived well into the 15th century. However, much was built in sandstone rather than brick and supported by exceptionally strong foundations. Inspired by classical architecture, this was a symmetrical style using such motifs as

form a lacy latticework.

As for church architecture, from the 14th century, the intricate floriated Gothic style became common. The Frari is the most glorious of Venetian-Gothic churches, based on a Latin cross plan with three aisles. It has a severe facade with a curved crowning and cross-vaulted roof with sturdy tie-beams. Santi Giovanni e Paolo, known as Zanipolo, is almost as grand, with a similar cross-vaulted roof. Exposed beams are a feature of many Gothic city churches, with the finest taking the form of

LEFT: the Renaissance Contarini-Bovolo staircase.
ABOVE: "Campo Santa Maria Formosa", by Canaletto.

Corinthian capitals, fluted columns, projecting roof cornices and rustication.

The Arsenal, with its crenellations and ceremonial land gate, is considered to be the first flowering of Renaissance architecture. Built in 1460, the land gate leads to the armaments and shipbuilding complex. Other key structures were Antonio da Ponte's Rialto bridge and the Giants' Staircase in the Doge's Palace.

The delightful church of Santa Maria dei Miracoli and Ca' Dario were designed by the Lombardi brothers, master-craftsmen. If the Venetian Renaissance was a compromise between classical precision and local convention, then Ca' Dario expresses its essence. The palace conveys an Oriental richness with its coloured marble reliefs and interlacing design. The flowing arabesques were inspired by Byzantine mosaics in the Basilica of San Marco. Venice owes much to Mauro Coducci (1440–1504), an architect from Bergamo who was inspired by the city. He imposed symmetry on the Venetian model but did not dispense with Byzantine decorative reliefs. His Palazzo Vendramin-Calergi, now the city casino, is a magnificent work, subtly introducing Tuscan sophistication to Gothic Venice. His designs were used for the Clocktower by San Marco and the grandiose Palazzo Zorzi. In addition, he

is also responsible for several buildings at San Marco, from the Zecca (Mint) to the Libreria Sansoviniana, his great library.

If the Renaissance was the apogée of refinement, Baroque Venice belonged to a bold yet less-inspired age. By turns ponderous and whimsical, this was a relatively sober form of Baroque, tempered by Palladianism. The style is characterised by stone rustication and heavy ornamentation. It revels in exuberant stuccowork and flamboyant friezes, with every surface studded with garlands, cherubs, coats of arms or grotesque masks. The inner courtyard became a grand feature of a palace, with gar-

rebuilt the church of Santa Maria Formosa and created the graceful facade of San Zaccaria, his masterpiece.

High Renaissance and Baroque

The High Renaissance was led by Jacopo Sansovino (1486–1570), who quickly adapted to the Venetian sensibility despite his Tuscan background and Roman training. In his role as Superintendent of the Works, he had great influence over Venetian architecture. Ca' Grande on the Grand Canal is a magnificent classical triumph. Here, as in other Venetian palaces, Sansovino established triple water-entrance arches and spandrels adorned with sculpture. He

dens often disappearing. As the prime exponent of Venetian Baroque, Baldassare Longhena (1598–1682) created the theatrical church of La Salute, with its grandiose plan indebted to Palladio's Il Redentore. In both churches and palaces, Longhena was noted for his sense of chiaroscuro, with dynamic and dramatic facades, heavily charged with rich carving. He is also responsible for breaking the three-part rhythm of the Venetian palace by introducing a continuous sequence of windows. Ca' Pesaro has a theatrical inner courtyard and a rusticated Grand Canal facade rich in ornamentation and chiaroscuro effects. Ca' Rezzonico, which was also designed by Longhena, is more restrained.

Classical revival

During the 18th century there was a reaction against Baroque and a return to Palladian values. Grandiose palaces were designed for wealthy *arrivistes*, with dignity and stateliness emphasised by monumental staircases.

Palazzo Grassi, for example, was based on Baroque plans by Longhena but completed by Massari (1686–1766), an architect who was drawn to the new spirit of the Classical revival. Massari created the Palladian facade of the Gesuati church and his masterpiece, the church of La Pietà.

The building of La Fenice opera house in

1790 was one of the last significant Neo-Classical structures to be built in the city.

The end of the Republic signalled an end to building, although there was a slight blip during the Napoleonic era. Modernist plans by architects such as Le Corbusier and Frank Lloyd Wright were rejected as out of place in a conservative city. Yet local fears were probably unjustified. By tradition, non-Venetian architects tend to go native, attuning their designs to the aesthetic sensibility of the city and the uniqueness of the lagoon. ❑

LEFT: interior of Santa Maria della Salute.
ABOVE: facade of Palladio's Il Redentore.

PALLADIO

Andrea Palladio (1508–80) was the leading architect of his day yet his radical classicism was too bold for Republican tastes. As a result, he received few public commissions and no commissions for palaces, making him dependent on the patronage of the religious orders. Palladio was born in the Veneto and worked as a mason on Mannerist monuments but only fully formulated his classical philosophy after visiting Rome in the 1540s. He dedicated the end of his career to transforming the Venetian skyline with his bold buildings.

Although his sublime churches were consigned to the outskirts, with their creation Venice's waterfront vista was complete. His churches are there framing the space where the sky meets the sea. This is true of San Francesco della Vigna, the church and hospice of Le Zitelle and Palladio's two masterpieces: San Giorgio Maggiore *(see page 268)* and Il Redentore *(see page 271)*.

San Giorgio, built in 1565, is a model of stylistic unity and coherent classicism. Created by a master of harmony and proportion, this monastic stage-set has a cloister more fitting to a sumptuous palace than a place of prayer. Il Redentore, built in 1576, is a model of rigour and restraint. Inspired by the Pantheon in Rome, it is designed along the lines of a votive temple.

An unwavering sense of proportion and perspective is reflected in the facades, the pedimented porticoes and the bold yet airy interiors. The subtle, spare designs are enhanced by broad domes, graceful columns and Corinthian capitals. Taken as a whole, Palladio's work on Venetian churches and the villas of the Veneto make him one of the outstanding architects of all time. His country villas, designed for patrician families outside the city, in the Veneto, influenced architectural styles all over the Western world, especially in the United States, England (notably Chiswick House) and Ireland. His use of the Graeco-Roman temple front, with pillars and pediment forming a portico, was probably his most imitated feature.

His treatise, *The Four Books of Architecture,* was also hugely influential in popularising classical architecture. If the term "Palladian" has entered the language, it is a compliment both to his superb buildings and to his legacy as a scholar.

THE VENETIAN PALACE

The grand palaces that line the city's canals give a remarkable insight into the way the Venetians once lived

The Venetian palace, whether decrepit or ruthlessly restored, remains a cornerstone of city life. Closed in and compact, surrounded by water on up to three sides, it seems a hermetically sealed world. For patrician families, the palace was a showy symbol of prestige, a lofty but practical seat of power and the

the Lion of St Mark, medallions and mosaics, even reliefs salvaged from Roman temples or raided from Byzantium during the Crusades.

All were built with both a land and a water entrance, even if the filling in of some canals meant that a few palaces later lost their water entrances. Colourful painted posts, called *paline*,

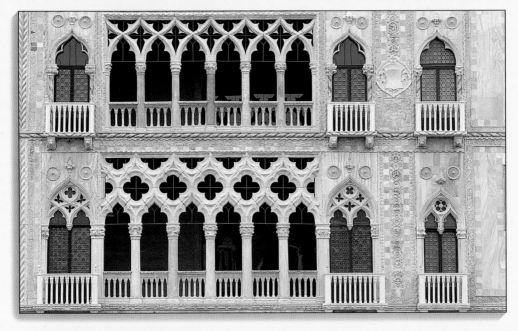

key building in the parish. Designed for commercial and ceremonial purposes, the palace reflects the city's mercantile character. Yet it was also the product of an avowedly aesthetic sensibility, with beauty the main criterion: buildings were "made to look good" ("*che el sia fata che el staga ben*", as the Venetians say).

Unlike the palaces of Florence or Rome, Venetian building principles remained constant. The building blueprint reflects the city's innate conservatism, with Byzantine features still influencing Renaissance and Baroque palaces. Although the style of facades and windows reflects the period, facade "furniture" is a constant. Decorative motifs include coats of arms,

mark the entrance to great palaces and were decorated in the family colours. The waterside entrance is always the principal facade, decorated with Byzantine *paterae*, roundels or precious marbles. The flatness of the facade is relieved by balconies (*pergoli*) rather than loggias or colonnades.

The watergate opens on to the *androne* or great hall. Once lit by torches or heavy lanterns, this gallery runs the depth of the palace. A general misconception is that the ground floor was part boatyard, part entrance hall, the place where family gondolas were stored in winter and where merchants stacked their bales of silks. This romantic notion is dispelled by the damp and draughty reality; gondolas were always in use, while precious fabrics were probably safer stored in adjoining, drier rooms. These dark rooms on either side of the hall often housed the kitchens as well, as indicated by the presence of heavy fireplaces and stone water troughs in some palaces. Nowadays, canalside ground floors are rarely lived in because of the damp.

Some palaces had a mezzanine floor, known as the *mesà* or *mezza*, where the offices were situated and accounts and archives stored. As the commercial function of the palace gave way to noble living, these quarters were transformed into libraries and treasure rooms.

By the 17th century, the draughtiness of the main reception room caused nobles to convert these quarters into cosy sitting rooms. The *piano nobile*, the elegant first floor, which has the most elaborate windows in the palace, contains the *portego*, the main drawing room, and a series of reception rooms and bedrooms leading off it. Suitable for lavish banquets, this central gallery often runs the length of the house, culminating in a balcony. Later forming a loggia, this provided the ventilation necessary to survive both the winter humidity and the stifling summer heat.

Luxurious fabrics

Despite ostentatiously frescoed ceilings, this was a spartan interior offset by the use of luxurious fabrics. From Gothic times, stamped and gilded leather lined the walls, with the *portego* hung with brocades, damask and silks. These products of trade with the Levant were preferred to tapestries. Although stuccowork and paintings became popular in the 17th century, the *portego* has traditionally spurned comfort. *Objets d'art*, Murano glass chandeliers, a *chaise-longue* and a clutch of Oriental rugs still encapsulate the austere elegance of the grandest Venetian palaces. But damp is a deterrent to over-elaborate decoration and the high humidity means that constant refurbishment is required.

Flooring is typically made of *terrazzo*. Layers of powdered marble, in a clay and lime paste, are strewn with fragments of coloured marble and then smoothed down and polished. Elaborate floors included glass, mother of pearl

or fragments of gold mosaics. This impressive but costly flooring solution is still used today.

Servants' quarters

The upper floors were reached by secondary staircases and housed a warren of rooms for relatives and children. The attics tended to be used as servants' quarters and for the kitchens, which were often situated here to allow smells to escape. The decorative chimney pots were also highly functional, the tall upended cone acting as a spark-trap. Chimney pots could take the form of an inverted bell, double stack, obelisk or even the funnel-shaped pots seen in the paint-

ings of Carpaccio. Linked to inner chambers, complicated double flues with bulbous external chimney breasts, these quirky chimney pots still enliven the Venetian rooftops.

Perched on the terraced roof was an *altana*, a wooden platform where noblewomen relaxed in private. Internal courtyards were introduced in the 17th century, although Gothic palaces may have had courtyards at the back. These were reached by imposing land gates displaying the owner's coat of arms. Space constraints meant that many courtyards were swallowed up by encroaching buildings. However, delightful courtyards and secret, wisteria-clad gardens remain, often the preserve of cats. ❑

LEFT: the latticework facade of the Ca d'Oro.
RIGHT: grand stairway in the entrance hall of the Baroque Ca' Rezzonico.

ARTISTS OF COLOUR AND LIGHT

Colour, light and texture distinguish Venetian painting
and reflect the city's watery world

Venetian sensibility reflected a shimmering, watery world. The constantly changing lagoon light created a fluid sense of space, fostering a mood of impermanence, a suspicion of form and an ambiguity that is absent from landlocked schools of art. Partly in response to the environment, the Venetian school embodies a poetic, painterly sensibility at odds with the rational, monumental and sculptural Florentine style. By the same token, Venice turns its back on the classicism and intellectual rigour of the Romans. To the Venetians, colour, light, texture and space were more important than form.

Venice's status as a great trading empire exposed it to new artistic influences, first from Byzantium and later from Flanders and the Italian schools of Padua, Mantua, Ferrara and Florence. However, Venetian insularity prevailed, with new ideas seeping in slowly and artistic developments transformed into a uniquely Venetian way of seeing things. Paradoxically, thanks to the inclusiveness of the Venetian vision and the varied sources of patronage, Venetian art was less formulaic than other schools, with the greatest painters free to form their own inimitable personal styles.

The Bellini family

Giovanni Bellini (c1430–1516) was the leading exponent of Renaissance art in Venice. Although his brother, Gentile Bellini (1429–1507), rose to be official state painter, Giovanni ("Giambellino") was the genius, an unworldly painter less concerned with fulfilling a patron's wishes. In later years, he succeeded his brother as state painter and was also buried in the church of Santi Giovanni e Paolo, the resting place of the Doges. Venice was slow to absorb Renaissance values but, largely thanks to Bellini, evolved its own expressive style.

With Bellini, oil paint displaced *tempera* (egg-based pigment). Its slow drying time

LEFT: detail from the sublime Bellini altarpiece (1505) in San Zaccaria. RIGHT: Bellini's "Madonna and Child" altarpiece (1488) in the Frari.

encouraged experimentation, with oils offering more subtle tonal gradation and a greater simulation of textures.

Influenced by Mantegna, his Paduan brother-in-law, Bellini had an understanding of perspective and was one of the first Venetian artists to include landscapes in the background of his

paintings. He revitalised Venetian painting, infusing his art with light, literally seen as a medium of grace. (*For a guide to Bellini's finest works, see page 70.*)

Carpaccio

Vittorio Carpaccio (c1465–1523/6) is arguably the most Venetian of painters, though by no means the greatest. Unlike Giovanni Bellini, Carpaccio was more interested in everyday life than in mood. Compared with Giorgione and Titian, Carpaccio was not innovative and his paintings have a static quality beneath the surface bustle. Yet the influence of Flemish art is apparent in his miniaturist precision, the details

In the steps of Bellini

Giovanni Bellini is often considered the founder of the Venetian school. "Giambellino", as he was called, admired Flemish art for its realism and Florentine art for its purity and perspective. Apart from his technical mastery of painting without modelling in line, his contribution was expressiveness, conveying moods of grace, tenderness and poignancy. Bellini's success in freeing Venetian painting from Byzantine stiffness can be appreciated in the masterpieces he made for his home city. Although much in demand in

IOANNES   BELLINVS

Padua, Ferrara and Verona, Bellini turned down commissions if he felt unable to conform to strict schedules. In Venice, his work in the Doge's Palace was so painstakingly slow that officials were despatched to monitor his daily progress.

A stroll centred on Bellini's masterpieces is an illuminating way to sense his rapt stillness of mood or to while away a wet day. A number of works are known as *sacre conversazioni* ("holy conversations") because they depict saints in a silent spiritual dialogue. The Accademia is the natural place to appreciate his mystical work before moving on to explore the city churches. These are not all limpid, idealised Madonnas: in his poignant *Pietà*, the suffering Virgin cradles her son in her arms, her

careworn face a testament to the painter's expressive powers; the city of Vicenza looms in the background, showing Bellini's love of landscape and his skill at opening out a canvas.

Also in the Accademia is the San Giobbe altarpiece, intended for the Renaissance church of St Job. Painted at the height of Bellini's powers, this is a cunning illusionistic space with a coffered ceiling heightening the perspective.

After pausing for refreshment in Le Belle Arti bar beside the Accademia, take *vaporetto* lines 1 or 82 two stops to San Tomà and follow signs to the Frari, a barn-like church housing a Bellini masterpiece. The *Madonna and Saints* is a subtle and luminous triptych of the Virgin flanked by Saints Peter, Nicholas, Mark and Benedict, who carries the Benedictine book of monastic rule. Illusionistic effects are created by the *trompe l'oeil* moulding. A couple of cherubic angels *(pictured on page 79)* play at the feet of the Madonna with flute and drum. The musical motif recurs in Bellini's work, reinforcing the notion of music as a symbol of order and harmony.

After returning to San Tomà, catch *vaporetto* lines 1 or 82 in the opposite direction to San Zaccaria. The delightful church of San Zaccaria contains a superb Bellini altarpiece. The work shows a beguiling interplay of colour and light in a rich blend of reds, golds and blues. This soft and lyrical *sacra conversazione* embodies the inner harmony implicit in the finest works of Quattrocento and High Renaissance art. As in Bellini's work in the Frari, there is a musical motif, one of the loveliest elements of the painting. For lunch, try Al Vecio Canton, a charming pizzeria close to San Zaccaria (*see page 323 for details*).

Next stop is the vast church of Santi Giovanni e Paolo. Inside is Bellini's *St Vincent Ferrier* altarpiece, a work of rapt devotion, showing the saint flanked by St Christopher and St Sebastian. Created between 1460 and 1465, the panel painting charts the passage from Gothic to Renaissance art since, although the figures are presented in separate panels, the painting is given a unity by the new use of perspective. Finally, follow Barbaria delle Tole eastwards to the church of San Francesco della Vigna, set slightly off the beaten track. The *Madonna and Saints* is another "holy conversation", set in a luminous landscape. The dedicated can finish the day in style with a Bellini cocktail in Harry's Bar. ❑

ABOVE: Giovanni Bellini, the family genius.
RIGHT: Carpaccio's "St George and the Dragon" in the Scuola di San Giorgio degli Schiavoni.

of faces and scenery. While no great master of perspective, he captured the texture of Venetian life and mastered the minutiae without ever losing the unity of the scene. Critics claim that in some respects this is a fantasy Venice in which colours are brighter than in real life and the architecture more extravagant. This is to neglect the celebratory spirit of an artist whose paintings offer an enticing vision of Venetian life: canal-sides crowded with onlookers; corners of palaces, from pinkish-hued porticos to curious casements and chimneys. There are ceremonial galleys and gondolas; the noble profiles of confraternity worthies; prelates resplendent in damask copes; cocky young blades in red hose and black Venetian caps; ambassadors conforming to strict protocol; cool Venetian ladies at leisure. A sense of the city as cosmopolitan melting pot is achieved by background figures, from enigmatic Moors to Jewish merchants and turbaned Turks. In the corners lurk a multitude of animals: symbolic lions, doves and dragons compete with whippet-like hunting dogs, Arabian mounts and pampered Maltese lap-dogs.

Symbol of Venice

Carpaccio specialised in pictorial cycles for the Scuole and also painted for the State. His Lion

THE BYZANTINE TRADITION

The Byzantine tradition confirmed Venetian art in its conservatism and love of ornate decoration. One of the city's earliest known artists, Paolo Veneziano (c1290-c1360), created static symmetrical works set against a shimmering Byzantine gold background. His great work in the Accademia is the gloriously decorative *Coronation of the Virgin,* in which the central figures are rendered nearly invisible amongst the large amounts of decorative gold.

Veneziano is credited with introducing the taste for panel paintings to Venice, particularly into the churches. His methods also made sacred art more intimate, with panels placed at eye-level to their admirers, by contrast with the inaccessiblity of mosaics and murals, which either decorated floors or were tucked away at the top of lofty domes.

Iconic Byzantine influences resurface in Venetian Renaissance art: in Bellini's decorative backgrounds or Veronese's shimmering surfaces. The Byzantine tradition was at one with the Venetians' painterly sensibility and love of surface colour. These are luminous, vibrant, harmonious colours: rich reds, glittering golds and warm sepias. Veronese added to this repertoire with his velvety greens and deep blues, while Tiepolo brought with him a palette of subtle pastels, including mauves and pinks, creams and pale greens.

of St Mark in the Doge's Palace is both a symbolic depiction of the might of the Republic and an animated portrayal of the winged beast dominating St Mark's and the Doge's Palace. Today his works can mostly be admired in the Accademia and in the Scuola di San Giorgio degli Schiavoni.

Giorgione

Giorgione (c1478–1510) has been called "the first modern artist" thanks to the subjectivity of his vision. There are tantalisingly few of his paintings in

RENAISSANCE MAN

"Titian (Tiziano Vecellio) was the complete Renaissance artist. His range remains unsurpassed in Western art." – Berenson

vision, seeing the depth of shadow as a sign of the strangeness of personality itself. Modern critics are tempted to project a vulnerability, loneliness and existential angst upon this Renaissance artist.

Titian

Titian (c1487–1576), known as Tiziano Vecellio in Italian, was the polished master of the Venetian High Renaissance style. After Bellini's death, Titian became the undisputed leader of Venetian painting. Indeed, he was the complete Renaissance

existence and those that remain are resolutely labelled enigmatic. In Venice, he is noted for two works in the Accademia. *La Vecchia* is both a realistic portrait of an elderly woman and a meditation on old age, accompanied by the telling inscription "with time". Poignantly, Giorgione died young, probably of the plague. The *Tempest* is a poetic and puzzling work that conveys a sense of enchantment disturbed by a mysterious inner tension.

In a sense, Giorgione was a Romantic before his time. His understanding of *sfumato*, the soft gradations from light to dark, weaves a spellbinding atmosphere. Some critics impose a psychologically modern interpretation on his

artist, with ineffable technique, varied subject matter and mastery of different media. His range remains unsurpassed in Western art, encompassing portraits, paintings, mythological *poesie*, allegories and altarpieces. His style is characterised by a monumentality akin to Roman painting, by bold design, sweeping forms and sensuous modelling. Allied to this is his expressive style, gorgeous use of colour and the carnal confidence of his nudes. In spite of this enormous scope, he preferred the soft contours of the Venetian school to the sculptural monumentality of the Roman school.

Titian's virtuosity and prolific output made him much in demand throughout Europe. At the height of his career he received commissions from the Pope, the Emperor Charles V and Philip II of Spain. If he is not particularly well represented in his home town, it is partly because Napoleon commandeered a clutch of Titians as the spoils of war – Venice's loss was the Louvre's gain.

Titian's greatest paintings in Venice are in the Frari, with the revolutionary nature of The *Assumption* vying with the secular opulence of the *Pesaro Altarpiece*. The *Assumption* echoes the vital confusion of life itself, reinforced by the image of mortals being swept up by the spiritual world. The Accademia possesses several

described his painting style as, "extravagant, unpredictable, fast-working and resolute: the most formidable brain that painting has ever known". As a Mannerist artist praising another of the same persuasion, his view may be viewed as slightly subjective.

Tintoretto's own aims were equally immodest: he wished to "reconcile the drawing of Michelangelo with the colours of Titian". Michelangelo's influence is clear in Tintoretto's virile compositions and battles with perspective: the bold foreshortening, the striking poses struck by his subjects, the passion for paint. Indeed, it is not fanciful to call the Scuola

of Titian's works, notably his powerful *Pietà*, which he had intended for his own tomb. Elsewhere, a luminous *Annunciation* graces the Scuola Grande di San Rocco while the Doge's Palace has several Titians, including a dramatic St Christopher, which is frescoed over a door of the Philosophers' Chamber.

Tintoretto

Tintoretto (1518–94) acquired his nickname ("the little dyer") after his father's trade as a silk-dyer. Vasari, the father of art criticism,

LEFT: Titian's "Annunciation". **ABOVE:** Tintoretto's "Visitation". Both are in the Scuola Grande di San Rocco.

Grande di San Rocco Tintoretto's Sistine Chapel.

Tintotetto's debt to Titian is clear in his love of colour and mood but these are from a bold, less-subtle palette, dominated by virtuoso chiaroscuro effects. In short, Tintoretto's Mannerist sensibility sacrifices luminosity for overwhelming contrasts and theatrical effects. But Tintoretto should not be underrated: he brought a new passion and religious fervour to Venetian painting.

Although unworldy, he worked on sumptuous decorative schemes for the State, including mythological battles interpreted as allegories glorifying the Serene Republic. Scenes such as his *Paradise* in the Doge's Palace revel in the majesty of Christ and the Madonna, accentuated by the halo effect of swirling clouds. (*For a tour of his works in the city, see the Tintoretto Trail on page 242.*)

Veronese

Veronese (1528–88) was nick-named after his native city of Verona, but his concerns were utterly Venetian. As the art critic John Steer says: "If colour is the most characteristic quality of Venetian art, then the most essentially Venetian artist of his period

SOUVENIR HUNTERS
Canalettos were prized souvenirs for the Grand Tourists and his works were exported by the crateful: few remain in the city today.

once to get the full cumulative effect. Veronese captured the taste of the times and was chosen to work on the decoration of the Doge's Palace: *The Apotheosis of Venice* is one of his finest mythological scenes. To great acclaim, he created the sumptuous painting in the church of San Sebastiano (*see page 255*), where the artist is appropriately buried. After the death of Veronese, art in Venice declined, and more than a hundred years passed before La Serenissima was able to produce another great painter.

is Veronese." As a colourist, he was the true successor to Bellini while in his striving for splendour and decorative detail, his works echoed the Byzantine style.

As a society painter, he portrayed the patrician ideal, a civilised life of leisure, a parade of sumptuous fabrics and Palladian decors. It is a fantasy world of formal and spiritual harmony, grace and Olympian perfection. These heroic, classical paintings are concerned with pictorial effects rather than narrative: on such dazzling stage-sets colour is used to convey mood, often one of eternal spring. However, in the hands of such a studied, subtle artist, these are slow-burning pictures, which need to be viewed more than

Canaletto

Antonio Canal (1697–1768), known as Canaletto, was greatly admired for his limpid landscapes and photographic observations. In Venice, he worked from nature, which was unusual for the period, creating detailed views (*vedute*) which influenced generations of landscape painters. Yet his early career as a painter of stage-sets meant that a theatrical approach coloured these scenes. Canaletto's "photographic eye" captured cloud formations and changing light but was not averse to creating exaggerated perspectives. The desired effect was a subtly idealised stage set, replete with a sense of order and realism, grandeur and prosperity. Venice was beloved by Grand Tourists, notably the English, French and Germans. As the forerunners of modern souvenir-hunters, these acquisitive nobles became collectors of Venetian keepsakes, of which the most prized were paintings. Given that Canaletto's work was exported or copied by the crateful, little remains in Venice itself, apart from a few works in Ca' Rezzonico and the Accademia. Although his depiction of San Giacomo di Rialto is better known, Canaletto's architectural whimsy in the Accademia was the work that won him membership of this august body.

Tiepolo

Giambattista Tiepolo (1696–1770) is celebrated for his sublime artifice, heroic style and a virtuosity reminiscent of the Old Masters. Tiepolo was taken under the wing of the Venetian aristocracy: his heroic style, inventiveness and bravura display of skills struck a chord with his patrons, leading to commissions to decorate the finest palaces. Art critic Adriano Mariuz comments on Tiepolo's desire to become another Veronese, "steeped in the flamboyance and airiness of the Baroque as well as in the elegance and playfulness of the Rococo".

Tiepolo was a fresco painter with a love of grand designs. Created in a Venice on the wane, these tottering pyramids of allegorical figures aspire to Olympian grandeur. The art is decadent in that it is not life-assertive but bound by conventions, albeit forged by an unfettered imagination. Critics claim that Tiepolo lacked real passion, replacing it with bursts of motiveless intensity. Certainly, he was a master of elusive mood, excelling at langorous figures whose moods are not matched to the narrative reality.

Tiepolo's palette consisted of pastel tones; delicate, airy colours make the space within his pictures shine with an unearthly radiance. This has earned him the epithet of "poet of light". Yet despite the ethereal settings, his figures have a fleshy, corporeal quality. His was a beguiling and grandiose vision but also one throbbing with sensuality. Such mastery of the medium of fresco made him much in demand, with his career taking him from Venice to the royal court of Charles III in Madrid and the German court

of the Prince-Bishop of Wurzburg. In an era that exalted virtuosity and the glorification of the patron, Tiepolo's triumphal allegories gave visual expression to the autocratic political ideology that dominated the Europe of his day.

The end of an era

The death of Tiepolo marked the end of an era. However, even after the fall of the Republic, Venetian "minor" painters were still superior to many "major" painters elsewhere in Europe. The final flowering came with perspective and genre painters. Venetian painters followed in Canaletto's footsteps, focusing on picturesque,

seemingly photographic views, pastiches custom-made for the collecting mania of the aristocracy. Francesco Guardi (1712–93) was an impressionistic painter whose views and caprices are, according to the art critic Michael Levey, an "intense response to Venice as a watery setting, its scattered islands, its sense of illimitable distance and silence amid crumbling fragments of ruin". Longhi (1733–1813), was most at home languishing in patrician palaces: as the leading genre painter, he mirrored Venetian high society with charm and intimacy. ❑

● *The best places to see Venetian art are the Accademia (see page 259), the Frari (page 222) and the Scuola Grande di San Rocco (page 223).*

LEFT: Tiepolo's flights of fancy in the Carmini.
RIGHT: Longhi's celebrated "Rhinoceros" (1751) in the Ca' Rezzonico.

THE OPERATIC TRADITION

The city of masks, romance and drama comes together in opera, which has long been a high point in Venice's cultural life

As one of the world's most operatic cities, Venice has a distinguished tradition in this field, which seems only natural. A decisive factor in establishing the genre in the city was the opening of the first public opera house. Taken out of the private chamber, this complex and sophisticated music entered the public domain and was no longer exclusively the preserve of the nobility.

Venice's status as a state with a Republican constitution, beyond the control of outside forces, also played an important role in making opera a popular national art form. The leading composers of their day wrote works for Venice, from Rossini and Bellini to Verdi and Wagner. Handel and Scarlatti both conducted their own operas in Venice. Opera remains close to the Venetian heart despite the tragic fire at La Fenice (*see page 80*).

Operatic origins

Although opera first emerged in 16th-century Florence, the baton was quickly passed on to Venice. The 17th and 18th centuries were the golden age of Venetian music, celebrated by Monteverdi and Vivaldi and, by the time opera had been defined as a special genre, the city had become the most important centre in Italy.

In the last 20 years of the 17th century more than 150 operas were performed in the city, including 20 new ones.The operas of the early period perfectly reflected the tastes of Venetian society. Although Classical mythology provided the colourful plots, the characterisation reflected the great scandals of the day. This realism was one of the reasons for opera's success in the city, with Venetians only too familiar with the traditional operatic themes of intrigue, conspiracy and betrayal.

In time, it was Venetian composers who developed the sensuous melodies that have

come to be considered the quintessential hallmark of all Italian opera.

Monteverdi in Venice

Claudio Monteverdi (1567–1643) is regarded as the founder of Venetian opera. Summoned to Venice after an early musical career at the Man-

tuan court, he was appointed choirmaster of San Marco and Master of Music for the Republic, remaining in his post for 30 years. He was the traditional successor to Andrea Gabrieli (1510–86) and his nephew Giovanni Gabrieli (1557–1612), the early masters of massed choirs and Baroque polyphonic music. Monteverdi wrote seven of his operas in Venice, proving his command of musical characterisation, especially in *Poppea*, a late work.

Opera goes public

Teatro San Cassiano, founded in 1637, was the first of many grand public opera houses. By the 18th century, there were 19 such opera houses

LEFT: poster for a performance of Verdi's "Aida" in La Fenice opera house (1881). **RIGHT:** monument in the Giardini Pubblici to Giuseppe Verdi, who wrote five operas while engaged by La Fenice.

in Venice, including La Fenice. These theatres were owned by prominent Venetian families who mounted short seasons, hence the constant renewal of the repertoire.

The Venetians were a demanding audience who expected strong librettos and elaborate staging. They got what they craved, and audiences were held spellbound by fantastic stage effects, which could convey dreams and ghostly visitations. Buildings were made to collapse, waves, thunder and lightening could all be simulated, and the clouds on which the gods were enthroned could divide into three as they sank, then re-form as they rose.

Bravos and rotten eggs

In the 17th century the craze for opera swept the city but the stage action often played second fiddle to the social aspects: the opera was the place to pick up the latest gossip, play cards, or simply to dine in the privacy of one's box. Yet outstanding vocal performances could provoke storms of applause. The spectators vied with one another in their cries of Bravo! or threw roses and lace handkerchiefs at the feet of the prima donnas. After the première of Rossini's *Semiramis*, an enthusiastic crowd escorted the maestro home in a convoy of gondolas while an orchestra reprised melodies from the opera.

VERDI IN VENICE

Giuseppe Verdi (1813–1901) was a patriot who found a responsive audience in Republican-minded Venice. As one of the greatest composers of his age, Verdi inflamed Venetian passions with five of his finest dramatic works. After diplomatically announcing that Milan's La Scala needed a rest from him, (with four of his operas in as many years), Verdi signed a contract with La Fenice. Although La Fenice was a leading opera house, Verdi's motives had more to do with his impatience at the incompetence of La Scala's management. Milan's loss was Venice's gain and *Hernani* was premiered there in 1844. The public were enchanted by Verdi's music and left humming the melodies. Seven years later, the season's popular hit was "*La donna è mobile*" from *Rigoletto*.

The heroic composer gave his operas stirring undertones during Italy's struggle for national unity. From 1848, Verdi's name became a rallying cry for his countrymen in the fight for freedom from Austrian domination. The acronym **V**(ittorio) **E**(manuele) **R**(e) **D'I**(talia) was used as a reference to the first king of Italy, eventually crowned in 1861. In 1866, during a performance of *Il Trovatore*, the stage was bombarded by bouquets of red, white and green, the colours of the Italian tricolour.

Singers who were indisposed, however, felt the public's wrath with a fusilade of rotten eggs and tomatoes, radishes or leeks.

The appointment of Verdi was a milestone in the history of La Fenice; here was the greatest composer of Italian *bel canto* creating works for Venice. But all was not lost after the passing of this golden age. La Fenice sustained its reputation, staging the Italian premiere of Wagner's *Rienzi* in 1873 and, after the composer's death in 1883, presenting the entire Ring cycle in Ger-

LEFT: Giuseppe Verdi and Claudio Monteverdi.
BELOW: angelic musicians in a Bellini altarpiece, Frari.

man. While most European opera houses could only offer makeshift programmes during World War II, La Fenice presented 68 premières. In 1930 the opera house created a festival of contemporary music, proof that Venice was committed to more than the classical canon. Its innovative approach reaped rewards: the world premières of Stravinsky's *The Rake's Progress* (1951), Britten's *The Turn of the Screw* (1954) and Gershwin's *Porgy and Bess* (1935). The illustrious tradition continues today, even if the burning down of La Fenice has forced the opera house to decamp temporarily to a tented affair, mounted alongside the Tronchetto car park. ❑

PRIMA DONNAS AND CASTRATI

The 18th century saw the emergence of the concept of the star soloist, the female prima donnas and the castrati, their curious male counterparts. Their way was paved by the enrichment of operatic forms, the creation of fine arias and coloratura, or virtuoso, voice passages. The *primo uomo* (leading man) was usually a castrated male singer. Giving the leading male character a treble voice was a popular custom which started in the 16th century and was all the fashion in 18th-century Italy, only finally dying out in the 19th century.

The custom of castrating young boys before puberty to preserve their clear soprano or contralto voices may have been linked to an earlier prohibition against women singing opera in public. The castrato possessed a unique tone of voice, as well as the lung capacity necessary to sing with great power, and the skill to scale the opera's most florid vocal passages.

Castrati and prima donnas were so worshipped by their public that they became capricious divas. As over-indulged soloists, they decided which arias to sing and which to leave out, as well as laying down the coloratura passages which best suited their own vocal virtuosity, regardless of the composer's original intentions.

LA FENICE: THE FIRE AND THE PASSION

In 1996, Venice's premier opera house burned down for the third time.

Was it an act of God – or was there a more sinister plot?

On 29 January 1996 fire raged through La Fenice opera house. Many Venetians, including the Mayor, sobbed as their beloved Phoenix burnt down before their eyes. Normally self-controlled citizens could not contemplate the loss of this jewel-box of a theatre. The rest of the city awoke in shock to discover

that the conflagration had engulfed musical instruments, paintings, costumes and sets; 200 years of history were reduced to four smoke-charred walls. Dame Joan Sutherland, the celebrated diva, was stunned: "It was probably the most beautiful opera house in the world; singing in the Fenice felt like being inside a diamond." Franco Zeffirelli, the film director, saw the tragedy both as "a cultural outrage" and a challenge: "An opera house is like a sponge that can absorb the best of man's creativity; but art must survive and so the Phoenix will rise again."

In a sense, this was the third fire in its history. The first Fenice replaced a 17th-century theatre which had burnt down in 1774. The former

owners named the new theatre La Fenice (The Phoenix) in reference to the family's own survival after a fire and forced re-location. Inaugurated in 1792, the opera house lived to rue its name when, in 1836, fire razed it to the ground. However, just a year later, La Fenice rose like the proverbial phoenix from the ashes, rebuilt as before. Despite renovations in 1854 and 1938, the theatre retained its Classical 18th-century appearance. Yet in 1996 the "Phoenix" must again have rued its unlucky name.

Feast for the senses

The first theatre was built by Gianantonio Selva. After the fire, it was recreated by two of his pupils, thus ensuring architectural continuity. For its time, La Fenice was a sober and highly functional building with two facades: an understated main facade and an arcaded canal-side entrance. A clever use of space was achieved by means of a grand staircase and an ingenious series of concealed stairways. By contrast with the restrained exterior, the richly decorated auditorium was a feast for the senses: a red and gold Rococo confection in a horseshoe-shaped design. On gala occasions, the balconies and five tiers of boxes were adorned with sweet-smelling roses. Beyond the gilt and stucco surface, performers appreciated the acoustics and intimacy, with the Imperial Box much closer to the stage than at La Scala.

The recent fire would resemble the plot of a comic opera if the consequences were not so grave. The blaze broke out at night, when Campo San Fantin was deserted; the theatre's smoke alarms and sprinkler systems had been mysteriously turned off; the night-watchman was nowhere to be found so there was a delay in calling the fire brigade. The draining of the canals left fire-fighters suffering from a water shortage; the water pressure was too low to reach the upper floors. When helicopters finally tackled the blaze, the theatre was a lost cause.

An electrical fault was soon ruled out and a more sinister story emerged. As flames engulfed the building, a photographer took pictures showing the fire had started in two separate places, pointing towards arson. Conspiracy theorists were quick to make links with the cultural terrorism that struck Italy in the 1990s: the torching of Turin Cathedral, the burning down of the opera house in Bari, and the bombing of the Uffizi Gallery in Florence. The Mafia or shadowy terrorist groups are held responsible, choosing such targets as a blow against the State and a sign of their power. The Mafia have a low profile in Venice but are believed to own hotel interests in the city and to hold a stake in the lucrative water transport business. The blaze coincided with the capture of a Mafia boss in the Veneto region and the Mafia theory has been supported by police informers and witnesses.

A simpler theory attributes the disaster to a bungled attempt to defer building deadlines. The fire took place during renovation work on the theatre. The builders, behind schedule and due to face financial penalties, might have started a small blaze to cover their tracks, a ploy which backfired. There was also speculation that Italian separatists might have been involved. However, given the slow pace of Italian justice and the political pressures put upon judges, the truth may never be known.

Facing the music

The aftermath of the fire had serious consequences for the city. The orchestra was made homeless, forced to play in small Venetian churches or to give charity concerts in other cities. Instruments and costumes were scattered throughout the Scuole, the former guild houses. The Mayor sought to sustain the bonds between the opera house and the public: "A theatre is more than a building, it is also artists, musicians, a workforce, a programme." Clutching their musical instruments, the orchestra dutifully posed for a solemn photograph in the shell of their beloved theatre. The wreck was later combed for clues and salvage: pieces of plasterwork, shards of mirrors, chandeliers and gilded doors would be of use in the restoration.

The decision was swiftly taken to rebuild the theatre before the year 2000, "*com'era, dov' era*" (as it was, where it was). The Italian State, aware that the eyes of the world were on Venice, acted with less sloth than usual: funds were

quickly released, even if rebuilding was delayed for 18 months, supposedly to allow the criminal investigation to run its course. Friends of La Fenice rallied to the cause and a series of benefit concerts were staged. The efficient international agencies also went into action, spurred on by the British Venice in Peril Fund and the American Save Venice Committee. Venice itself responded with alacrity, selling Phoenix memorabilia, creating a press office and publishing a popular magazine dedicated to charting plans for the future of La Fenice.

Meanwhile, conservative Venetians were asked to change the habits of a lifetime and

attend a new auditorium. Chic opera lovers initially turned up their noses at the PalaFenice, a tented structure on the grim garage island of Tronchetto. However, Venetians over the water welcomed the theatre's reasonable prices and its proximity to the mainland. The acoustics left much to be desired, with performances of *Don Giovanni* punctuated by the foghorns of passing ferries. Even so, city pride eventually prevailed and the audiences returned.

With the re-opening of La Fenice by the Millennium, opera lovers can expect a change in musical fortunes. Although surpassed by today's first division opera houses, optimists hope the Phoenix can again perform wonders. ❏

LEFT: "the most beautiful opera house in the world".
RIGHT: clearing up after the 1996 fire.

COSMOPOLITAN CUISINE

There's a feast for the stomach as well as the eye. Venice is noted for top-quality seafood, accompanied by sparkling wine and followed by delicious desserts

When it comes to commenting on Venetian cuisine, food critics tend to damn Venetian food as overpriced and underachieving. Certainly, the difficulty of transporting fresh produce adds 15 per cent to restaurant prices. Mass tourism also means that the city can get away with grim "tourist menus", indifferent service and inferior breakfasts. Yet for seafood lovers, the cuisine can be memorable, with soft-shelled crabs from Murano, plump red mullet, pasta heaped with lobster or black and pungent with cuttlefish ink.

According to Alastair Little, the British gourmet chef and Italophile, "The city's cosmopolitan past and superb produce imported from the Veneto have given rise to Italy's most eclectic and subtle style of cookery." Fine praise indeed. Like their southern neighbours the Sicilians, the Venetians absorbed culinary ideas from the Arabs; they also raided Byzantium and, according to the Middle Eastern cookery writer Claudia Roden, translated it into their own simple style: "If you could see the fish come in live at dawn in barges on the Grand Canal straight on to the market stalls, you would understand why all they want to do is lightly fry, poach or grill it."

As the hub of a cosmopolitan trading empire, Venice was bristling with foreign communities, each with its own culinary tradition. As a bazaar city, Venice raided the recipe books of the Arabs, Armenians, Greeks, Jews and Turks. Venetian trading posts in the Levant gave the city access to spices, the secret of subtle Venetian cookery. Pimento, turmeric, ginger, cinnamon, cumin, cloves, nutmeg, saffron and vanilla show the oriental influences; pine-nuts, raisins, almonds and pistachios play their part.

Reflecting later conquests of Venice, these exotic ingredients are enriched with a dash of French or Austrian cuisine. From the end of the

18th century, French influence meant that Oriental spices were supplanted by Mediterranean herbs. The French brioche was eagerly added to the breakfast repertoire, as was the Belgian waffle and the Turkish *crescente* (literally "a crescent"). The appearance of this croissant dates back to the Turkish defeat outside the walls of

Vienna in 1683. The Austrian conquest may have left Venice with a bitter taste in its mouth but it also left the city with an appetite for sweet apple strudel and *krapfen* (doughnuts).

Eclectic tastes

A classic Middle-Eastern inspired dish is *sarde in saor*, tart sardines marinated in the standard Venetian sauce, *saor*. *Melanzane in saor*, made with aubergines, is the vegetarian version. *Saor* can mean savoury or tasty, possibly derived from the dialect word for *sapore*, meaning flavour. It is a spicy sauce made with permutations of onions, white wine, raisins, vinegar, pine-nuts and olive oil.

PRECEDING PAGES: fresh catch from the Adriatic; fish features on menus more often than meat.
LEFT: the Erberia, the Rialto fruit and vegetable market.
RIGHT: eating out in the heart of the Rialto.

For visitors who spurn the "tourist menu", there is often a choice between basking in the beauty of Venice over an exorbitantly priced dinner or hunting down an unpretentious *trattoria* in a malodorous back canal. Without unlimited means, it is hard to satisfy soul and stomach in one sitting. This is the syndrome known as not having one's cake and eating it: dinner with a view and Diner's Card or authenticity on a plate in a cramped cellar. However, with perseverance (and probably on the last day of your visit), you will join discriminating Venetians in finding an elusive table with a courtyard, a view, subtle service and genuine home cooking.

The *antipasti* (appetisers) will feature fresh seafood, raw, fried or boiled, including *tartuffi di mare* (sea truffles) or *peoci salati*, mussels cooked in the pan with parsley and garlic. Those who don't care for seafood should try *crostini* or roast vegetable dishes.

A typical *primo* (first course) is a *minestra* (soup) such as *pasta e fasioi,* a murky brown sludge, based on pasta and beans, and tasting better than it looks, thanks to the blend of borlotti beans, celery, carrots, onions, rosemary, basil and sage. If eating pasta, check that it is home-made (*fatta in casa*). Popular pasta dishes are *bigoli in salsa* (wholewheat spaghetti in a spicy sauce), *pappardelle alla granseola* (pasta with crab), and *spaghetti con astice* (with lobster). Expect a variety of seafood dishes using tiny sea snails (*lumache*), mussels (*cozze*) and cuttlefish (*seppie*).

As a *secondo* (second course), there is fish of every description, including *seppie alla veneziana*, cuttlefish cooked in its own ink. This dish is served with polenta, maize porridge, white or yellow according to the *trattoria*. Contorni (side dishes) include a whole palette of vegetables to choose from. The best are grilled or fried, such as *radicchio ai ferri*, red endive fried with oil and pepper. Toast-sized chunks of polenta are served as an accompaniment to many dishes.

As for *dolci* (desserts), a typical one is *crema fritta alla veneziana*, custard which is cooled, cut into squares, and refried in egg and breadcrumbs. Those with a sweet tooth will like *tiramisu*, which is now enjoying international popularity, but which was originally brought from Byzantium by the Venetians.

Riso (rice), rather than pasta is the predominant canvas for a culinary display. Rice was introduced by the Arabs and remains the most versatile aspect of the local cuisine. Creamy Venetian risotto offers endless possibilities, flavoured with spring vegetables, meat, game or fish. *Risi e bisi* ("rice and peas") is a thick soup flavoured with ham, celery and onion, the star of rice dishes. Highly recommended are the seasonal vegetable risottos, cooked with asparagus tips, artichoke hearts, fennel, courgettes or pumpkins. An Oriental variant involves the addition of sultanas and pine-nuts. To achieve the creamy consistency, the rice is fried with

onions and ladled over with stock and wine. Venetians look out for a rippling wave effect forming on the silky surface of the risotto; called *all'onda*, it is proof that the rice is cooked to perfection.

Fishy dinners

Given the European climate of health scares, some visitors avoid the lagoon fish, fearing mercury contamination. However, the fish on most local menus, from mullet to sea bass and mackerel, comes from the Adriatic. Inland fishing also occurs in *valli*, fenced off sections of the lagoons, mainly for mullet (*dorade*) and eel (*anguilla*). It is hard to better *antipasti di frutti di mare*, a feast of simply cooked shellfish and molluscs, dressed with olive oil and lemon juice; prawns and soft-shelled crabs vie with baby octopus and squid.

A trademark dish is cuttlefish risotto, served black and pungent with ink, or *granseola*, a large crab, boiled and then dressed simply in lemon and oil. Another staple is *baccalà* (also known as *stoccafisso*) dried salt cod, prepared with milk and herbs, or parmesan and parsley, and served in countless ways, including on toasted bread. In Venice, fish features more often than meat but offal is favoured, particularly in *fegato alla veneziana*, calf's liver sliced

kin pancakes served hot. *Torta nicoletta*, named after the Nicoletti, impoverished Venetian residents, is vaguely like French *pain perdu*, a poor man's cake of bread, milk and spices, often sold under different names. The best ices can be found in *gelaterie* (ice-cream parlours) on the Zattere, behind the Salute church. Nico (Zattere ai Gesuati, Dorsoduro 922) boasts fruity summer water ices and *gianduiotto*, a chocolate-drenched Venetian ice-cream.

Wine

Prosecco, the sparkling wine from the Veneto, makes a fine *aperitivo* whether you prefer it dry

into ribbons and cooked with parsley and onion in olive oil.

Sweet tooth

Pastries, cakes and desserts are a forte, flavoured with exotic spices ever since the Serene Republic first discovered cinnamon and nutmeg. The Venetians introduced cane sugar to Europe and have retained their sweet tooth. Spicy sweets are popular, including *fritelle di zucca*, sweet pump-

LEFT: you know what you're getting at a pizzeria; the best ones have a wood-fired oven.
ABOVE: market produce from the Veneto provide the ingredients for *minestra* or *crostini*.

(*secco*) or medium sweet (*amabile*). As such, it is the Italian equivalent to Champagne but drunk at the drop of a hat in Venice. The Veneto produces a number of superior (DOC) wines, from the fruity, garnet-red Bardolino to the less prestigious Valpolicella. Soave is the Veneto's best-known white, which emanates from some fine vineyards dotted along the eastern shores of Lake Garda. Dry white wines from the Veneto and Friuli, such as Soave, Verduzzo or Pinot Grigot, all bring out the best in seafood dishes. Regional wines should be sampled in traditional bars: these *bàcari*, as they are called, are a Venetian institution dating back to the Middle Ages. ❏

CAFÉ SOCIETY

St Mark's Square is the epitome of café life, but the city's cafés and bars offer much more, from glitzy hotel haunts to friendly bars fit for a "wine crawl"

After a morning spent enthusing and emoting in churches and museums, it is easy to while away the rest of the day in a chic Venetian bar. St Mark's Square is still the place to bask in the beauty of Venice over a drink. Under the arcades of the Piazza are a cluster of distinguished coffee houses: Florian, Quadri

and Lavena. In winter, the cafés turn in on themselves and, during *acqua alta* (high water), when the piazza is often submerged, are only accessible by rickety duck-boards. Yet as soon as the first rays of spring sunshine promise warmer weather, the tables and chairs are set out on the square and the spectacle begins.

Like Paris and Vienna, Venice relishes its reputation as a café society, with all the spurious glamour that attaches to the idea of conversation and the meeting of minds. Yet historically, Venice is first and foremost a coffee society, ever since the Serene Republic's trade with the Orient brought the Arabian stimulant to Europe. Venetian officials in 16th-century Constantino-

ple were introduced to the Ottoman taste for "black water boiled up as hot as they can bear it, which has the property of making a man stay awake". As the Venetians began to import arabica coffee beans in the 17th century, the invigorating black drink was first regarded as a medicine. It soon became a delicious addiction, with the itinerant coffee-vendor a familiar figure in the city. The first *bottega del caffè* (coffee bar) opened on Piazza San Marco in 1638.

In spite of high prices, contemporary visitors to Venice should not spurn San Marco's opulent cafés. With their stagey string quartets, pirouetting waiters and pretentious airs, they are part of the performance art that is Venice. Each café has its charms: Quadri's basks in the morning sun and an 18th-century ambience while Florian's, its more celebrated rival, lies in the shade until noon; Lavena simply serves the best coffee without the *beau monde* atmosphere.

Prince of coffee houses

Caffè Florian, considered the prince of coffee houses, was founded in 1720 and is the oldest surviving café in Italy. Although heavily restored, Florian (accented on the last syllable: Floriàn), is a tribute to 18th-century splendour. As an erstwhile literary haunt, it has welcomed Byron and Dickens, Goethe and Thomas Mann, Marcel Proust and George Sand, not to mention the ubiquitous Ernest Hemingway. The café has long numbered musicans among its patrons although Richard Wagner kept away from Florian's for fear of running into Giuseppe Verdi. Writers and artists still meet in Caffè Florian, though more for show than to listen to the melancholic airs of the cello and violin *virtuosi*.

Although trading on its past, Florian's air of *fin-de-siècle* Habsburg nostalgia is misplaced. After the Austrian army, led by Field Marshal Radetsky, had quelled the 1848 Venetian uprising, Florian's became the meeting place for republican patriots. The Austrians preferred to survey their uncowed subjects from Caffè Quadri across the square. Outside, the victors regularly paraded to martial music, provoking a mass exodus from Florian's. Today, with no visible trace of irony, this most Venetian of cafés sets its band to playing Johann Strauss's *Radetsky March*, written to celebrate the vanquishing of Venice. Quadri's rival band, ever ready to accommodate the whims of the latest wave of overseas invaders, responds by playing requests for popular American favourites.

Even out of season, these historic haunts captivate. Here one can sip hot chocolate in a café adorned with elegant stucco-work, red damask walls, Murano chandeliers and gilded mirrors. Through the windows are visions of Venetian matrons swathed in fur coats, trailing along through the mists.

Beyond St Mark's

To ponder on the ghosts of Venice, you can choose from a number of sophisticated stage sets at the glitsiest hotels: the Gritti Palace, overlooking the Grand Canal, was one of Hemingway's haunts; or the Art Deco Hotel des Bains, where Visconti shot *Death in Venice*. Sipping a chilled Prosecco from the summer terrace of the Londra Palace is not to be sniffed at: the pleasure of gazing at San Giorgio Maggiore across the canal is made more intense by the memory that it was in this palazzo that Tchaikovsky composed his Fourth Symphony.

Outside the grand hotels, the Venetian café clientele is not easily stereotyped. In Campo Santa Margherita, for instance, customers range from trendy college students to housewives returning from market. Traditional neighbourhood bars, such as Paolin in Campo Santo Stefano, are also favoured by sleek architects and scruffy academics. Paolin's position, on the well-beaten path from the Accademia to the Rialto, exposes it to swathes of Venetian society. Equally appealing are the humble bars with battered chrome tables, often hidden down a narrow alley. Venetian wine bars, known as *bàcari*, double as bistrots and serve a tempting array of snacks, often stretching to filling platefuls of pasta and risotto. These are the places to indulge in the bitter cough mixture that passes for *amaro*, the classic Italian aperitif. More Venetian is a *spriz*, an aperitif which is made with white wine, *amaro* and soda water. Nor is a

beer out of the question in Venice, whether a *biròn*, a tiny glass, or the slightly bigger *birèta*.

Only slightly off the beaten track lie humble, long-established bars, such as those off bustling Strada Nova. Tucked into tiny *calli*, the bars have intimate, rustic interiors, with the odd ceiling hung with heavy oars and boating paraphernalia. These are classless places with the *vecchio veneziano*, the Venetian born and bred, rubbing shoulders (or even cards) with left-wing intellectuals.

Traditional bars offer *ciccheti e l'ombra,* snacks and wine, literally "a little bite and the shade". A glass of wine is known as *un ombra,*

or "shade", because it was originally served under the shady awnings of St Mark's Square. A *giro di ombra*, as they say in dialect, is a serious "wine crawl", with each tasting accompanied by *ciccheti*, a local *tapas*, eaten at the bar. Delicacies include *crostini* covered with cheese, salmon or *baccalà* (dried salted cod). More substantial nibbles include *sorprèssa*, a dark-red creamy black pudding, home-cured country salami, and *sarde in saor*, sardines in a marinade of onions, vinegar, wine and pine-nuts.

"Venetians do not know how to eat or drink," declared Pietro Aretino, a visitor to Venice in the 16th century. He clearly had not been invited on a wine crawl. ❑

LEFT: historic Caffè Florian's gilded interior.
RIGHT: rival Caffè Quadri, in St Mark's Square, enjoys more sun but has less style.

REGATTAS AND WATER FESTIVALS

The Doges have gone and the great navy is no more, but Venice still celebrates its festivals by staging great water pageants

Water festivals are the glory of Venice, with palaces on the Grand Canal festooned with streamers and bedecked in silks, redolent of the pomp and pageantry of the Republic. Festivals were always a unifying factor, binding the patricians and people together to honour the state. As such, all festivals celebrated the spiritual and political life of Venice. The lagoon provided a stunning stage set for the Republic's maritime prowess, suitable for glittering processions and palatial receptions. Even today, there is a watery element to most major Venetian festivals.

Military exercise

As befits a great naval power, the grandest festivals took the form of regattas or ceremonies linked to the sea. Water-borne pageants were accompanied by the Doge and Dogeress and sometimes led by the Captain of the Sea, the naval commander-in-chief. The regattas trace their origins back to naval exercises or military training for crossbowmen on the Lido. The first official regatta was inaugurated in the early 14th century and regattas have proliferated ever since. The traditional finishing post was Ca' Foscari on the Grand Canal, the palace of a former Doge, now the seat of Venice University. Then as now, regattas typically end with the eating of polenta and fish.

To appreciate the festive nature of Republican Venice, there is no substitute for immersion in the picture galleries of the Accademia and the Museo Correr. One lovely painting (this time in the Querini-Stampalia Museum) by Bella (1730–99) records *The Women's Regatta*, with a scene of costumed girls standing up and rowing fiercely down the Grand Canal. First held in 1493, in honour of Beatrice d'Este, wife of the Duke of Milan, the race is still run today.

From March to September, the lagoon is

awash with regattas, ranging from the traditional Regata Storica (Historical Regatta) to smaller regattas at Mestre, Murano, Burano and the minor islands. More recent is the summer series of floating concerts known as Fresco Notturno (Summer Nights). Dining cruises and boats with musicians on board parade down the Grand Canal. A young people's regatta is in the pipeline, using *puparini*, small light craft.

La Festa di San Marco, held on 25 April, is when the Venetians honour their patron saint. The Feast of St Mark was once one of the most important of La Serenissima's feast days and the festival is still special. Marco Cè, the Patriarch of Venice, ushers in the occasion with solemn celebrations at San Marco which echo the Republic's skill at binding state, secular and religious affairs into one ceremony. The occasion still locks Venetian officialdom into a tight embrace, old and new powers alike. The Patriarch greets each dignitary in the Cappella di San Teodoro: the Mayor, the Prefect, the Armenian

---

PRECEDING PAGE: "Regatta on the Grand Canal" by Luca Carnevalis (1663–1730).
LEFT: contemporary Grand Canal regatta.
RIGHT: poster advertising the Historical Regatta.

MESSING ABOUT IN BOATS

The variety of everyday Venetian craft is best appreciated from the water or from the vantage point of a bridge or a Grand Canal palace: the *motoscafi, vaporetti,* water taxis and service boats will all eventually chug or sweep by. The police, ambulance and fire services all have official craft. Retreat to the smaller canals to see gondolas glide under bridges beneath your feet.

On quieter canals look out for the often despised working boats: the ingenious refuse barges (which use lifts to move rubbish) and the powerful dredgers at work clearing the canals of centuries of filth. However, for familiarity with ceremonial and traditional boats, there is no substitute for attending a regatta or water festival. The Festa del Redentore (see opposite page), with barges laden with fireworks and a cavalcade of everyday and ceremonial craft, is the most moving night spectacle.

The greatest Venetian boat of all was the State barge, the Bucintoro, dismantled after the fall of the Republic in 1797. On ceremonial occasions since, Venetians have had to make do with such paler imitations as the *bissona veneziana,* an eight-oared boat with a Lion of St Mark figurehead on the prow. At the other end of the scale is the *s'ciopon,* a rustic-looking craft that features in many pastoral paintings. It was originally used on duck shoots thanks to its ability to navigate the shallower waters of the lagoon.

The *bragazzi,* linked to neighbouring Chioggia, are colourful fishing boats decorated with paintings. Every space is adorned, from the stern to the distinctive sail: the imagery embraces heraldic devices and mythological motifs.

All classes of Venetian craft appear in regattas, from gondolas to *sandali,* flat-bottomed boats, and *sanpierote,* stable fishing vessels. Other traditional craft include the *topo,* a sailing boat first intended for fishing, and the *puparin,* a narrow boat, 10 metres (33 ft) long, built, like the gondola, in an assymetrical design; the rower stands on a platform at the back. As small, light craft, *puparini* are often considered suitable for young racers. The symmetrical *caorlina,* manned by six oarsmen, was intended to navigate mainland canals but is now used for racing. *Gondolini* are fast, racing gondolas, present in the popular gondoliers' race in the Regata Storica. By contrast, the *mascareta* is a light skiff often used as a women's racing boat.

abbot, the Knights of the Order of Malta, and leaders of the Scuole, the historic guilds and confraternities.

The tradition of giving one's sweetheart a rosebud, *il bocolo,* on this day goes back to a sentimental legend. During a battle against the Turks, a Venetian soldier was mortally wounded, but he managed to pluck a white rosebud for his beloved, far away in Venice. The flower, dyed red with his blood, miraculously reached the maiden after his death. Today, because Venetians still seek the protection of St Mark, girls take any rosebud tokens of love they have been given and place them on the saint's

grave. Given the watery nature of Venice, the festival is also marked by a gondola race across St Mark's Basin, between the island of Sant'Elena and Punta della Dogana, the Sea Customs Point. The race and the day culminate in the eating of *risi e bisi,* thick rice-and-pea soup.

Marriage with the sea

La Sensa, held the Sunday after Ascension Day, celebrates Venice's Marriage with the Sea. From the year 1000 until the fall of the Republic, the Doge would sail off from San Marco to the Lido in the Bucintoro, the ceremonial state barge. With great pomp he proclaimed in Latin: "We wed thee, O sea, in token of true and lasting dominion"; a ring was cast into the Adriatic, symbolising the sacred union with the sea. (Variants include the Doge also casting a cup or a laurel crown into the sea.)

Venetians sing of the city as *"Gemm'adriatica, sposa del mar"* (gem of the Adriatic, bride of the sea). As the Adriatic ruffles the lagoon waters, the citizens say, *"il mar la chiama"*, the sea is calling, calling eternally for its bride. Although this is a heartfelt festival, today's re-enactment is a pale version of the past: even though the traditional words are spoken, the Mayor of Venice, accompanied by the Patriarch, makes a poor substitute for the Doge.

and cup into the sea, at which a loud acclamation is ecchoed from the greate guns of the Arsenal and at the Lido."

Endurance race

La Vogalonga, a race of endurance of more recent creation, takes place on the Sunday following La Sensa. Founded in 1975 in response to popular demand, La Vogalonga means 'The Long Row'. Hundreds of oar-powered craft take to the water in a marathon regatta starting from St Mark's Basin and proceeding as far as Burano and San Francesco del Deserto before turning back towards the city. The 32-km (20-

The diarist John Evelyn attended La Sensa in 1645 and wrote: "The Doge, having heard masse in his robes of state (which are very particular, after the Eastern fashion), together with the Senat in their gownes, imbark'd in the gloriously painted, carved and gilded Bucentora, inviron'd and foll'd by innumrable gallys, gondolas, and boates, filled with spectators, some dressed in masquerade, trumpets, musiq, and canons; having rowed about a league into the Gulph, the Duke at the prow casts a gold ring

LEFT: boat-shed with suspended boat, off Campo dei Mori. **ABOVE:** "The Women's Regatta" by Gabriele Bella (1730–82).

mile) procession returns via Cannaregio and the Grand Canal, with boats finishing any time from mid-morning onwards.

La Festa del Redentore, the Feast of the Redeemer, takes place on the third Sunday of July and is at once the most romantic and intimate of Venetian festivals. Begun under Doge Alvise Mocenigo, the festival focuses on Il Redentore, (the Redeemer), the Palladian church built as a token of thanks after salvation from the plague of 1576.

Then as now, processing Venetians wend their way to the church, carrying candles and reciting the rosary. A sweeping bridge of boats stretches across the Giudecca canal to the church, enabling people to attend Mass and listen to the chanting monks.

The nocturnal fireworks display on the eve of the feast day has been a feature since the 16th century. At night, crowds line the Zattere and the Giudecca or take to boats of every description. From stately yachts to refuse barges and gondolas, the watercraft are bedecked in finery and glow like festive gazebos. Children jump into the lagoon while boisterous families and friends enjoy on-board picnics of duck, lobster, mulberries, mandarins and sparkling Prosecco. Foghorns are sounded to signal the crowd's impatience and the kaleidoscope of colour and

clamour explodes. Under the fireworks, Venice becomes a bewitching Baroque dream.

Venetians with views retire to well-positioned terraces, known as *altane*. From these eyries, they eat watermelon while watching the fireworks blaze over the cityscape. Visitors who are not pulled into picnic boats by high-spirited Venetians must content themselves with the "redemptive" dinners on offer at Harry's Bar and the Hotel Cipriani. Energetic souls picnic and carouse all night before rowing to the Lido for a dawn swim and bed.

Writer Mary McCarthy reports a gondolier's poetic reasoning on the post-fireworks flight across the waters: "The true colours of nature refresh the eye after the fires of artifice." The American writer Mark Twain first visited in 1867, nine months after the annexation of Venice to the Kingdom of Italy. He was impressed by the moonlit festival, a vision of coloured lanterns suspended over bobbing boats, "like a vast garden of many-coloured flowers". As for the on-board banquets, revellers brought 'their swallow-tailed, white-cravated varlets to wait upon them... their tables tricked out as if for a bridal supper. They had also brought along the costly globe lamps from their drawing-rooms, and the lace and silken curtains from the same places, I suppose."

Gondoliers on parade

La Regata Storica, the Historical Regatta, held on the first Sunday in September, is one of the most magnificent festivals, featuring participants in Renaissance costume. The regatta dates from 1825, the year after the gutting of the last Bucintoro, and was a way of preserving the great memories of the Republic. The waterborne parade of traditional and ceremonial craft begins in the Giardini quarter before processing along the Grand Canal.

The prizes are presented outside Ca' Foscari, where dignitaries gather on a decorated barge. (Plans are afoot to change the route, with the regatta ending at La Salute church; this would give visitors a better view, especially those staying in Grand Canal hotels.) The parade is followed by separate races involving different craft, including the Disdotona rowing competition, a trial of strength and skill.

La Festa della Madonna della Salute, celebrated on 21 November, commemorates the city's deliverance from the plague of 1630. Much like the Festival of the Redeeemer, there is a votive procession to the church, reached by a pontoon bridge from Santa Maria del Giglio. Venetians make the pilgrimage to La Salute to light candles in gratitude for the continuing good health of the city and its citizens. This Baroque church makes a spectacular sight, its main doors finally flung open and crowds ascending the steps. The art critic Bernard Berenson loved La Salute as "the building which occupies the centre of the picture Venice leaves in the mind". Certainly, the church makes a fitting final impression of the festive city. ❑

LEFT: a gondola on the Grand Canal.

Deadly floods

Although the sight of hordes crossing duck-boards in St Mark's Square seems pic-turesque, it is deeply disruptive of city life. *Acqua alta* (high water) is considered one of the city's greatest problems, with bad floods on the increase. *Acqua alta* occurs with the combination of persistent south-easterly sirocco winds and seasonal tides. The effect is worse if the high pressure sirocco wind from Syria coincides with the low pressure bora wind from the Steppes. The action of wind and tides traps the high water in the Lagoon, leading to a deadly welling up around the city's buildings. In one recent year there were 120 days affected by high water.

Venice has always been threatened by floods, with the greatest floods between April and September, following sirocco storms. However, the massive flood of 1966 mobilised the world. A tidal wave breached the sea walls and the water level rose by 1.9 metres (6 ft) above mean high tide. St Mark's Square, the lowest point in the city, was submerged under 1.2 metres (4 ft) of water, a fithy tide of debris, with water seeping through the Basilica doors and waves thrashing against the Doge's Palace. Since then, the city has entrusted the management of the Lagoon to a new authority. Many grander houses close to San Marco and the Rialto, areas prone to flooding, have installed ingenious flood gates. The flood alert centre gives at least a day's notice, with serious tidal flooding being signalled by sirens.

Although floods have increased of late, the precise reasons are in dispute. Some blame global warming, the melting of the polar ice cap and other meteorological shifts. However, the environmentalists are not alone in pointing the finger at human intervention and the industrialisation over the water. The 20th century has seen the delicate balance of the Lagoon disturbed by land reclamation, the deepening of shipping channels and by the enclosure of sections of the Lagoon for fish farming.

The latest solution to the floods is a tidal barrier, named Mose after Moses, the Biblical master of the waves. It is masterminded by the Venezia Consorzio Nuova, a consortium of engineering companies eager for the prestige and profit to flow from the scheme. The idea is to place submerged mobile barrages at the three *porti*, the entrances to the

---

RIGHT: the disruptive *acqua alta* in Piazza San Marco. It can occur on more than 100 days a year.

Lagoon. A prototype has been tested but the final model may not be ready until the year 2010. The project has fallen foul of vested interests, political lobbying, scientific scepticism and environmental disapproval. One argument against the barrier is that it would reduce the beneficial effects of the tidal flow. Conservationists are not convinced of its efficacy, a view shared by Italia Nostra, Italy's heritage body. They argue that the best solution is a return to the *status quo ante*. By halting land reclamation and returning the shipping lanes to their original paths, they reason that the tides will regulate themselves.

The authorities have gone part of the way down

this path, allowing some reclaimed land to be flooded and seeking to ban oil tankers from the Lagoon. Other suggestions for curing the problem range from restoring those canals that were filled in during the Austrian occupation, to creating one vast marine park, from which ships and industry are banned. Venetian writer Damiano Rizzo is resigned to a long wait: "In the meantime, the city will go on fighting the high tides with traditional weaponry: wailing sirens, wooden duck-boards, wellington boots and buckets of patience. Some day visitors might be able to look back nostalgically at the quaint experience of high tide." But today it's a reality – certain Japanese tour groups come especially to sample the aquatic perils of *acqua alta*. ❏

LIFE AS A MASQUERADE

Carnival in Venice is supreme self-indulgence, a giddy round of masked balls and private parties suggesting mystery and promising romance

Carnival in Venice is a 10-day pre-Lenten extravaganza, culminating in the burning of the effigy of Carnival in Piazza San Marco on Shrove Tuesday. As an expression of a topsy-turvy world, carnival is a time for rebellion without the risk of ridicule. The essence of the "feast of fools" lies in the unfolding Venetian vistas: masked processions heading towards Piazza San Marco past shimmering palaces, with surreal masqueraders tumbling out of every alley. As the revellers flock to Florian's café in Piazza San Marco, the air is sickly-sweet with the scent of fritters and the sound of lush Baroque music. Carnival capers include costumed balls, firework displays and historical parades, all staged by the carnival societies.

SPIRIT OF RESISTANCE

Carnival is often dismissed as commercialised and chaotic but Venetian traditionalists view it differently. The leader of a venerable carnival company sees the event as saving his city: "Life in Venice is inconvenient and costly. With the carnival, we give a positive picture and show the pleasure of living here. Carnival is a form of resistance. By resisting the temptation to leave, we are saving the spirit of the city for future generations."

▽ THE GREAT LEVELLER

A mask makes everyone equal. Masqueraders are addressed as *"sior maschera"* (masked gentleman) regardless of age, rank or even gender. One way of preserving some individuality is face-painting.

△ SELECT CARDS

A select group of Venetians still appears as *tarocchi*, fortune-telling tarot cards. These famous cards supposedly reached Europe from the East, through Venice. The star of the pack is the Queen of Swords, her costume rich in silver cabalistic signs.

▽ WINDOW DRESSING

Masks originally allowed the nobility to mingle incognito with the common people in *casini* (private clubs), but are now an excuse for all-purpos revelry. This shop window displays fantasy masks, which are creative rather than authentic, and appeal to individual tastes.

MASTERS OF DISGUISE

△ THE NOBLE LOOK
Costumes can be historical, traditional or simply surreal. The classic Venetian disguise of the 17th and 18th centuries was known as the *maschera nobile*, the patrician mask. The carnival companies wear noble Renaissance and Rococo costumes *(left)* as a matter of course.

▽ VOLTO FACE
The patrician *maschera nobile* and witty *commedia dell'arte* masks are among a number of authentic disguises. While this cumbersome ruff is pure fantasy, the white mask looks to the past for inspiration: it is a modern variant on the slightly sinister *volto*, the traditional Venetian mask.

Mask-makers had their own guild in medieval times, when a *mascheraio* (mask-maker) helped a secretive society run smoothly. Modern masqueraders must choose between masks in leather *(cuoio)*, china *(ceramica)* or papier-mâché *(cartapesta)*. Papier mâché and leather masks are the most authentic.

Antique masks are rare since neither material readily stands the test of time or the Venetian climate. Authentic mask-makers both reinterpret traditional designs and create new ones. In the case of papier-mâché masks, the pattern is made from a fired clay design, which generates a plaster of Paris mould. Layers of papier-mâché paste are used to line the mould and thus create the mask. When dry, the glue gives the mask a shiny surface akin to porcelain. Polish and a white base coat are applied before the eye holes are cut and decorative detail added. This painting process can be simple or highly artistic.

The alternatives to papier-mâché include leather masks, which are hard to fashion, or ceramic designs, ideal as hand-held masks or wall decorations, often adorned with fine fabrics. Places to browse include Laboratorio Artigiano Maschere (Barbaria delle Tole) founded by a family of puppet-makers, and the bohemian workshop of Ca del Sol (Fondamenta dell'Osmarin).

CARNIVAL

The colourful, pre-Lenten carnival, dating from pagan times, is a 10-day extravaganza of masked balls, pantomime and music

Every year the city indulges in a 10-day masked ball, a Lententide "farewell to the flesh". A combination of poseurs and voyeurs come to wallow in the ghostly beauty of Venice as La Serenissima awakes to a whirl of colour, masks and costumes. Venice Carnival is virtual reality for dreamers and insomniacs. Expect to spot a Doge flaunting a drink habit in Florian's café, a libidinous nun locked in an embrace with an 18th-century fop, or Casanova threading the dark canals with a Venetian alley-cat in tow.

Carnival has much to answer for: prices soar and the city boasts more mask shops than butcher's; fashion shoots and foreign film crews swamp San Marco; cavorting crowds of motley Europeans dress as gondoliers and bosomy courtesans. Amidst air-kissing and cries of *"bellissimo"*, there are displays of pan-European bad taste. These are all travesties of carnival but carnival is a time for travesty. Despite the commercialism, this kitsch masquerade retains its magic. In the swirling mists, the city exudes a feeling of decadence and faint menace. Carnival unfolds with strangely sinister scenes: cadaverous creatures rowing to the rhythm of the church bells.

Memories of carnival may include a mysterious group of white-masked merry-makers, glimpsed on a moonlit terrace; a spangled yet sad Harlequin posing on a jetty; or a ruff of debauched Pierrots strolling up and down the Riva degli Schiavoni. More poignant is the winged lion striking simpering poses against the outline of St Mark's, the symbol of the Republic turned into a tame pussy cat.

Lords of misrule

The carnival features a host of rival narcissists but also some genuine characters. Count Targhetta d'Audriffet is a carnival-goer who has become a celebrity. During carnival, this frail, Quentin-Crisp of a figure can be seen bewigged,

LEFT and **RIGHT:** revellers mix fashion and fantasy with the mysterious and sinister white mask.

pomaded, and carried in a sedan chair by his faithful companion, an Abyssinian servant.

His palace, facing the cemetery island of San Michele, is close to where Casanova was arrested on charges of freemasonry. The city is prepared to subsidise his eccentricities on the understanding that he will bequeath his palace to his fellow-citizens. However, the Prior of the Antichi carnival company says: "The Count lives with a Negro servant who will probably inherit everything. He enjoys a timeless existence in an immortal palace which he only leaves at carnival time. Come rain or snow, this elderly figure, with his cloak flying, strides across the Accademia bridge so as not to "keep Contessa Marcello waiting". He is living Venetian history and once a year invites us all to a huge party."

Not that the city is closed to outsiders: indeed the finest costumes are often worn by gay Germans or French transvestites. Camp send-ups include appearances of La Très Sainte Compagnie Secrète du Tiramisou (the Very Holy Secret Company of the Tiramisu). The alternative carnival, beginning with erotic verse and ending in an orgy, is slightly harder to gain access to.

However, licence and excess are also much in evidence in the main carnival. A Venetian school-teacher who dresses up as various parts of the body is regularly arrested for obscenity. It seems that, as in the Serene Republic, not all carnival transgressions are readily tolerated. Yet while La Serenissima denounced subversion, today's city council draws the line at a phallus hung with plastic grapes. To think that the 18th-

century was supposed to be the nadir of Venetian decadence.

Carnival lore

Epiphany in Venice was once a time of gentle melancholy, with the city wreathed in winter sleep. The recent revival of carnival, after an interval of several centuries, has dispelled the mellow mood.

When Napoleon conquered Venice in 1797, the carnival went the tragic way of the Venetian Republic. Although revived sporadically in the early part of the 20th century, it was only fully restored in 1979. The event was eagerly reclaimed by Venetians, with playful processions

and masquerades. According to Lady Clarke, a leading light of Venice in Peril, the British restoration fund, "Then it was very much a family affair".

It is fashionable to mock the carnival as a commercial fabrication but its roots go deep in the Venetian psyche. The city has an instinctive love of spectacle and dressing up, dating back to the glory days of the Republic. The carnival reaches back to medieval times and represents a cavalcade of Venetian history, tracing political and military events, factional rivalries and defeats.

Moveable feast

In the past, the Venetian carnival was something of a moveable feast, beginning as early as October or Christmas and lasting until Lent. This long carnival season incorporated an element of "bread and circuses", with crowd-pleasing performances intended to curry favour with the populace. In addition to masquerades, there were rope dancers, acrobats and fire-eaters who routinely showed their skills on Piazza San Marco.

The diarist John Evelyn visited Venice in 1645–6 and reported on "the folly and madness of the carnival", from the bull-baiting and flinging of eggs to the superb opera, the singing eunuch and a shooting incident with an enraged nobleman and his courtesan, whose gondola canoodling he had disturbed. During the 1751 carnival, everyone gathered to admire an exotic beast, the rhinoceros, captured in a famous painting by Longhi, which is now displayed in the Ca' Rezzonico.

Carnival was not without barbaric flourishes, including spectacular blood sports with Venetian twists. As well as bear-baiting and Spanish-style bull chases, dogs were shot out of cannons for the crowd's amusement.

Another gory event commemorated the conquest of Aquileia in 1162, when the Patriarch of Venice was captured along with 12 of his priests and ransomed for 12 pigs and a bull. After this incident, 12 pigs were flung from the *campanile* at every carnival, while a bull was beheaded. Today, such bloody-thirsty scenes are confined to the butcher's shops where even pig's heads may be masked.

LEFT: masks in papier-mâché and porcelain make memorable souvenirs.

Commedia dell'arte

Many of the most distinctive carnival costumes are inspired by the *commedia dell' arte*. The essentially comic genre emerged in 16th-century Italy and featured improvisation, a fast pace and witty regional parodies. Given the physical nature of the comedy, the actors had to be skilled mime artists and acrobatic tumblers. In addition to stagecraft, the genre relied on stock characters who wore costumes and masks to differentiate their roles. In 1574, King Henri III of France was so impressed by the Venetian *commedia dell'arte* troupe that he invited them to perform at the French court.

A typical feature of the popular comedy was that characters spoke in regional dialects, leading to comic contrasts and misunderstandings. Thus, the classic pair of manservants, Harlequin *(Arlecchino)* and *Brighella* come from Bergamo and speak the local dialect. The merchant *Pantalone* speaks Venetian while the Doctor *(Dottore)* favours Bolognese and the lovers Tuscan. The manservants, known as *zanni*, include *Brighella*, the wily servant, and are always plotting and intriguing. The bilious green colour of his mask shows his bitter nature, as does his broken nose and ugly face. He wears white livery, with green diagonal stripes. The acrobatic *Arlecchino* is often the butt of *Brighella's* jokes. Harlequin's costume of colourful rags is a symbol of his poverty, and later became his red, orange and green suit.

Harlequin's master is the miserly old Venetian merchant, *Pantalone*. Anglicised to "Pantaloons", this was a nickname for Venetians, derived from the name of a popular city saint. The image was reinforced by the character's trousers *(pantaloni)*, worn with a black cloak and red stockings. A brown mask with a bristling moustache and a long crooked nose complete the ensemble.

The foil to *Pantalone* is the pompous and lecherous *Dottore*. As a tedious doctor-at-law, his trademark is pedantry and tirades larded with Latin tags. His black half-mask features a bumpy forehead simulating an injury caused by a disgruntled student. The Captain *(Capitano)* is a braggart of Spanish extraction who has a huge ruff, plumed hat and a mask with a protruding nose.

Many other characters have sprung from these main types, including the maid-servant *Columbina*,

---

RIGHT: the miserly merchant Pantalone (1550).

Harlequin's partner, and *Pulcinella*, the lovable clown, ever popular with children. In England he has turned into Mr Punch, half of the seaside Punch and Judy puppet show, while in Germany he has become jolly Kasper.

Other characters are seen in France, including the winsome *Pierrot*, a pantomime extension of Harlequin. As well as laying the foundations for puppet shows throughout Europe, the *commedia dell'arte* greatly enriched Continental comic drama, and led to mime in France, and to pantomime in England and Denmark.

However, by the 18th century the *commedia* was in decline, with the characters frozen in time.

Carlo Goldoni (1707–93) raided the repertoire to create his Venetian comedies of manners, plays which are still performed in the city.

Yet he chafed against the constraints of the *commedia*, resenting the lowly role of the writer and the straight-jacket of using masks: "I quietly sought the freedom to write whole plays of my own, and despite the hampering effect of masks, I quite quickly succeeded." In fact, he subverted the genre, skilfully using it to satirise the laziness of the leisured classes.

Visitors of a consumerist bent can buy the cute velour slippers used by *commedia* characters, including *Pierrot* and *Columbina*, (at La Pantofila, Calle della Mandola, San Marco 3718. ❑

Carnival companies

The Venetians had a propensity for societies, from the guilds to the myriad carnival companies. Known as Compagnie della Calza, these date from Renaissance times and played an important part in the rebirth of the carnival. These companies gained their name from the custom of wearing an emblem on the right stocking (*calza*). All the societies bore strange names, such as *Antichi* (the Ancient), *Ardenti* (the Ardent), *Pacifici* (the Peaceable) and *Modesti* (the Modest). The official organisation of the carnival was in the companies' hands until Doge Gritti transferred control to the state in the mid-16th century. The companies retreated into *ridotti* or *casini*, private clubs where, in the rarified world of the palaces, their members preserved the old carnival customs until the present day. The Antichi company traces its origins to a group of narcissistic Renaissance noblemen who staged festivals for the people. To this day, the company holds masked balls and literary readings, interspersed with classical music and dance (and, when the mood takes them, licentiousness).

As one of the best-known mask-makers in Venice, the Prior of the Antichi lives and breathes carnival. He sees the company's role

FAREWELL TO FLESH

The Carnival revels are accompanied by such rustic fare as spaghetti in anchovy sauce, squid risotto, salted herring, eels or *baccalà* (salt cod) with polenta. Although accompanied by spicy sweets and washed down with white Veneto vines, this is hardly an orgy of indulgence.

The early Christian church banned the use of butter and eggs during Lent so sweet delicacies became synonymous with carnival as cooks rushed to use up their old supplies. During carnival, cake shops are piled high with crisp *galani* (also called *crostoli*), wafer-thin, sugar-dusted strips of pastry. Equally traditional are the springy,

deep-fried fritters (*fritole* in dialect). The fritters (*fritelle* in standard Italian) are actually more like doughnuts, stuffed or topped with apples, aniseed, raisins, pine nuts and candied peel.

Such is the popularity of these sweet snacks that there was even a medieval guild of *fritoleri* to protect the secrets and status of the craft.

Nowadays, carnival fare can be found on sale on the various side streets close to San Marco and Castello districts. As a result, for several days in the month of February, tiny kitchens in the backstreets exude aromas of frying batter, zingy peel and spicy fillings.

as creating a more authentic carnival to complement the public festivities. "We incline towards a Renaissance interpretation rather than the Rococo one favoured by the official carnival. Although Venice carnival generally presents its 18th-century face to the world, we mustn't forget that carnival already existed in Renaissance times".

A typical theme was the 1997 "End of the Republic", which commemorated the extinction of the Serene Republic in 1797. The company created elaborate costumes, tableaux and performances to mark such poignant moments as the "last supper with the Doge" and " the last

robustly defends his choice of themes: "We don't believe in making any distinction between high and low culture."

Festive calendar

"The finest drawing room in Europe" was Napoleon's overworked description of Piazza San Marco. Here the carnival opens in the presence of thousands of masqueraders, with a different theme each year. The uniqueness of the "feast of fools" in Venice lies in the character of the city itself: no theatre could provide a better setting. During the ten-day spectacle leading up to Shrove Tuesday, revellers come tumbling out

day of the Republic". The company stresses its Venetian nature by honouring the spirit of the carnival with historical re-enactments closer to the heart of the citizens.

However, just to show that pre-Lenten licence cannot be kept in check, the company recently staged an outdoor festival of erotic 18th-century verse on Campo San Maurizio, outside the palace where Baffo, the spirited 18th-century poet, once lived. The Prior

of every alley, with the sound of Renaissance and Baroque music echoing from every courtyard. Pantomime, operetta, concerts and literary readings are held in theatres and in the open-air spaces of the city *campi*. Campo San Polo, one of the largest squares, is a popular site for outdoor events, thus maintaining a role it has played here since medieval times. Many of the finest masked balls, fireworks and historical happenings are led by the Compagnie della Calza, the local carnival companies.

The public face of carnival used to be Giovedi Grasso (Maundy Thursday), when the Doge, nobility and ambassadors congregated on the balcony of the Ducal Palace. However, the

LEFT: posing in primary colours against the pallid stone colonnade of the Procuratie; fantasia mask.
ABOVE: masked revellers in the winter sunshine parading through Piazza San Marco.

high point of the modern festival is on Shrove Tuesday when revellers gather for a masked ball on St Mark's Square before moving onto private parties or, in the case of celebrities, to the ball at the Cipriani, across the water. In the past, the midnight fasting bell would ring out from San Francesco della Vigna, signalling an end to licence and the onset of atonement. Come Ash Wednesday and Venetians usually have much to atone for. The end is signalled when the effigy of Carnival is burnt on St Mark's Square.

Devilish disguises

From Epiphany to Ash Wednesday *"Sior Maschera"*, the masked reveller, reigns supreme. Venetians love to attend the carnival in groups, all wearing the same costumes. Revellers are addressed as *Sior Maschera* since carnival erases distinctions in rank and sex. During the Republic's official ceremonies a strict order of precedence had to be observed but carnival was a time for the breaking of social taboos: the mask makes everyone equal.

Venetian carnival masks seem timeless. In fact, the most traditional masks form a dramatic monochrome disguise, often harking back to periods of Venetian history or the *commedia dell'arte*. Masks not based on traditional

PAGAN RITES

The Venetian carnival is the inheritor of a rich folk tradition, embracing pagan and Christian motifs. Linked to the Winter Solstice and fertility rites, such mid-winter folk festivals pre-date Christianity. According to pagan rites, winter was a force to be overcome, with the sun persuaded to return by a show of life at its most vital.

Thus in Rome, the fertility rites of Saturnalia were celebrated with a riotous masquerade in which even the slaves took part. Christianity gave the carnival new significance: the words *carne vale*, the Latin for 'farewell to meat', meant a last blow-out, particularly on Giovadi Grasso or Mardi Gras (Fat Tuesday), before the start of the long and rigorous Lenten period, marked by abstinence from the pleasures of the flesh and a focus on the spiritual.

From the beginning, Carnival was a challenge to the fear of death and decay. It also encouraged the breaking of social rules. The wearing of masks allowed revellers to question authority or ridicule the establishment without fear of punishment. Throughout Italy, extravagant masked balls were in fashion from medieval times. Today carnival is celebrated mainly in countries and regions with a strong Roman Catholic tradition, in both Europe and in Latin America.

designs are generally known as *fantasie*, fantasy masks. One of the finest is the *maschera nobile*, the white sculpted mask, with black tricorn and black silk cloak. *Columbina* (Columbine) is the name given to the elegant Venetian domino mask; more catlike and seductive is the mask commonly called *civetta* (flirt).

Some of the masks look quite sinister. One of the most menacing is undoubtedly the Plague Doctor, with his distinctive beaked nose and black gown, once worn as a protection against the plague.

It is worth visiting one of the traditional made-to-measure mask shops where they can

exquisite carnival paintings, which are in the Ca' Rezzonico).

Lavish lifestyles

Today's carnival plays homage to the lavish lifestyles of 18th-century Venice. It is ironic that the carnival's heyday coincided with the terminal decline of the Republic. Costumes currently in vogue extol the voluptuous femininity of 18th-century dress for both sexes. The classic costume of the 17th and 18th centuries was *maschera nobile*, the patrician mask. The head was covered with *bautá*, a black silk hood and lace cape, topped by a voluminous cloak

whip you up anything from a festive Harlequin to a Medusa wreathed in snakes or even a sinister death mask.

The most traditional masks are made of leather (*in cuoio*) or papier-mâché (*in cartapesta*) with modern creations in ceramics or covered with luxurious fabrics. Leather masks are hardest to fashion, while hand-held masks make effective wall decorations. (If you are seeking inspiration for historically authentic carnival costumes, study Pietro Longhi's

LEFT: ghostly revellers in the wintry snow.
ABOVE: masqueraders, including one wearing a *volto*, the traditional white half-mask.

(*tabarro*), in black silk for the nobility and in red or grey for ordinary citizens. The *volto*, the white half-mask, covered the face, with the finishing touch provided by a black tricorn hat adorned with feathers.

The elegant *maschera nobile* and *commedia dell'arte* masks are not the only authentic disguises. Masks representing or ridiculing the Republic's enemies, such as an exotic Moor or swarthy Turk, remain popular, as do esoteric costumes associated with the carnival companies. Certainly, the Venetian love of disguise masks a desire to slip into a different skin. As Oscar Wilde said, "A man only reveals himself when wearing a mask." ❑

IACOB. HIERON. CHS̄ SAVM̄US VENETVS ANNO ÆT: SVÆ. LXIII.

I. Berka del. et scalpsit Prag.

CASANOVA'S VENICE

Casanova, the libertine and supreme seducer, symbolises the decadence of 18th-century Venice

Casanova (1725–98) is a name synonymous with seduction, the Latin lover incarnate. Yet despite the numbers of his conquests, this complex character cannot be dismissed as an amorous rogue. Not that the versatile Venetian was averse to roguery, whether in the form of illicit bed-hopping or forgery and deception. Havelock Ellis accurately praised him as being "the Venetian genius of sensuous enjoyment, of tolerant humanity, of unashamed earthliness. Soldier, gambler, necromancer, adventurer, profligate and man of letters". Venetians prefer to think of Casanova as embodying the spirit of the Serenissima, a certain decadence tinged with genius, balanced half-way between the twin poles of comedy and tragedy.

As for seduction, charm as much as guile won him conquests. His reputation as libertine lives on. The eccentric Count Targhetta (*see page 101*) cultivates Casanova's memory, in particular his amorous exploits. He lives close to where Casanova was arrested and claims to possess his bed (hotly disputed by the Metropolitan Museum in New York). Casanova would have chuckled over such arguments: beds were never a problem while there were willing partners in gondolas, opera boxes, carriages and churches.

The facts of his life

Casanova lived in the crested Palazzo Malpiero, close to Campo San Samuele and his baptismal church where, ironically, he preached his first sermon in a misguided attempt at a career in holy orders. Fittingly, the church contains an altar dedicated to St Valentine, the god of love. In nearby Calle Malpiero a plaque records that: "in a house in this street, previously known as Calle della Commedia, Giacomo Casanova was born on 2nd April 1725." From his home, the city's finest clubs and salons were within easy walking distance.

Daniele Varè, the Venetian diplomat, calls his

LEFT: Giacomo Casanova, the ultimate lover.
RIGHT: "Courtesan with a Parrot" by Rosalba Carriera (1720).

fellow-citizen, "an adventurer by choice and by necessity". Born into a theatrical background which served him well, Casanova had to be independent from an early age. Although absentee parents left him to his own devices, he studied law, using wealthy patrons to further his career. Yet his failure to follow a religious or

legal vocation eventually led to more intriguing pursuits as a musician, gambler and spy. In Venice, he earned his living first as a violinist for the nobility, and later returned in a new guise as a spy for the state.

He was welcome in the best Venetian circles, befriended by poets and patricians alike. So charmed was Pope Clement XIII, who was a Venetian and a member of the aristocratic Rezzonico family, that he invested Casanova with the Order of the Golden Spur. His adventures took him from literary salons, princely palaces and royal courts to noblewomen's beds, nunneries and prisons. On a typical day he dined with the nobility, then visited a wine shop near

San Marco before disappearing to the gambling dens on the Frezzaria (also the place for romantic assignations).

Republican Venice was liberal socially but utterly intolerant of political dissidence. A satirical pamphlet laid at Casanova's door reveals the deadly atmosphere: "A foreigner who travels to this Republic should leave his tongue in Fusina and arrive in Venice mute. Silence is the emblem of this government; everything is secret and cloaked in mystery. In Venice, those who talk are buried alive in a tomb covered with lead". In the eyes of society, Casanova was subversive and all the more plausible because of his

worse. Accompanied by an incompetent monk, Casanova consulted an oracle to determine the most propitious time for his escape and scaled the Venetian rooftops close to the Bridge of Sighs. After tumbling through a skylight into the state archives in the ducal chancery, he changed into "an exquisite hat trimmed with Spanish lace", outwitted the doorman and took a gondola to Mestre, where he wrestled with a Venetian spy before reaching the safety of Treviso, and from there on to Munich and Paris.

Casanova often led a clandestine existence, evading capture from political enemies and former friends. In 1774, he returned to Venice,

charm and cosmopolitan finesse. Yet he also led a dissolute life that was entirely in keeping with the decadence of his age.

Arrest and imprisonment

In 1755, Casanova was arrested on charges of freemasonry and denounced for "impiety, imposture and licentiousness" by a spy of the Venetian Inquisition. Imprisoned in the notorious "Leads", the lofts of the Doge's Palace, he managed a daring escape in 1756, which he recounts in his *Memoirs*. The "Leads" (*Piombi*) are named after the plates of lead that covered the ceilings – not that the Leads were the hellhole of legend – the "Wells" (*Pozzi*) were far

craftily acting as a spy for the Venetian Inquisition. However, a libel suit caused him to be expelled from his home city forever. (This became a familiar refrain, with his expulsion from several European countries, including France, on the grounds of financial fraud.)

Lottery director and librarian

Casanova was a true citizen of Europe, crossing borders and exchanging masters with ease, ranging from London and Paris to the Russian court of Catherine II. In between, he worked as a diplomat in Vienna, a financier in Paris (where he was director of the state lottery) and a librarian in Waldenstein Castle, Bohemia. There he wrote his *Memoirs*, dabbled in alchemy and died in penury. His last words were: "I lived as a philosopher, and I die as a Christian".

Casanova's Venice is still largely intact: you can see his birthplace in the romantic San Samuele quarter or saunter along the bustling Frezzaria to savour the dingy Corte Lugenegher where he later had rooms; or visit the Ridotto, the famous former casino where Casanova learnt his trade as a gambler, a profession he later practised to great effect in Paris.

FELINE FIGURE

"Casanova was a charlatan and a dilettante, as mercurial as the water in the Venetian lagoon, with more lives than a Venetian cat."

appreciate the glistening freshness of the morning market. Campo Santi Giovanni e Paolo recalls Casanova's encounter with a masked nun, briefly free from her convent in Murano. To meet the libertine as a boisterous young man, stroll around the ill-lit Campo Sant'Angelo, much as it was in Casanova's time. Here he indulged in childish pranks, untying moored gondolas or summoning sleeping midwives and priests to imaginary emergencies. Even in his day, critics dismissed Casanova as a liber-

Palazzo Soranzo on Campo San Polo was where, as a professional musician, the young chancer fell in with Senator Bragadin, soon his chief patron in Venice. After saving the Senator from "a fit of apoplexy", Casanova had the nobleman bled by a physician, and then went on to bleed his grateful patron dry.

It is hard to see the Rialto through Casanova's eyes: after a night's gaming at the Ridotto when he had lost all he owned ("plus 500 sequins on my word"), the jaded gambler could hardly

LEFT: "The Ridotto", the famous casino, by Guardi (1699–1761) in Ca' Rezzonico. ABOVE: The notorious Pozzi, the basement prisons in the Doge's Palace.

tine, charlatan and dilettante. Yet he was mercurial as the water in the Venetian lagoon, with more lives than a Venetian cat. Casanova was in his element in this chameleon city, an habitué of the best salons, convents and casinos. In a warped way he was a Rococo version of the Renaissance man: capable of mastering anything but choosing to squander his gifts. But what glorious squandering.

To follow further in Casanova's footsteps, join the so-called "Secret Tour" of the Doge's Palace *(see page 149)*, which takes in the Leads where he was jailed, or try the Casanova Walk (enquire at the tourist office). Alternatively, come for Carnival and join the throng. ❏

THE CASINI

For many, the private club is a quintessentially English establishment,

but the Venetians, too, have a strong tradition of exclusive retreats

Often considered the preserve of the English, clubbiness and gentlemen's clubs form a distinct Venetian tradition. By contrast, their clubs were more cosmopolitan, hedonistic and inclusive, places to play and transgress under the safety of a mask. Known as *casini*, these were originally clubs (although

the word means brothels or casinos in modern Italian). Even in the dying days of the Republic the Venetians were devoted to these retreats from reality. Several *casini* existed in the St Mark's area from medieval times onwards. Here, worthy procurators and state officials would retire for a bit of light relief after a hard day at the office. However, it was in the decadent 17th and 18th centuries that such establishments really came into their own.

The finest *casini* were decorated by great Renaissance and Mannerist artists, from Tintoretto and Veronese to Giandomenico Tiepolo. Casino Venier al Ponte dei Baretti, once a famous club and now the French Institute, is adorned with a fine frescoed ceiling by Jacopo Guarana. As well as offering music, meals and witty company, the clubs also became known as places for gambling, illicit liaisons, and, innocent though it sounds, for sipping hot chocolate, the fashionable tipple.

The subversive element to such gatherings lay in the opportunities for social mixing away from the eyes of the ever-watchful state. Not that the clubs were free from spies, as the career of Casanova, libertine, gambler and victim of the Venetian Inquisition, proves.

To amorous Venetians such as Casanova, there were also welcome erotic undertones to certain clubs, with suggestive paintings on the walls, the reading of salacious verse, and the pleasure of female company. The optional wearing of masks, the multitude of mirrors and secret doors added to the frisson of excitement. Although essentially home to cultivated young nobles, the clubs were visited during carnival by masked revellers from across the social classes. At the other end of the scale were the rough-and-ready clubs which were patronised by the populace. These were regularly closed down for licentious behaviour or excessive gambling.

A chance of encounters

By the 18th century, Venice had more than a hundred *casini*, a cross between gentlemen's clubs and gambling dens. Some were genuine literary salons, where nobles and intellectuals gathered to discuss the political issues of the day. For obvious reasons, the Venetian state was hostile to such developments and preferred the notion of the clubs as artistic salons where privileged women held court to men of the world – and a fair number of libertines. (For free-thinking women, hitherto cloistered at home, this was also an opportunity for fashionable encounters.)

More overtly artistic salons in the French mould were led by Venetian noblewomen. Byron, the Romantic poet, and Canova, the Classical sculptor, patronised the salons led by Isabella Albrizzi. Writers of the calibre of

Byron, Stendhal and Longfellow also gathered at Countess Marina Querini-Benzon's salons, held in Palazzo Benzon on the Grand Canal.

Although not open to the general public, several erstwhile clubs survive, including Casino degli Spiriti, the evocatively named House of the Spirits. Still a desolate place, it stands isolated at the edge of the lagoon, its gardens facing the funeral island of San Michele. The name is supposed to refer to the high spirits of club habitués, although the building also has a reputation for being haunted. Set in part of the Renaissance Palazzo Contarini dal Zaffo, this was once a pleasure palace for select gatherings. The 16th-century gardens were reputedly patronised by the architect Sansovino and artists of the stature of Titian. Casino Corner in Mur-ano, and its companion club on the Giudecca, were also welcome retreats from the heat. Sea breezes swept through the splendid gardens, festivities focused on the elegant loggias.

The first public casino

Threatened by the influence of the *casini*, the Republic clamped down on the clubs, imposing fines and even prison sentences on officials who patronised such haunts. Many clubs were closed, provoking such uproar that in 1638 Doge Marco Dandolo was forced to open the first public casino. Set on Calle del Ridotto near San Moisè, this was the celebrated Ridotto, now a theatre. The casino soon became the meeting place of patricians, merchants and usurers, libertines and adventurers, courtesans and cardsharps. Pompeo Molmenti, an 18th-century visitor, sets the scene: "At each table sat a nobleman, in robe and wig, with piles of sequins and ducats before him, ready to hold the bank against all-comers provided they were patricians or masked" (to preserve the players' good names, masks were compulsory in the casino).

In the mid-18th century gambling mania swept Venice and took its toll on the nobility, bankrupting many. The Ridotto even included a "chamber of sighs" where vanquished lovers or defeated gamblers retreated to lick their wounds. Lorenzo da Ponte, Mozart's librettist, fell asleep there after a terrible evening spent in the company of his beloved's brother, an invet-

erate gambler. In 1774, partly in response to the ruination of the nobility, the Maggior Consiglio (Great Council) voted virtually unanimously to close the Ridotto. Ever vigilant, the state could not tolerate such a subversive influence or the indirect drain on the state coffers.

However, the effect was simply to drive Venetian pleasures underground, to private clubs scattered throughout the city. In this the carnival companies, such as the Compagnie della Calza, played a leading role. As well as keeping the carnival spirit alive, they provided the unique blend of refinement and fun that once characterised the Venetian clubs.   ❏

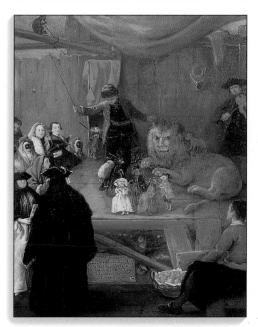

A CONTEMPORARY VIEW

"This was where, amid gossiping, gaming and sneering, debauchery called itself gallantry, impudence urbanity, and vice pleasure; where the lustful behaviour of the women was brought to new heights by the rivalry of others who sought to replace them; where, almost to a man, the winners laughed in the face of the losers; where the losers yelled in vexation at every card, some blaming themselves, others someone else, and so loudly and with such violence that they were sometimes on the edge of coming to blows" – MUTINELLI.

LEFT: gamblers in Il Ridotto, a painting in the Querini-Stampalia gallery. RIGHT: Pietro Longhi's "Il Casotto dei Leoni" in the same gallery.

THE JEWISH GHETTO

Shakespeare gave Jews a bad press in "The Merchant of Venice",
but they were already stigmatised in the original "ghetto"

According to the 1875 *Cook's Handbook,* "The houses are immensely tall, the streets ridiculously narrow, and a great deal of filth abounds." Thus was the world's oldest Jewish ghetto dismissed. Today, the Ghetto is quiet and unobtrusive, far from the typical tourist attractions. Nothing about the neglected facades of these drab tenements would suggest that until the 17th century this was one of the major Jewish communities in Europe. Jews were first mentioned in Venetian records in the 10th century, as passengers forbidden from travelling on Venetian ships. As an ambitious trading city, Venice feared competition from astute Levantine merchants. Persecution soon drove waves of refugees to Venice in search of a safe haven but they often sought in vain: over the centuries, Venetian policy was ambivalent, wavering between toleration and protection, persecution and expulsion.

Second-class citizens

While Jews who practised as doctors, traders or textile merchants were tolerated, pawnbrokers and money-lenders were resented. Jewish "banks for the poor" opened in 1366, first in Mestre on the mainland, then in Venice itself. Venetian self-interest played its part: persecution reached its height in the 15th century, when the collapse of private banks forced Venetians to use money-lenders, a practice forbidden to Christians. Hefty levies on money-lending meant that the Serenissima naturally profited from this arrangement. Although Jewish profits were high, credit was strictly regulated by the state. However, Jews were still treated as second-class citizens, forbidden from settling in Venice. As Shylock says in Shakespeare's *Merchant of Venice*, "I will buy with you, sell with you, talk with you, walk with you... but I will not eat with you, drink with you, nor pray with you".

Even changing faith failed to release Jews from their shackles: converts were forbidden to practise non-Jewish professions "on pain of hanging, whipping, imprisonment or pillory".

Racial prejudice was also fuelled by religious scruples: the Jews often took Christian religious objects into pawn.

From the 14th century, there were attempts to restrict Jews to the mainland, resulting in the decree of 1423 forbidding Jews to own property. Jews were forced to wear a distinguishing

badge, yellow skull cap or red hat. When Mestre was destroyed by enemy troops in 1509, the Jews sought refuge in Venice and were allowed to stay for a time. Seven years later the expanding Jewish community was given its own closed living quarters, both a reward for contributing funds for the defence of the city and as a means of future control. While other ethnic communities had settled in different districts, only the Jews were segregated, forced to move into an unhealthy area. This new home was within sight of the former foundry or *ghetto*. Thus the term came to mean a closed Jewish quarter.

The Ghetto was ringed by canals, like a moated prison. By day, many Jews worked outside the Ghetto but night curfews prevailed. The locked gates were manned by Christian guards the Jews were forced to pay for. The Ghetto was damp and dark and the living space cramped because the local community multiplied in spite of persecution. In time, the houses grew as high as the foundations permitted. For fear of subsidence, houses were generally no higher than three storeys. Ceilings were made low in order to cram in seven floors, leading to the buildings being dubbed "medieval skyscrapers".

The population density was three times greater than in the most crowded Christian suburbs. After the Ghetto Nnuovo (1516), two

newer settlements, the Ghetto Vecchio (1541) and Ghetto Nuovissimo (1633) only provided temporary relief from overcrowding.

The Venetian ambivalence to Jews was mirrored in the Ghetto itself. Jews often favoured splendid clothes and jewellery, the sole way of displaying status for a community excluded from land and property ownership. While the synagogues, mostly situated on the second floor as a protection against floods, were outwardly modest, the interiors were sumptuous, reflecting the great reserves of Jewish wealth. How-

ever, the Ghetto's elected representatives had limited powers: they obeyed their contract with the Venetian state, collected taxes, settled legal problems and dealt with new immigrants. There were numerous charitable organisations and free schooling was taken for granted in an age when few Christians were literate; the Ghetto also ran a renowned printing centre for Jewish books. Christians often patronised the Ghetto, visiting respected doctors or the three local banks, called the red, yellow and green after the colour of their promissory notes. Yet even in death, the Jews were segregated: they were rowed down the Canale degli Ebrei to the Lido, the cemetery for outcasts.

Brief liberty from Napoleon

While Venice's greatness declined during the 16th and 17th centuries, the Jewish community thrived. Their main source of wealth was trade with Levantine Jews, but they also dealt in second-hand goods and clothing. In troubled times, Venice found the Jews useful consumers. Yet the decline of Venice ultimately affected the Jews; in 1655 there were almost 5000 people in the Ghetto, with numbers falling to 1500 a century later. The Jewish tax burden often led to bankruptcy or emigration. This long farewell ended in 1797 with the Napoleonic invasion when the Ghetto gates were flung open and everyone was entitled to liberty, equality and fraternity. This dream was soon dispelled by the restoration of Austrian rule. But times had changed and Jews were among the most passionate upholders of the revolutionary aims of 1848. Jews became full citizens in 1866, when Venice became part of the Kingdom of Italy.

Jews found no peace in the 20th century: a bronze relief in the Ghetto Nuovo recalls the deportations and death of 200 Venetian Jews. Grim though the Ghetto is, it must be seen in the context of the times. Venice was one of the few states to tolerate the Jewish religion: the city was a liberal enclave compared with the brutal regimes of 15th-century Spain or the Ottoman Turks. Today the local Jewish community numbers 600, with few choosing to live in the former Ghetto. Nonetheless, the Ghetto remains at the heart of Jewish life, with fine synagogues and a cultural centre, a nursery, an old people's home, workshops selling liturgical objects and a kosher bakery. The Jews may live elsewhere but this is where they still break bread. ❑

LEFT: the bridge leading into the Ghetto.
ABOVE: the nearby Museo Ebraico, the Jewish Museum.

DEATHS IN VENICE: FACT AND FICTION

Thomas Mann and Luchino Visconti have much to answer for: Death in Venice *has spun a morbidly beguiling web around the lagoon*

Death and Venice go together. While the lagoon is a familiar backdrop to modern murder mysteries, romantic foreigners may even see Venice as beckoning them to a watery grave. The city's taste for the macabre is partly a figment of the foreign imagination, a romanticised notion fed by visions of sinister alleys, the inkiness of a lagoon night or a cortège of mourning gondolas gliding across the water. However, Venetian history does provide tales of murdered Doges and deadly plots nipped in the bud by the secret police. Be that as it may, the Venetian cult of death stems from the struggle for survival. The city built no fewer than five churches in thanksgiving for the passing of the plague.

During the glory days of the Republic, funeral cortèges were a magnificent sight. Nowadays, coffins are usually transported on motor launches. The Venetian love of living is matched by their respect for the dead. Commuters visit the cemetery island of San Michele *(above)* to leave flowers for loved ones before travelling to work. The cemetery is officially full but exceptions can be made. Unless one can afford to lease a family plot, coffins are dug up after 10 years to make space for new arrivals and the bones are placed in a public ossuary. Burial at sea is unheard of, so many Venetians are now buried on the mainland. "I could kill Ezra Pound," declares Rose Lauritzen, an old Venice hand. Since the American poet's tomb takes up nine plots in the cemetery, the city had difficulty squeezing in Sir Ashley Clarke, who had worked tirelessly for the Venice in Peril charity. His funeral in 1995 was suitably stately, with a procession down the Grand Canal.

▽ **RICHARD WAGNER**
After separating from his first wife, Richard Wagner (1813–83) retreated to Venice, where he composed *Tristan und Isolde*. He later lived in the splendid Palazzo Vendramin-Calergi (now the Winter Casino) until his death. Although buried in Bayreuth, the composer is celebrated by the Wagner Society in his Venetian home.

△ **MANN'S WORK**
Dirk Bogarde stars as the moodily introspective German composer von Aschenbach in Visconti's *Death in Venice* (1971), based on the evocative novella by Thomas Mann *(right)* (1875–1955).

◁ **FUNERAL BARGE**
Adorned with gold-winged angels and draped in grand livery, these flower-bedecked biers once set out for San Michele, followed by a floating cortège of mourning gondolas.

▽ **ROBERT BROWNING**
Robert Browning (1812–89) wrote his poetry in Palazzo Barbaro but died in style in Ca' Rezzonico, which was then owned by his son.

▽ **IGOR STRAVINSKY**
Igor Stravinsky, the stirring composer (1882–1971), is buried close to his compatriot and collaborator Diaghilev in the Russian and Greek Orthodox section of San Michele cemetery, a haunting spot.

△ **GENIUS IMPRESARIO**
Sergei Diaghilev (1872–1929), the dazzling founder of the Ballet Russe, is buried amidst foreign royalty in San Michele cemetery.

THE CANAL'S FATAL ALLURE

There is a morbid interest in Venice's reputation as a suicide destination. A recent illustrious victim was industrialist Raul Gardini who shot himself in Ca' Dario *(above),* which is particularly accursed. Venetians are shocked that their picture-postcard city should be a magnet for would-be suicides. The stoical natives have one of the lowest suicide rates in Italy. Germans and Scandinavians are in the forefront, followed by the British and Americans, with lovers' pacts common. Typical candidates are couples (homosexual and heterosexual) and middle-aged single women. But death by drowning is only successful in about 10 percent of cases: the canals are so shallow that gondoliers regularly fish people out in time.

Psychiatrists distinguish between "lucid suicides", programmed for death in a place of supreme beauty, and the borderline cases, deeply troubled people seeking to escape into a city of dreams. A leading psychiatrist suggests that Venice is seen as "a beautiful, unreal city at the end of the line. The dark mixture of death and water provides a deadly allure".

GHOSTS OF THE LAGOON

Poets, novelists and philosophers have been haunted by Venice,

portraying it as a city trapped in its past

O f all the ghosts of the Rialto, "the first is Venice herself, for Venice died on 17th October 1797", declared Daniele Varè, the Venetian chronicler. History aside, a visitor to Venice is always aware of ghosts, literary spectres, shadowy Doges, memories of films, the clichéd gondola ride never taken. Venice is the city we have all been to, if only in our imagination. Given the palpable fiction of Venice, its appeal to writers is tangible. Painters have seen a Venetian state of grace in the interplay of light and water, musicians have found poetry and philosophers have found music. Venice lends itself to lyricism. Even Nietzsche said that if he searched for a synonym for music, he found "always and only Venice".

Heavenly paradox

In this floating, insubstantial world, "most visitors move among her wonders mindlessly" claims Jan Morris. Yet she is one of many gifted writers who have tried to come to terms with this shimmering but elusive subject. Venice is a paradoxical place, with its unpromising setting at the heart of the mystery. Machiavelli (1469–1527), the political philosopher, made a study of the city: "Being in a marshy and unwholesome situation, it became healthy only by the number of industrious individuals who were drawn together".

"A commercial people who lived solely for gain – how could they create a city of fantasy, lovely as a dream or a fairy tale?" asks Mary McCarthy, posing one of the central puzzles of Venice. Writer Jonathan Keates attributes this fantastical creation to the citizens' indomitable spirit: "For Venice's very existence derives from a simple human yearning to make things happen against the odds."

Venice can play cultural one-upmanship better than most cities. Even the cafés of St Mark's Square are awash with famous ghosts. Almost everyone who is anyone has been here, and

tourism is almost as ancient as the city itself. As an essential port of call on the Grand Tour, Venice attracted visitors drawn to the notion of slowly crumbling splendour. The Romantics were concerned with the pathos, transience and futility of existence. Venice rewarded them with a feeling of having come too late to a world too

old. In Venice, the Victorians indulged their predilection for the whimsical, Gothic and romantic. While perceiving Venice as a city in decay and decline, some felt sentimental sadness while others were resolutely unmoved.

Solitary city

Connoisseurs compare the poetry of Venice with the plain prose of the mainland. Henry James thought that "everyone interesting, appealing, melancholy, memorable or odd" gravitated towards Venice: "The deposed, the defeated, the disenchanted, the wounded, or even only the bored, have seemed to find something that no other place could give." Writer Ian

LEFT: the Lagoon that holds the spirits of the past.
RIGHT: memorial next to the basilica in Murano.

Littlewood elaborates: whereas Florence was the haunt of couples, Venice became "the haven of individuals", a place for solitary figures. There, writers as different as Proust and James "seemed to find in its passivity and its decadence and its ambiguous femininity an atmosphere that allowed them to breathe more freely". It is only too easy to see a decline since the glory days, to deplore a commoner type of visitor. Crotchety critics find the city brutalised, commercialised, a cliché of itself: "The city once welcomed princes and Doges, Henry James and Hemingway. For romance, you can literally walk in Casanova's footsteps; for Baroque passion, succumb to a Vivaldi concerto in Vivaldi's church, or savour the gondoliers' songs that inspired Verdi and Wagner. If feeling adventurous, explore the world of Marco Polo in his home city, or bargain in the Rialto with latter-day Merchants of Venice, pick up the cobalt blue cabbages that sent Elizabeth David into culinary raptures, or roam the

> ## SWEET DREAMS
>
> "You can sleep in Tchaikovsky's bed or wake up in the apartments that welcomed Doges, Henry James and Hemingway."

becomes ever more ersatz. Venice's reason for existing is to celebrate the absence of a reason for existing. It will be for urban necrophiliacs" rails UK journalist Simon Jenkins. Yet in some respects, the necrophiliacs are already there.

Theme park for the soul

Venice finally "slipped her moorings from time and became the first of the world's theme parks", declares critic Gilbert Adair. Yet Venice is no mere fantasy land but a superior theme park for the soul. The city offers a cradle-to-the-grave experience in the best possible taste. You can sleep in Tchaikovsky's bed in the Londra Palace or wake up in cavernous apartments that

world's first Ghetto with a wily Shylock in tow. If feeling contemplative, ponder the passing of time with Proust's ghost in Caffè Florian. If fortunate, capture Canaletto's views with your camera, or see Titian's painting in the church it was designed for. If feeling gregarious, savour the gossip and martinis at Harry's Bar, Hemingway's favourite. If feeling Byronic, you can swim from the Lido (but only retrace the poet's Grand Canal exploits if you can face a stomach pump afterwards). The morbid can play roulette in Wagner's death chamber, now the city casino; the melancholic can even die in Thomas Mann's Venice, followed by a costly but atmospheric burial in Stravinsky's cemetery.

Yet one person's theme park is another's time capsule. Wealth and leisure mean "we spend it searching out capsules of past cultures, if only because the past is another country and we like to travel", says Simon Jenkins of Venice, the perfect time capsule. Ian Littlewood agrees: "No city but Venice lends itself so powerfully to nostalgia because no other city resists time so faithfully or marks its passage so clearly". Old Venice hands regret the passing of the city's presumed melancholy, nostalgia and yearning for empire. Such critics take a maudlin delight in charting the city's continuing social decline: Venice is no longer a voluptuous dowager on a same token, the cult of the ruin may have obsessed the Romantic poets but was fostered by the earliest Venetians.

Written on water

Indeed, to many writers, the most poetic Venetian end would be for "the Serenissima to subside below the waves, only its towers and domes sometimes to be glimpsed as in legend, waved around in seaweed in the depths of the lagoon". Jan Morris's sentiments were widely shared by earlier writers: the Victorians saw Venice as dying while contemporary doom-mongers, laden with *fin de siècle* sorrow or millennium

drawing-room sofa but a tawdry show run by guides and gondoliers. Yet as Jan Morris concedes, "The sadness of Venice is a much more nebulous abstraction, a wistful sense of wasted purpose and lost nobility, a suspicion of degradation, a whiff of hollow snobbery, the clang of the turnstyle and the sing-song banalities of the guides." The "decline" of Venice has been a common refrain down the centuries. Many travellers have seen moral turpitude in Venice, equating it with the city's physical decay. By the

LEFT: Francesco Zuccarelli's "Pastorale".
ABOVE : Monet's "Palazzo da Mula at Dusk", painted in 1908 when his eyesight was failing.

angst, now seek to bury the city anew. This whining sense of regret characterises much Venetian commentary. While entombment by the sea would show symmetry, those who know Venice well see the city's skill at resisting atrophy and degeneration. On a recent visit Jan Morris said: "I think the city today is more like the Venice of the Republic, the mercantile, sovereign Venice, than I have ever known it. Gone is the tristesse, gone is the uncertainty". In fact, melancholy and nostalgia await around most dark canal corners, if a ghost town is what one is seeking. Venice is a state of mind, a canvas for projecting one's poetic fantasies. The city reflects and intensifies one's moods, aided by changeable light and a capricious climate. Jonathan Keates tellingly sees Venice as "the great masseuse of our hankerings and illusions: she discovers us not for what we are but for what each of us would like to be".

Secret Venice

Amongst connoisseurs, Venice provokes a possessive passion, an elitist striving for a "secret Venice". Mary McCarthy, in her delightfully ironic book, *Venice Observed*, warns against the vanity of thinking one has discovered a hidden Venice: "Contrary to popular belief, there are no back canals where a tourist will not meet himself, with a camera, in the person of the other tourist crossing the little bridge". Lest one should think that the creators of this shimmering paradise are paragons of virtue, she points out that the Venetians were responsible for inventing income tax, statistical science, state censorship, anonymous denunciations, the gambling casino and the Ghetto.

Venice captured the hearts of the Anglo-American colony who moved to the city at the turn of the century and bought dilapidated palaces for a song or stayed with generous friends. Henry James (1843–1916) was happiest in Palazzo Barbaro. In a gracious compliment to his hosts, he used the setting for *The Wings of a Dove*. The dying heroine longed for "no dreadful, no vulgar hotel; but... part of a palace, historic and picturesque, but strictly inodorous, where we shall be to ourselves, with a cook, servants, frescoes, tapestries, antiquities, the thorough make-believe of a settlement".

The subjective views of Henry James act as a lively counterpoint to the academic precision of John Ruskin (1819–1900), the art critic and aesthete. Ruskin's passion for Gothic glories cast a pall over his contemporary's delight in Venice: "We feel at such moments as if the eye of Mr Ruskin were upon us; we grow nervous and we lose our confidence". Sated by palaces, James found himself perversely beguiled by gardens: "Of all the reflected and liquefied things in Venice, I think the lapping water loves them most... Venice without them would be too much a matter of the tides and the stones".

Ruskin's art and architecture books were highly influential for generations of visitors to Venice. As the son of a preacher, his vision was finely attuned to evidence of sin and virtue in stone. According to the ethos of the times, art was meant to be edifying not enjoyable. Much like a censorious school-teacher, Ruskin praised the "pure currents of Christian architecture" and set the Venetian artistic agenda in stone: Renaissance art was scorned and Gothic art celebrated as the pinnacle of creative genius. As historian John Pemble says, "Ruskin transformed the art treasures of Italy into a Christian preserve, a source of edification and reassurance for Christian travellers". However, Ruskin's commentaries would now be consigned to dust if it were not for his genuine passion for art; indeed, it is the creative conflict between his aesthetic sen-

sibility and Christian conscience that provides the questing tone to his work. Not that visiting artists paid the slightest heed to his strictures.

Artistic paradise

Venice is a painterly city, beloved by artists, particularly the French Impressionists. Renoir (1841–1919) naturally chose to portray the city bathed in light rather than paint the slick grey surface of the canals. The English Romantic painter Turner (1775–1851) captured the city's iridescence in his marine studies. Turner's atmospheric watercolours of Venice were much admired. In turn, the art critic Bernard Berenson (1865–1959) loved the humanity of the

Venetian artists: "They were painting handsome, healthy, sane people like themselves, people who wore their splendid robes with dignity, who found life worth the mere living and sought no metaphysical basis for it". This view is debatable but proof that Venice blinds the senses: we all paint our own Venice.

"Each nation has made its own Serenissima, like something cut out with scissors and glued together," asserts Jonathan Keates. "There is a German Venedig, replete with *sehnsucht*,

> ### ILL LUCK
> "Thomas Mann visited Venice while it was gripped in a cholera epidemic, and he used this as the backdrop for his novella."

Aschenbach broods while his gondola glides past "slippery corners of wall, past melancholy facades with ancient business shields reflected in the rocking water". His judgment on the city struck a chord with later travellers: "Yes, this was Venice, this the fair frailty that fawned and that betrayed, half fairy tale, half snare".

The French have a vision of Venice which is both wistful and lyrical. Maupassant (1850–93) likened the city to "an old, charming *bibelot d'art*, poor, ruined but proud". As a focus for

schwarmerei and *weltschmerz*" (yearning, waxing lyrical and world-weariness). Wagner (1813–83), working on *Tristan und Isolde*, tapped into such romantic emotions, admitting that the chants of the gondoliers "may even have suggested the plaintive trailing clarinet at the beginning of Act Three". Thomas Mann (1875–1955) remains the touchstone for the German experience of Venice. He visited the city while it was gripped by a cholera epidemic and used this as a backdrop to his haunting novella, *Death in Venice*. The troubled von

LEFT: Palazzo Barbaro, once home to Henry James.
ABOVE: Canaletto's "San Giacomo di Rialto".

nostalgia, Venice inevitably drew Marcel Proust (1871–1922), who translated Ruskin's works on Venice and then conjured up the city himself in *Remembrance of Things Past*. He dreamily recalls "the palaces of porphyry and jasper… tall houses with their tiny Moorish windows… the quatrefoils and foliage of Gothic windows".

His compatriot, George Sand (1804–76), succumbed to the enchantments of a Venetian spring, and this despite her disastrous love affair here with Alfred de Musset: "The base of the palaces, where oysters clustered in the stagnant moss, is now covered with the most tender green and gondolas float between two banks of this verdure".

Americans and English abroad

By contrast, American writers have tended to have an inexplicably less sentimental view of Venice over the years. Mark Twain (1835–1910) recorded his impressions in *The Innocents Abroad,* castigating his uncouth gondolier but serenading Venice, the one "a mangy barefooted gutter-snipe" and the other moonlit romance "with music floating over the waters – Venice was complete".

To an even greater extent, Ernest Hemingway (1898–1961) focused on life rather than on his literature while in the city: the result of this is a somewhat lightweight novel but heavyweight

alcohol consumption in Harry's Bar. As a young man, Hemingway was wounded in the First World War in the Veneto, becoming the first American casualty. In 1948, he returned to live on Torcello and wrote of the adjoining island: "Burano is a very over-populated little island where the women make wonderful lace and the men make *bambinis*". Hemingway and Venice make rather an odd pairing: the macho man abroad in a feminine city.

Charles Dickens (1812–70) was also drawn to Venice's seductive decline. "Sometimes, alighting at the doors of churches and vast palaces, I wandered on… through labyrinths of rich altars, ancient monuments, decayed apart-

ments". But among English writers and poets, Lord Byron (1788–1824) is exceptional in giving equal weight to the decadence of Venice and its undeniable vivacity:

Statues of glass – all shivered – the long file
Of her dead Doges are declined to dust;
But where they dwelt, the vast and sumptuous
  pile
Bespeaks the pageant of their splendid trust.

The Romantic poet slips effortlessly from high-flown verse to high-spirited vernacular: "The bathing, on a calm day, must be the worst in Europe, water like hot saliva, cigar-ends floating into one's mouth, and shoals of jellyfish". Byron occupied various Grand Canal palaces amidst "a shifting population of servants, acquaintances, hangers-on and half-tamed animals". Ian Littlewood's view of Byron is matched by contemporary accounts which have the Romantic poet swimming the length of the Grand Canal, conducting illicit affairs with a string of mistresses, writing, or talking to Shelley long into the night.

Ghostly farewells

According to Jan Morris, most visitors leave Venice "sated but puzzled" with "a sensation half of relief, half of sadness, strongly tinged with bewilderment". Henry James, standing on the steps of La Salute, the Baroque basilica, was beguiled by the seductive city, "all the sweet bribery of association and recollections". Nor could Théophile Gautier tear himself away: "I delayed my departure from week to week… In vain did light vapours begin to rise in the morning over the lagoon, or sudden showers compel me to take refuge in a church … In six weeks I had worn out three pairs of eyeglasses, a pair of opera glasses, and lost a telescope. Never did anyone indulge in such an orgy of sightseeing; if I had dared, I would have continued my visiting by torchlight." Many writers conclude that Venice will outlive us all and, at the deepest level, will never leave us. As Jan Morris says: "Wherever you go in life, you will feel somewhere over your shoulder a pink, castellated, shimmering presence, the domes and riggings and crooked pinnacles of the Serenissima." ❑

LEFT: Lord Byron, poet and adventurer, who saw both the decadence and vivacity of the city.

City on celluloid

The city's mythic status has inspired countless directors, from the Lumière brothers in 1896 to a host of foreign directors a century later. Although art-house movies and period dramas predominate, the odd adventure movie provides a change of pace. One James Bond movie, *Moonraker* (1979), includes a frenzied gondola chase with the agent 007 discovering an enemy hide-out in St Mark's Clocktower. *Indiana Jones and the Last Crusade* (1989) features a crypt full of crusader knights under the paving stones of the church of San Barnaba. In the French *Le Guignolo* (1980), Jean-Paul Belmondo, playing a daring smuggler, zooms into the famous Hotel Danieli in a motorboat.

Antonioni's masterpiece, *Identification of a Woman* (1982), shows Venice as a magical yet murky world, with scenes set in the misty lagoon and the historic Hotel Gritti. Fellini's *Casanova* (1976) charts the adventures of the Venetian libertine with great aplomb while *Don Giovanni* (1979), based on Mozart's opera, shows atmospheric scenes of masked figures in the mist.

By contrast, Luchino Visconti's *Senso* (1954) traces a doomed romance in the days of Austrian occupation. While the Italian countess hurries through the gloomy Ghetto Nuovo to meet her Austrian lover, the courtesan heroine (Jeanne Moreau) waits in chic Caffè Lavena on Piazza San Marco. David Lean's *Summertime* (1954) cast Katherine Hepburn as an American who falls in love with an antique dealer and falls into the San Barnaba canal.

A more recent period drama is *The Wings of a Dove* (1997), based on the dying heroine in Henry James's classic. The film makes magnificent use of the palaces along the Grand Canal, including the Palazzo Barbaro, where James once lived.

However, the undisputed Venetian masterpiece is Visconti's *Death in Venice* (1970), based on the Thomas Mann novel. Dirk Bogarde plays the leading role of the lugubrious composer, von Aschenbach, who mutely adores Tadzio, the Polish golden boy. Yet almost 30 years later, Bogarde wryly attributes "starvation and exhaustion" to the mood of "loneliness and sense of loss" that he portrayed so poignantly. Visconti's decision to use dawn and night shoots left Bogarde sleepless during the day, "with all the blasted bells clanging across the water

and the novice monks in the gardens of the Redentore jumping up and down in their brown cassocks".

Visconti wanted "the light of the sirocco, the pale, still, pearl light". The result is exquisite, with an atmosphere of decay conveyed by scenes shot in the early morning light of the Lido. The film is mainly set on the Lido's busy Alberoni beach and in the majestic Hotel des Bains. However, Bogarde, staying in Count Volpi's summer villa on the Giudecca, recalls his solitary life, spent coming to terms with the "prissy, fastidious, ugly, lonely old German composer". Every dawn, the speedboat ride from the Giudecca marked the emotional voyage towards his "prissy playmate": "It was about

4 km across to the Lido, and for that time I was splendidly and amazingly myself. I even managed a cigarette, knowing with increasingly sickening lurches that von Aschenbach was waiting ahead".

Nic Roeg's *Don't Look Now* (1973) is the only other portrayal of the city that seeps into one's bones. Although in thrall to Venice, he captures the faintly menacing mood of the city in winter: "Of course beauty has its sinister side. For example, one of the strange things about walking in Venice is that you can hear people but don't see them." In this terrifying film, the austere church of San Nicolo dei Mendicoli is an important location while the dark passageways frequented by the hooded dwarf lie close to Campo Santa Maria Formosa. ❑

RIGHT: Woody Allen, ever the romantic, in his film "Everybody Says I Love You", set partly in Venice.

Venetian Lagoon

0 — 5 km
0 — 5 miles

N

Monastier di Treviso
Udine, Trieste
Caposile
San Dona di Piave
Sile
Iesolo
Lido dei Lombardi
Vallio
Meolo
Lanzoni
Valle Doga
Valle Grassabo
Valle Dragaiesolo
Capo del Guardiano
Sile
Treviso
Vallio
Porto di Piave Vecchia
Roncade
Portegrandi
Palude Maggiore
Cavallino
La Valle
Santa Fosca
Sile
Valle di Ca'Zane
Treviso, Vittorio Veneto
Quarto d'Altino
Zero
Casale sul Sile
L. Veneta
Litorale del Cavallino
Palude di Cona
Torcello
Treporti
Gaggio
Dese
Burano
Ca'Savio
Colmello
San Francesco del Deserto
Sant' Erasmo
Punta Sabbioni
Terzo
Marco Polo International Airport
Le Vignole
Porto di Lido
Marocco
Favaro Veneto
Murano
G o l f o
Campalto
S. Michele
MESTRE
San Giuliano
Lido
Zelarino
S. Servolo
S. Lazzaro degli Armeni
d i
Porto Marghera
S. Maria delle Grazie
Lazzaretto Vecchio
Marghera
Poveglia
V e n e z i a
Chirignago
VENEZIA (VENICE)
Malamocco
Spinea
Fusina
Litorale di Lido
Malcontenta
Alberoni
Brenta
Porto di Malamocco
Oriago
San Pietro in Volta
Litorale di Pellestrina
Mira
Padova
L. Veneta
Valle di Rivola
Dolo
Valle Seraglia
Laguna Viva
Pellestrina
Tagliò di Brenta
(Living Lagoon)
Camponogara
Valle dell'Averto
Laguna
Porto di Chioggia
Prozzolo
Campagna
Palude Fondello
Sottomarina
Fosso
Lova
Morta (Dead Lagoon)
Chioggia
Brenta
Valle di Millecampi
Valle della Dolce
Brondolo
Sant' Angelo
Compolongo Maggiore
Valle delle Morosna
Gonche
Strada Romea
Codevigo
Valle di Brenta
Piove di Sacco
Santa Margherita
Ca'Bianca
Ravenna, Rimini

Strada Romea
E 55
E 70
E 70
Zero
Sile

PLACES

*A detailed guide to the entire city, with principal sites
cross-referenced by number to the maps*

The first fleeting glimpse of Venice from the air is a foretaste of the watery puzzle that awaits below. At low tide, the lagoon reveals an expanse of mud flats, shifting sand banks and brackish marsh; the sunlight momentarily withdraws from the glassy greyish-brown waters, showing the same desolation that failed to daunt the early settlers. Yet as the plane circles the lagoon, the sinuous redbrick city floats into view, changing foreboding into fantasy.

Venice is traditionally divided into six *sestieri* (districts), a practice followed in this book. In addition, each main island is treated separately, as is the Grand Canal, which winds through all districts. Despite the watery insubstantiality of Venice, most time is spent walking rather than travelling by boat. However, a mastery of key ferry routes can save unnecessary circling of the lagoon: an error can cost an hour on a short journey. (*See the transport map inside the back cover and the Travel Tips section, page 297, for advice.*)

To find an address, ask the name of the closest parish church; this is more helpful than the postal address. Venetians will often escort you to your destination. Despite the kindness of strangers, all visitors eventually lose themselves in this labyrinthine city. Indeed, a distinctive Venetian pleasure is to *andare per le fodere*, "to move among the linings", creeping about the crevices of the city.

The uniqueness of the city geography is captured in Venetian dialect, with the names of streets providing clues to the nature of the city. Familiarity with these idiosyncratic terms will help in identifying places on your trails through the confusing backwaters. Venetian spelling is variable so expect alternative versions. ❑

A Venetian lexicon

Ca' – from *casa*, house/palace
calle alley
calle larga – wider alleyway
campo – square
campiello – small square
corte – external courtyard
cortile – internal courtyard
fontego or *fondaco* – historic warehouse
fondamenta – wide quayside
punta – a point
ramo – side street, often a dead end
rio (plural *rii*) – curving canal lined by buildings);

rio terrà – infilled canal
riva – promenade, quayside
ruga – broad shopping street
rughetta – small shopping street
sacca – inlet
salizzada – main street; means "paved" and dates from the days when few streets were
sottoportico (or *sottoportego*) – tiny alleyway running under a building;
squero – boatyard
stazio – gondoliers' station where they wait for clients

PRECEDING PAGES: panoramic view of the Doge's Palace; Palazzo Dolfin (on the left) and Palazzo Bembo; Cannaregio washing.

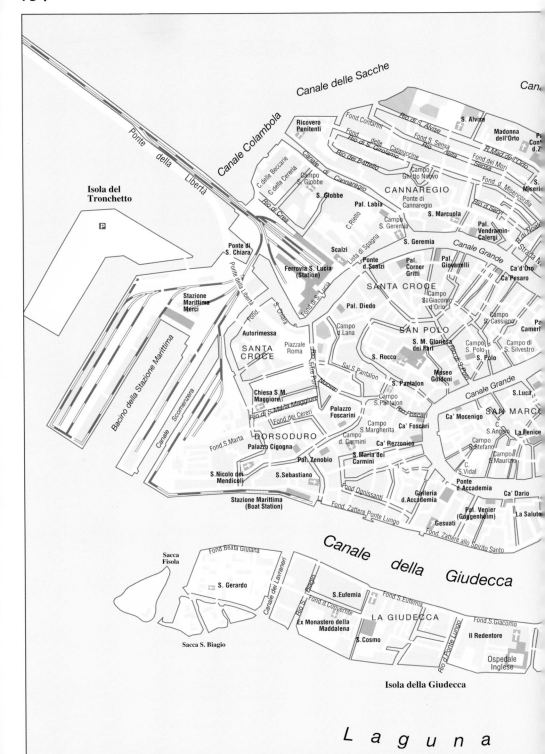

Isola del
Tronchetto

P

Ponte della Libertà

Ponte della Stazione Marittima

Canale Scomenzera

Bacino della Stazione Marittima

Stazione
Marittima
Merci

Ponte di
S. Chiara

Autorimessa

SANTA
CROCE

Piazzale
Roma

Chiesa S.M.
Maggiore

Palazzo
Foscarini

DORSODURO

Palazzo Cigogna

Pal. Zenobio

S.Nicolo dei
Mendicoli

S.Sebastiano

Stazione Marittima
(Boat Station)

Canale delle Sacche

Canale Colambola

Ricovero
Penitenti

Fond.Contarini

Rio di S. Alvise

S. Alvise

Madonna
dell'Orto

R.Mad.de l'Orto

Fond. delle Cappuccine

Rio dei Battello

Fond S. Sensa

Rio della

C.delle Beccarie
C.della Cereria

Campo
S.Giobbe

Canale di Cannaregio

Rio di S.Girolamo

Fond.dei Mori
Sensa

Fond. d. Misericordia

S. Miseri

S. Giobbe

Pal. Labia

C. Riello

Campo
Ghetto Nuovo

CANNAREGIO

Ponte di
Cannaregio

Scalzi

Lista di Spagna

Campo
S. Geremia

S. Geremia

S. Marcuola

Pal.
Vendramin-
Calergi

Rio d.Noal

Strada M

Ponte di Sacca

Rio di Crea

Rio di S.Lucia

Ferrovia S. Lucia
(Station)

Ponte
d.Scalzi

Pal.
Corner
Gritti

Pal.
Giovanelli

Canale Grande

Ca'd'Oro

Ca'Pesaro

SANTA CROCE

Pal. Diedo

Campo
S.Giacomo
d'Orio

Campo
S.Cassiano

Pal.
Camerl

S. Chiara

Fond.

Campo
d.Lana

SAN POLO

S. M. Gloriosa
dei Frari

Campo
S.Polo

Campo di
S. Silvestro

S. Rocco

S. Polo

Canale Grande

Sal.S.Pantalon

S. Pantalon

Museo
Goldoni

S.Luca

Rio Nuovo

Campo
S.Pantalon

Rio Foscari

SAN MARC

Rio di S.Maria Maggiore

Fond. dei Cereri

Campo
S.Margherita

Ca' Foscari

Ca' Mocenigo

C.
S.Angelo

La Fenice

Fond.S.Marta

Campo
d. Carmini

Ca' Rezzonico

Campo
S.Stefano

Campo
S.Maurizio

S.Maria dei
Carmini

C.
S.Vidal

Ponte
d.Accademia

Ca' Dario

Fond Ognissanti

Galleria
d.Accademia

Pal. Venier
(Guggenheim)

La Salute

Fond. Zattere Ponte Lungo

Gesuati

Fond. Zattere allo Spirito Santo

Sacca
Fisola

Fond.Beata Giulana

Canale della Giudecca

Canale dei Lavraneri

S. Gerardo

Rio di

S. Eufemia

Fond.d.Convertite

Fond.S.Eufemia

LA GIUDECCA

Fond.S.Giacomo

Ex Monastero della
Maddalena

S.Cosmo

Il Redentore

Rio di Ponte Lungo

Sacca S. Biagio

Ospedale
Inglese

Isola della Giudecca

Laguna

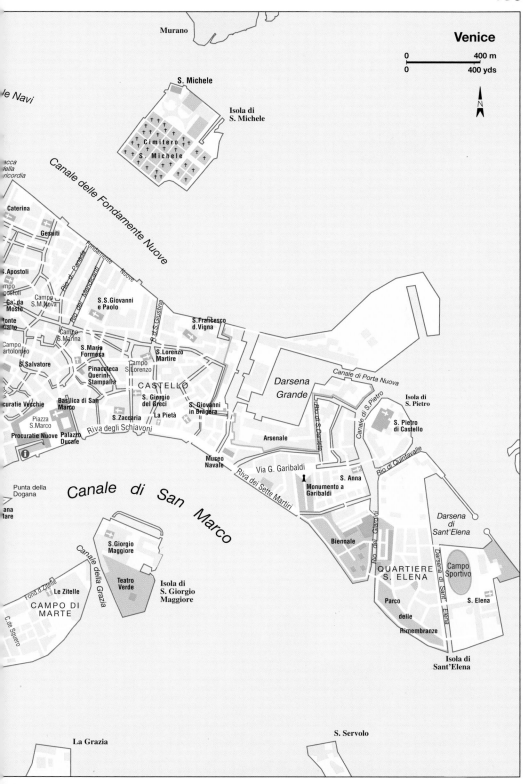

Murano

Venice

0	400 m
0	400 yds

N

S. Michele

Isola di
S. Michele

le Navi

Cimitero
S. Michele

acca
della
ricordia

Canale delle Fondamente Nuove

Caterina

Gesuiti

S.Apostoli

mpo
postoli

Ca' da
Mosto

Campo
S.M.Nova

S.S.Giovanni
e Paolo

S.Francesco
d.Vigna

onte
ialto

Campo
S.Marina

Campo
artolomeo

S.Maria
Formosa

S.Lorenzo
Martire

S.Salvatore

Pinacoteca
Querini
Stampalia

Campo
S.Lorenzo

CASTELLO

Darsena
Grande

Canale di Porta Nuova

Isola di
S. Pietro

curatie Vecchie

Basilica di San
Marco

S. Giorgio
del Greci

S. Giovanni
in Bragora

S.Pietro
di Castello

Piazza
S.Marco

S.Zaccaria

La Pietà

Procuratie Nuove

Palazzo
Ducale

Riva degli Schiavoni

Arsenale

Museo
Navale

Via G. Garibaldi

S. Anna

Punta della
Dogana

Canale di San Marco

Riva dei Sette Martiri

Monumento a
Garibaldi

Darsena
di
Sant'Elena

ana
lare

Biennale

S.Giorgio
Maggiore

QUARTIERE
S. ELENA

Campo
Sportivo

Le Zitelle

Teatro
Verde

Isola di
S. Giorgio
Maggiore

S. Elena

CAMPO DI
MARTE

Parco

delle

Rimembranze

Isola di
Sant'Elena

La Grazia

S. Servolo

AROUND SAN MARCO

St Mark's Square is the heart of Venice: here are the famous Basilica and belltower, the Doge's fabulous palace, the Correr Museum, Harry's Bar and the best cafés in town

Map, page 138

Piazza San Marco was famously dubbed "the finest drawing room in Europe" by Napoleon. Like many visitors to Venice, he then proceeded to repaint it in his own image, even rearranging the furniture and literally moving the walls. However, given the city's talent for fusing influences into a beguiling Venetian whole, the square has retained its essential character. Gentile Bellini's *Procession in Piazza San Marco* (1496) is the most reproduced view of Venice, a grand hierarchical affair of prelates and senators outside the Basilica. Yet unlike many official city squares, St Mark's belongs to the citizens as well as visitors. Venetians themselves will drink at the grand cafés, even if they often save money by standing up. Some may attend Sunday Mass at the Basilica or even dance at the open-air Carnival. However, for most of the day, St Mark's belongs to the pigeons, the crowds and the souvenir-sellers; only in early evening does it revert to a semblance of solitude.

LEFT: aerial view of the finest drawing room in Europe.
BELOW: on hand are the waiters from the grandest cafés.

Piazza San Marco acted as the heart of the Republic from the time the earliest settlement shifted from Torcello to central Venice. The piazza's essential design was determined by the building of the Byzantine St Mark's Basilica and the Doge's Palace. However, in the 16th-century, the square was remodelled to reflect Venetian notions of glory. The Basilica and Palace were embellished, with a new library, mint and administrative buildings clustered around the square. The design remained intact until the bombastic Napoleonic era, when churches and waterside monuments were demolished to create a Neo-Classical wing, a ballroom and public gardens.

Before braving the hordes in the Basilica, it is well to retreat to one of the grand cafés on the square. The most Venetian is **Caffè Florian**, spilling under the arcades of the Procuratie Nuove. **Caffè Quadri** faces its rival from the arcades of the Procuratie Vecchie. Quadri is only slightly less prestigious, decorated in Venetian colours, its interior adorned with elegant stucco-work, red damask walls, Murano chandeliers and gilded mirrors. This is the setting for a fine restaurant, the only proper one on the Piazza, serving Venetian specialities as well as creative twists on classic Italian cuisine. Yet with a glass of Prosecco and a fairytale setting, the colourful comings and goings on the Piazza are pleasure enough.

The Basilica

The Basilica di San Marco (St Mark's Basilica) ❶ *(9.30am–5pm, Sunday 1.30–5pm)* is the centrepiece of the square, a place the aesthete John Ruskin called "a treasure heap, a confusion of delight". Best visited in the early morning, at midday or in the early evening, the Basilica remains a glorious confusion. Given the crowds, the mysterious design, and the varied museums within, several visits are desirable. San Marco, mod-

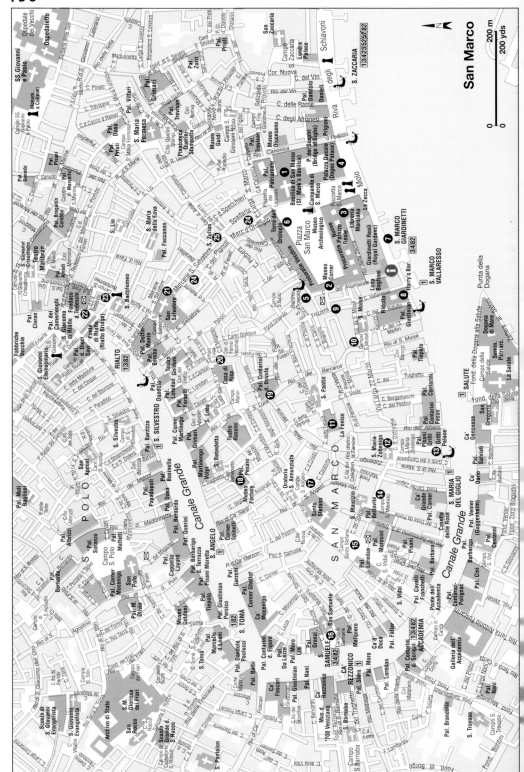

San Marco

elled on Byzantine churches in Constantinople, transposes the essence of an eastern basilica to the West. Indeed, to critic Mary McCarthy, it was "an Oriental pavilion, half pleasure house, half war tent, belonging to some great satrap". The French poet Théophile Gautier (1811–72) declared San Marco "a pirate cathedral enriched with the spoils of the universe" while Charles Dickens (1812–70) was spellbound: "opium couldn't build such a place… dim with the smoke of incense; costly in treasure of precious stones and metals; glittering through iron bars; holy with the bodies of deceased saints".

The Basilica was consecrated in AD 832, intended as a mausoleum for St Mark's relics and as the Doge's ceremonial chapel. In AD 976 the church burnt down after a riot but was rebuilt between 1063 and 1094, probably supervised by a Greek architect. Since Venice still recognised the cultural supremacy of Byzantium, the Basilica echoed eastern models. At the same time, Doge Selvo (1071–84) asked merchants to return with rare marbles and semi-precious stones to adorn the Basilica, from jasper to alabaster and porphyry. John Ruskin admired this "confused incrustation", which incorporated Roman fragments and looted Byzantine booty in an Oriental basilica which professed to be a Christian church. Yet for political reasons, this majestic building was technically designated the Doge's private chapel for most of the duration of the Republic. San Marco only succeeded San Pietro as the cathedral of Venice Cathedral in 1807.

Map,
page 138

Glittering mosaic in San Marco. For further details of the basilica, see pages 158–9

The Treasury and Museo Marciano

The Greek cross plan is inscribed in a square, and crowned by a cluster of five domes, set over each arm of the cross. These are linked to one another by loggias and arcades. The bewildering contrast is between the Oriental domes and rounded Byzantine arches and the Gothic ornamentation of the central roofline. Gothic arches and pinnacles were grafted onto 12th-century facades and completed by a gallery overlooking the square. Most of the garish mosaics on the facade are 17th-century copies, with the only intact 13th-century mosaic depicting the arrival of St Mark's relics in the Basilica (set above the doorway on the far left). A 17th-century mosaic also shows the smuggling of St Mark's remains from Alexandria, supposedly concealed under "a basket covered with herbs and swine flesh which the Muslims hold in horror".

BELOW: the domes of San Marco.

The Basilica was controversially restored in the 1860s and 1870s, which led to the removal of the mosaics on the north and south facades. In a letter to his father, Ruskin, who helped mobilise international opinion, literally wept: "They appear to be destroying the mosaics. I cannot draw here for tears in my eyes." Although these mosaics were lost, the international furore stirred up by Ruskin led to the reversal of other restoration blunders in St Mark's.

The exterior brickwork of the central apse is reminiscent of Santa Fosca in Torcello (*see page 279*). The southern side abuts the Doge's Palace and is currently being restored. The Baptistry doors are framed by the **Pilasters of Acre**, two ancient Syrian pillars plundered from Acre, in the Holy Land (modern Israel) after a victory over the Genoese in 1258. These sculpted 6th-century marble columns stand beside a porphyry stump

The domes of San Marco, with the banner of St Mark.

BELOW: San Marco, with the winged Lion of St Mark above the main doorway.

known as the *pietra del bando*, where the laws of the Republic were proclaimed. In the corner are the **Tetrarchs**, often known as Moors because of their dress, a 4th-century Egyptian sculpture representing Diocletian and his fellow rulers who governed the Roman Empire.

The Basilica is remarkable for its spatial complexity and stylistic synthesis, creating an eclectic yet harmonious design. From the inside, the 13th-century Oriental domes seem much lower and smaller than they really are. The **pavimento**, the Basilica pavement, is an oriental carpet interweaving floral, animal and geometric motifs. The undulating mosaics of marble, porphyry and glass depict allegorical and naturalistic scenes. After the conquest of Constantinople in 1204, Venice celebrated its triumph with lavish cycles of mosaics and the display of Byzantine booty. Some of the greatest treasures in San Marco were plundered from Constantinople, including the **Madonna Nicopeia**, a sacred 10th-century icon, adorning the Altar of the Virgin. The **Treasury** incorporates a 9th-century corner tower from the first Doge's Palace and displays Byzantine gold, silver and glassware. Since this collection began with the Venetian looting of Constantinople, it seems only poetic justice that French plundering should have depleted the treasury. However, much remains, despite a forced sale of jewels and the Napoleonic melting down of *objets d'art*.

The Classical **horses** were also Byzantine booty. The rearing horses stood on top of a triumphal arch in Rome before gracing the hippodrome in Constantinople and finally adorning the facade of San Marco. Given that the horses symbolised the Venetian Republic's untramelled independence, Napoleon had them harnessed to a chariot in Paris for 18 years. The humiliation ended with their return to Venice in 1815. Jan Morris mourned the fate of "the supreme talismans

of Venetian power, the Golden Horses of St Mark, chafing their gilded hooves in the humiliation of decline." Yet despite the demise of the Republic, the prancing horses are still proud and remain the only team pulling a chariot to survive from Classical times. They are now displayed in the **Museo Marciano**, on the floor above the entrance portal, allowing one to pause for a fine view of the *piazza* and exterior mosaics from the loggia on the way up.

Map, page 138

The mosaics and altarpiece

Officially, St Mark's remains are encased in a sarcophagus under the altar but sceptics believe that these were destroyed in the fire of AD 976. Behind the altar, often swamped by crowds, is the **Pala d'Oro**, a superb medieval altarpiece studded with gems and covered in sacred scenes. The panels are enclosed in a gilded frame and encrusted with emeralds, rubies, sapphires and gleaming, translucent enamels bound by a filigree of gold; each *tessera* is a separate segment of colour. This 10th-century masterpiece was created by Byzantine goldsmiths but embellished in 1209 and 1345 by the Venetians and Siennese; panels from a sacked church in Constantinople also added to the lustre.

The interior is studded with **mosaics**, one of the chief glories of San Marco. Unfortunately, in summer, visitors are channelled along set routes, making lingering difficult. The secret is to come early or late, conceivably even passing oneself off as a practising Catholic (the Basilica is open from 7am for worshippers but only welcomes tourists after 9.30am). The mosaics date from 1071, first created by craftsmen from Constantinople; while the majority are from the 11th to 14th centuries, mosaics continued to be added until the 18th century. The result is a bewildering and beguiling tapestry, an illustrated Bible using

Film director Woody Allen came to Venice in 1997 to marry Soon-Yi Previn, the adopted daughter of his former partner Mia Farrow.

BELOW: the basilica's glittering interior.

The star of the Correr museum is Carpaccio's "Two Venetian Ladies", pictured on page 45.

4,000 square metres of mosaics. Even the windows of this Oriental extravaganza were walled up to make more space for mosaics.

The mosaics are rich in geometric forms and symbolic meaning, part decorative, part naturalistic. Relatively naturalistic Old Testament scenes in the **narthex** (atrium) are contrasted with the more stylised figures of the central domes. As a rule of thumb, the lower walls depict saints, with the middle section featuring the Apostles, and the domes dedicated to Christ Pantocrator, the Creator of All. The atrium mosaics in the **Genesis dome** show the Creation, unravelled in concentric circles. The **Pentecost dome**, rising above the nave, depicts the descent of the Holy Ghost as a dove, and was perhaps the first to be adorned with mosaics. The paired figures between the windows represent the nations in whose languages the Apostles evangelised after Pentecost. The central **Ascension dome** shows Christ in Majesty, a 13th-century scene embracing the Apostles and the Virgin Mary. The 14th-century mosaic-encrusted **Baptistry** and adjoining Zen Chapel remain closed for restoration.

The Museo Correr

Facing the Basilica on the far side of Piazza San Marco is the **Museo Correr** ❷ *(9am–7pm)*, the museum of Venetian civilisation (it is much less crowded than the Doge's Palace, and can be visited with a combined ticket). The museum is housed in the Procuratie Nuove, with the entrance in the Ala Napoleonica, the Napoleonic Wing. The Neo-Classical rooms make a fitting setting for Canova's sculptures. The first section is a romp through Venetian history, illustrated by representations of the Lion of St Mark, paintings of festivities and examples of ceremonial costume. The final historical section covers the trou-

BELOW: the facade of San Marco at one end of the square.

RESTORATION OF SAN MARCO

St Mark's Square is rarely completely free from scaffolding. Amongst recent projects, Olivetti has funded the restoration of the bronze horses of St Mark, with the originals controversially placed within a museum inside the Basilica and copies left on the facade. The British have subsidised the cleaning of the capitals on the Doge's Palace, the restoration of the Loggetta at the foot of the belltower and the Porta della Carta, the ceremonial gateway to the Doge's Palace.

The grand gateway and the crypt of the Basilica have been well-restored but Sansovino's Loggetta is posing a problem. The resins used to protect the restored marble have begun to discolour the building so work is under way to flush the resins out. The facade of the Basilica and the belltower are currently being restored, as is the lovely Clocktower at the landward end of the piazza.

The partly boarded-up facade of the Basilica hides the damage caused by sulphur dioxide and pollutants. The curved reliefs, dating to at least the 13th century, represent the most important cycle of stone sculpture in Venice. Restoration involves the removal of encrustations by hand or using micro sand-blasting techniques. It will be for future generations to judge whether the result is a success.

bled times from the fall of the Republic to French and Austrian domination and the Risorgimento. Those without a taste for coins and battle memorabilia can proceed to the more accessible picture gallery. This chronological display focuses on Venetian art from the 13th to the 16th century. Highlights include Byzantine-influenced works by Paolo Veneziano and Bartolomeo Vivarini and paintings by Giovanni Bellini, especially the poignant *Pietà*. However, the symbol of the museum is Carpaccio's *Two Venetian Ladies* (1507), depicted in a pleasure garden, surrounded by birds and dogs. Although often seen as courtesans, these are probably languid noblewomen, given the presence of the Torella family crest; yet also present is a pomegranate, a symbol of love and fertility.

The Libreria Marciana ❸ *(9am–1pm by appointment only, tel: 041-520 8788),* or Marcian Library, is a cool Classical building set in an extended loggia around the corner. Designed by Sansovino in 1537, the library is also known as the Libreria Sansoviniana. This long, low building is lined with arches and expressive statues, and graced with a sumptuous stairway. Indeed, Palladio praised it as the richest building since Classical times. The library was designed to house the precious collection of manuscripts bequeathed by Petrarch in the 14th century and by Cardinal Bessarione, the Greek humanist, in 1468. The superb salon of the original library is covered with paintings by Veronese and Tintoretto. Visitors can best appreciate the scene by attending one of the occasional classical concerts that are staged here.

The *piazza* is bounded by the Procuratie, the offices and residences of the Procurators of the Republic, the highest government officials. The **Procuratie Vecchie** is an elegant porticoed building stretching along the north side of the square. Dating from 1500, this functional affair was modelled on Coducci's

Map, page 138

St Mark's roofline is encrusted with pinnacles, statuary and ornamentation.

BELOW: Museo Correr, at the other end of the square.

Ceiling of the Scala d'Oro, Sansovino's gilded staircase in the Doge's Palace.

designs but finished by Scarpagnino. The Marciana was a model for the **Procuratie Nuove**, the adjoining offices on the south side of the square. The long building was begun in 1586 but finished by Longhena in 1640. Although echoing the Marciana, it is more sober and less graceful than the earlier buildings. Napoleon converted it into a royal palace, creating a ballroom by demolishing a neighbouring church. The **Ala Napoleonica**, the Napoleonic Wing, closes the piazza, sandwiched between the Procuratie Nuove and Vecchie.

The **Museo Archeologico** *(9am–2pm)* is housed in part of the Procuratie Nuove and the Libreria Marciana. The core collection consists of Greek and Roman sculpture bequeathed by Cardinal Grimani in 1523, a gift which influenced generations of Venetian artists who came to draw and study here. Amongst the Roman busts, medals, coins, cameos and portraits are Greek originals and Roman copies, including a 5th-century Hellenistic *Persephone*.

The Doge's Palace

The **Palazzo Ducale** (Doge's Palace) ❹ *(April–Oct 8.30am–7pm; Nov–March 9am–5pm)* vies with San Marco for most attention and plaudits. A recent reorganisation, introducing a bar and bookshops, means that visits are more efficient. A number of new rooms have been re-opened, including a museum of sculpture and sections hitherto off-limits; temporary exhibitions are also held in the Doge's Apartments. In adddition, a special pre-booked "secret itinerary" tour (in Italian only) explores the palace behind the scenes. (Since 1996, public access has been through Porta del Frumento, the waterside entrance).

BELOW: waterfront facade of the Doge's Palace.

The Doge's Palace was the seat of the Venetian government from the 9th century until the fall of the Republic in 1797. Yet while rival mainland cities were

building grim fortresses, the Venetians indulged in a light and airy structure, confident of the natural protection afforded by the lagoon. Apart from being the Doge's official residence, it acted as the nerve centre of the Republic, containing administrative offices and armouries, council chambers and chancellery, courtrooms and dungeons. The Palace was a symbol of political stability and independence, as well as a testament to Venetian supremacy and a glorious showcase of Venetian art, sculpture and craftsmanship. Yet there was also a shadowy side to the palace, a secretive machine staffed by state inquisitors, spies and torturers-in-residence.

First built as a fortress in the 9th century, there is now no trace of the original Byzantine building, although the massive walls echo its previous role. The Palace was enlarged over the course of several centuries, from the 12th-century onwards, and was essentially complete by 1438. However, sections were further embellished between the 14th and 16th centuries. Architecturally, the Palace is a Venetian hybrid, a harmonious fusion of Moorish, Gothic and Renaissance.

Although often considered the symbol of Gothic Venice, the Palace's distinctive facades were inspired by the Veneto-Byzantine succession of porticoes and loggias. However, the Gothic inversion of spaces and solids reached perfection in the floriated style of the southern corner, with a mass of masonry seemingly floating on air. The Palace boasts two of the finest Gothic facades in existence, a vision of rosy Verona marble supported by delicate Istrian stone arcades. With its noble loggia and arcading, the facade overlooking the Piazzetta embodies the majesty of State. Gothic tracery on the loggia became the model for palaces throughout the city. The harmonious waterfront facade is a Venetian Gothic masterpiece, including the porticoes and ceremonial balcony over-

Map, page 138

Strange but true: 50 per cent of visitors to Venice fail to stray further than St Mark's Square.

BELOW: a corner showing Gothic tracery.

The lions of Venice

The city "crawls with lions, winged lions and ordinary lions, great lions and petty lions... lions rampant, lions soporific, amiable lions [and] ferocious lions". The writer Jan Morris conveys a sense of a city under the wing of a triumphalist lion. For over a thousand years, the lion and the city were inseparable. The Venetians took the symbol in honour of St Mark, traditionally represented by a lion. As a symbol, it was less pagan than the Roman wolf or the rampant *marzocco* of the Florentines. The Venetians were also inspired by eastern models, converting chimeras and basilisks into Christian symbols. Yet the Venetian lion was often domesticated, even literally: patricians kept lions as pets in their palace gardens.

Pacific, playful or warlike, lions dominate paintings, sculptures, crests and illuminated manuscripts; they adorn buildings, bridges, balconies, archways and doorways. Lions pose majestically on flags unfurled over Grand Canal palaces; they soar over the seas as ship's ensigns; they curl up in mosaics on the floor of St Mark's or crouch as statues in secret gardens. In the days of the Republic, the leonine standard was carried into battle, fires and plagues; it guarded palaces, prisons and citadels, fluttering over Venetian ships of war and overseas dominions. A golden winged Lion of St Mark still adorns the city standard, while the lion remains the symbol of the Veneto region. Whereas the seated lion represents the majesty of state, the walking lion often symbolises Venetian sovereignty over its dominions. The winged lion was a formidable symbol of primacy, force and justice. Propagandists presented the lion as a symbol of their peaceful Christian state, a Republic sustained by the intercession of St Mark.

The Lion of St Mark bears a traditional greeting of peace. Yet in times of war, the lion is depicted with a closed book, as it is in the arch over the Arsenal gateway. A few lions are even shown clutching a drawn sword in one of their paws. The Napoleonic forces were fully aware of the symbolism of lions and destroyed many prominent images. As a result, some, such as those on the Porta della Carta, the Gothic gateway to the Doge's Palace, are replicas.

The greatest concentration of lions lies in the San Marco and Castello districts, closest to the centre of power. One writer has counted 75 lions on the Porta della Carta alone. One of the greatest winged lions stands atop the Column of St Mark . At the top of the Clocktower, a slightly sorrowful beast stands against a star-studded backdrop. Bold lions naturally adorn the Doge's Palace. In Castello district, a soporific lion is depicted on the equestrian statue on Riva degli Schiavoni.

In San Giorgio degli Schiavoni (*see page 196*), Carpaccio depicts St Jerome removing a thorn from a wounded lion's paw. The facade of the Scuola Grande di San Marco (*see page 194*) bears a portal guarded by threatening lions. Torcello, the oldest Venetian settlement, has a sarcophagus adorned with a winged lion; a lovely iconostasis is also supported by sculpted lions and peacocks drinking from the fountain of life, symbolising, perhaps, the eternal spirit of Venice. ❑

LEFT: standing sentinel by Palazzo Franchetti.

looking the quays. The **Sala del Maggior Consiglio** was rebuilt in 1340, transforming this waterfront wing. The intricately sculpted capitals and statuary on the facade are a tribute to Venetian Gothic craftsmanship (but some capitals are copies, with the originals on display inside).

The Porta della Carta, the main ceremonial gateway, is a triumph of Flamboyant Gothic style, named after resident archivists or clerks who copied petitions nearby. Above the portal is the sculpted figure of Doge Francesco Foscari, who commissioned the gateway, kneeling before the winged lion. Sadly, the sculpture is partly reconstructed, since the lions were obliterated during Napoleonic times. In the Renaissance, attention turned to the eastern wing, courtyard and interior. After a fire in 1483, this wing, tucked between the courtyard and the canal, was remodelled to improve the Doge's Apartments and provide grander magistrates offices. This smooth transition is marked by the meeting of the two styles in the **Foscari Arch**, between the Porta della Carta and the Scala dei Giganti. This deep arch is adorned with the figures of Adam and Eve, copies of the 15th-century originals. Beyond lies an elegant courtyard with Renaissance well-heads. The **Scala dei Giganti**, the Giants' Stairway, was built in 1486 to provide access to the loggia on the first floor. In 1567, this triumphal staircase was lavishly sculpted with monumental figures of Mars and Neptune, symbolising Venetian supremacy on land and sea. Doges were crowned, with a ceremonial jewel-encrusted cap, at the top of the stairs.

Many of the carved capitals on the portico have been replaced by 19th-century copies, but the restored originals can now be seen in the **Museo dell'Opera** beside the entrance hall. Set in the former prisons, this collection has recently reopened after a 30-year closure. After admiring these narrrative columns, visi-

Map, page 138

"If a Doge does anything against the Republic, he won't be tolerated, but in everything else, even in minor matters, he does as he pleases."

− GIROLAMO PRIULI, 16TH-CENTURY NOBLEMAN

BELOW: Scala dei Giganti (1554), Doge's Palace.

The clock aided merchants and crews about to sail from St Mark's Basin.

tors are usually directed to the more decorative columns, of musicians, warriors and flowery caprices, that once adorned the loggia. The profusion of wood panelling, coffered ceilings and paintings meant that fire was a constant hazard and destroyed many treasures on several occasions. For this reason, there are few paintings that predate the 1570s. Nonetheless, the interior is magnificent.

The palace interior

The rooms reveal the inner workings of the Serene Republic, from the voting procedures to the courts of law. The **Scala d'Oro**, designed by Sansovino in 1555, is a ceremonial staircase linking the *piano nobile* with the upper floors. The glittering, gilded setting is a prelude to the superb state rooms, intended to overawe visiting dignitaries. The **Sala del Collegio** was where the Signoria met and ambassadors were received.

Other highlights include the **Collegiate rooms**, lavishly decorated with Tintoretto's mythological scenes. The **Sala del Consiglio dei Dieci** was the chamber of the feared Council of Ten (*see page 34*) and boasts a ceiling decorated by Veronese. The **Sala del Maggior Consiglio**, the Grand Council Chamber, is a highlight of the tour, a grandiose affair studded with coffered ceilings, paintings and embossed surfaces. The paintings in the chamber both reassured Venetians of Republican glory and reminded them of their boundless duties to serve the State.

An entire wall is covered by Domenico and Jacopo Tintoretto's *Paradise*. Veronese's *Apotheosis of Venice* is one of his finest mythological scenes: with his glowing colours, carefree and graceful pictures, Veronese captured the taste of the times. A frieze which runs around the upper walls features the first 76 Doges,

BELOW: sumptuous Sala del Maggio Consiglio.

with the noticeable exception of the traitor, Marin Falier. The portraits of Doges continue in the adjoining Ballot Chamber, where votes were counted.

The **Secret Itinerary** *(Itinerari Segreti)* is well worth following and is recommended to anyone with even the slightest smattering of Italian. Few could fail to be enthralled by this exploration of the "shadow-palace", with its maze of alleys, secret passageways, and general air of murk and mystery. The civil service worked behind the scenes here to ensure the smooth-running of the Republic and was supported by a police state.

En route, one sees the state inquisitors' rooms, torture chamber and prisons, including the famous **Pozzi**, the basement cells. Also visible are the stifling **Piombi** or Leads, under the eaves of the Palace; it was from here that Casanova made his daring escape in 1755 *(see page 110)*.

Gondola depot

Just west of the square is the **Bacino Orseolo** ❺, the main gondola depot, which provides an opportunity to watch the comings and goings of the boats with a minimum of fuss. The Basin backs onto the **Procuratie Vecchie**, the earliest of the Procurators' offices.

At the far end of the severe building stands **Torre dell'Orologio** ❻, the **Clocktower**, currently being restored by Piaget, the watchmakers. Based on designs by Coducci, this Renaissance tower (1496) boasts a large gilt and blue enamel clockface which displays the signs of the zodiac and the phases of the moon. Naturally, it also tells the time, with two bronze figures of Moors striking the bell on the hour. In 1646, the diarist John Evelyn records the death of the clock-keeper, hit by the hammer as it struck the hour: "and being stunned, he

Map, page 138

TIP

The Bacino Orseolo is the most central place to begin a gondola ride but don't pay more than the official rate. Bargain beforehand if you want to book a musical serenade or to see anything outside the gondolier's set route *(see page 181)*.

BELOW: sinister Sala del Consiglio dei Dieci.

BELOW: taking a break from serenading.

reeled over the battlements and broke his neck". Behind the Clocktower, inveterate shoppers can plunge into the dark alleys of the Mercerie (*see page 156*).

Unlike the Clocktower, the **Campanile** *(10am–6pm)* can be climbed and provides a superb view across the city and lagoon. Curiously, one cannot see the canals, although on a clear day even the Dolomites are visible. In the past, foreigners were only permitted to climb the tower at high tide to prevent them from espying secret navigational channels. Standing on the site of an earlier watchtower and lighthouse, the belltower was rebuilt in the 12th century and crowned by a pyramid-shaped spire. During the Republic, each of the bells played a different role, with one summoning senators to the Doge's Palace and another, the execution bell, literally sounding the death knell. As a symbol of the city, the belltower occupies a special place in Venetian memory: in 1902 it suddenly collapsed but was rebuilt exactly as before. The only casualties were the custodian's cat and the **Loggetta**, the Classical loggia at the base of the tower, which was completely crushed. Originally a meeting place for the nobility, it was redesigned as a guardsroom by Sansovino in the 1540s. The Campanile was at the centre of controversy in 1997 when it was briefly captured by a Separatist group before being retaken by Venetian commandoes (*see page 51*).

Clustered around San Marco are numerous official buildings, including **La Zecca** (the Mint), facing the island of San Giorgio. The severe 16th-century rusticated building is attributed to Sansovino. Venice minted silver and gold ducats from 1284, with the latter known as a *zecchino*, the accepted currency until the fall of the Republic. The mint and treasury functioned until 1870, but the building is now part of the Libreria Marciana, with the inner courtyard covered over and used as a reading room.

HOTEL CAVALLETTO

THE TOURIST TRAP

Although cosmopolitan and tolerant, Venetians will also admit to an impatience with mass tourism. Every few years a new administration flirts with the idea of controlling access to the city by means of computerised entry cards. Tourists have always been deplored yet remain part of the picture. Not that Byron, Ruskin, Proust or Wagner would have tolerated such a vulgar term for themselves. But as the cliché runs: Venice without visitors would not be Venice.

The locals resent back-packers and day-trippers who spend little and leave quickly; are puzzled by foreigners who drink a cappuccino with everything, even a savoury; and amused by tourists who remain rooted to the floating pontoons until told that, in order to travel, they have to actually board a boat. The emergency services are occasionally called to fish hapless tourists out of the canals (the main culprit is seaweed-covered steps).

Claudia Ruzzenenti, who runs a cosy bar off Riva degli Schiavoni, deplores the summer deluge: "Any Venetians who can, go away – we have to stay and work. Still, *però non si sputa dove si mangia* – you don't spit where you eat, as we say, and tourism is all Venice has got". Spoken like a truly philosopical (and pragmatic) Venetian.

Bounded by the Mint, the Basilica and the Doge's Palace is the **Piazzetta** (the Little Square), overlooking the **Molo**, or waterfront. This functioned as the former inner harbour, with ships unloading on the quays. Now a square, it is framed by the **Columns of San Marco and San Teodoro**, which marked the sea entrance to Venice. The columns were named after the city's two patron saints, with St Mark replacing St Theodore in AD 828. The granite columns, from the Levant, were reputedly erected in 1172, and the engineer's reward was the right to set up gambling tables between the two columns – a lucrative spot for business. This was also the site of public executions, and superstition has it that bad luck follows anyone walking between the columns.

While the statue of St Theodore is a modern copy (the original Classical statue is in the Doge's Palace), the Lion of St Mark is genuine. This ancient winged beast with agate eyes may be a Middle-Eastern hybrid or a Chinese chimera. After the lion was rescued from Napoleon's clutches in Paris, the damaged beast was restored and returned to his pedestal with a Bible placed under his paw. Thus was a beast "from the pagan east converted from a savage basilisk to a saint's companion," remarks the writer Jan Morris.

Grand café retreat

Before exploring the San Marco district, retreat to one of the grand cafés on the *piazza* or to one of the modest bars situated off **Piazzetta dei Leoncini**, the tiny square beside the Basilica. Named after the marble lions who guard it, the Piazzetta is home to a pathetic and long-suffering pair of lions used as play horses by countless generations of children. Michel Butor, the French novelist, is sanguine about those who despair of finding solitude or sanity in Piazza San

Map, page 138

The Lion of St Mark, which was restored in London in 1990.

BELOW: the band performing at Florian's.

Marco, saying: "The basilica, like the city around it, has nothing to fear from this fauna or from our own frivolity; it was born under the perpetual gaze of the visitor, and so it has continued."

The San Marco district

Signposts to the Ferrovia (train station) and Piazzale Roma (bus station).

The San Marco district is obviously overshadowed by the attractions of St Mark's Square. Nonetheless, the *sestiere* is noted for its bustling *campi* and the maze-like Mercerie, a beguiling shopping quarter. Some of the finest palaces also lie along this stretch of the Grand Canal. The loop in the canal occupied by San Marco is known as "the seven *campi* between the bridges", a succession of theatrical spaces, each with chic or welcoming bars. The noblest square is undoubtedly Campo Santo Stefano, one of the most prestigious addresses in Venice. This suggested circular route embraces the heart of the city before sweeping back to St Mark's.

Heading west along the waterfront you will pass the **Giardinetti Reali** (Royal Gardens) ❼ and the central **tourist office**, housed in a pavilion. These cool public gardens were supposedly created by Napoleon's nephew, in pursuit of his desire for a sweeping view from his palace in the Procuratie Nuove. On Calle Vallaresso, the next alley, awaits **Harry's Bar** ❽, the world-famous watering hole (*see page 157*). The *calle* is awash with designer boutiques and forms part of a chic shopping district. On Calle del Ridotto, which runs parallel, stands the **Ridotto**, Venice's licentious casino for masked revellers, now a theatre. Just north is the **Frezzeria** ❾, a bustling shopping street named after the arrows it sold in medieval times, but also notorious for its prostitutes who would "open their quivers to any arrow". Not that all clients were satisfied. John Evelyn, the

BELOW: dazzling Neo-Classical pavilion on the waterfront.

diarist (1620–1706) was informed that Venetian women were *"mezzo carne, mezzo ligno"* – half flesh, half wood.

Campo San Moisè ❿, which lies at the southern end of the Frezzeria, opens onto the most exclusive, but least characteristic, shopping quarter. The square is framed by an ugly modern hotel and the florid Baroque facade of **San Moisè** *(3.30–6.30pm)*, a church which is almost universally disliked. The novelist L.P. Hartley was one of the few to admire the exuberance of the architecture, with its "swags, cornucopias and swing boat forms whose lateral movement seemed to rock the church from side to side." The ponderous interior is not redeemed by a Tintoretto.

Sophisticated shoppers may be drawn to the district around **Campo Largo XXII Marzo**, with its antique shops, fashion boutiques and jewellery stores. From here, Calle delle Veste leads north to **La Fenice** ⓫, the site of the famous opera house *(see page 80)*. Although it was destroyed by fire in 1996, the "Phoenix" should rise from the ashes by the year 2000. In the meantime, a bookshop and booking office for the temporary opera house are installed beside the ravaged site. It remains an appealing district, with atmospheric restaurants tucked around the encircling canals.

Just south lies **Santa Maria Zobenigo** ⓬ *(9am–noon, 3.30–6pm)*, confusingly also known as Santa Maria del Giglio. The church was named after the Jubanico, a patrician Slav family who funded the first building, yet it is more closely associated with Antonio Barbaro, a 17th-century patron who rebuilt the church in Baroque style. With its depictions of the Virtues, the facade glorifies the Barbaro dynasty rather than God. On the lower columns are reliefs depicting the dominions governed by the Barbaro in the name of the Republic – Candia (Heraklion), Split and Corfu – as well as Rome and Padua, places in which the family held ambassadorial posts. Inside are paintings which are attributed to Rubens and Tintoretto .

The adjoining square leads back to the waterfront and the **Gritti Palace** ⓭, a famous Venetian hotel *(see page 167)*. Ruskin, the art critic and aesthete, wrote his influential *Stones of Venice* while staying in both the Gritti and the Danieli. The Gritti terrace offers a grandstand view of the Grand Canal, lying diagonally opposite the church of La Salute. Just west of Santa Maria Zobenigo is the charming **Campo San Maurizio** ⓮, with its discreet palaces, a Neo-Classical church and an occasional antiques market. An enticing Fortuny fabrics shop is the Venetian outlet for the Giudecca factory. For a view of the curiously truncated Guggenheim Museum and the haunted Ca' Dario *(see page 176)*, follow Calle del Dose to the waterside and then look across the canal.

Around Santo Stefano

On the far side of Rio del Santissimo is **Campo Santo Stefano** ⓯, a long, theatrical space lined with palaces and cafés. This spectacular square makes a seamless link with the Accademia, the great Venetian gallery on the far side of the bridge *(see page 259)*. Confusingly also known as Campo Morosini, after a famous Dogal family, the wide square was a backdrop for bull-baiting until 1802, but is now more closely associated with the

Map, page 138

TIP

The waterfront tourist office is where to pick up a list of current exhibitions or book concerts. But for booking city trips or island tours, try the more helpful private travel agencies on the streets off Calle Vallaresso, just behind the tourist office.

BELOW: the controversial San Moisè church.

TIP

Fiore, both a bar and a reliable *trattoria*, lies on Calle delle Botteghe, just off Santo Stefano. Venetian dishes include *risotto nero*, coloured by cuttlefish ink, *risotto di pesce*, made with Adriatic fish, and *spaghetti alle vongole*, with clams and a spicy chili sauce.

BELOW: Campo Santo Stefano and Paolin.

chic evening *passeggiata*, with the occasional baiting of music students by mischievous lawyers. The overwhelming Palazzo Pisani, now the Venetian conservatoire, dominates **Campiello Pisani** at the Grand Canal end of the square. Next-door stands Palazzo Morosini, a Gothic Dogal palace remodelled in the 17th century, while opposite lies the severe 16th-century Palazzo Loredan, an artistic institute. A clutch of cafés occupy the space between the palaces and the tilting belltower of Santo Stefano. The clientele changes with the time of day, but at the cocktail hour, Santo Stefano's bars tend to be full of sleek Venetian professionals. **Paolin** has passed into local lore as one of the most prized Venetian bars, but the two adjoining cafés are far friendlier, while **Nico**, on the Zattere, just five minutes away serves much finer ice cream.

At the far end of the square stands the Gothic church of **Santo Stefano** (*7.30am–noon, 4–7pm*). This Augustinian monastic church has a Gothic main portal facing a café-lined alley. Unusually, a canal flows under the church, which gondolas can pass under if the tide is low. The interior boasts an entrancing ship's keel ceiling, carved tie beams and notable paintings by Vivarini and Tintoretto. The tomb of Doge Francesco Morosini (1694) is also prominently displayed in the nave. The cloisters, now appropriated by public offices, are accessible through a gateway in Campo Sant'Angelo.

If you lack the energy to visit the Accademia (*see page 259*), then ignore the bridge over the Grand Canal in favour of an engaging quarter on the bend of the canal. **Campo San Samuele** ⑯ was Casanova's parish, with Lord Byron's former home nearby, in Ca'Mocenigo, overlooking the canal. San Samuele, Casanova's baptismal church, is graced with a Byzantine belltower (currently being restored). Beside the ferry landing stage looms the formidable **Palazzo**

Grassi, a major exhibition centre. From here, a circuitous route winds back to San Marco, beginning with **Campo Sant'Angelo** ⓱, a noble quarter lined with the very palaces where Casanova played his practical jokes. Two fine Gothic palaces with mullioned windows face each other across the square.

From Sant'Angelo, follow Calle Spezier and take the first turning left to **Palazzo Pesaro** ⓲, home to the **Museo Fortuny** (currently closed). The late-Gothic palace boasts contrasting facades, one gracious and the other distinctly fortress-like. A courtyard with an arcaded staircase leads to a shrine to Mario Fortuny (1871–1949), the Spanish-born painter and designer who lived here. Although the museum houses an appealing and quirky collection, it pays little homage to Fortuny's pleated silk dresses, his chief claim to fame. Such are the vagaries of the fashion world that these flowing robes, delicately stencilled and weighted with chains of Murano glass, are considered to have liberated women's fashion from constraint. A Fortuny factory continues to produce his patterned silks and velvets (*see Campo San Maurizio on page 153*).

From here, cross Rio di San Luca into **Campo Manin**, named after a Venetian patriot who led the ill-fated revolt against the Austrians in 1848. Just south, concealed in a maze of alleys between Calle Vida and Calle Contarini, is **Palazzo Contarini del Bovolo** ⓳ *(10.30–5.30pm)*, a late Gothic palace celebrated for its romantic arcaded staircase. *Bovolo*, meaning snail-shell in Venetian dialect, well describes the delightful spiral staircase which is linked to loggias of brick and smooth white stone.

Campo San Luca ⓴, the bustling square east of Campo Manin, is a popular student haunt. The marble plinth supposedly marks the centre of the city, while Teatro Goldoni, named after the Venetian playwright, must compete with

Map, page 138

BELOW LEFT: Palazzo Pesaro (not to be confused with Ca' Pesaro, **above**) and the Museo Fortuny. **BELOW:** staircase in Palazzo Bovolo.

Map, page 138

The Mercerie is prime shopping territory. For a consumerist tour of the quarter see *Shopping Spree* on page 330, with helpful Italian phrases listed on page 337.

BELOW: clocktower of San Marco.

breezy cafés. Close to the Rialto, on the far side of Rio di San Salvador, stands **San Salvatore ㉑** *(10am–noon, 5–7pm)*, a luminous Renaissance church. Beyond the Baroque facade is a harmonious interior graced with striking perspectives and a delicate inlaid floor; in the 1560s, lanterns were added to create more light.

Close to the Mannerist monument to Doge Francesco Venier (1561) hangs Titian's impressionistic *Annunciation*, a late work; his *Transfiguration* adorns the high altar. The church was a place for romantic assignations in the 18th century, a function the square outside now performs for fickle Venetian youth.

Further north, just beyond the Rialto bridge, is the **Fondaco dei Tedeschi ㉒**, once an impressive trading centre for German merchants but now the city post office *(see page 175)*. On warm evenings, **Campo San Bartolomeo ㉓**, the adjoining square, resembles an open-air club: the statue of the playwright Goldoni, the half-hidden church and the basic bars are usually surrounded by chattering youngsters.

The Mercerie

From here, follow Via 2 Aprile to the **Mercerie ㉔**, the shadowy maze of alleys running between the Rialto and San Marco. Named after the haberdashers' shops that once lined the route, these alleys were amongst the first paved city streets to be found anywhere in the world. In 1624, John Evelyn was entranced by "the most delicious street in the world", displaying "cloth of gold, rich damasks and other silks… perfumers and apothecaries shops and the innumerable cages of nightingales". Today, it remains an engaging bazaar, even if the perfumes of old have been replaced by Calvin Klein's latest unisex body lotion. Some of the goods are tawdry, but you can also buy such traditional souvenirs as marbled paper, Murano glass and carnival masks of every description. Here, designer leather goods and hand-crafted jewellery also compete for space with kitsch glass gondolas.

For Venetians, the Mercerie has long been displaced by the district around **Via Largo XXII Marzo** as the smartest shopping address in town *(see page 331)*. Even so, many office workers choose this route between St Mark's Square and the Rialto bridge, as they stream home from work via Venice railway station. Narrow these alleys may be, but they are brightly lit and packed. The Mercerie comes out under the **Clocktower** on Piazza San Marco, but en route lies the church of **San Zulian ㉕** *(9am–noon, 4.30–6pm)*, a refuge from commercialism. Dedicated to St Julian, the church was rebuilt in the 16th century and recently restored thanks to Venice in Peril. The unsatisfactory exterior is hemmed in by buildings but the interior boasts gilded woodwork and a late work by Veronese. The old Armenian quarter is around the corner, based around **Santa Croce degli Armeni**, the well-hidden Armenian church. For the truest understanding of this ancient community, visit their monastery island of San Lazzaro degli Armeni *(see page 293)*. This church can safely be missed in favour of a welcoming bar. As writer Jan Morris says, "There are 107 churches in Venice, and nearly every tourist feels he has seen at least 200 of them." ❑

Harry's Bar

On the basis that Harry's Bar is the best bar in the best city in the world, the famed Bellini cocktail is cheap at any price. This is a legendary bar, resolutely unglitzy, apart from a clientele of visiting celebrities and celebrity-watchers. The lure of classic cocktails and a good gossip have drawn prominent personalities, from Churchill and Charlie Chaplin to Bogart and Bacall, Fellini and Mastroianni, Frank Sinatra and Madonna. Ernest Hemingway, footloose in Venice, could always find inspiration or oblivion in his favourite bar. As a macho man in a macho bar, he slugged the Montgomery, a martini made with 15 measures of gin to one of vermouth, the same potent ratio of troops to enemy employed by the military strategist.

Sketches of famous guests appear in a book dedicated to the founder. Indeed, writer Gore Vidal claims that, since the closure of the American Consulate in the 1970s, "Harry's Bar is sometimes the only place for Americans in acute distress to go to for comfort and advice." Yet, uniquely in Venice, the bar has become accepted by the locals.

Founded by Giuseppe Cipriani in 1931 and still run by the family, Harry's was financed by Harry Pickering, a Bostonian dissatisfied with Venetian bars. Cipriani is famous for the creation of the Bellini, a cocktail of crushed, puréed peach and sparkling Prosecco. He is also credited with inventing *carpaccio*, a dish of finely sliced raw beef fillet doused in oil and lemon. (The dish was named after the 15th-century Venetian painter Carpaccio, whose paintings favoured a beefy red.)

Set in a small converted storeroom and still visually unmemorable, Harry's Bar is crowded and cosmopolitan. The wood-panelled rooms house a bustling bar and a more sedate restaurant above. The view from upstairs is of the glorious baroque church of Santa Maria della Salute and, from another window, the Dogana di Mare, the 17th-century sea customs post. But Harry's is about food and fun not views. The unfussy menu includes such staples as scampi risotto.

RIGHT: Harry's gateway to heaven is still visually unmemorable.

Harry's Bar prides itself on a clubby atmosphere underpinned by superb service. Whereas other prestigious restaurants have taken to issuing stern warnings against smoking and other sins, Harry's prefers humorous signs: "The use of mobile phones could seriously damage the health of your risotto."

Today, the Bellini is made by Claudio Ponzio who has presided over the bar since the late 1960s and learnt the secrets from the creator of the cocktail. His technique involves pouring his secret potion into numerous glasses six times each, ensuring a complete mix. Nor has his boss, Arrigo Cipriani, betrayed the founder's expertise.

Arrigo (Harry), the dapper son of the founder, claims to be the only person ever named after a bar. He works the room with great panache, welcoming guests and chatting plausibly in Eurospeak.

Harry's Bar is at Calle Vallaresso 1323 (tel: 041-528 5777). If it is sunny, cross over to the Giudecca for an outdoor table at Harry's Dolci, Fondamenta San Biagio, Giudecca 773 (tel: 041-522 4844), the companion bar. ❑

THE WORLD'S GRANDEST PRIVATE CHAPEL

Everyone who comes to Venice visits San Marco. It is not surprising. This golden , marbled pleasure pavilion is simply the city's greatest site

Although intended as the private chapel of the Doges, San Marco soon became a symbol of Republican splendour, set beside the Doge's Palace, the centre of Venetian power. The basilica has always been at the heart of city life, the focus for the greatest celebrations, from thanksgiving for foreign conquests and victories at sea to redemption from the Plague. In recent years, San Marco has been a place of remembrance, with the city commemorating the 30th annniversary of the tragic 1966 floods through a series of spectacular concerts. After the burning down of La Fenice, the beloved opera house, similar fund-raising events followed, attracting famous politicians and foreign stars.

The eastern inspiration of the basilica is clear from its oriental domes and lustrous mosaics. Charles Eliot Norton, a 19th-century American scholar, marvelled at this eclectic basilica, "fused into a composition neither Byzantine nor Romanesque, only to be called Venetian… No building so costly or so sumptuous had been erected since the fall of [the Roman] Empire". French writer George Sand, visiting in 1844, found it "a grand and dreamy structure, of immense proportions; golden with old mosaics; redolent with perfumes; dim with the smoke of incense; costly in treasure of precious stones and metals; holy with the bodies of deceased saints".

△ **MAIN ENTRANCE**
Thirteenth-century carvings on the central doorway (part of the sumptuous decoration added between the 11th and 15th centuries) depict the Labours of the Month and the signs of the zodiac.

◁ **ZEN CHAPEL**
Cardinal Zen bequeathed his fortune to Venice on condition that he was buried in the basilica. His chapel (1504) is decorated with naturalistic Byzantine mosaics.

◁ **ST MARK ARRIVES**
A Byzantine mosaic in the Zen Chapel depicts St Mark's arrival in Alexandria. In 828, his relics were smuggled out to Venice, cleverly hidden under barrels of pork – which no Moslem would touch.

▷ **PLUNDERED TREASURE**
Spoils of war, such as the two Turkish pilasters and the 4th-century Egyptian sculpted Tetrarchs, contribute to the eclectic façade.

△ **THE FIRST DOME**
This seated Apostle from the Pentecost Dome, probably the first to be decorated, is from the early 12th century.

▽ **BEJEWELLED DOORWAY**
A glittering lunette of Baroque mosaics is set above the richly decorated west doorway.

THE FOUR HORSES OF SAN MARCO

"Below St Mark's still glow his steeds of brass, their gilded collars glittering in the sun". Byron was one of many travellers to admire the four bronze horses, 3rd or 4th-century Hellenistic or Roman sculptures, which stood guard over the basilica's central doorway. Like the lion of St Mark, these noble horses were a symbol of independence. Yet the tale of their travels is a story of imperial envy and an allegory of the Republic's rise and fall.

The horses, which had graced a triumphal arch in Rome, were standing guard over the stadium in Constantinople when the city was sacked by the Venetians in 1204. Centuries of peace in the lagoon city ended in 1797, when they were plundered by Napoleon. This final insult to the crushed Republic was compounded by further humiliation: Napoleon had the noble steeds harnessed to a chariot in Paris for 18 years. After returning to Venice in 1815, the horses decorated the Loggia dei Cavalli on the basilica. The Venetians, never ones to look gift horses in the mouth, were delighted.

The originals are now displayed in the Museo Marciano inside the basilica, with rather paltry replicas placed on the façade. Many Venetians felt that the beasts should be left in situ, but conservationists thought the bronzes ought to be protected for posterity from the corrosiveness of the Venetian climate.

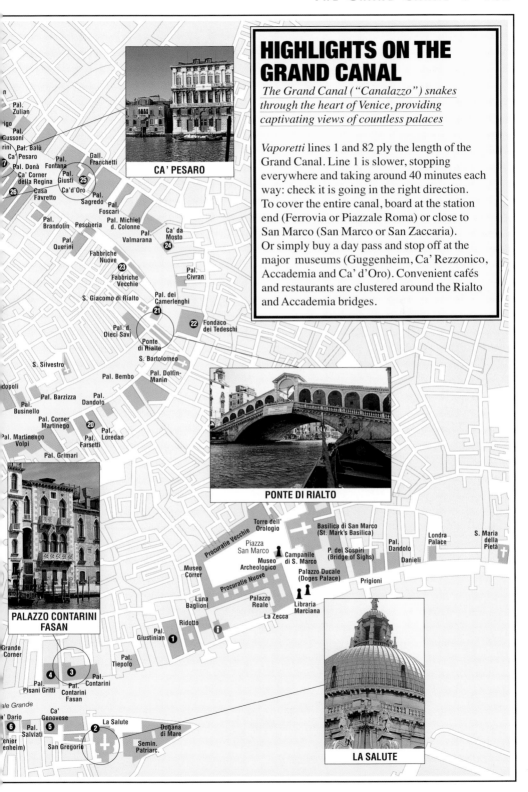

CA' PESARO

HIGHLIGHTS ON THE GRAND CANAL

The Grand Canal ("Canalazzo") snakes through the heart of Venice, providing captivating views of countless palaces

Vaporetti lines 1 and 82 ply the length of the Grand Canal. Line 1 is slower, stopping everywhere and taking around 40 minutes each way: check it is going in the right direction. To cover the entire canal, board at the station end (Ferrovia or Piazzale Roma) or close to San Marco (San Marco or San Zaccaria). Or simply buy a day pass and stop off at the major museums (Guggenheim, Ca' Rezzonico, Accademia and Ca' d'Oro). Convenient cafés and restaurants are clustered around the Rialto and Accademia bridges.

PONTE DI RIALTO

PALAZZO CONTARINI FASAN

LA SALUTE

Map labels:

Pal. Zulian
Pal. Gussoni
Pal. Balù
Ca' Pesaro
Pal. Donà Fontana
Gall. Franchetti
Ca' Corner della Regina
Pal. Giusti ㉕
Casa Favretto
Ca' d'Oro
Pal. Sagredo ㉖
Pal. Foscari
Pal. Brandolin
Pescheria
Pal. Michiel d. Colonne
Ca' da Mosto ㉔
Pal. Querini
Pal. Valmarana
Fabbriche Nuove ㉓
Pal. Civran
Fabbriche Vecchie
S. Giacomo di Rialto
Pal. dei Camerlenghi ㉑
Pal. d. Dieci Savi
Ponte di Rialto
Fondaco dei Tedeschi ㉒
S. Bartolomeo
S. Silvestro
S. Bartolomeo
Pal. Bembo
Pal. Dolfin-Manin
dopoli
Pal. Barzizza
Pal. Dandolo
Pal. Businello
Pal. Corner Martinego ⑳
Pal. Loredan
Pal. Martinengo Volpi
Pal. Farsetti
Pal. Grimani
Torre dell' Orologio
Basilica di San Marco (St. Mark's Basilica)
Londra Palace
S. Maria della Pietà
Procuratie Vecchie
Piazza San Marco
Campanile di S. Marco
P. dei Sospiri (Bridge of Sighs)
Pal. Dandolo
Museo Correr
Museo Archeologico
Palazzo Ducale (Doges Palace)
Danieli
Procuratie Nuove
Prigioni
Luna Baglioni
Palazzo Reale
Libraria Marciana
La Zecca
PALAZZO CONTARINI FASAN
Ridotto ①
Pal. Giustinian
Grande Corner
Pal. Tiepolo
④ ③
Pal. Pisani Gritti
Pal. Contarini
Pal. Contarini Fasan
ale Grande
Ca' Genovese
Dario
Pal. Salviati ⑤
⑥
La Salute
Dogana di Mare
enier enheim)
San Gregorio
Semin. Patriarc. ②

THE GRAND CANAL

Map, page 162

*A trip on the Grand Canal, Venice's fabulous highway,
reveals the full pageant of the city's most opulent palaces, from the
Ca' Grande to the Ca' Foscari, the Guggenheim to the Ca' d'Oro*

Venice is a place "where the simplest social coming and going assumes at the same time the form and charm of a visit to a museum and a trip to the sea". Marcel Proust captures the entertaining yet educational aspect of a trip along the Grand Canal. Known affectionately as the "Canalazzo" (Little Canal), the canal follows the course of an ancient river bed. It is nearly 4 km long (2½ miles) and up to 70 metres wide (230 ft). The surprisingly shallow highway is spanned by three bridges and lined by ten churches and over 200 palaces. This great waterway sweeps through the six city districts (*sestieri*), with its switchback shape providing changing vistas of palaces and warehouses, markets and merchant clubs, courts, prisons and even the city casino.

Once a waterway for merchant vessels and great galleys, the canal now welcomes simpler craft, from gondolas to garbage barges. However, the palaces remain as a testament to the city's imperial past. The Grand Canal was considered the register of the Venetian nobility, with the palaces symbolising their owner's status and success. Yet the sea is a great leveller, with low tide revealing the slimy underpinnings of the noblest palace. Venetian eclecticism and the habit of recycling elements from various periods makes the dating of palaces difficult. Indeed, the writer Jan Morris wryly observes that guidebook writers are the only people who seem capable of distinguishing between the different styles.

A peculiarly Venetian phenomenon is the number of palaces with the same or similar names. Palaces were often the seats of separate branches of the family so their names bear witness to Venetian fortunes, feuds and intermarriage; a family member sometimes added the name of the parish or new dynasty to avoid confusion. The Contarini, for instance, built over twenty-five palaces; thus the Grand Canal reveals the Gothic Contarini-Fasan and Contarini-Corfu as well as the Renaissance Contarini-Polignac. The city is littered with palaces linked to the patrician or Dogal dynasties of the Corner, Giustinian, Grimani, Mocenigo, Pesaro and Pisani families.

PRECEDING PAGES: Santa Maria della Salute at the end of the Grand Canal. **LEFT:** Fondaco dei Turchi. **BELOW:** Palazzo Cavalli-Franchetti.

Palatial homes

Thanks to inheritance laws, financial vicissitudes and the extinction of the old Dogal families, few families inhabit their ancestral homes. Yet a number of impoverished aristocrats languish in part of a palace or live in one which, while not bearing their name, has been in the family for centuries. Many palaces have become hotels or prestigious showcases for banks and major companies, especially for Venetian glass and textile manufacturers. Others belong to residents who relish the soft opulence of their second homes. Many superb buildings have been bequeathed to the city so, restora-

Only police boats are allowed to travel at speed.

tion work permitting, visitors are spoilt for choice. Several of the grandest art collections border the canal, notably the Accademia (Venetian art of all periods), the Guggenheim (modern art), the Ca'd'Oro (medieval and Renaissance art), the Ca' Rezzonico (18th-century art) and Ca' Pesaro (oriental and modern art). The charm of these palaces lies in their variety. As Henry James remarks: "The fairest palaces are often cheek-by-jowl with the foulest, and there are few, alas, so fair as to have been completely protected by their beauty".

Grand Canal procession

Purchase a day pass and trail up and down the Canal to your heart's content, stopping at sights as the fancy takes you. (*Vaporetti* No1 and No 82 both cover the route but check the direction and be sure to get off before the boat sweeps away to the Lido). Ideally choose the slower route No 1 and take a return trip to appreciate both banks (it takes about 40 minutes each way). As well as providing a cavalcade of Venetian pageantry, the Canal offers a slice of local life. Architecturally, the Grand Canal is a feast for the senses. (*See Architectural Style, page 59, for a fuller account.*)

From San Marco to the Accademia Bridge

From the **San Marco Vallaresso** stop, the *vaporetto* sweeps into St Mark's Basin, with romantic views across to **San Giorgio Maggiore** (*see page 267*). Set on the right bank, facing the **Customs Point** (*see page 251*), **Palazzo Giustinian ❶** is the first significant palace on the Grand Canal. The Giustiniani were an illustrious dynasty tracing their origins to the Roman Empire. Legend has it that, in the 12th century, the line was threatened with extinction and the sole

BELOW: Grand Canal to La Salute.

remaining heir was persuaded to leave his monastery for marriage to the Doge's daughter. After saving the line by siring 12 offspring, he returned to a life of celibate seclusion. His sacrifice was a success: the Venetian branch only died out in 1962. In the 19th century, the palace was a hotel where Proust, Turner and Verdi stayed. As a newly-wed, George Eliot stayed here with her unstable husband until he jumped from their window into the canal. The palace is now the headquarters of the Biennale exhibition organisation, the international art showcase staged every two years (*see page 209*).

On the left bank, the Baroque church of **La Salute ❷** (*see page 250*) guards the entrance to the Canal. Slightly further on, **Palazzo Contarini-Fasan ❸** appears on the right bank. This model of late-Gothic design in miniature boasts subtle carved cable moulding on the facade. It is nicknamed Desdemona's House since it supposedly inspired the setting for Desdemona's home in Shakespeare's *The Merchant of Venice*. As soon as the boat stops at Santa Maria del Giglio, **Palazzo Pisani-Gritti ❹** comes into view on the same bank. Otherwise known as the Gritti Palace, this is one of the most sumptuous hotels in Venice, linked to writers as diverse as Hemingway and Graham Greene. Ruskin and his wife stayed here rather than being tempted by the decadent notion of "hiring a house or palace – it sounds Byronish or Shelleyish".

Virtually opposite is **Ca' Genovese ❺**, a neo-Gothic palace, and **Palazzo Salviati**, with its distinctive mosaics set in an ochre facade; these gaudy showrooms belong to wealthy Murano glass-makers. On the same side, several palaces further down, is the gently listing **Ca' Dario ❻** (*see page 176*), one of the most delightful spots on the Grand Canal. Henry James adored the palace, then let to motley foreigners, for its "little marble plates and sculptured circles".

Map, page 162

"I will buy with you, sell with you, talk with you, walk with you, and so following; but I will not eat with you, drink with you, nor pray with you"

– SHYLOCK
IN SHAKESPEARE'S
THE MERCHANT OF VENICE

BELOW: glittering Palazzo Salviati.

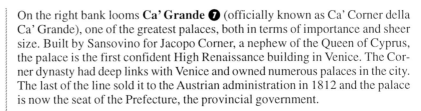

"A man's life often resembles these palaces on the Grand Canal, which begin at the base with an array of stones proudly sculpted in diamond points, and end with the upper floors hastily cobbled together from dry mud."

PAUL MORAND

On the right bank looms **Ca' Grande ❼** (officially known as Ca' Corner della Ca' Grande), one of the greatest palaces, both in terms of importance and sheer size. Built by Sansovino for Jacopo Corner, a nephew of the Queen of Cyprus, the palace is the first confident High Renaissance building in Venice. The Corner dynasty had deep links with Venice and owned numerous palaces in the city. The last of the line sold it to the Austrian administration in 1812 and the palace is now the seat of the Prefecture, the provincial government.

Palazzo Venier (the Guggenheim Foundation)

Facing Ca' Grande is the **Palazzo Venier ❽**, a white, truncated structure also known as "Nonfinito" (unfinished). Legend has it that the owners of Ca' Grande forbade further building as it would block their view, but it is more likely that the project simply ran out of funds. Although now restricted to two-storeys, the original palace was intended to rival the city's grandest. This 18th-century palace was built for one of the oldest Venetian dynasties who produced three Doges and numerous naval commanders. The Veniers' lion nickname *(dei Leoni)* comes from their habit of keeping a pet lion chained in the courtyard. The building now houses the **Guggenheim Foundation** *(11am–6pm, closed Tuesday)*, named after the American millionairess, art collector and benefactor, Peggy Guggenheim (1898–1979), who lived in Venice from 1949 until her death.

It is appropriate that this startlingly modern-looking building should house a superb collection of modern art. This is a deservedly popular collection, displaying work by such names as Chagall, Dali, Klee, Braque, Giacometti, Kandinsky, Bacon and Sutherland. Most major movements are represented, from Picasso's Cubist period to Severini's Futurism; from Mondrian's Abstract

BELOW: Marini's provocative "Angel of the Citadel".

THE CANAL BY NIGHT

A t night, after most tourists have returned to the mainland, is the time for a leisurely look at the Grand Canal. Pick up a No 1 *vaporetto* and slip into one of the coveted seats on the prow. The palaces present a seductive face at night: the illuminated windows are an invitation to dream, revealing gleaming Murano glass chandeliers, red silk-clad walls and the odd summer party spilling onto the balconies.

On the water, you may catch a fleeting glimpse of a *sandolo*, a twin-oared rowing boat, scudding by, its prow lit by a rustic lamp. Afterwards, the tiny *campielli* near the shore provide a good vantage point for watching the water traffic: try the bench on Campo San Vio, between the Guggenheim and the Accademia, or just stand on the Rialto Bridge. Writer Jonathan Keates revels in the elemental delight of walking in Venice after dark, with the city's ghostly stage sets bathed in "muted brilliance, shadow and absolute murk".

Mark Twain, writing in 1878, was equally entranced: "Under the mellow moonlight the Venice of poetry and romance stood revealed... ponderous stone bridges threw their shadows athwart the glittering waves... Music came floating over the waters – Venice was complete". A conversational stroll or a boat ride are classic Venetian pastimes, activities that pass for nightlife in sleepy Venice.

works to Surrealist masterpieces by De Chirico, Delvaux and Magritte. Max Ernst, Guggenheim's second husband, is well-represented. Other highlights include De Chirico's *Red Tower*, Brancusi's *Bird in Space*, Magritte's *Empire of Light* and Pollock's *Alchemy*.

Map, page 162

Although Guggenheim helped launch the reputation of Jackson Pollock, there is little Expressionist work here since it did not find favour with the otherwise discerning collector. The gardens are filled with sculptures, including works by Henry Moore and Marino Marini. (Curiously, the watergates are often closed to conceal the provocative erection sported by the rider in Marini's *Angel of the Citadel*.) Several palaces further along is **Palazzo Barbarigo**, notable for its gaudy 19th-century mosaics, and **Campo San Vio**, a pleasant spot from which to watch the traffic on the Grand Canal.

Guggenheim poster

On the same left bank, two palaces before the bridge, lies **Palazzo Contarini-Polignac ❾**, one of the first Renaissance palaces in Venice. In fact, a new facade, decorated with precious marble roundels, was added to the original Gothic building. The Princesse de Polignac ran a sophisticated 19th-century salon here and the palace remains in the same family.

On the right bank, virtually opposite, is **Palazzo Barbaro ❿**, a charming Gothic gem where Monet, Browning and Henry James stayed as guests of the American Curtis family. James wrote *The Aspern Papers* here and set *The Wings of a Dove* in his rooms: "part of a palace, historic and picturesque but strictly inodorous". The wheel came full circle recently with the making of the film of the same name in the palace. Next-door is **Palazzo Cavalli-Franchetti**, a grandiose Gothic palace with an appealing garden. Now a bank, the interior was remodelled in neo-Gothic style.

BELOW: Palazzo Venier dei Leoni.

The Tiepolo trail

Tiepolo's credo was that "the mind of the painter should always aspire to the sublime, the heroic and perfection". According to art critic Adriano Mariuz, in practice this meant: "a sophisticated clientele who could appreciate the wit and sensuality of Tiepolo's interpretations of mythology". However, the greatest of Rococo painters also produced a riot of picturesque detail and enough charm to seduce the most casual observer. In Ca' Rezzonico, Tiepolo proves himself a master of scenic illusion, creating mirages of light and air and orchestrating figures in large compositions. Apart from the *trompe l'oeil* paintings here, Tiepolo's work can be admired in numerous Venetian churches and confraternities, several in the Dorsoduro district.

A short walk or *vaporetto* ride (one stop from Ca' Rezzonico to Accademia) leads to Rio Terra Foscarini and the Gesuati church (*see page 252*) on the breezy shores of the Zattere. This Dominican church in Dorsoduro

has illusionistic Tiepolo frescoes and a subtle painting. The ceiling features the *Life of St Dominic and the Institution of the Rosary* since, according to Dominican lore, the Madonna first offered the rosary to St Dominic. In a side chapel is a joyous altarpiece of the Madonna with three saints favoured by the Order. From here, it is a pleasant stroll through Dorsoduro to the Scuola Grande dei Carmini (*see page 257*). This confraternity is home to Tiepolo's *Madonna of the Scapular*, a sensuous visionary scene of the Madonna and the Blessed Simon Stock, surrounded by graceful Virtues. Such mature Tiepolo frescoes not only hark back to Veronese but transcend his ceiling paintings.

After refreshment on one of the cafés on neighbouring Campo Santa Margherita, a short stroll takes you to an even grander confraternity in the San Polo district. The Scuola Grande di San Rocco (*see page 223*), although primarily a shrine to Tintoretto, also shows Tiepolo in a softer light. Here he is seen as a painter of subtle and sensuous portraits and altarpieces, notably *Abraham Visited by the Angels*. The San Tomà *vaporetto* stop is a stone's throw away, and offers a choice of Tiepolo pilgrimage sites, both easily reached by ferry. In the direction of the railway station, a No 1 ferry leads to the Ca' d'Oro stop and an overlooked church in Cannaregio. The church of Santi Apostoli (*see page 238*) contains one of Tiepolo's loveliest paintings, *The Last Communion of St Lucy*, memorable for its glowing colours and the saint's expression.

If, instead, you prefer to end the journey closer to the centre, from San Tomà take ferry 1 or 82 (San Marco direction) to the San Zaccaria stop in the Castello district. A walk along the bustling Riva degli Schiavoni leads past inviting waterfront cafés to La Pietà (*see page 198*). The church is a feast for the senses, with Tiepolo's celebrated frescoes best seen during a concert of Vivaldi's music. Art critic Philip Rylands praises the vibrant effects of the ceiling fresco in Vivaldi's church: "The acoustics cause the sacred music to reverberate from the ceiling so that Tiepolo's celestial angels seem to have burst into a trumpeting cantata." ❑

LEFT: Tiepolo's "Agar and Ismail".

Between the Accademia and Ca' Foscari

Beside the palatial bank is the distinctive wooden **Accademia Bridge**, a popular meeting-place for Venetians. Beside it is the Accademia boat stop, with the world's greatest collection of Venetian paintings housed in the neighbouring **Accademia ⓫** gallery *(see page 259)*. (If you are suffering from a surfeit of palaces, pause for a coffee or a snack at the Belle Arti bar beside the gallery.) Also on the right bank is **Palazzo Falier ⓬**, an early Gothic palace with typical Venetian loggias *(liaghi)* facing the canal. This was supposedly the home of the infamous Doge Marin Falier, beheaded for treason in 1355.

Ca' Rezzonico and the Museum of 18th-Century Life

Ca' Rezzonico ⓭ lies on the left bank by the boat stop of the same name. Henry James likened this bold building to "a rearing sea-horse" because of its upward-thrusting cornices. This Baroque masterpiece, designed according to Longhena's plans *(see page 64)*, is slightly more restrained than Ca' Pesaro. This is probably the most famous palace in the city and one of the few on the Grand Canal open to the public. The newly ennobled Rezzonico banking family bought the unfinished palace in 1750 and supervised its completion in conservative Baroque style. The effect is harmonious, if rather ponderous, with heavy rustication on the ground floor and a grand courtyard. It was in this palace that the poet Robert Browning (1812–89) died. (His son, Pen, owned the palace in the 1880s and did much to restore it.) After lying in state in the ballroom, the poet was transferred to San Michele *(see page 288)* and then to London's Westminster Abbey. A wall in the palace bears words taken from Browning's epitaph: "Open my heart and you will see /Graved inside of it Italy".

Ca' Rezzonico houses the **Museum of 18th-Century Life** (Museo del SettecentoVeneziano, *10am–4pm, closed Friday*). The palace has been well-restored in recent years, with the addition of a chic café and bookshop tucked into the ground floor. (The third floor opened in 1998 after several years of refurbishment.)

The opulent Baroque building makes a suitable showcase for Tiepolo's *trompe l'oeil* ceilings and Guardi's 18th-century genre paintings. The interior is magnificent, boldly restored, daringly frescoed and richly embellished with glittering chandeliers and period pieces. In keeping with Venetian style, the rooms are sparsely but lavishly furnished, with the mirrored wall brackets, lacquered furniture and chinoiserie that characterised the period. A ceremonial staircase leads to the ballroom on the *piano nobile*, added by Massari.

Below a splendidly frescoed ceiling are ebony vase-stands borne by Moors. Off the ballroom is the *Sala dell'Allegoria Nuziale* (1758), a homage to Tiepolo. The frescoed ceiling depicts a nuptial allegory, the *Marriage of Ludovico Rezzonico*. Careering horses are seen tumbling through the billowing heavens accompanied by angels and cherubs; this illusionistic allegory links the family to the Olympian gods. In the same year, a Rezzonico count was elected Pope, thus putting the seal on the family's social acceptability. Elsewhere there are further lofty Tiepolo frescoes depicting *Nobility and Virtue* and *Fortitude and Wisdom*.

Map, page 162

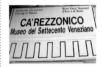

Carlo Rezzonico, born in a Grand Canal palace in 1693, became Clement XIII, the fifth Venetian Pope.

BELOW: Statue in Ca' Rezzonico courtyard.

*Entrance to
Ca' Foscari, home
to the university.*

BELOW: powerful
Palazzo Balbi.

Apart from Tiepolo's frescoed ceilings and the lavish ballroom, the highlights are paintings by the greatest of the 18th-century genre painters. Guardi's *Ridotto* (1748) is an animated picture of masked gamblers and revellers in the state casino . His *Nuns' Parlour* (1768) depicts the spirited and worldly nuns whose reputation for lasciviousness made Venetian convents a byword for dissolute living. Longhi's superior salon pictures show patrician Venice at play. The most famous is the *Rhinoceros Show*, depicting masqueraders entranced by this exotic beast. Also on display is one of the few works by Canaletto in Venice: his *View of Rio dei Mendicanti* (1725). There are also subtle paintings and miniatures by Rosalba Carriera, the 18th-century portraitist. The top floor is home to a Rococo boudoir and a quaint apothecary's shop. Sadly, the mezzanine apartments linked to Robert Browning are usually closed.

Set on the right bank, the **Palazzo Grassi** ⓮ and the church of **San Samuele** can be seen from Ca' Rezzonico. **Palazzo Grassi** is an imposing patrician palace and model of Neo-Classical restraint. Although designed by Longhena, there is no trace of Baroque exuberance; Massari completed the palace with due regard to the correct Classical orders. The palace belonged to a patrician family who died out in the 19th century. Now owned by Fiat, it is used as a showcase for international exhibitions and the interior has been stunningly converted into an art gallery to compete with the best in the world. On the same bank lies a cluster of three historic palaces. Together they command the sharp bend on the canal known as the Volta del Canal. **Palazzo Giustinian** ⓯ is one of no less than fifteen city palaces once owned by the Giustiniani clan. This showpiece of Gothic architecture is a double palace adorned with delicate tracery and linked by a watergate. Here, in 1857–59, Wagner composed his opera *Tristan und Isolde*.

Between Ca' Foscari and the Rialto Bridge

Next door, **Ca' Foscari** presents similar Gothic coherence, with a waterside facade graced by the Foscari arms. Built at the height of Venetian power, this is a monument to the ambition of Doge Foscari, who ruled from 1423 to 1457. Tommaso Mocenigo, a previous Doge, distrusted him: "He sweeps and soars more than a hawk or a falcon". But Foscari survived to pursue expansionist goals until a conspiracy, led by a powerful clique, caused his downfall. The Doge was dismissed and died a broken man in this palace.

The Foscari name aside, this Gothic stage-set witnessed countless pageants. During a state visit prior to being crowned, Henri III of France stayed in Ca' Foscari and was fêted by the Venetians. The mosaic floor of his bedroom was remodelled according to Veronese's designs; Titian painted his portrait and Palladio was commissioned to build a welcoming triumphal arch. Now the grandest part of Venice University, the palace has suffered from tampering but is being restored. On the far side of the Rio (side canal) lies **Palazzo Balbi**, the grandiose seat of the Venetian regional government, distinguished by its twin pinnacles.

Around the Rialto

Henry James found this middle stretch of the Canal evoked a "melancholy mood", likening it to "a flooded city". Be that as it may, there is an intriguing contrast between the bold palaces and the bustling quayside close to the Rialto market. As the boat stops at the **San Tomà** landing stage, look across to **Ca' Mocenigo** ⓲ on the right bank. This cluster of palaces belonged to the influential Mocenigo family who produced seven Doges. Byron stayed here while writing his mock-heroic poem *Don Juan* (1819–24) and had an affair with the

Under the strict Sumptuary Laws, the size and decoration of palaces was carefully controlled, with ornamental balustrades and statuary forbidden.

BELOW: historic Ca' Mocenigo.

Map, page 162

*"Streets full of water,
please advise"* was
the famous cable sent
home by the
American humorist
Robert Benchley on
his first visit to
Venice.

baker's wife, a woman "wild as a witch and fierce as a demon". On the left bank a little further along, is **Palazzo Pisani-Moretta ⑱**, with its Gothic tracery reminiscent of the Doge's Palace. Curiously, the palace has two *piani nobili*, two patrician floors instead of the more common one. The palace is also exceptional in still belonging to descendants of the Pisani family. On the right bank, beside the **Sant'Angelo** stop, is **Palazzo Corner-Spinelli ⑲**, the prototype of a Renaissance palace. It was designed by Coducci and boasts a rusticated ground floor as well as his trademark windows, two bold round-arched lights framed by a single round arch. Like Ca' Grande , the palace was owned by the Corner family, the royal Cypriot dynasty. The ownership passed to the Spinelli, important dealers in golds and silks, and still serves as the showrooms of noted Venetian textile merchants today.

As the boat stops at **San Silvestro** by the church, look across to the right bank to appreciate the **Palazzo Farsetti** and **Palazzo Loredan ⑳**. These twin buildings are two of the finest Veneto-Byzantine palaces in Venice. Ca' Loredan, in particular, is graced with the original capitals, arches and decorative plaques. The pair are occupied by the City Council and the Mayor of Venice. The banks between here and the **Rialto Bridge** are lined with restaurants and usually crowded with market-bound tourists and traders.

From the Rialto bridge to Ca' d'Oro

The **Rialto bridge** was the only one to span the Grand Canal until 1854. Today, the bridge provides the chance to watch the water traffic, from gondolas to garbage barges. The Rialto district is also an ideal place for lunch in a *bacaro*, a rough and ready Venetian version of the Spanish *tapas* bar. On the left bank,

BELOW: Palazzo
Loredan.
BELOW RIGHT:
Fondaco dei
Tedeschi.

just upstream from the Rialto, the severe **Palazzo dei Camerlenghi** ㉑ curves round the canal bend. Now a courthouse, it was built in 1525 as the seat of the Exchequer, with the ground floor used as a debtors' prison. Like many multifunctional Venetian buildings, it also served as a merchants' loggia, a sort of semi-covered market, and an administrative centre.

On the right bank, facing Palazzo dei Camerlenghi, lies the **Fondaco dei Tedeschi** ㉒, named after the German merchants who leased the building. A healthy trade in precious metals from German mines meant that this privileged community used the warehouse as a cross between an emporium, commercial hotel and social club. Set conveniently close to the Rialto commercial quarter, this self-contained haven for the mercantile community even boasted its own chapel and casino. After a fire in 1505, it was rebuilt in traditional fashion, with an inner courtyard and towers that echo an earlier defensive function. The merchants only left in 1812, leaving the palace to its banal fate as the city post office.

On the left bank looms the **Fabbriche Vecchie e Nuove** ㉓, a long arcaded frontage which contained a pair of mercantile institutions . The buildings around the Rialto were destroyed by fire in 1514 but were rebuilt in Classical style. The ground floors functioned as shops while the upper floors acted as administrative offices and courts. The porticoes of **Fabbriche Vecchie** housed sectors devoted to fruit and vegetables, fish, banking, cloth and upholstery. Above were offices and tribunals to settle trading disputes. Sansovino's larger **Fabbriche Nuove**, built about 30 years later in 1555, echo the design of the earlier buildings. Now the Court of Assizes, these formed the Republic's trading centre, with offices on the upper floors devoted to commerce, navigation and food distribution. Virtually opposite the Fabbriche Nuove and the covered Neo-Gothic fish

Map, page 162

Mail home in Fondaco dei Tedeschi.

BELOW: hub of the Rialto.

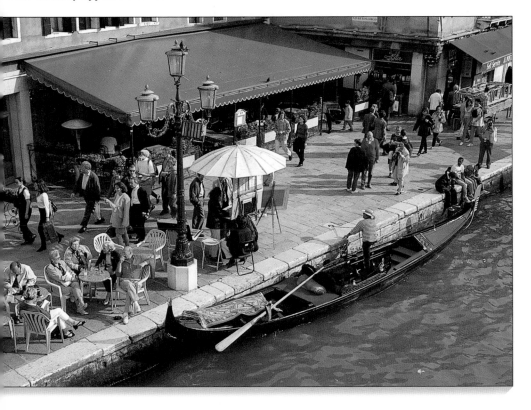

The curse of Ca' Dario

Five centuries of scandals, suicides and suspicious deaths have left Venetians wary of this unfortunate canalside palace. Yet it feels secretive rather than sinister. Known as a "*cielo-terra*", a self-contained structure, it is only accessible by water or through a door in the walled garden. The gently listing facade is an intricate pattern of roundels and plaques of precious marble and porphyry. As usual in Venice, it represents a subtle fusion of styles: a Gothic design is graced with round Renaissance arches and pilasters, while the sweep of Oriental tracery echoes the Byzantine tradition.

The Gothic palace belonged to Giovanni Dario, a Venetian chancery secretary who negotiated peace with the Turks in 1479. As a privileged member of the citizen class, Dario was richly recompensed for diplomatic success in Constantinople. He built this sym-

metrical Renaissance facade in a jewel-box design, adding the inscription: 'to the spirit of the city'. The house's history suggests that the spirit is malign.

The curse supposedly started after Dario's daughter died of a broken heart after marrying into the patrician Barbaro family. Although the Barbaro dynasty retained the palace until the 19th century, they suffered scandals and disasters, the most dramatic if which was the massacre of most of the family in the 17th century.

Venetians were reluctant to buy the palace but it was eventually sold to an Armenian diamond merchant who went bankrupt and died in penury. After squandering money on restoring Ca' Dario in the 1840s, Rawdon Brown, an Englishman and a friend of the aesthete John Ruskin, committed suicide in the drawing room. One hundred years later, in 1936, the melancholic French poet, Henri de Régnier, died shortly after moving in.

More recently, Charles Briggs, a colourful American, held homosexual orgies in the palace and was expelled from the city. In the early 1970s Kit Lambert, manager of The Who pop group, was murdered in a dispute with a drugs dealer shortly after selling Ca' Dario. In 1979 the jinx supposedly led to the death of Count Giordano delle Lanze, who was battered to death with a candlestick by his male lover. The next owner, a Venetian, went bankrupt and his sister was murdered. The most recent illustrious victim was Raul Gardini, an Italian industrialist, who committed suicide in 1993 after being caught up in corruption scandals.

Since then, the palace has lain empty. Prospective purchasers may well overlook the curse and be tempted by the superb interior. Dario's Oriental leanings caused him to add an "Arab kiosk", an enclosed terrace and minaret-style effect. Purchasors may even have time to appreciate the silk-hung drawing room, coffered ceilings, chandeliers of Murano glass and carved columns of Istrian stone. The American film maker Woody Allen and a famous tenor have both expressed interest in Ca' Dario but in the end they wisely decided not to court disaster. ❑

LEFT: Ca' Dario, the beguiling but bewitched palace where many have met their fate.

market is **Ca' da Mosto** ㉔, a shining example of Veneto-Byzantine architecture. This 13th-century palace was the birthplace of the explorer Alvise da Mosto (1432–88) credited with discovering the Cape Verde islands (Senegal) and exploring coastal west Africa. The original facade is adorned with cusped arches, plaques and a frieze of vines.

The Ca' d'Oro (Palace of Gold)

On the same side is the **Ca' d'Oro** ㉕, one of the loveliest Gothic palaces, set beside the landing stage of the same name. Architecturally, this is a landmark building and a sumptuous version of a Venetian palace. On the facade, the friezes of interlaced foliage and mythological beasts were originally picked out in gold, leading to its popular name, "the Palace of Gold". The Veneto-Byzantine influence is clear in the design, from the oriental pinnacles to the ethereal tracery. The palace boasts an arcade rather than the pointed watergate favoured by Gothic palaces. This was a single family courtyard, unlike palaces designed for several branches of the same family which commanded twin watergates and double courtyards. As well as the watergate on the Grand Canal, the palace retains its original land gate in a brick courtyard. In 1845 Ruskin wept while watching the brutal "restoration" of the palace demanded by the owner, a famous ballerina. Fortunately, Baron Franchetti, a later owner, restored the Ca' d'Oro to its original glory, even tracking down the original staircases. While suffering from an incurable illness, the Baron committed suicide in 1922, but not before bequeathing his beloved palace to the city.

The Ca' d'Oro houses the **Franchetti Gallery** *(9am–2pm daily)*, arguably the most appealing city art museum. If the collection is idiosyncratic, it reflects the refined taste of the owner. The courtyard contains the original Gothic well-head that Franchetti finally retrieved from a Parisian dealer. Although the interior is no longer recognisably Gothic, the coffered ceilings and fine marble floors make a splendid showcase for the medieval and Renaissance exhibits.

The gallery is adorned with Flemish tapestries as well as Gothic and Renaissance furniture. The highlights of the collection include a delightful *Annunciation* by Carpaccio, Guardi's views of Venice and Titian's *Venus*. Andrea Mantegna's *St Sebastian* is the most poignant of his paintings, with other versions existing in Paris and Vienna; this was Franchetti's favourite work. Yet the minor Venetian works give the greatest pleasure, ranging from the 12th-century sculptures of interlaced peacocks to the poetic Byzantine style paintings executed by Vivarini.

The *portego,* or gallery, opens onto the Grand Canal. In fine weather, the loggia makes a delightful place to sun oneself and watch the Canal: looking towards the Rialto, there is a splendid view of the **Pescheria**, the fish market. A wooden Gothic staircase leads to the top floor and works by Guardi and Tintoretto. Also on display are the faded frescoes by Giorgione and Titian that once adorned the facade of the Fondaco dei Tedeschi (*see page 175*). To appreciate this section, arrive in good time since the staff, in their eagerness for lunch, tend to sweep visitors out early.

Map, page 162

"A Venetian palace that has not too grossly suffered and that is not overwhelming by its mass makes almost any life graceful that may be led in it."

– HENRY JAMES

BELOW: Mantegna's "St Sebastian".

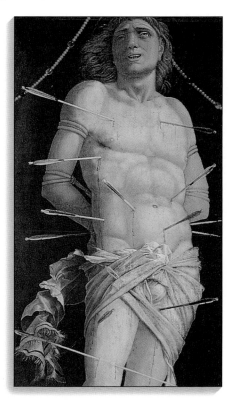

From Ca' d'Oro to the Station

"Its palaces did seem like fabrics of enchantment piled to heaven"

– PERCY BYSSHE SHELLEY

Just upstream on the left bank is **Ca' Corner della Regina** , the birthplace of Caterina Corner, Queen of Cyprus, in 1454. Corner was the victim of a cynical Venetian plot to gain control of Cyprus. The island was, as a result of French conquests during the crusades, ruled by King James of Lusignon, whom Corner married in 1468. When James died, leaving her Queen of Cyprus, Venetian ambassadors persuaded her that it was her patriotic duty to abdicate and grant Cyprus to the Republic. In return, she was given dominion over Asolo, a beautiful, but minor, town in the Veneto. In the 17th century, descendants of this illustrious family rebuilt the palace, which is now owned by the Biennale organisation (*see page 209*).

Ca' Pesaro ㉗, the next palace but one, is a stately Baroque pile which bemused Henry James: "I even have a timid kindness for the huge Pesaro, whose main reproach, more even than the coarseness of its forms, is its swaggering size." In building Ca' Pesaro, Longhena was inspired by Ca' Corner. The recently restored Grand Canal facade offers a play of chiaroscuro effects created by recessed windows and sharply delineated cornices. The rusticated ground floor facade is interrupted by a triple-arched water entrance. The theatrical inner courtyard is lined by balconies, loggias and a portico; in the centre is a grand wellhead that was originally in the Mint. In 1899, Duchess Bevilacqua La Masa bequeathed the palace to the city. It is now home to the **Museum of Oriental Art** *(9am–2pm, closed Monday)* and the **Museum of Modern Art** *(closed for restoration until the year 2000)*. Upon completion of the works, the Oriental Museum will probably be transferred to Palazzo Marcello. (For now, anyone wanting to visit the museum should leave the boat at the San Stae stop.)

BELOW: Ca' d'Oro, the sumptuous Palace of Gold.

The Museum of Oriental Art is based on the eclectic 19th-century collection assembled by the Count di Bardi on his travels to the Far East. The collection contains Japanese art of the Edo period (1614–1868) and Oriental decorative works, including painted screens and lacquer-work. There are also precious fabrics, musical instruments, costumes and armour, plus masks and puppets.

The **Museum of Modern Art** is being redesigned to create a better showcase for contemporary art. Although the fate of earlier modern art is safe, the first floor will be devoted to temporary exhibitions, with sculpture displayed in the courtyard. The rotating permanent collection will be shown on the second floor, including works by Klimt and Chagall, Klee, Kandinsky, Matisse, Rouault and Morandi. On the same bank is the church of **San Stae** , with its striking Palladian facade. A couple of palaces further on is **Palazzo Belloni-Battaglia**, which stands out for its stylish facade and distinctive pinnacles. It was designed by Longhena for the *parvenu* Belloni family who bought their way into the local aristocracy.

On the right bank is **Palazzo Vendramin-Calergi** , a testament to the changing fortunes of the Venetian nobility. It was built before 1500 by Coducci for the patrician Loredan dynasty, but later belonged to the Calergi, a Cretan family who bought their way into the Venetian nobility. The Vendramin, scions of a banking and Dogal family, then owned the palace until 1845 when it was sold to the French Bourbon Duchesse de Berry. Here she based her court in exile, a Versailles on the lagoon, with the interior hung with Renaissance paintings. Wagner rented the mezzanine wing from the family and, with his father-in-law Franz Liszt, gave a concert at the Fenice opera. In 1883, Wagner suffered a stroke in his apartments and died in his wife's arms. Now the **Winter Casino**, the place

Map, page 162

TIP

To gamble in the impressive Casino, dress smartly and bring a passport (tel: 529 7111). It is open mid-September to mid-June, 4pm to 2am (vaporetto lines 1, 6, 52 and 82).

BELOW: Fondaco dei Turchi, a former Turkish emporium.

Map,
page 162

Henry James was stunned by the Museum of Natural History's "glare of white marble without and a series of showy majestic halls within."

BELOW: Distinctive ornamental prows.

is banned to Venetian residents in an uncanny echo of ancient Republican law. (To admire the palace from afar, leave the boat at San Stae but to chance your luck in the Casino, get off at San Marcuola.)

Architecturally, the palace is inspired by classical principles and built in familiar three-part design and faced with Istrian stone. It is notable for its horizontal line, Tuscan projecting cornices, sweeping balconies and a frieze studded with shields and heraldic eagles. The palace still possesses a spectacular interior, despite the sale of the original furnishings by the de Berry heirs. The casino boasts coffered ceilings, chandeliers, marble fireplaces and Mannerist paintings as well as a hall decorated with jasper columns from the fabulous Turkish ruins of Ephesus. A Wagner society is housed in the composer's former quarters.

On the far bank stands the fortress-like **Deposito del Megio** ③⓪, the state granary. Now a school, the austere 15th-century granary is crenellated, in keeping with the Venetian approach to many public buildings. The Lion of St Mark emblem on the facade is a reconstruction, since Napoleonic troops effaced whatever Republican symbols they found. Next door is the **Fondaco dei Turchi**, a former trading base for Turkish merchants. It was built in 1227 for the noble Pesaro family but was leased to the Ottomans in 1621, partly as a means of supervising them. Bedrooms, shops and servants' quarters were created. In keeping with Muslim custom, doors and windows were sealed off, and the building boasted a mosque and Turkish baths. The Venetian State insisted that all weapons should be surrendered on entry and forbade Christian women and children from crossing the threshold. The Fondaco only fell into disuse in 1838 and, after an insensitive restoration, became the **Museum of Natural History**. Henry James was stunned by "the glare of white marble without and a series of showy majestic halls within". The museum contains the sarcophagi of previous Doges but one bears no inscription since it belonged to the disgraced Marin Faliero, the Doge decapitated for treason in 1355.

The buildings are less impressive on the next humdrum stretch of the canal. Opposite is **San Marcuola** ③①, an unfinished 18th-century church (*see page 239*). On the same bank, further upstream, stands **Palazzo Labia** ③②, recognisable by its square tower. This eclectic palace is the regional headquarters of the RAI state broadcasting network. The superb decorations and Tiepolo frescoes can be visited by appointment (*Tuesday, Thursday, Friday 3–4pm, tel: 041-524 2812*).

Next door is the domed church of **San Geremia** and, just beyond, the severe **Palazzo Flangini** ③③ marks the last of the major palaces. On the same bank, virtually at the station, stands the Rococo **Scalzi** ③④ church "all marble and malachite, all a cold hard glitter and a costly, curly ugliness". Henry James may have thought little of the church but it has a place in Venetian hearts as the sole monument to survive the building of the grim **Railway Station** ③⑤ which only serves to remind us of what the real world is like. Leave the boat at the **Ferrovia** (Station) stop, with a glance at **San Simeone Piccolo** ③⑥ on the far bank. This 18th-century domed church was modelled on the Pantheon in Rome and intended as a counterweight to La Salute, framing the Grand Canal with a Baroque church at either end. ❏

Gondolas and gondoliers

According to the writer Mary McCarthy, everything in Venice has an "inherent improbability, of which the gondola, floating, insubstantial, at once romantic and haunting, charming and absurd, is the symbol". The gondola may be as old as Venice itself, and although probably of Turkish origin, it is uniquely adapted for the Lagoon waters: it is streamlined yet sturdy, able to navigate the shallowest waters and narrowest canals. To Thomas Mann the gondola conjured up "visions of death itself, the bier and solemn rites and last soundless voyage". Although red was the traditional Venetian colour of mourning, funeral gondolas were eventually painted gold and black.

The gondola took its definitive form by the 17th century; before then, the craft was less streamlined. A gondola is made of eight different sorts of wood, finished off with 10 coats of black paint. The *ferro*, or metal prow, is the most distinctive feature, much admired by Mark Twain: "The bow is ornamented with a steel comb with a battle-axe attachment." The front of this projection supposedly symbolises the *corno*, the Doge's cap, with the six forward prongs representing the six *sestieri* (districts) of Venice, and the seventh the Giudecca. In practical terms, the prow serves as a counterweight to the gondolier and aligns the boat around narrow corners.

Until the 16th century, boats were lavishly decorated, bedecked with satins and silks, brocade and brass sea-horses. The Sumptuary Laws consigned gondolas to perpetual mourning. The gilded cherubs and noble crests on the stern and prow were banished in favour of black livery. Luxurious gondolas were equipped with a *felze*, an upholstered wooden cabin that gave protection from prying eyes and winter weather. (These are on show the Naval Museum, *see page 205*.)

In the 16th century, Venice had about 10,000 gondoliers but, now the number has fallen to 400. Nowadays, the Japanese are the keenest customers, always ready to try a gondola ride in all weathers and to pay a premium for a "music boat", rowed by a serenading gondolier.

The *gondolieri* are a breed apart: only native-born Venetians can apply for a coveted licence, and the trade is often passed down from father to son. Many are noted for their singing, but serenades are often spiced with lewd language, including lascivious appreciation of brides. (Since this is in Venetian dialect, few visitors are likely to be offended.)

Spokesman Mario Ventin also defends fellow gondoliers against criticisms of colourful language: "Foreign visitors love to hear us shout at each other. If a water-taxi narrowly misses us, are we to bow and say politely, 'Sir, your keel was too near?' No! We despatch the captain to hell!" Yet gondoliers do occasionally live up to their romantic image. Roberto Nardin met his Californian wife when she took a ride on his gondola. When Roberto described her eyes as "more beautiful than those September days when the sky dissolves into the lagoon", one more heart melted into the Venetian sunset. ❑

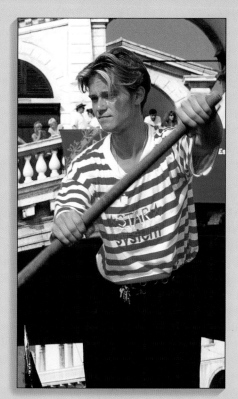

RIGHT: a gondolier plying his trade by the Rialto.

CASTELLO

*Lying to the north and east of San Marco, Castello is a mix of
sophistication and local charm. It has the city's best-known
waterfront, the sumptuous Scuola Grande and Vivaldi's church*

Map,
page 186

Henry James's evocation of the essence of Venice easily applies to Castello:
"a narrow canal in the heart of the city – a patch of green water and a surface of pink wall… a great shabby facade of Gothic windows and balconies". Yet this fails to do justice to the diversity of the district. As the most
varied Venetian *sestiere*, Castello offers a spectrum of sights, from the sophisticated bustle along Riva degli Schiavoni to the quaint fishing village ambience
of San Pietro. Castello's seafaring heritage may be strong but so are its cosmopolitan roots and mercantile spirit. Sailors, shipwrights and merchants came
from Dalmatia, Eastern Europe, Greece and Egypt, attracted by the prospect of
work at the Arsenal shipyards and great quaysides. The cosmopolitan legacy
lingers on, with the district still home to sizeable Greek and Slav communities
as well as a small Armenian quarter.

Like Cannaregio, Castello offers domesticity and a slice of everyday life, with
Sundays ringing with church bells, and dark alleys opening onto bright, bustling
squares. Two of the most homely areas are centred on Campo Santa Maria Formosa and San Giorgio dei Greci, the Greek church. Yet culturally the *sestiere*
can compete with any in Venice. The district is home to La Pietà, Vivaldi's
church, and the Gothic majesty of San Giovanni e Paolo (San Zanipolo). The
distinctive Venetian confraternities *(scuole)* are well-
represented, with San Giorgio degli Schiavoni the most
intimate and San Marco the most prestigious. The Arsenale is the focal point of the eastern district, with its
looming walls and defensive towers visible from afar.

Sadly, the remoter parts of Castello are falling silent
as workshops close and apartments remain untenanted.
However, the eastern area is also the greenest in Venice,
with classical gardens, wide waterfronts and the site of
the Biennale exhibition. Castello's diversity is encap-
sulated by its bars: choose a drink in the Danieli, the
haunt of the literati, or an *ombretta* of white wine in a
secluded neighbourhood bar, under the sole gaze of a
Venetian cat.

The Bridge of Sighs

Just beyond the Doge's Palace is the **Ponte dei Sospiri**
❶ (the Bridge of Sighs), the most famous bridge in
Venice. It crosses the canal to the "new" prisons, providing a link between the Doge's Palace, courtrooms
and cells, allowing interrogators to slip back and forth.
Built between 1595 and 1600, this covered stone bridge
acquired its legendary name after the lamentation of
prisoners as they confronted their inquisitors. In reality, by the standards of the day, the prisons were relatively comfortable. The **new prisons**, designed to hold
the overspill from the "old" prisons in the Doge's
Palace, occupy a sober, Classical building. The **old pris-**

PRECEDING PAGES:
The Danieli hotel
on the Riva degli
Schiavoni.
LEFT: the Bridge of
Sighs, linking the
Doge's palace to
the "new" prison.
BELOW: a stylish
maitre d'hotel.

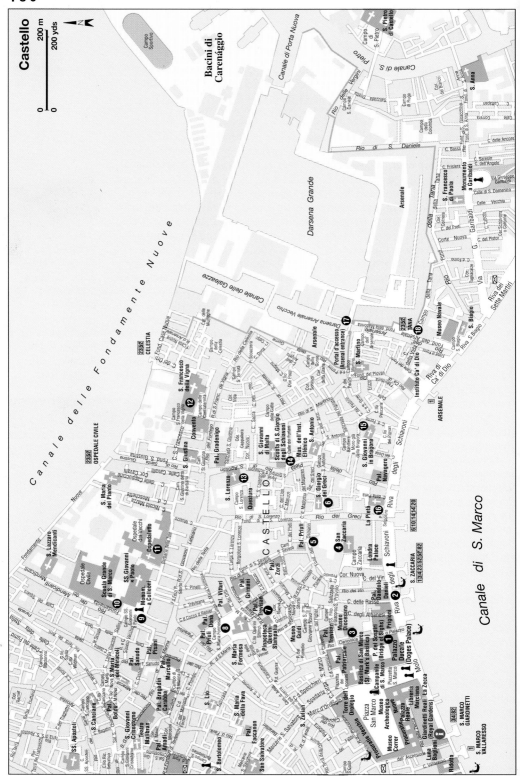

ons, from which Casanova (*see page 109*) made his dramatic escape, were known as *I Piombi* (the Leads), because they were built right under the lead roofs of the Palace.

The bridge marks the beginning of **Riva degli Schiavoni ❷**, the best-known stretch of Venetian waterfront. Now bustling with tourists and souvenir sellers, this sweeping quayside once thronged with slave-dealers and merchants. Its name refers either to slaves or Slavs, who were often synonymous in Venetian minds. Certainly, the term came to embrace the Dalmatian merchants from Schiavonia, modern-day Croatia, who settled in Venice in great numbers during the 15th century. The quayside was widened and paved in 1782 and has been a popular Venetian promenade ever since. Nor can visitors avoid the waterfront, since it is the focal point of ferry routes, and of the latter-day merchants of Venice who erect souvenir stalls along its length. As the hub of the upmarket tourist trade, the Riva is lined with distinguished hotels.

The Hotel Danieli

The **Danieli** is the most historic hotel in Venice, with even Proust enchanted by his room: "When I went to Venice I found that my dream had become – incredibly but quite simply – my address". The Danieli was also the scene of an unhappy love affair between George Sand and Alfred de Musset in 1883. During the Liberation, in 1945, many of the grandest hotels were commandeered as officers' clubs, with the Danieli becoming the New Zealand headquarters. The Danieli terrace still remains a superb place to toast the ending of a war or the beginning of a romance.

Over the next bridge stands a well-known landmark, the horseback monument to Vittorio Emmanuele, the first king of a united Italy. Behind lies the **Londra Palace** hotel, with balconies overlooking the island of San Giorgio and lights reflected in the lagoon waters. The waterfront is awash with literary and musical links, from Wagner and Tchaikovsky to Dickens. Henry James stayed further along the Riva (at 4145) while finishing the *Portrait of a Lady*. Here, "in the fruitless fidget of composition", he was distracted by "the waterside life, the wondrous lagoon spread before me, and the ceaseless human chatter at my windows".

The **Museo Diocesano di Arte Sacra ❸** *(10.30am–12.30pm; closed Sunday)*, the Museum of Sacred Art, is tucked away on Ponte della Canonica, behind the Doge's Palace and Riva degli Schiavoni. The Romanesque cloisters of this canalside museum form an oasis of calm amidst the bustle of San Marco. Ranged around the cloisters are fragments of early medieval sculptures from San Marco, as well as Roman and Byzantine statuary. The museum upstairs displays works salvaged from deconsecrated churches and paintings redeemed by the restoration centre. The permanent collection includes Mannerist and Baroque religious paintings, crucifixes, gold and silver chalices, and a crystal tabernacle.

From here follow Salizzada San Provolo east to Campo San Zaccaria. En route are several simple restaurants including Alla Rivetta, a popular inn serv-

Map, page 186

"A Venetian gondola? That singular conveyance came down unchanged from ballad times, black as nothing else on earth except a coffin".

— THOMAS MANN

BELOW: one of the city's best known hotels.

ing cuttlefish and polenta (on Ponte San Provolo 4625, the bridge across Rio del Vin). **San Zaccaria ❹** *(10am–noon, 4–6pm; closed Sunday)* is a delightful church graced by Coducci's curvilinear facade. This Renaissance masterpiece conceals a far older basilica, with Byzantine and Gothic churches fused into a harmonious Renaissance whole. Fortunately, elements of earlier incarnations remain. The church was founded in the 9th century and acted as a Venetian pantheon, with eight early Doges buried in the crypt. The original Byzantine basilica forms the crypt below San Tarasio chapel, an atmospheric spot usually lying under water. The chapel itself is decorated by Gothic frescoes and three lovely 15th-century altarpieces. In the north aisle of the main church, which is essentially Gothic, is Bellini's glowing altarpiece of the *Madonna and Child*. The charming square is completed by a Gothic belltower.

It is hard to associate this peaceful square with its sinister reputation for skulduggery and licence. Three Doges were assassinated in the vicinity, while the adjoining Benedictine convent was a byword for lascivious living. Since noblewomen were frequently dispatched to nunneries to save money on dowries, tales of libertine nuns were rife. Venetian attempts to stem the scandals were halfhearted: although chaplains and confessors had to be in their fifties or older, younger sons were made welcome at the convent's masked balls; the aristocracy encouraged such illicit liaisons as a means of keeping the family estate intact. The nuns' parlour became a celebrated social salon, as portrayed in Guardi's famous painting in Ca' Rezzonico. Men are still made welcome in the former convent: the Carabinieri barracks sacrilegiously occupy the Renaissance cloisters, linked to the church by a graceful open loggia.

A Gothic portal leads to Campo San Provolo, which opens onto the wide quay-

Poisoned daggers were used by Venetian secret police: when inserted into a victim's body, the glass dagger would snap off and leave virtually no trace of the fatal wound.

BELOW: courtyard in the Danieli.

ROOMS WITH A VIEW

St Mark's Square was described by Napoleon as the "drawing-room of Europe", which must make the **Riva degli Schiavoni** its sumptuous bedroom. Here the good **Danieli** was favoured by Wagner, Dickens, Proust, Debussy, Cocteau and Balzac. Here, too, George Sand and Alfred de Musset famously fell in and out of love. Today the Danieli still attracts the wealthy and famous. Next-door is the charming **Londra Palace**, boasting "a hundred windows on the lagoon". In splendid rooms overlooking San Giorgio, Tchaikovsky composed his *Fourth Symphony*. The grand Venetian hotels are still the place to strike a pose, perhaps starting with the **Luna Baglioni**, which claims to be the oldest hotel in Venice, dating back to Templar times.

On the Grand Canal is the **Gritti Palace**, once favoured by Ruskin, Hemingway and Graham Greene. Over the water on the Giudecca is the **Cipriani**, the choice for guests who want luxurious seclusion. Yet even the most illustrious visitors once faced night-time horrors: "The great business before going to bed is the hunt for insects, vicious mosquitoes that particularly torment foreigners, on whom they hurl themselves with the sensual appetite of a gourmet." Fortunately, poet Théophile Gautier's experiences are lost to modern visitors.

side of **Fondamenta dell'Osmarin ❺**, notable for the **Palazzo Priuli**, a superb late-Gothic palace commanding the corner of Rio di San Severo and San Provolo. From the bridge over Rio dei Greci is a view of the over-restored Gothic **Palazzo Zorzi** on the right, the university faculty of foreign languages.

Across the bridge is **San Giorgio dei Greci ❻** *(10am–5pm)*, the Greek Orthodox church, distinguished by its dome and tilting Baroque tower. The Greeks represent one of the oldest ethnic communities in Venice, even if they have only been established within this enclosure since 1526. After the Turkish conquest of Constantinople in 1453, the Venetian Greek community expanded greatly, working as merchants, scribes and scholars. In fact, only the Jews formed a larger ethnic group. The Greek contribution to Venetian culture can be seen in scholarship and printing, and in the artistic production of icons and mosaics.

The 16th-century church has a tall, narrow facade and early Renaissance purity. In keeping with Orthodox tradition, the interior boasts a *barco* or *matroneo*, a women's gallery, and an iconostasis, an exotic 16th-century screen separating the sanctuary from the nave. This intimate church comes alive during the vibrant Easter festivals when the stylised, golden interior and the scent of incense create a heady exoticism. Wagner visited the church shortly before his death and was disturbed by the oriental pomp and the mysterious mood created by the dark dome and flickering haloes of saints. An elegantly walled square encloses the church and a cluster of cultural buildings, including the Hellenic Institute, a museum of icons and a tiny Greek cemetery.

The **Museo Dipinti Sacri Bizantini** *(9am–1pm, 2–4.30pm)*, the icon museum, is housed in the former Greek *scuola,* or confraternity house, now run by the Hellenic Institute. The confraternity chapter house has kept its Baroque decor,

Map, page 186

Statues celebrated the State rather than individuals.

BELOW: view from Tchaikovsky's bedchamber in the Londra Palace.

The Baroque campanile of Santa Maria Formosa.

while the museum displays an outstanding collection of 16th and 17th-century Cretan works, which illustrate the synthesis of Greek and Venetian art.

Just around the corner is Da Remigio, a cosy trattoria noted for its home-made *gnocchi* (Salizzada dei Greci 3416). From here, cross Rio dei Greci to Fondamenta dell'Osmarin, before taking the second bridge on the right into **Ruga Giuffa**, a narrow alley with overhanging roofs. This is both an everyday shopping street and Venice at its most insular. Although only a stone's throw from San Marco, it feels like a private world, deeply Venetian yet historically linked to the Armenian community. The street, once populated by Armenian cloth merchants, was named after an Armenian enclave in Persia.

Pinacoteca Querini-Stampalia

Just before Santa Maria Formosa, turn left into Calle dietro Magazen, which rounds the canal to Calle Querini and comes out at **Pinacoteca Querini-Stampalia ❼** *(10am–1pm, 3–6pm; Friday and Saturday open until 10pm, often with concerts; closed Monday)*. This is one of the best small galleries in Venice, intimate, eclectic and uncrowded. The Querini belonged to the ancient nobility, the families who elected the first Doge. However, a foiled plot led to the Querini's banishment to the Greek island of Stampalia, a title they later appended. The last count died in 1868 and bequeathed his home to the city.

Count Giovanni left his stamp on this Renaissance palace, from the new library to the gallery hung with family portraits and Venetian paintings, mainly 17th and 18th-century genre scenes. Highlights include a poetic Bellini painting and the festive and domestic scenes of Gabriele Bella (1730–99). Several famous works by Longhi include *The Geography Lesson* and the *Ridotto*, depicting mas-

queraders at the casino. The count's taste in furniture is typical of the refined yet relatively spartan interiors favoured by the nobility. Given such pared-down chic, it is perhaps fitting that the ground floor should be remodelled by Carlo Scarpa, the celebrated modernist architect, in the 1960s, creating an airy atrium and a Japanese minimalist garden. Evening classical concerts are held in the frescoed main salon, allowing one to combine a gallery visit with musical appreciation.

Santa Maria Formosa

Campo Santa Maria Formosa ❽, the next square north, is a lovely assymetrical space dotted with flower, fruit and junk stalls. Rivalled only by Campo Santa Margherita and Campo San Polo this is the archetypal Venetian square. Set in the heart of Castello, this *campo* provided a backdrop for traditional festivities, from masked balls to bear-baiting. Today, the square rests on its laurels, sure of each Venetian element: the shadowy alleys running into a sunlit space, a striking Renaissance church, palaces from three different periods, a covered well-head surrounded by pigeons, everyday cafés filled with stallholders and visitors alike, and even a gondola station *(stazio)*. The **Palazzo Vitturi** (5246) is a 13th-century affair decorated with Gothic and Moorish motifs, while the **Palazzo Trevisan** (5250) is a Renaissance palace studded with slender columns and ornamentation. On the Rialto end, above Ponte del Paradiso, stands a delicately sculpted Gothic archway.

The parish church of **Santa Maria Formosa** *(8.15am–12.15pm, 5–7pm)* is an endearing sight, with its eccentrically bulging apses. The foundations may date from the 9th century but the church was redesigned by Coducci, the great

Map, page 186

"I love the cats of Venice, peering from their pedestals, sunning themselves on the feet of statues."

– JAN MORRIS

BELOW: cool alley cat.

*Stained glass in
San Zanipolo.*

Renaissance architect, and acquired a Baroque belltower with a grotesque mask at its base. While the canalside facade is by Coducci, the *campo* facade was added in 1604. The cool grey and white marble interior contains a Vivarini *Madonna* (1473) and a chapel set aside for students "to pay a little visit on the way to school". The canalside café beside the church makes a good coffee stop, the place to listen to passing musicians or the backchat of gondoliers waiting for business on their *stazio*.

San Zanipolo (Santi Giovanni e Paola)

From the square, follow Calle Santa Maria Formosa north across Rio di San Giovanni to **Campo Santi Giovanni e Paolo ❾**. Familiarly known as Zanipolo, this is one of the most monumental squares in Venice. While less intimate than Santa Maria Formosa, it is far more impressive architecturally. This spectacular square occupies land given to the Dominicans by Doge Orseolo in 1234 and encloses a great Gothic church and Renaissance confraternity, as well as the finest equestrian statue in northern Italy. This restless horse and rider commemorate **Bartolomeo Colleoni** (1400–76), a celebrated *condottiere* (mercenary soldier) whose bequest to the city came with a stipulation that a monument be erected to him on St Mark's Square. The rider has reason to be restless: the authorities cunningly relegated the idealised Renaissance statue to this lesser spot, outside St Mark's confraternity.

The square possesses another Renaissance treasure, a sculpted well-head which is attributed to Sansovino. The imposing *campo* can be admired from Rosa Salva, an historic café on the ground floor of a Gothic palace. The café itself dates back to 1750, making it one of the oldest in Venice. The sweet pas-

BELOW: Colleoni
equestrian statue.

tries and fruit aperitifs form a prelude to feasting on the city's most authentic Gothic church.

Santi Giovanni e Paolo *(7.30am–12.30pm, 3–6.30pm; Sunday 3–6pm only)* is also known as **San Zanipolo**, a conflation of Saints John and Paul, to whom the church is dedicated. Sheer size and scale invite comparisons with the Frari, its fellow giant *(see page 222)*. This, too, is an austere church, founded in the late 13th century but only later consecrated in 1430. The Gothic pinnacles can be seen from both banks of the Grand Canal, with the roofline displaying statues of the Dominican saints. Close to, the plain brickwork of the church is enlivened by a 14th-century polygonal apse. The main portal incorporates Byzantine columns and ornamentation salvaged from Torcello. While characterised by a lofty nave and sparse decoration, the interior is initially more coherent and welcoming than the Frari. The cross-vaulted ceilings are supported by wooden tie beams and stone pillars.

The church is considered the Pantheon of Venice, honouring illustrious leaders, from admirals and noblemen to the occasional state artist, notably Bellini. Above all, this was the last resting place of the Doges, with the pomp of state funerals matched by magnificent monuments to 25 Doges. Amongst the profusion of funerary monuments is the sculpted Renaissance tomb of Doge Giovanni Mocenigo, close to the main portal. Made by the Lombardi family of master-craftsmen in 1500, it is one of many monuments to the powerful Mocenigo dynasty. In the right aisle, also close to the main portal, is a memorial to Marcantonio Bragadin, the garrison commander flayed alive by the Turks in Cyprus in 1571. In the chancel, by the Baroque high altar, lies the finest Renaissance funerary monument in Venice, dedicated to Doge Andrea Ven-

Map, page 186

The Colleoni equestrian statue was sculpted by Verrocchio but in his rage at only being asked to sculpt the warhorse, not the rider, he smashed his first attempt.

BELOW: tomb of Giovanni Mocenigo.

Call home with a phone card ("scheda telefonica").

dramin, who died in 1478. Diagonally opposite is the tomb of Doge Michele Morosini, a victim of the 1382 plague. This was the Gothic monument most admired by Ruskin.

The Chapel of the Rosary, at the end of the north transept, was built to commemorate the Venetian victory over the Turks in 1571. Over the entrance is the funerary monument to Doge Sebastiano Venier, who commanded the fleet at Lepanto. The chapel once contained works by Titian and Tintoretto but, after a tragic fire, these were replaced with ceiling panels by Veronese, considered the most pagan and joyous of Venetian painters. The church interior is enriched by other works of art, including Vivarini's *Christ Bearing the Cross* (1474). A controversial Veronese *Last Supper* was painted for this church but is now in the Accademia (*see page 259*). In the right aisle, Bellini's gorgeous *St Vincent Ferrier* altarpiece survives, set in its original gilded frame.

The Scuola Grande di San Marco

The unadorned facade of Zanipolo is flanked by the ornate **Scuola Grande di San Marco** ⑩, once the richest Venetian confraternity. This *scuola* is the exception to the rule that Venetian interiors are finer than exteriors. The confraternity retains its *trompe l'oeil* Renaissance facade as well as its assembly rooms and chapter house. Coducci designed the curved crowning of the facade in 1490, conceivably inspired by the domes of St Mark's. The sumptuous marble lower section was decorated by the Lombardi brothers. In keeping with the charitable aims of the confraternity, it is fitting that the city hospital should now be based here. A grand portal framed by illusionistic lions leads into the hushed hospital, with the foyer occupying the cloisters of the former Dominican foundation. To

BELOW: the church of San Francesco della Vigna.
BELOW RIGHT: a local artisan's shop.

Map, page 186

visit the former *scuola*, slip past reception and walk upstairs to check the current opening times posted on the door of the medical library, housed in the panelled, 16th-century assembly rooms.

From here, **Fondamenta dei Mendicanti** leads past a *squero,* or gondola boatyard, and the hospital chapel of San Lazzaro. Beyond lie the bleak jetties of **Fondamente Nuove**, with fast boat services to the islands. From the canalside are occasional views of hospital cases arriving by water ambulance. Alternatively, from San Zanipolo follow Barbaria delle Tole to the cunningly concealed **Ospedaletto ⑪** *(Friday–Sunday 3–6pm)*, set in a hospice. Also known as Santa Maria dei Derelitti, this was one of four famous Ospedali, charitable institutions that acted as orphanages and prestigious music conservatoires. The frescoed Sala della Musica formed the main concert hall and can still be visited, ideally for a concert. The ponderous Baroque facade of the adjoining Ospedaletto church is attributed to Longhena. Ruskin dismissed these leering masks as "the most monstrous example of the Grotesque Renaissance… the sculptures on its facade representing masses of diseased figures and swollen fruit". The church interior is decorated with 17th and 18th-century paintings, which include an early Tiepolo.

Barbaria delle Tole leads east across Rio di Santa Giustina to **San Francesco della Vigna ⑫** *(8am–noon, 3.30–7pm)*, set in an isolated, somewhat shabby area. Goethe even required a compass to reach this remote spot. However, this Franciscan church represents an architectural milestone, both Sansovino's first creation in Venice and the first flowering of the High Renaissance in Venice. The facade and crowning pediment were designed by Palladio while the tall belltower is a familiar city landmark. San Francesco is a hallowed site, built on

Although the "scuole" (see page 220) were confraternities not guilds, the arts and crafts were well represented, from glassmakers to goldsmiths, stone-cutters to fritter-makers.

BELOW: Scuola Grande di San Marco.

To find a ferry or gondola, return to the Riva degli Schiavoni.

vineyards associated with a mysterious visit by St Mark. The present building was founded in 1534 by Doge Andrea Gritti, the Renaissance scholar and notorious womaniser. "We cannot make a Doge of a man with three bastards in Turkey", declared one envious rival. The church was built in accordance with Neo-Platonic ideals, using the precision of proportional relationships based on the number three: even the width of the aisles corresponds to a third of their height. The cool but harmonious interior contains a monument to the Doge (who died from a surfeit of grilled eels) as well as a clutch of paintings by Venetian masters, from Vivarini to Tiepolo. Highlights include sculptures from the Lombardi school, Veronese's *Holy Family*, and a *Madonna and Child* by Negroponte (1450). The charming Gothic cloisters lead on to the Cappella Santa where a Bellini *Madonna* can be found.

Behind the church lies a depressing stretch of urban wasteland, with canalsides abutting one of the oldest walled sections of the Arsenale, out of bounds to visitors. From here, cross Rio del Fontego to the south and reach **San Lorenzo** ⓭, the presumed burial place of Marco Polo. Since the discovery of ancient foundations in 1987, the deconsecrated church has been undergoing a lengthy restoration. San Lorenzo was also the site of another lax convent while the canal is flanked by fine palaces, including the police headquarters, which often feature in contemporary thrillers.

From here, Fondamenta San Giorgio hugs the canal south to **San Giorgio degli Schiavoni** ⓮ *(9.30am–12.30pm, 3.30–6.30pm; Sunday 9.30am–12.30 only; closed Monday)*. Tucked into Calle dei Furlani is the loveliest confraternity seat in Venice. The *scuola* was intended to protect the interests of Slavs from Dalmatia (Schiavonia), the first Venetian colony. This community of sailors,

BELOW: San Giorgio degli Schiavoni.
BELOW RIGHT: goods to deliver.

skilled artisans and merchants was first accommodated by the Knights of Malta in the building behind San Giorgio before prosperity spurred them to build their own headquarters. On its completion in 1501, the confraternity commissioned a painting cycle in honour of the Dalmatian patron saints, St George, St Tryphon and St Jerome. As the foremost painter of cycles, Carpaccio was chosen to decorate the upper gallery but, after the *scuola* was rebuilt in 1551, his masterpieces were moved downstairs. Despite remodelling, the *scuola* retains its authentic atmosphere and boasts the only Venetian pictorial cycle to have survived in the original building for which it was painted.

Carpaccio's narrative cycle

Carpaccio's vibrant works are displayed in a mysterious, intimate setting, below a coffered ceiling. Unlike his superb cycle in the Accademia (*see page 262*), a portrayal of pomp, pageantry and everyday life, this cycle is characterised by dramatic storytelling. In particular, the *St George and the Dragon* paintings are bold chivalric scenes, with a captivating depiction of a veritable knight in shining armour, a dying dragon, and a place of desolation, with the ground littered with skulls, vipers and vultures. Equally beguiling is the St Jerome Trilogy, with *The Miracle of the Lion* showing the saint extracting a thorn from the lion's paw. Despite the scene's presumed eastern setting, Carpaccio has included San Giorgio and the Knights of Malta.

The Vision of St Jerome is both one of the most engaging works and his masterpiece, conveying a mood of contemplative calm and a Tuscan sense of space combined with Flemish realism. St Augustine is depicted in his study writing to St Jerome when a heavenly voice announces his imminent death. Carpaccio

Map, page 186

TIP

Corte Sconta, set on Calle del Pestrin near San Giovanni in Bragora, is a perennial favourite with Venetian diners, so book in advance (tel: 522 6546, closed on Sunday and Monday).

BELOW: Carpaccio's "Vision of St Jerome".

**Map,
page 186**

Pulpit of La Pietà.

BELOW: the altar
of Pietà, Vivaldi's
church.

shows his customary accuracy in the depiction of a Renaissance humanist's
study, from the bookspines to the astrolobes and musical scores. The perky Maltese dog by the saint's feet evokes the Knights of Malta, whose headquarters
still lie next-door. The upstairs room, hung with minor works and the confraternity pennant, is more memorable for the panelled ceiling and sound of cooing
doves. Behind San Giorgio stands **San Giovanni di Malta**, the secretive seat
of the Knights of Malta. The members not only contributed to San Giorgio but
continue to have close links with the confraternity.

Fondamenta dei Furlani winds south to Salizzada Sant'Antonin and **San Giovanni in Bragora** ⓑ *(8–11am, 3–5pm; Saturday 8–11am only)*. This treasured
parish church is set on a quiet *campo* beside a handsome Gothic palace. The
austere church is essentially late Gothic, despite 9th-century foundations and a
Renaissance presbytery. The interior is notable for its ship's keel ceiling and
Renaissance works of art, a style which reached Venice later than elsewhere.
While Bartolomeo Vivarini's *Madonna and Saints* (1478) is a stiff Byzantine-style work, his nephew Alvise shows humanist leanings in his *Resurrection*
(1498), a dynamic High Renaissance altarpiece. Adorning the high altar is Cima
da Conegliano's *Baptism of Christ* (1492), set against a realistic mountain landscape. Mouldering in a chapel on the right lies the mummified corpse of St John
the Almsgiver. However, the church of St John is keener to proclaim birth than
death: Vivaldi was baptised in the red marble font, as the proudly displayed
copies of the baptismal register prove.

Calle del Dose leads back to bustling Riva degli Schiavoni and **La Pietà** ⓖ
(9.30am-noon), a church with even stronger Vivaldi connections. The Ospedale
della Pietà was the most famous of the Ospedali, institutions that combined the
roles of orphanage and musical conservatory. The
church was the backdrop for the concerts given by the
choir of orphan girls under Vivaldi's tutelage. The
church was superbly remodelled by Massari in the 18th-century and transformed into the city's leading concert
hall. The cool, oval interior was designed with acoustics
in mind, aided by curving lines, low vaulted ceilings, a
vestibule which muffled the street noise, and the filigree-like choir galleries. Since Massari won the commission to rebuild the church in 1735, while Vivaldi was
still in residence, it is perhaps not too fanciful to presume that the composer advised the architect on
acoustic refinements.

The magnificent gold and white interior is crowned
by Tiepolo's *The Triumph of Faith* (1775). In the dazzling fresco, the figures appear to come alive and billow into the church itself. Ironically, Vivaldi never lived
to see the completion of this church but the young
chamber orchestra that plays here now does its best to
invoke the master's spirit. The fine acoustics can be
appreciated during one of the frequent Baroque concerts. In Vivaldi's time, the ranks of orphans from the
adjoining orphanage were swelled by nuns from local
convents. Contemporary accounts found the massed
female presence beguiling: "I swear nothing is so
charming as to see a pretty young nun dressed in white,
a sprig of pomegranate blossom behind one ear, leading the orchestra." ❑

Antonio Vivaldi

Rarely does *The Four Seasons* fall on fresh ears, but it often falls on deaf ones. As one of the world's best-known pieces of classical music, its fate has been sealed. Its sin was to be too successful. The concerto is a cliché of tasteful background music, signalling anything from seduction to a sophisticated dining experience. The Venetian composer, no slouch at seduction or the celebrity stakes, would have been secretly pleased at such popularity.

Although his work acted as a model for future followers, J.S. Bach among them, Vivaldi's music soon suffered a decline, and was only rescued from oblivion in 1926. It seems inconceivable that the works of such a celebrated composer could have been lost for nearly 200 years. To contemporary critics, Vivaldi (1678–1741) is one of the most important composers of late Baroque music. Now a new generation of classical violinists has managed to infuse his work with passion.

Vivaldi's great musical talent was encouraged by his father, Giovan Battista, a barber whose playing was good enough to gain him a place in the orchestra of St Mark's Cathedral. His son was nurtured in the Venetian musical tradition and, as a budding violin virtuoso, allowed to stand in for his father. The young man entered the priesthood, which gave him time to devote to music, and he was known as "*il prete rosso*", the red-haired priest.

Vivaldi devoted himself to composition and obtained a post as composer and violin teacher at the Ospedale della Pietà, a famous charitable institution. At once an exclusive girls' conservatoire and an orphanage, it was one of several schools where gifted orphans were elevated from poverty to careers in music. It proved so popular that a plaque had to be erected threatening heaven's wrath on parents who passed off their offspring as foundlings. Vivaldi spent almost 40 years here, coaxing fine performances from choir and orchestra and introducing his compositions to a wide public.

Right: "*il prete rosso*", the musical red-haired priest, whose downfall was caused by a soprano.

Vivaldi's relationship with the Ospedale began superbly, with universal acclaim for his Sunday concerts of concerti, sonatas and sacred music, including oratorios. His gift for melody made him successful in most fields of music but his favourite instrument remained the violin. However, within 10 years the administration had become aggrieved by the maestro's frequent absences, caused by his new star status, his excuses for avoiding Mass and his general worldliness.

His reversal of fortune came with allegations of improper conduct with a pupil from Mantua, Anna Girò, a soprano who sang in several of his operas. The affair damaged his reputation as a teacher, priest and establishment figure. In his disappointment, Vivaldi, turned his back on Venice and went on extended concert tours to Paris, Dresden, Prague, Amsterdam and finally Vienna, where he died in poverty in 1741.

La Pietà, Vivaldi's musical base in Venice, was remodelled shortly after his death. His chamber music is regularly performed beneath a splendid Tiepolo ceiling. ❑

EASTERN CASTELLO

Dominated by the Arsenale shipyards, Eastern Castello has a scattering of important sites, including the excellent Naval Museum and the exhibition pavilions of the Biennale

Map, page 202

Eastern Castello is a curiously indefinable outlying district, with soulless modern quarters interspersed with lively working-class neighbourhoods. The sights are scattered, with much space occupied by the legendary Arsenale, the unknowable void at the heart of the district. Urban regeneration schemes, from craft enterprises to cultural centres, are regularly proposed for the Arsenale, but initiatives are hampered by the secrecy surrounding the site.

Recently, these shipyards have received an economic boost, with scientific centres encouraged, including a new company devoted to marine research housed in the historic dockyards of the Darsena Nuovissimo. The Mayor of Venice has described his plans for the Arsenale in somewhat opaque terms: "Maximum conservation is only achieved by maximum innovation."

The district around the naval complex contains a stretch of early modular housing designed for the former *arsenalotti*, the Arsenale workers whose skills were so valued that they were offered jobs for life. One of the newest quarters of Venice lies further east, with the ancient island of San Pietro on the outskirts.

Napoleonic redevelopment and land reclamation schemes created the streets and the public gardens that line the eastern waterfront. Following French demolition projects, the Austrians were responsible for reclaiming swathes of the watery marsh off Sant'Elena. Originally intended as a military parade ground, this former island has now succumbed to development.

The Arsenale

Arsenal is a term that the Venetians have bequeathed to the Western world. Although the oldest dockyard of the Venetian **Arsenale**, the Darsena Vecchio, still exists, the Darsena Nuovo and Nuovissimo now form a single basin, swallowed up by the Darsena Grande. Today the site is mainly used as a sheltered anchorage for battleships. In the late 1990s, ships were despatched from Venice to Albania and former Yugoslavia. Previously a forbidden zone, public access remains restricted but two ferries pass through the naval complex. Since the Arsenale remains a working base, naval school and shipyards, officers and crew can be seen strolling around.

The best way to see the Arsenale is to take a walk or boat ride to **Tana ❶**, the landing stage for the 52 or 23 boats that run through the heart of the naval complex. After exploring the immediate surroundings on foot, take a boat to see the closed military zone. Apart from befriending a sympathetic naval officer, this is the only way to see this evocative area, lined with a mixture of abandoned warehouses, and both functioning and derelict docks. The sense of desolation is partly due to the Napoleonic devastation, when buildings and ships were set on fire and cannons and bronzes melted down.

LEFT: the grand entrance to the Arsenal.
BELOW: a lion guards the gates.

Just east, running along Rio della Tana, stands the hulking **Tana** (or **Corderie**), the former rope and cable factory that was founded as a hemp warehouse. Here, hemp plants were carded and spun before being passed to master cordwainers who made the ropes and hawsers. This functional space was redesigned in the 1540s by da Ponte, the architect of the Rialto bridge. The barn-like building is used as an occasional exhibition space during the Biennale but may become a cultural centre.

As Venetians grew wealthier, it became harder to find native oarsmen. By the 16th century, Dalmatian and Greek crews gave way to convicts who were dragooned into service.

From Campo della Tana, Rio dell'Arsenale leads to **Campo dell'Arsenale ❷**, the entrance to the naval complex, with its impressive fortifications bounded by 16th-century walls and towers. Beyond the footbridge lies the water entrance, framed by crenellated brick towers. These picturesque waterside towers were rebuilt in the 17th century. Beside the watergate stands the ceremonial **Porta Magna**, the majestic land entrance to the Arsenal. Built in 1460, this triumphal arch is celebrated as the first Renaissance monument in Venice. Yet, with typical Venetian eclecticism, the gateway recycles stolen statuary as well as four Greek marble columns and their Byzantine capitals.

Notwithstanding the Venetian victory at Lepanto in 1571 the Republic undertook defensive fortifications in response to fears of Turkish expansion. As a sign of the warlike mood, the winged Lion of St Mark over the gateway holds a closed book, rather than displaying his traditional message of peace. The gateway was embellished with statues at the same time, with the allegorical figures added a century later. These are believed to have been carved from marble looted from the Parthenon during the Venetian bombardment of Athens in 1687. The land gateway is guarded by two lions pillaged from Piraeus during the same attack by Doge Morosini, Admiral of the Venetian fleet. The lion sitting upright

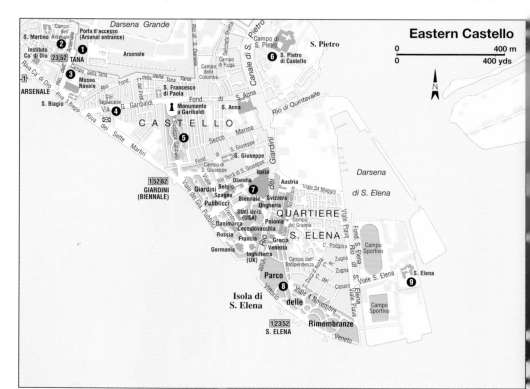

to the left of the gateway bears a runic inscription on his shoulder and haunches, probably carved by 11th-century Norse mercenaries who were defending the Byzantine emperor against Greek rebels. The smaller pair of lions on the far right may be Greek booty from Delos dating from the 6th century BC. In 1682, a terrace replaced the medieval drawbridge, setting the seal on this ambitious modernisation programme.

Map, page 202

The Arsenal by boat

Although this is as far as unauthorised visitors are allowed to go, the inquisitive can resort to water-borne glimpses of the Arsenal. The 52 *vaporetto* crosses the naval complex, along with all authorised water-borne craft, including Caribinieri speedboats. After slipping between the towers of the grand water entrance, the ferry affords a view of the docks. Also on the right-hand side stands a monumental 16th-century boathouse, designed by Sanmicheli, the noted civil and military engineer. It housed the legendary Bucintoro, the ceremonial state barge, until Napoleon stripped it, and is now home to a pale imitation (*see page 206*).

"Why don't they put outboard motors on them?" is a common reaction to gondolas from the more naive tourists.

On entering the **Canale delle Galeazze**, named after the oar-propelled Venetian galleys, the boat passes 18th-century shipyards where frigates were made. The journey also allows glimpses of the **Cantiere delle Gaggiandre** docks on the right, with their dignified 16th-century arches. These were created after the 1571 Venetian victory at Lepanto and were capable of dispatching a fleet of warships at a moment's notice. The most significant building here is Sansovino's magnificently roofed boathouse designed for the armed patrol craft that protected the lagoon ports.

BELOW: a quiet, characteristic corner.

Before or after the short boat trip, consider visiting the underrated Naval

The Arsenale

The Arsenale was the symbol of Venetian maritime might. Founded in 1104, this secretive military and naval complex became Europe's largest medieval shipyard and a power-house of industrial planning. The term "Arsenal" derives from the Arabic *darsina'a*, or house of industry, a most suitable description of this Venetian production line.

The Arsenal was a functional city within a city, bounded by 3 km (2 miles) of walls, with wet and dry docks and ordnance depots that were envied abroad. It was also an armaments site, although originally an arms and munitions depot rather than a factory.

At its height, 16,000 people toiled in the foundries, gunpowder mills and munitions depots, the hemp and sail factories, the ropeworks and grain stores. Industrial bakeries produced the horribly dry Venetian biscuits that were admirably suited to preservation for consumption on long sea voyages but less acceptable to modern palates. The

Arsenal's industrial caulkers' vats so impressed Dante that he described them in his *Inferno*, making immersion in the bubbling cauldrons of pitch a hellish punishment for corrupt officials.

Before the creation of the Arsenal, shipbuilding and repairs were often carried out in St Mark's Basin. However, even at the height of its production capacity, the Arsenal was supported by numerous private repair yards, including some on the neighbouring islands, especially Murano. However, as far as shipbuilding work was concerned, the state exercised a monopoly, with the Arsenal constructing war and merchant fleets. This was a vast enterprise that stretched over three docks and spawned several hundred successful chartered shipping companies.

The Arsenal acted as a medieval production line, manufacturing light galleys, ships of war and merchant vessels. Hulls constructed in the "new" Arsenal were towed past a series of openings in the "old" Arsenal where they were rigged and fitted out with munitions and food supplies. "From one window the cordage, from another the bread, from another the arms, and from another the mortars", as one impressed visitor described the conveyor belt system in 1436.

Everything from oars and sails to barrels of biscuits would be loaded by means of a pulley system; at the end, the galleys would be ready to sail. In its 16th-century heyday, the Arsenal could deliver a fully rigged galley within a day. As a party trick in 1574, the Venetians impressed Henri III of France by producing a seaworthy vessel complete with a 16,000-pound cannon in the time it took him to devour a state banquet.

Such pioneering methods of prefabricated construction were dependent on a highly skilled workforce. The *arsenalotti* comprised an artisans' elite of master ship-builders, caulkers and carpenters. They were staunch loyalists, with a privileged section acting as the Doge's guards of honour or pallbearers, and another group operating as firemen. So greatly did the state value the experience and skill of these men, that workers were guaranteed jobs for life. ❑

LEFT: The towers and bridge around the city's mighty Arsenal.

Museum. A small detour from the Arsenal takes one back to the waterfront via the site of the former Arsenal bakeries. These stand at the St Mark's Basin end of **Riva Ca' di Dio** (number 2179–80). Set on the east bank of the canal, the **Forni Pubblici** date from 1473 and are distinguished by a marble frieze.

According to historian Pompeo Molmenti, one batch of long-lived Venetian navy biscuits was left in Crete in 1669 and was discovered to be perfectly edible in 1821. Nearby stand workers' houses first designed for the *arsenalotti*, the Arsenal shipwrights and skilled craftsmen.

The Museo Navale (Naval Museum)

Further along the waterfront stands the dignified **Museo Navale ❸** *(daily 8.45am–1.30pm, except Tuesday and Thursday 2.30–5pm)*. Given the tantalising elusiveness of the Arsenale, the Naval Museum is the only place where you can fully appreciate the greatness of maritime Venice. Before its present incarnation, the 16th-century building was used as a naval granary and biscuit warehouse. The Austrians created the collection from those few remnants to survive French depredations. (Many Venetian naval treasures are now displayed in the Parisian naval museum.)

The Naval Museum is greatly underrated.

The Venetian museum is deceptively spacious so you may wish to restrict your visit to the lower floors; the top floor is devoted to uniforms, pennants and insignia. Unusually for Venice, exhibits are labelled in English and French. Apart from naval maps and nautical instruments, the collection includes a range of weaponry, from 17th-century breech-loaders to heavy cannons and World War II torpedoes. The antiquarian maps are specifically Venetian, depicting the development of the Arsenal and the lagoon defences. Venetian naval supremacy is

BELOW: Admiral Morosini's fleet encounter the Turks in 1659, from the Naval Museum.

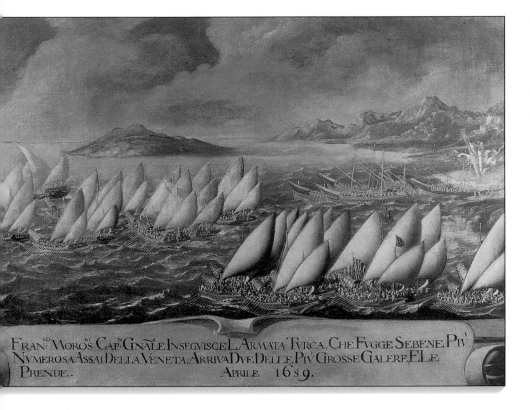

FRAN:ᶜᵒMOROˢ:CAP:ᴺᴵGNALE INSEGVISCE L'ARMATA TVRCA, CHE FVGGE SEBENE PIV' NVMEROSA ASSAI DELLA VENETA, ARRIVA DVE DELLE PIV' GROSSE GALERE, E LE PRENDE. APRILE 1659.

Map, page 202

Garibaldi in his gardens.

Below: Canale di San Pietro di Castello.

illustrated by scenes of naval battles, such as Lepanto, and by models of fortresses around the Mediterranean. Venetian shipyards generally built boats from models rather than drawings. Models on display range from early Egyptian and Phoenician craft to Greek triremes and a Venetian galley. Gondolas naturally play a prominent role, including examples of boats built with a *felze*, the wooden cabin that protected passengers from prying eyes and winter weather. One highlight is a scale model of the last Bucintoro, the legendary state barge.

From here, a walk through one of the quietest and greenest parts of the city leads to the site of the Biennale exhibition and to the former city fortress, marooned on the island of San Pietro. Strolling east along **Riva San Biagio** takes you past the colonnaded San Biagio, a Greek church now used as the naval chapel. On the left is **Via Garibaldi ❹**, the widest street in Venice, occupying an filled-in canal. As the commercial hub of eastern Castello, this workaday street is lined with basic food shops and bars. On the right is the former home of the Venetian navigators, John and Sebastian Cabot, who explored Newfoundland together in 1497.

Viale Garibaldi ❺, a tree-lined avenue further down on the right, is a model of French rationality. Napoleon embellished this area, incidentally demolishing churches and monasteries. The avenue runs down to the Napoleonic gardens, a tree-lined promenade dotted with monuments. In 1834 the novelist George Sand found the park as deserted as most Venetian parks, populated only by "grumbling old men, some senseless smokers or some bilious melancholics".

From here, one can cross the gardens to the Biennale site, or retreat to an established canalside *trattoria* at the end of Viale Garibaldi – a good choice is the Hostaria da Franz (Fondamenta Giuseppe 754), which was opened in 1842 by an

THE BUCINTORO

Venetian maritime traditions glorified the Doge and the Republic, with no regatta complete without the presence of the Bucintoro, or state barge. This boat resembled a gilded dragon or some other mythical beast, with the symbolic winged Lion of St Mark on the prow.

The Doge occupied a throne close to the ship's figurehead, which was carved with the image of Justice, personifying the city of Venice. John Evelyn, the 17th-century diarist, marvelled at the size and design of a craft manned by up to 200 galley slaves: "Here stands the Bucintoro, with a most ample deck, and so contrived that the slaves are not seen, having on the poop a throne for the Doge to sit".

The last barge was built in 1728 but was destroyed by Napoleon during the fall of the Republic in 1797–8. However, in 1828 a scale model was made from past records and is on display in the Naval Museum, along with period paintings of the great craft. On La Sensa, Ascension Day, a replica of the Bucintoro still sets sail for the Lido in honour of the Marriage with the Sea, one of the city's most important celebrations (*see page 94*). The traditional words are spoken during the ceremony and the mayor and patriarch stand in for the absent Doge.

Austrian soldier who fell in love with a Venetian woman (*see page 322*). Once refreshed, return to Via Garibaldi and cross the bridge to San Pietro, set in the far reaches of Castello. At the first bridge at the end of the street is a distant view across to the Arsenal, with its cranes, walls and defensive towers. This shabby district is enlivened by the jaunty fishing boats, workshops and boatyards lining the Canale di San Pietro.

San Pietro and the Biennale

A wooden bridge leads to the island of **San Pietro**, the site of the original castle (*castello*) which gave its name to the district. **San Pietro di Castello ❻** (*9am–noon, 3–6pm*) rests on ancient foundations but is essentially Palladian, topped by a central dome. From the foundation of Venice until 1807, the church was the city cathedral, with the title only passing to St Mark's after the demise of the Republic. Ironically, this remote island church was the official seat of religious power while the splendid St Mark's Basilica was merely the Doge's private chapel. This was the Venetian way of keeping the power of the Papacy at one remove, with temporal power centred on the St Mark's district.

The disappointing interior contains a late work by Veronese and the distinctive Throne of St Peter, a marble seat decorated with Moorish motifs and Koranic inscriptions, cut from an Arab *stele*. On the grassy *campo* beside the church is the patriarchal palace, converted into a barracks by Napoleon. Also on the square stands a tilting Renaissance belltower by Coducci.

Retracing one's steps through the nondescript suburbs leads back to the Napoleonic gardens and the site of the **Biennale ❼**. The Biennale is based in the **Giardini Pubblici**, gardens lined by paths leading to designer pavilions.

Map, page 202

"There are few more soothing places than a Venetian garden on a blazing summer morning."

— JAN MORRIS

BELOW: Guardi's "Festival of the Doge" depicts the Bucintoro (state barge) leaving the Lido.

Map,
page 202

XLV
Esposizione
Internazionale
d'Arte

*Poster advertising
the Venice Biennale*

BELOW: Terrapins in
the fountain, Via
Garibaldi.

About 40 countries are housed in these permanent pavilions, with space set aside for international exhibitions. The pastoral nature of the site makes a pleasing contrast to the slick modernism of the exhibits.

A number of pavilions have been built by famous architects, notably Josef Hoffman's Austrian pavilion (1934), Carlo Scarpa's Venezuelan pavilion (1954) and Alvar Aalto's Finnish creation (1956). The best spots are taken by the old world powers. According to art critic Waldemar Januszczak, distortions of national rivalries are alive and well: "The British pavilion stares across at the German"; yet while the British space is classically Palladian, the German building is "one of the few bits of full-blown Nazi architecture to survive outside Germany". The newest star is James Stirling's Book Pavilion (1994), facing the vast Italian pavilion. Clearly inspired by naval design and intended to echo the neighbouring Arsenale, this spacious glass and copper structure resembles an overgrown *vaporetto*.

On the waterfront, the Giardini-Biennale boat stop returns one to the San Marco area. Energetic walkers can follow the shoreline east through **Parco della Rimembranze** ❽ and the redeveloped island of **Sant'Elena**. The Austrian parade grounds have since been turned into sports fields while the medieval monastery and seamen's hospital have succumbed to urban sprawl.

Dating from the 1920s, these streets bear the names of famous battlefields of the First World War. The goal is the Gothic church of **Sant' Elena** ❾, with its restored belltower, cloisters and Renaissance portal. Afterwards, the Sant'Elena *vaporetto* ferries visitors back to the Lido or San Marco, offering superb views of the Doge's Palace, the Giudecca and San Giorgio Maggiore, framed by a constellation of minor islands. ❑

The Biennale

The Biennale has been described as Disneyland for adults: art-lovers want to play with everything at once and end up suffering from sensory overload. This glamorous forum for contemporary art is held from June to September in odd-numbered years. Sponsorship is always precarious and organisation fraught, but the Biennale remains a highlight in the international art calendar. The event is garish, sprawling and pretentious but also chic, challenging and commercially successful. There is a place for everything, from post-modernist lampshades and erotic photography to Armenian video installations, Romanian folk art and a 3D Japanese tea ceremony. As at Venice Carnival, the festival attracts eccentrics, including two bald Germans who always attend dressed as angels.

The Biennale was designed to give Venice a fresh identity as a lively cultural metropolis within the new Italian nation. It aimed to attract leading artists, boost tourism and introduce an international audience to the wonders of Venice. The Biennale was inaugurated in 1895 by King Umberto I and raised a furore because of Giacomo Grosso's Symbolist work depicting women draped lasciviously over a corpse.

The event has been controversial ever since. In 1910 a work by Picasso was rejected for being too scandalous; the great artist was only finally deemed acceptable in 1948. Nevertheless, in the early 1920s the Impressionists were well-received, as were Degas and Toulouse-Lautrec.

The Fascist period marked the lowest point of the Biennale, with Hitler declaring his "disgust" at the degeneracy of the art. Since World War II, however, the festival has paraded its avant-garde credentials. In 1948 the first post-war Biennale displayed works by Picasso, Klee, Schiele and Magritte as well as by the Metaphysical painters, Carrà, De Chirico and Giorgio Morandi. Here too, the Impressionists vied with Otto Dix and other German Expressionists banished by Nazism.

In 1964, an American artistic invasion and the advent of Pop Art marked another great turning point. Robert Rauschenberg received the major prize, despite protests by staid French Academicians.

In recent years, visitors have been suitably scandalised by an Israeli pavilion overrun by a flock of sheep, only outdone by an Italian slaughterhouse. The centennial Biennale in 1995 staged an impressive retrospective, juxtaposing the masters of the 20th century with lesser-known painters. Recent exhibitions have seen the triumphant return of American artists as well as the last major showing of Roy Lichtenstein, who died in 1997.

The Biennale is tied in with parallel events at the major galleries and at such curious exhibition spaces as a former leper colony, the salt warehouses on the Zattere and the Corderie, the old rope factory in the Arsenale. The unofficial fringe still acts as a prestigious springboard for struggling artists. The 1997 aesthetic agenda was as bizarre as ever: the best artist's prize went to a British sculpture of a rusty bath. To make full use of the Giardini pavilions, plans are afoot to create a Biennale just for architecture, which will take place in the intervening years. ❑

RIGHT: installation in the Japanese pavilion.

SAN POLO AND SANTA CROCE

Map,
page 214

*These left-bank districts, centred on the Rialto, are a warren
of alleys and markets which hide the great treasures of Bellini,
Titian and Tintoretto in the Frari and Scuola Grande di San Rocco*

San Polo and Santa Croce form adjoining districts (*sestieri*) curved into the
left bank of the Grand Canal. Together they encompass the bustling Rialto
market and a modest yet picturesque artisans' quarter towards the station.
The hub of the left bank is the Rialto, "the marketplace of the morning and
evening lands". Goethe's poetic description is fleshed out by writer Jan Morris,
who loved the Rialto's "smell of mud, incense, fish, age, filth and velvet".

The labyrinthine Rialto, with its network of dark alleys and tiny squares
(*campielli*), makes a sharp contrast to the more open spaces around Campo San
Polo. In theory this is *Venezia minore*, lesser-known Venice, yet humble is an
inappropriate description of an area that contains two of the city's greatest sights:
the Frari is a huge Franciscan church containing masterpieces by Titian and
Bellini while the Scuola Grande di San Rocco is a shrine to Tintoretto. Nor is
"minor" a fair summary of the stretch of the Grand Canal from the Rialto Bridge
to the station. The waterside is lined by historic warehouses and notable palaces,
including several Veneto-Byzantine gems. (*Best seen from the water, this section
is covered in the Grand Canal chapter, page 165*).

PRECEDING PAGES:
Rialto waterfront
LEFT: chatting by the
Rialto Bridge.
BELOW: "Venice's
kitchen and
back parlour".

The Rialto

"What's new on the Rialto?" was Antonio's cry in
Shakespeare's *The Merchant of Venice*. Gossip remains
a popular Venetian pastime in this curiously provincial
city and the **Rialto ❶** , with its market and mass of tiny
bars, is still a talking shop. To Venetians, the Rialto is
not restricted to the graceful bridge but embraces the
district curved around the middle bend of the Grand
Canal. The Rialto (derived from *rivo alto* or high bank)
also refers to the first settlement of central Venice and
became the capital from AD 814.

As the oldest district, the Rialto has the greatest number of Veneto-Byzantine palaces. From its earliest foundation, this was the powerhouse of the Venetian empire,
a crossroads between East and West. On a practical
level, it also acted as a commercial exchange and meeting place of wholesale and retail merchants. As such,
the Rialto is often described as "Venice's kitchen, office
and back parlour".

Even outbreaks of fire failed to crush the city's mercantile spirit. In the past, the Rialto was as prone to fire
as it is to flooding today. The fire of 1514 razed the
Rialto to the ground in six hours, sparing only the stone
church. However, the commercial district quickly
recovered and was rebuilt much as before. Thanks to
liberal laws and an entrepreneurial culture, the Rialto
was a cosmopolitan centre, home to a mixture of races
and a babble of tongues. The Venetians were middle-
men, making a profit from the sale of everything in this

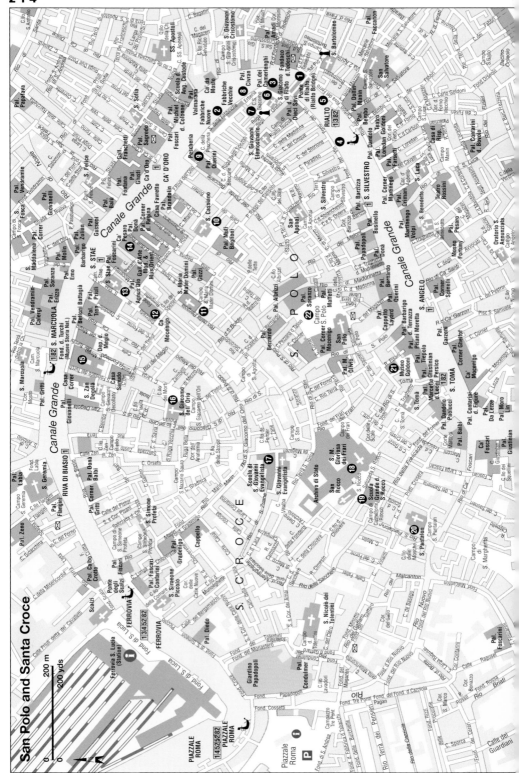

San Polo and Santa Croce

emporium. Long before Shakespeare's Shylock, the Venetians had a reputation for guile and business acumen. In this exotic marketplace, cargoes of spices and silks from the Levant were sold, along with Slav slaves. Here, northern Italian grain dealers and Flemish wool merchants rubbed shoulders with Jewish money-lenders, Arab spice traders and German metal traders, as well as with Florentine and Lombardic cloth merchants.

Map, page 214

Trading centre

The district was also home to a cluster of highly functional mercantile buildings that supervised trade and administered justice. From the 13th century onwards, various magistracies governed the Rialto commercial centre, granting leases or supervising fiscal, financial and legal affairs. Foremost amongst these state institutions were the **Fabbriche Nuove** and **Fabbriche Vecchie** ❷ (*see Grand Canal, page 175*), trade offices and tribunals, which stand between the two main Rialto markets. Another key civic building was the **Palazzo dei Camerlenghi** ❸ the former state treasury and debtors' prison, housed in a Renaissance hulk built of Istrian stone.

Also on the Grand Canal are the trading houses for German and Turkish merchants. Craftsmen were equally protected by the authorities, with many guilds located in the Rialto, including those for jewellers, woodcutters and goldsmiths.

The ancient market was also the hub of a foreign exchange and banking centre, with a cluster of private banks around the bridge. The Venetian *ducat* was a stable currency and the Rialto dominated international exchanges. Private banks flourished from the 12th century onwards, with a forerunner to the Banco di Giro, the earliest state deposit bank, opening in 1157. The *giro* took the form of

BELOW: "What's new on the Rialto?"

a written transfer from one account to another; no receipt was given since the bank register was considered an official record. At night, the money was moved to the Mint under an armed escort. With ready access to capital, the Rialto merchants funded fleets and made use of maritime insurance services and a commodity stock market.

The **Rialto Bridge** traditionally divides the city into two, with the right bank, the San Marco side, known as the *Rialto di quà* (this side) and the left bank known as the *Rialto di là* (that side). The Rialto Bridge spans the Grand Canal with a strong elegantly curved arch of marble. This single span bridge is lined with shops selling shoes, silk scarves and jewellery. Henry James appreciated the "small shops and booths that abound in Venetian character" but also felt "the communication of insect life".

The place for fish: sample "brodo di pesce", fish soup, flavoured with saffron.

The Rialto Bridge is merely the last in a series of bridges that began with simple pontoons and progressed to wooden bridges with a drawbridge section to allow the passage of tall ships. A new bridge was created in 1588–91 by Antonio da Ponte following the collapse of the previous one. Tradition has it that the greatest architects of the day, including Michelangelo and Palladio, competed for the commission but the aptly-named da Ponte was chosen. The result is a light, floating structure with shops nestling in the solid closed arches. From the bridge one can admire the majestic sweep of palaces and warehouses swinging away to la Volta del Canal, the great elbow-like bend in the Grand Canal.

BELOW: Antonio da Ponte's famous bridge.

The quayside

Henry James, who stayed in a palace nearby, admired "the old pink warehouses on the hot *fondamenta*". The Grand Canal palaces and warehouses are gener-

ally difficult to appreciate from the land but on this stretch the waterside is lined with *fondamenti* or *rive*, accessible quaysides. Here one can walk along both banks, weaving amongst the crowded terraces. The **Fondamenta del Vin ④**, where barrels of wine used to be unloaded, is now a quayside overrun by colourful restaurants and souvenir stalls. Facing it is **Riva del Ferro ⑤** where German barges unloaded iron (*ferro*). Their trading house, the Fondaco dei Tedeschi, was close by (*see page 175*). Also on the right bank is Riva del Carbon where coal merchants moored their barges.

San Giacomo di Rialto ⑥, the church nestling comfortably amongst the fruit and vegetable stalls, is linked to St James, the patron saint of goldsmiths and pilgrims. Both were much in evidence in the Rialto, even if the pilgrims were often in search of gold rather than God. Affectionately known as San Giacometto, this is reputedly the oldest church in Venice, founded in the 5th century but rebuilt in the 11th century.

Its most distinctive features, apart from the market bustle, are the Gothic portico, belltower and bold 24-hour clock. The 16th-century restoration respected the original domed Greek cross plan, the ancient Greek columns and Veneto-Byzantine capitals. The cramped interior is disappointing but enlivened by the presence of resting market traders and dishevelled customers.

Campo San Giacomo ⑦ preserves its mercantile atmosphere, an echo of Republican times when money-changers, bankers and insurance-brokers set up their tables under the church portico. The **Gobbo di Rialto**, the Hunchback of the Rialto, is a curious stooped figure supporting the steps opposite the church: it was on the adjoining pink podium that Republican laws were proclaimed, with the financial burden borne, literally and metaphorically, by this figure, a kind

Map, page 214

TIP

The Poste Vecie, in the Pescheria, is a fairly pricy fish restaurant and a Venetian institution approached by its own bridge from the fish market (tel: 721822, closed on Tuesday).

BELOW: detail of San Giacomo.

of Venetian everyman. Petty criminals were also chased through the streets from St Mark's to the Rialto and were only given sanctuary from the bloodthirsty crowds when they reached these steps.

Market life

Threading the labyrinthine alleys of the Rialto is an intoxicating experience, especially by morning. The alleys and quays bear witness to the Rialto's mercantile past, with names such as *olio* (oil), *vino* (wine), *spezie* (spices), *polli* (poultry) and *beccarie* (meat). Ruga degli Orefici, "Goldsmiths' Street", begins at the foot of the Rialto Bridge while Ruga degli Speziali, "Spice-traders' Street" is nearby. Today, smelly alleys often triumph over spicy perfumes but the market is rarely squalid and makes a refreshing change from the monumental Venice of St Mark's. Indeed, the market is one of the few places where Italian prevails, along with the guttural sing-song of Venetian dialect.

The Rialto remains a hive of commercial activity, with everything on sale between here and the Mercerie in the San Marco district. Ignore the tourist tat in favour of angora sweaters, supple shoes and foodstuffs galore, including pasta, cheese and salami shops. Ruga Vecchia di San Giovanni is home to some good food shops (which keep normal shop hours) and close to some typical bars.

The **Erberia** ❽ is the colourful fruit and vegetable market overlooking the Grand Canal. Brightly-painted boats from the Lagoon supply the main markets with fish and fresh vegetables. Close by is the watergate, the "tradesman's entrance" to the markets. Casanova (*see page 109*) spoke of the Erberia as a place for "innocent pleasure", even if latter-day foodies find sensuous pleasure in the profusion of medicinal herbs, flowers and fruit, not to mention the local aspara-

Visit the Erberia to see bunches of red peppers, succulent salad leaves and peachy borlotti beans. Apart from spring artichoke hearts ("castraura"), tasty vegetables are grown on the island of Sant' Erasmo or imported from mainland Veneto, just across the water.

BELOW: servicing the Venetian stomach.

gus, radicchio and baby artichokes. Elizabeth David, the celebrated English cookery writer, was entranced by "the light of a Venetian dawn so limpid and so still that it makes every separate vegetable and fruit and fish luminous with a life of its own".

The markets extend along the bank to the **Pescheria ❾**, the fish market, set in an arcaded Neo-Gothic hall by the quayside, a design inspired by Carpaccio's realistic paintings. Under the porticoes, fishermen set their catch on mountains of ice. Elizabeth David waxed lyrical about, "ordinary sole and great ugly skate striped with delicate lilac lights, the sardines shining like newly-minted silver coins". The sight of so much appetising food is an invitation to a lively lunch in a local *bacaro,* a Venetian wine bar. The adjoining Campo delle Beccarie, once a public abattoir, now contains market overspill and a lively bar.

Just over the canal lies **San Cassiano ❿** (*8am–noon, 5.30–7.30pm*), an eclectic but slightly oppressive church which suffered from 17th-century remodelling. It dates from the 9th century and retains a pair of marble pilasters from the period. The interior contains Tintoretto's eerie *Crucifixion* as well as pillars swathed in red and grey damask. The district between here and Campo San Polo enjoyed a dubious reputation, with bare-breasted courtesans leaning from their windows to attract clients. In 1608 the visitor Thomas Coryate was impressed by the profusion of prostitutes who "are said to open their quivers to every arrow".

From the former fleshpots, tiny alleys lead across the next canal to **Campo di Santa Maria Materdomini ⓫**, a harmonious square with a Gothic wellhead hemmed in by medieval palaces. Set back from the square is the equally beguiling Renaissance church of **Santa Maria Mater Domini** (*10am–noon, 3–5pm*). Often overlooked, it has a well-restored interior, a cool but distinctive

Map, page 214

There are gondola stands on Riva del Carbon (the Rialto) and at Santa Maria del Giglio.

BELOW LEFT: cargo of thirst quenchers. **BELOW:** The cheery, arcaded Erberia.

The Scuole

Dating back to the Middle Ages, the *scuole* were charitable lay associations close to the heart of Venetian life. Until the fall of the Republic, they acted as a state within a state, looking after members' spiritual, moral and material welfare. Anything could be provided, from a dowry or loan, to alms, free lodging and medical treatment.

Serving the citizen class, from lawyers and merchants to skilled artisans, the *scuole* were expected to support the State, play a part in processions and contribute to good causes. The richest foundations even recruited and financed military expeditions. For the merchant class, excluded from government, this was an opportunity to show their civic pride and communal spirit.

In fact, these associations were the main focus of social life for citizens beneath the patrician class. In a regimented and rather claustrophobic society, the *scuole* also served as a useful safety-valve.

While there were great distinctions between the prestigious *scuole grandi* and the humble *scuole minori*, they were essentially democratic, with rich and poor able to join at different rates of subscription. Four of the *scuole grandi*, the major institutions, originated as flagellant societies in the 13th century. While the *scuole grandi* were more overtly religious, all the *scuole* were devotional associations: they prayed together and performed charitable works in the name of the patron saint. Such confraternities appealed to the Venetians' puritanical streak as well as to their fondness for self-government. The *scuole* promoted pious living and forbade blasphemy, adultery, gambling, "frequenting taverns and lewd company".

The *scuole grandi* possessed great wealth and prestige and played a leading role in the ceremonial life of the city. Apart from San Rocco, these include the Scuole di San Giovanni Evangelista, I Carmini, San Marco and Santa Maria della Carita, now home to the Accademia gallery. There were also associations for foreign communities, such as the Scuola di San Giorgio degli Schiavoni, intended for workers from Dalmatia, present-day Croatia. All *scuole* wished to glorify their patron saint and themselves by employing the great artists who had decorated the Doge's Palace. Corporate funds were lavished on the interiors of meeting-houses, of which the grandest is San Rocco. Set on two floors and linked by a magnificent staircase, a typical headquarters had halls decorated by the finest artists of the age, rich in narrative scenes and in dazzling processions.

By the 18th century there were almost 500 confraternities. Although Napoleon sacked their headquarters and disbanded the confraternities themselves in 1806, several have since been revived and still more former meeting houses are now open to the public. The *scuole* remain highly distinctive, whether used as living confraternities, permanent museums or occasional concert halls. One has become a school sports hall, and the Scuola Grande di San Marco, one of the greatest, is currently home to the city hospital, thus still serving the community in the broadest sense. ❏

LEFT: Lombardi's portal to Scuola Grande di San Giovanni degli Evangelisti.

atmosphere enhanced by clean Roman lines, a Byzantine cube shape and Baroque cornices. There are fine 16th-century paintings, including a Tintoretto.

From here, Calle del Spezier leads across the next canal north to the patrician palace of **Ca' Mocenigo** ⓬ *(10am–4pm, closed Monday)*. The museum is decorated in 18th-century style, with rich furnishings and period fabrics. The palace is linked to one of the greatest Dogal families and to other Mocenigo homes on the Grand Canal. The palace was so well-preserved that, after Alvise Mocenigo bequeathed it to the city in 1954, it became a fitting showcase of gracious 18th-century living. The palace, lavishly decorated with frescoed ceilings, antiques and Murano glass chandeliers, houses a collection of costumes and precious fabrics. A stone's throw from the palace is the church of **San Stae** ⓭ *(8am–noon, 3–6pm)* overlooking the Grand Canal. The design is closer to Palladian than Baroque, with Corinthian columns set on high plinths.

Just east of the church is **Ca' Pesaro** ⓮, a palace housing museums of modern and oriental art *(see page 178)*. To the west, also on the Grand Canal, lies the **Fondaco dei Turchi** ⓯, one of the greatest of the city's merchant's warehouses, now home to the Natural History Museum *(see page180)*.

Behind the Fondaco, Fondamenta del Megio leads to the church of **San Giacomo dell'Orio** ⓰ *(8am–noon, 5–7.30pm)*, tucked into a corner of the square of the same name. Although slightly off the beaten track, this charming parish church conveys an inviting Romanesque atmosphere lit by diffuse light. The coherence is particularly remarkable given the eclectic nature of the church.

Although founded in the 9th century, the church building spans many centuries. Behind the pulpit and in the right transept are several Byzantine capitals raided from Constantinople, including one made of greenish Greek marble. The poet Gabriele d'Annunzio likened it to "the fossilised compression of an immense verdant forest". Architectural eclecticism is apparent in the Veneto-Byzantine belltower and columns, wooden Gothic arches and Renaissance apses; the *pièce de résistance* is the Gothic ship's keel roof. The finest artworks are a rare 14th-century wooden Tuscan crucifix and, in the New Sacristy, a Veronese ceiling. A stroll round the building reveals the characteristic bulbous absides.

Labyrinthine quarter

The church is part of a labyrinthine quarter of narrow *calli* and covered passageways (*sottoporteghi*). A short but confusing stroll south leads to the home of one of the surviving *scuole* or powerful lay confraternities. The **Scuola di San Giovanni Evangelista** ⓱ *(Monday 4–6pm by prior appointment, tel: 713498)* still serves its original purpose and, while difficult to gain access to, is worth seeing from outside. Ruskin readily admired this architectural gem, which dates from the 14th century. The distinctive Renaissance marble portal and courtyard is watched over by an eagle, the symbol of St John, the confraternity's patron saint. The interior is graced by a monumental staircase, a barrel-vaulted, double-ramp affair attributed to the great Coducci. Most of the paintings that once adorned the oratory are now in the Accademia *(see page 259)*. Opposite is the much 15th-century church of San Giovanni Evangelista.

Map, page 214

TIP

Avoid the ubiquitous "tourist menus" and search out the authentic Antica Bessetta (Salizzada Zusto, near San Giacomo dell'Orio), a fairly pricey temple of home cooking (tel: 721687, closed on Tuesday and Wednesday).

BELOW: painting from the 18th century in San Stae.

The Frari, mother church of the Venetian Franciscans.

BELOW: Titian's "Assumption" in the Frari.

From here, Calle del Magazzen leads to the greatest church on the left bank, the **Frari ⓲**, officially known as Santa Maria Gloriosa dei Frari (*weekdays 9am–noon, 2.30–6pm; weekends 3–6pm*: the route is signposted from San Tomà *vaporetto* stop, line 1 or 82). Rivalled only by San Giovanni e Paolo, this is the largest and greatest of all the Venetian Gothic churches. The hulking Franciscan complex, founded in the 13th century, was rebuilt in the 14th and 15th centuries. The adjoining monastic cloisters house the state archives and 1,000 years of Venetian history. Outside and in, the bare brick church is virtually devoid of decoration. The writer Jan Morris likens it to "a stooping high-browed monk, intellectual and meditative". Such simplicity lies in the strictness of Franciscan building rules: poverty was the guiding principle of the great mendicant orders.

Only the three Gothic turrets crowned with pointed gables act as a reminder of the richness of Venetian architecture. Yet inside, even the restricted colour range is used to great effect, with red-brick walls relieved by creamy Istrian stone, colours repeated in the red and white marble floor.

The barn-like interior is a stark, spare framework for the artwork, a pantheon of Venetian glories. The choir chapels are lined with tombs of the Doges, including the monument to Doge Francesco Foscari, deposed in 1457. The side chapels display glittering, conservative works by members of the Vivarini family.

The nave is dominated by a Gothic choir screen and lovely choir stalls, the only such ensemble to survive in Venice. The high altar beyond is the focal point of the Frari, a space illuminated by Titian's *Assumption*, his masterpiece, flanked by Dogal tombs. His other great work, the *Pesaro Altarpiece*, lies in the north aisle of the nave. Beside it is the *Pesaro Monument* to Doge Giovanni Pesaro (1658), currently being restored. This funerary piece honours the patrician

TITIAN

Titian was the supreme artist. The Frari contains two of his masterpieces, including the *Assumption*, a work whose revolutionary nature caused it to be rejected by the Friars; when they relented, the work made Titian's international reputation. The altar is dominated by this vibrant and eye-catching work, painted between 1516 and 1518. The Virgin floats heavenwards on a wreath of clouds borne aloft by cherubic angels. Unlike his rivals, Titian could make his illusionistic work command attention from afar. Vibrant colours helped: the counterpoint of the golden sky against the glowing red of the Virgin's robes. Titian aligned the work exactly with the opening of the rood screen so that one's eye is drawn through the Gothic choir towards this magnificent altarpiece.

The *Pesaro Altarpiece* depicts members of the Pesaro family, Titian's patrons, with the steady gaze of the young heir to the family fortune looking out towards us. Titian was a shrewd businessman who flattered his many patrons. This is a Venetian *sacra conversazione* with a difference: worldliness. For the first time, the portraits of a patron and his family were made part of a devotional painting, thus breaking the strict division that had previously existed between the sacred and the secular worlds.

dynasty who were once Titian's chief patrons. Ruskin disliked the Baroque in general and this sculpture in particular, decrying it as "a huge accumulation of theatrical scenery in marble… [its] negro caryatids grinning and horrible".

Titian's bombastic tomb, erected almost three centuries after his death, is set in the right-hand (south) aisle, close to the main portal. Directly opposite is the mausoleum of the Neo-Classical sculptor Canova, who died in Venice in 1822. Canova designed this as Titian's tomb but it became a monument to himself. Canova's sinister open-doored pyramid contains the sculptor's heart; the tomb feels cold and even heartless. The querulous Ruskin dismissed it as "ridiculous in conception, null and void to the uttermost in invention and feeling".

To the right of the high altar lies the entrance to the Pesaro family chapel, which has always served as the sacristy. The space is dominated by Bellini's altarpiece, a radiant *Madonna and Child*. Henry James adored the triptych: "It is as solemn as it is gorgeous as it is simple as it is deep". Also delightful is an early 14th-century Byzantine-style *Madonna* by Paolo Veneziano . The writer Ian Littlewood recommends seeing the church in the evening when "the smoking candles and the softness of the light offer the giddy experience of slipping from one world to another".

The Scuola Grande di San Rocco

The apse of the Frari abuts Campo San Rocco, home to the **Scuola Grande di San Rocco** ⓭ (*9am–5.30pm*), one of the greatest city sights. San Rocco is the grandest of the *scuole* or charitable lay confraternities. The society is dedicated to St Roch, the French saint of plague victims, who so impressed the Venetians that they stole his relics and canonised him. The confraternity's mission was the relief of the sick, a noble aim that soon became conflated with the prestige and social standing of the *scuola*. The early 16th-century building is also a shrine to Tintoretto, the great Mannerist painter, whose pictorial cycle adorns the walls. (*See The Tintoretto Trail, page 242*). In the evening, this splendid stage acts as a backdrop for Baroque recitals. Visitors are supplied with a relatively clear plan of the paintings in various languages. Hand-held mirrors are also provided to help one view the ceiling paintings; even so, most visitors will find that they suffer vertigo and sensory overload.

Tintoretto won the competition to decorate the interior, clinched by his cunning submission of a perfectly completed panel rather than the requested cartoon. The painter's overpowering Biblical scenes, executed between 1564–87, provoke strong responses. Henry James found "the air thick with genius" yet palpably human: "It is not immortality that we breathe at San Rocco but conscious, reluctant mortality".

New Testament scenes are displayed in the Sala Inferiore, the Ground Floor Hall, including the *Annunciation*, a dramatic chiaroscuro composition. Such works show the painter's profound Biblical knowledge and manipulation of Mannerist iconography. Yet, according to art historian Bernard Berenson, "the poetry which quickens most of his works is almost entirely a matter of light and colour".

A gilded staircase leads to the Sala Grande, the Great

Map, page 214

TIP

Concerts are often performed in churches and confraternities, including the Frari, San Rocco, La Pietà, San Stae and the Ospedaletto.

BELOW: Titian's "Pesaro Altarpiece".

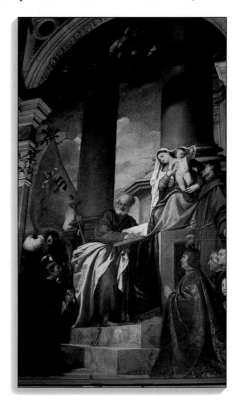

Upper Hall, and the Sala dell'Albergo, the smaller assembly room. This upper floor is framed by an inlaid marble floor and by surfaces studded with one of the finest painting cycles imaginable. Tintoretto's genius is revealed in these dynamic orchestrations of colour and light, works marked by drama and strong composition. Even the artist's faults, from a gaudy palette to the strenuous posturing of his figures, are a product of his visionary imagination, restless style and volatile changes of mood. The Sala Grande uses telling Biblical scenes to accentuate the confraternity's mission to heal. Stagily set on easels by the altar are several great paintings, notably Tiepolo's *Abraham and the Angels* and Titian's poetic *Annunciation*, matched by his *Christ Carrying the Cross*, previously attributed to Giorgione. The Sala dell'Albergo contains allegories linked to the society's patron saint, including *St Roch in Glory*, the ceiling panel that won Tintoretto the entire commission. Facing it is the *Crucifixion*, both a vast masterpiece with a charged atmosphere and a poignant drama.

San Rocco, temple to Tintoretto.

Henry James contrasted the "portentous solemnity" of the paintings with "the bright light of the campo, the orange-vendors and gondolas". The orange-vendors have gone, but there are enough bars nearby to restore one's spirits.

San Rocco and San Pantaleone

The church of **San Rocco** (*7.30am–noon, 2–4pm*) is tucked into the tiny campo of the same name. Sadly, after the Scuola di San Rocco, the church cannot fail to be an anticlimax. The late 15th-century building was remodelled in 1725 and has a Classical facade. The gloomy interior is lined with works by Tintoretto and Pordenone, another major Mannerist artist. On the right, *The Pool of Purification* is a dramatic Tintoretto. However, most works suffer from poor lighting

BELOW: fishy lagoon fare.

BACARI: TRADITIONAL BARS

There are plenty of good local places to eat in this area. For a simple lunch, snack or drink, try Da Pinto (Campo delle Beccarie, tel: 522 4599), one of many rough and ready places on the Rialto. A window overlooks Campo della Pescheria allowing traders to have an *ombretta* (glass of wine) without coming in. This is the place for *ciccheti*, snacks such as salami, *polpettine* (meat balls) and cheese or *baccalà mantecato* (cod paste) and fried fish (*see Cuisine, page 85*). Antica Bessetta (Salizzada di Ca' Giusto 1395, tel: 523687, closed Tuesday and Wednesday) lies just north of San Giacomo dell'Orio. This is a deceptively rustic Venetian *trattoria* where standards (and prices) are suitably high. Da Fiore (Calle del Scaleter 2202a, tel: 721308, closed Sunday and Monday) lies off Campo San Polo and is a stylish restaurant popular with Venetians and foreigners.

The Rialto is the ideal place to indulge in a Venetian bar crawl, a *giro di ombre* (*see Café Society, page 88*). Start at the Do Mori bar (Calle de Do Mori, 9am–1pm, 5–8pm, closed Wednesday) tucked just off Ruga Vecchia di San Giovanni. Then move on to Do Spade which lies at the end of the alley (Sottoportego delle do Spade, 9am–2pm, 5–11pm).

and indifferent restoration. From here, follow Calle Fianco della Scuola across the next canal south to **Campo San Pantalon**, an everyday square lined with crumbling palaces.

Set on this canalside *campo* is the church of **San Pantalon** ❷ *(3.30–5.30pm, closed Saturday)*. San Pantalon (or Pantaleone) is dedicated to an obscure saint, who was both Emperor Diocletian's doctor and a miraculous healer. The church follows common Venetian practice, whereby the interiors, with the exception of St Mark's or Palladian gems, are often finer than the exteriors. The bare, unfinished 17th-century facade gives no indication of the splendours within. This is one of most visually striking churches in Venice, a *tour de force* of perspective which projects the nave high into the sky.

The Baroque ceiling paintings by Fumiani (1650–1710) depict *The Martyrdom and Glory of St Pantalon*. Unlike in San Rocco, there is no need for mirrors since this majestic work was intended to be viewed from one single perspective, close to the entrance. This may be the largest painting on canvas ever completed, created on 60 panels and hoisted into place. The illusionistic ascent into heaven is populated by boldly foreshortened figures clambering, floating or ascending. On completion of the ceiling, the artist supposedly stood back to admire his work before slipping off the scaffolding to his death.

Veronese's last work, *The Miracle of St Pantalon,* is in a side chapel on the right, while one on the left houses several Byzantine-style paintings, including a delightful Paolo Veneziano *Madonna and Child* (1333). For a closer look, ask the sacristan to open the metal gate.

From here, cross the Rio Foscari canal, currently being cleaned, to explore the Dorsoduro district. Alternatively, if you are feeling a touch claustrophobic

Map, page 214

"What a funny old city this Queen of the Adriatic is! Narrow streets, vast, gloomy marble palaces, black with the corroding damp of centuries and all partly submerged".

– MARK TWAIN

BELOW: famously dry Venetian biscuits.

Map, page 214

and in need of a burst of everyday Venetian life, head towards spacious **Campo San Polo**, via **Campo San Tomà**. (San Tomà *vaporetto* stop is nearby, with lines 1 or 82 returning to the Rialto in one direction and San Marco in the other). On the far side of Rio San Tomà is the **Museo Goldoni ㉑** (closed for restoration) the birthplace of Goldoni, the 18th-century Venetian dramatist. Even if you are indifferent to the playwright, glance at the charming courtyard with its carved well-head and Gothic staircase. Inside is a collection of Goldoni memorabilia and a centre for theatre studies.

Campo San Polo ㉒, lying just across the canal of the same name, is the heart of a picturesque district. After San Marco, it is the largest Venetian square and one of the most appealing. Historically, this amphitheatre of a square was the scene of bull-baiting, tournaments and processions, even a great "bonfire of the vanities" in 1450. Still today it is a popular venue for film screenings or carnival balls. Like Campo Santa Margherita, it is a classic Venetian space. At different times of day, the workaday square becomes an impromptu football pitch or mother-and-toddlers' meeting place; in the evening, students gather on the benches or meet at the neighbourhood *birreria*. As the heart of the San Polo district, the square is home to university, school and financial buildings, including the School of Oriental Studies (at No. 2169).

BELOW: Ponte del Purgatorio by the Arsenal.
RIGHT: Backwater by Santa Maria Mater Domini.

The lofty, rusticated **Palazzo Corner Mocenigo** (No. 2128) is now the headquarters of the Guardia di Finanza, the financial police. However, in the past it was noted for having two doors so that the dead and the living would never pass through the same door. The Gothic **Palazzo Soranzo** (No. 2169–70), at the eastern end of the campo, was where Casanova's main patron lived. Here the humble violinist was adopted by an ailing senator. It is curious to think that this palace, along with the neighbouring Baroque **Palazzo Maffetti** (No. 1957), bordered the canal until it became *rio terrà* (filled-in land) in the 18th century.

In the south-west corner is the church of **San Polo** (*8am–noon, 3.30pm–6.30pm*), hemmed in by houses. The church dates from the 9th century but is essentially Gothic, despite a clumsy 19th-century restoration. Highlights include a Gothic rose window and ship's keel roof, as well as Tintoretto's *Assumption and Last Supper* and Tiepolo's *Apparition of the Virgin*. An early 17th-century plaque on the outside of the church forbids games, shopping and swearing "on pain of prison, the galleys or exile" but Venetians, then as now, paid little heed to limitations on their pleasures.

Heading home

From here, walk back to the familiar landmark of the Rialto Bridge or catch the line 1 *vaporetto* from San Silvestro. Alternatively, linger for a drink in this friendly neighbourhood. Calle della Madonetta is a charming alley that runs over bridges and under buildings towards the Rialto. This is one of several adjoining streets to boast overhanging roofs, a rarity in Venice.

The area comes alive in the early evening when locals stroll down Calle della Rughetta in search of fine foodstuffs (Aliani, in Ruga Vecchia, is a superb delicatessen and cheese shop). For dining, consider Alla Rivetta, a canalside *trattoria* (*see page 320 for details*). ❑

QUI ERANO LE CASE OVE NACQUE NEL 1417

PIETRO BARBO PATRIZIO VENETO

DAL 1464 AL 1471 SOMMO PONTEFICE

CON IL NOME GLORIOSO DI

PAOLO II°

"PACIS ITALICAE FUNDATOR"

NEL V° CENTENARIO DELLA MORTE

L'AZIENDA AUTONOMA SOGGIORNO E TURISMO

CANNAREGIO

The most northerly district, around the railway station, was once the most fashionable in Venice, though it's hard to believe it today. It was also the site of the world's first Jewish ghetto

Map, page 232

Théophile Gautier, the sensitive French poet, wrote: "From alley to alley we had got deep into Cannaregio, into a Venice quite different from the pretty city of watercolours." Far from wanting to escape from this run-down quarter, he lapped up the deserted squares, desolate wharves and green, sluggish canals. Cannaregio is a district for those who have tired of the monumental sights around San Marco. Walks in the melancholic backwaters at the edge of the city trace a landscape of peeling facades and humble workshops, broad canals and wind-buffeted quays; the sense of abandon creates a poetic atmosphere conducive to wistfulness.

The district's name comes from *canne*, meaning reeds, indicating Cannaregio's marshy origins. Cannaregio is the most densely populated district and the closest both to the railway station and to the mainland. Before the advent of the causeway, the Canale di Cannaregio was the main entry point to Venice; it is therefore fitting that the district remains a bridge between Venice and the mainland, between the historic city and modernity. This is an ancient quarter, often scorned by the snobbish in favour of the more stylish Dorsoduro. Certainly, the district's working-class credentials are beyond dispute. Ironically, this was once one of the city's most fashionable spots, dotted with foreign embassies and palatial gardens sloping down to the lagoon. The palaces may be faded but Cannaregio remains both a retreat for *cognoscenti* and the last bastion for working-class Venetians who have not moved to the Mestre mainland.

This is also the most northerly *sestiere*, bounded by the railway station in the west, by the windswept expanses of the northern quays, and by the upper sweep of the Grand Canal. Within this great arc are subtly different districts, from the world's oldest ghetto, in eastern Cannaregio, to the quaint, remote quarter around Madonna dell'Orto. The northern quays face the islands and are characterised by wide, melancholy, slightly menacing canals. By contrast, the Grand Canal district contains palaces as fine as any in Venice. Just inland, Strada Nuova is a bustling shopping district linking the station with historic Venice.

PRECEDING PAGES: birthplace of Pope Paul II Barbo in the 15th century. **LEFT:** washing day in Cannaregio. **BELOW:** The Moor, Campo dei Mori.

Washing and balconies

Cannaregio has a distinctly neighbourhood feel, with every parish possessing its own church and *campo*. Despite daunting post-war tenements on the fringes of the district, Cannaregio is alive with activity, with the space for chattering children and dozing cats. For visitors, there are glimpses of everyday life on secluded balconies or through half-shuttered blinds. Elderly Venetians chat to their neighbours, leaning out of windows hung with washing. The tangle of alleys reveals the odd *bottega* selling wood carvings, earthy, hole-in-

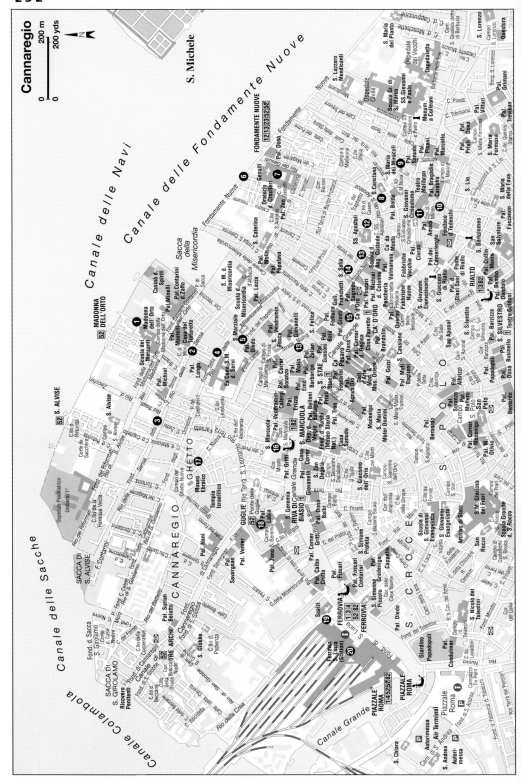

the-wall bars, and even *alimentari,* ordinary food shops which you will search for in vain in many more fashionable parts of Venice, where you can often get *vino sfuso* (draught wine). Far away from San Marco, a Sunday in Cannaregio is still spent streaming from church to a *trattoria* for lunch.

The northern quays

Cannaregio has a cluster of different neighbourhoods rather than an obvious heart. The northernmost tip, centred on the church of Madonna dell'Orto, is one of the most curious quarters. (Despite its sense of remoteness, the district is easily reached by *vaporetto* 52 from the San Zaccaria stop near San Marco.) Here parallel *fondamente* (quaysides) frame wide *rii* (canals) and are criss-crossed by *calli,* smaller canals. The three major canals (*rii*) were created from the Cannaregio marshes in medieval times, with Rio della Sensa arguably the most atmospheric. These faintly mournful waterways are flanked by houses and neglected palaces faintly reminiscent of Amsterdam, a great contrast to the tall tenements of the Ghetto further west. In the 1890s, the de Goncourt brothers were moved to describe these quays as "a whole district in decay, like an antique sculpture eaten away by rain and sun".

A miracle-working statue.

Madonna dell'Orto ❶ *(9.30am–noon, 3.30–5.30pm),* set on a harmonious square of herringbone design, is named after a miracle-working statue of the Madonna found in a nearby vegetable garden (*orto*). The three-part composition of the facade, enlivened by a frieze of garlands, is reminiscent of the Frari, albeit on a smaller scale. The quirky *campanile* is topped by an onion-shaped cupola; this is the first belltower to greet visitors as they speed across the lagoon from the airport. Often bathed in a warm light, the church is a masterpiece of Venetian Gothic. The austere, brick-faced interior, graced by Greek marble columns and a fine wooden ceiling, was well-restored by the British Venice in Peril Fund after the 1966 floods.

BELOW: Moorish statue on Tintoretto's House.

The church also makes a good starting point for exploring Tintoretto's temperamental genius: the painter lived nearby and this, his parish church, is decorated with works he created *in situ* (*see page 242*). His tender *Presentation of the Virgin* (1551) graces the Mauro Chapel, as does the over-restored statue of the "miraculous" Madonna. Two other Tintorettos dominate the chancel. The aesthete John Ruskin raved about *The Last Judgment,* seeing "the river of the wrath of God, roaring down into the gulf where the world has melted"; his new bride ran out of the church, traumatised by "a death's head crowned with leaves". A memorial bust of the artist watches over his grave in a side chapel.

Tintoretto aside, the church is a treasury of Venetian painting from the 15th to 17th centuries, despite the theft of a Bellini altarpiece, tragically stolen for the third time in 1993.

Adjoining the church is **Scuola dei Mercanti**, the 16th-century merchants' guild and confraternity. Unfortunately, nothing remains of the fine art treasures inside, which were ransacked by Napoleon Bonaparte. Before crossing the bridge over **Rio Madonna dell'Orto** to **Campo dei Mori** ❷, stand on the quayside and glance across at the Gothic **Palazzo Mastelli** opposite. To the

Map, page 232

Wrought-iron railings close to the Ghetto.

right of the filigree balcony is a charming relief of a laden camel, lending the palace an eastern flavour. The owners were Levantine merchants whose origins are alluded to in the worn Romanesque reliefs of turbaned Moors on the **Campo dei Mori** facade. The *campo* conceivably derives its Moorish name from the Fondaco degli Arabi, the Arab trading centre that once stood on the same spot.

Just beyond the *campo* is Tintoretto's house, marked by a plaque and bas-relief of the painter.

Quayside atmosphere

For a fine view, follow **Fondamenta della Sensa ❸** to **Corte Vecchia** and **Ponte di Sacca**. This bridge looks out over the northern lagoon and San Michele, island of the dead (*see page 288*). At twilight, especially when the boundary lights of the waterways are lit, this is the place for poignant thoughts. Another atmospheric spot is **Campo d'Abbazia** at the end of **Rio della Sensa**. Here, the sculpted facade of the former confraternity of the **Scuola della Misericordia** overlooks a quaint well-head and a tiled, herringbone-style square.

The quaysides can feel rather exposed but, if the weather is bleak, you can retreat to one of several bars and inns nearby, sampling the Syrian ambiance of **Barada** (2754 Fondamenta degli Ormesini, *evenings only, closed Sunday*) or the homeliness of **Bentigodi** (1423 Calleselle, *10am–3pm, 6–11pm, closed Sunday*). **Al Paradiso Perduto** (2540 Fondamenta della Misericordia, *evenings only, closed Wednesday*) is a typical inn offering filling plates of pasta, along with live music and occasional poetry readings.

Fondamenta della Misericordia ❹ and **Fondamenta degli Ormesini** are the next quaysides south of Fondamenta della Sensa. This bustling section of

BELOW: mournful Canale di Cannaregio.

quays overlooks **Rio della Misericordia**, with the middle section in particular lined by inns, bars and neighbourhood shops. Fondamenta della Misericordia is bordered by severe 17th-century palaces and the church of **San Marziale ❺** *(3–6pm; Sunday 9.30–11am)*, essentially a Baroque church built on medieval foundations. The austere exterior makes a sharp contrast to the boldly ornamented interior. Baroque altars and gilded cornices compete with the gaudy ceiling created by Sebastiano Ricci (1659–1734).

From here, head south to bustling **Strada Nuova** if the solitude of certain quaysides has seeped into your bones. Alternatively, to visit a Baroque church or the islands, stroll to **Fondamente Nuove ❻**, the quays bordering the northern lagoon. (Walk east along Fondamenta della Misericordia, crossing the bridge over the canal of the same name, then follow Calle della Rachetta to the waterfront.) The windswept Fondamente Nuove, or New Quays, were actually created in the 1580s. Before that time, this now rather desolate stretch was a desirable residential district, with summer palaces and well-tended gardens lapped by the lagoon waters.

Fondamente Nuove is the main stage for ferries to the islands, with the fastest journey times, as well as services to San Marco in the opposite direction. The quayside offers a smattering of basic bars, as well as a plaque marking Titian's home and the **Palazzo Donà delle Rose,** at 5038, a severe 17th-century palace that still belongs to the family that built it. Although the quays can seem inhospitable, especially in winter, the stirring lagoon views, encompassing the cemetery island of San Michele, count for much. On the proverbially clear day, the snowy Dolomite peaks are visible, seemingly suspended over the apparently featureless great plain of the Veneto.

Map, page 232

A "fondamenta" is a quayside beside a canal (often known as a "rio"). To familiarise yourself with Venetian place names, see page 133.

BELOW LEFT: on Salizzada San Giustina.
BELOW: The Scuola della Misericordia.

Gesuiti church

The **Gesuiti** church ❼ *(8am-noon, 5–7pm)* is often confused with the Gesuati, the other major Jesuit foundation, set in Dorsoduro district. The Jesuits were never popular in Venice, a city which put patriotism before the Papacy and famously declared: "Venetians first and Christians second". After their banishment was revoked, the Jesuits returned to Venice and, in 1715, started to rebuild this church on the site of its medieval predecessor. The Gesuiti is still run by the Order and is the seat of the American Jesuit University.

Set into a line of severe houses, the Baroque, angel-bedecked facade reveals an exuberant interior. This is a typical Roman Jesuit church, with a broad nave flanked by deep chapels and surmounted by a central dome. Gaudy stuccoes and frescoes set the tone for an interior decorator's delight, from the vaulted and domed ceiling to the lavish altars, including one encrusted with lapis-lazuli. The overwhelming impression is of a wedding cake swathed in green and white damask, even if it is marble masquerading as drapery. Théophile Gautier, the French poet, felt that the decor made "the chapel of the Holy Virgin look like a chorus girl's boudoir". The finest works of art are Titian's *Martyrdom of St Lawrence* and Tintoretto's *Assumption of the Virgin*. This was the painting that most inspired Tiepolo. The flashes of lightning, the daring, darting angels and the sheer creative passion had a lasting effect on the great Rococo artist.

Facing the Gesuiti is the **Oratorio dei Crociferi**, dedicated to the mendicant order of Crutched Friars. Once associated with the Crusades, the oratory and hospice were remodelled in the 16th century and later passed into Jesuit control. The interior has a subtle pictorial cycle by Palma il Giovane (1548–1628). Outside, **Campo dei Gesuiti** is dotted with houses associated with the guilds; on

Palaces were not permitted to have projecting eaves which might cast a shadow on the alleys below.

BELOW: arcade on the atmospheric Rio della Sensa.

the walls are symbols or inscriptions referring to coopers, tailors and weavers. Nearby is **Palazzo Zen**, a 16th-century palace with an eastern influence.

If you do not want to visit the islands (*see page 267*), leave the bleak quaysides of the Fondamente Nuove for commercial Cannaregio. From Campo dei Gesuiti, cross **Rio di Santa Caterina** and head south through a network of alleys, following signs for the Rialto. Well before the Rialto bridge, take **Calle Malvasia** across the canal of **Rio dei Santi Apostoli** to the church of **San Canciano ❽** (*8am–noon, 5.30–7.30pm*). Although of ancient foundation, it is decorated in bold Baroque style.

Just south, by the meeting of several canals, the lovely church of **Santa Maria dei Miracoli ❾** rises sheer from the water, marooned like a marble siren awaiting the call of the sea or the embrace of a foolish sailor. No wonder the church is a favourite with Venetian brides. Perfect proportions and seductive charm make this a Renaissance miracle in miniature, gleaming with a soft marble sheen. Its romantic setting invites such clichés as "Renaissance jewel box", an image for once justified. The church is often compared with Ca' Dario (*see page 176*), a palace also created by the Lombardi family of master-builders.

Certainly, this dazzling display of pastel marble is a far cry from the prosaic Venetian brick facade. Even Ruskin, no fan of the Renaissance, was forced to admit the Miracoli to be "the best possible example of a bad style". The interior boasts a *barco*, a nuns' choir gallery, and a barrel-vaulted and coffered ceiling, with the presbytery surmounted by a starry dome. The surfaces present a vision of pale pinks and silvery greys, and pilasters adorned with interlaced flowers, mythical creatures and cavorting mermaids. Visitors would be bedazzled by the cumulative effect of this bridal church, if they were able to get in.

Map, page 232

Santa Maria dei Miracoli looms above a moat-like canal.

BELOW: facade of Santa Maria dei Miracoli.

The belltower of Santi Apostoli, a familiar landmark.

Sadly, a flawed earlier restoration means that the Miracoli is closed for further analysis by an American-funded rescue programme.

Just south, sandwiched between the canals of **Rio Giovanni Crisostomo** and **Rio dei Tedeschi**, lie Marco Polo's former home and an historic church. **Corte del Milion ❿** is a quaint courtyard where the great explorer reputedly lived. While Marco Polo's house burnt down in 1596, the well-head remains, as does a courtyard and arch decorated by Veneto-Byzantine friezes.

On an adjoining square lies the church of **San Giovanni Crisostomo ⓫** *(8.30am–noon, 3.30–5.30pm)*. Although founded in the 11th century, this terracotta-coloured church owes more to the Renaissance. As the last work of Coducci, it is reminiscent of his other Venetian churches, with the tripartite facade echoing San Zaccaria. The dome, supported by pillars and arches, is a model of classical coherence. The restrained marble interior contains a delightful Bellini altarpiece (1515), possibly his last work. The surrounding maze of streets was the 17th-century preserve of "hired slaves, bravoes, common stabbers, nose-slitters and alley-lurking villains". Today, however, any aspiring nose-slitter probably finds selling souvenirs to tourists more profitable.

Shopping district

Cannaregio's main shopping district begins at **Campo Santi Apostoli ⓬**, across the canal of the same name. The sombre air of the church of **Santi Apostoli** *(8–11.30am, 5–7pm)* is offset by the liveliness of the surrounding square. The 16th-century church is built on ancient foundations but, apart from a prominent belltower, is architecturally undistinguished. However, this is the place to appreciate Tiepolo's *Communion of St Lucy*, if the work is not on loan to a foreign

BELOW: well-head on Campo dei Mori.

exhibition. The domed Corner Chapel, designed for the family of the Queen of Cyprus, is a product of the Renaissance restoration of the church. Queen Caterina Corner herself survived two burials, the first one here. The Corner dynasty also possessed numerous palaces on the Grand Canal.

Campo Santi Apostoli marks the beginning of the **Strada Nuova** ⓭, which forms the main thoroughfare to the station, undergoing several name changes along the route. Created under Austrian rule in the 1860s, the street represents the first piece of modern town planning in Venice. The Strada Nuova was carved through an ancient quarter, causing Campo Santa Sofia to be severed from its church. Running roughly parallel to the Grand Canal, the street offers tempting *bacari*, typical bars and food shops displaying juicy hams and home-made pasta. Side streets close to the **Campo Santi Apostoli** end of Strada Nuova conceal such traditional inns as **Alla Vedova** (3912 Ramo Ca' d'Oro) and **Promessi Sposi** (4367 Calle dell'Oca). Despite the demolition of houses to create the Strada Nuova, the church of **Santa Sofia** ⓮ survives, seamlessly merging into the streetscape. Only the ungainly belltower reveals that this is a church.

Campo Santa Sofia, with its two sidewalk cafés, provides a sunny spot for a rest. The small square is dominated by the gracious **Palazzo Sagredo**, a Veneto-Byzantine palace with Gothic flourishes.

The next left turn leads to the **Ca' d'Oro** ⓯ *(9am–2pm)* one of the finest palaces on the Grand Canal (*see page 177*); beside it is a boarding stage which whisks one to San Marco or the station. With several name changes, Strada Nuova continues eastwards towards the station; at **Campiello dell'Anconetta**, either turn left to visit the Grand Canal or right to explore the Ghetto. Turning left leads to the church of **San Marcuola** ⓰ *(8am–noon, 4.30–7pm)*, a Grand Canal

Map, page 232

TIP

When eating out in local *bacari* (bars), try *sarde in saor*, fried sardines in a spicy, sharp pickled vinegar sauce (marinated with onions and pine nuts).

BELOW: discreet boating backwater.

חוזרין
עברי
MUSEO
EBRAICO

The Jewish Museum: for a history of the Ghetto see page 114.

BELOW: banner advertising an exhibition on the history of the Ghetto.

landmark. The unfinished brick facade is a feature of many Venetian churches, as is the 18th-century form built on medieval foundations. The modest interior has a Tintoretto *Last Supper*. Nearby is a handy *vaporetto* boarding stage and, on the same bank, the magnificent **Palazzo Vendramin-Calergi** *(see page 179)*, home of the Winter Casino. Alternatively, turn your back on the waterfront and take **Calle Farnese** to **Campo del Ghetto Nuovo**, and the Venetian **Ghetto** ⑰.

Despite its name, **Campo del Ghetto Nuovo** (New Ghetto Square) stands at the heart of the world's oldest ghetto *(see page 114)*, a fortified island created in 1516. This moated *campo* contains evocative testaments to the deportation of Jews to the death camps in the form of memorial plaques on several of the buildings around the irregularly shaped square. Three of Venice's five remaining synagogues are set around the square, as unobtrusive as the Ghetto itself. Although hidden behind nondescript facades, the synagogues reveal lavish interiors, often with a Levantine feel. Gilt and stucco are used rather than marble, a material forbidden to Jews by the Venetians. The synagogues, known as *schole*, were Jewish counterparts to the Venetian *scuole*. The synagogues followed different rites and acted as community centres as well as places of worship.

The **Schola Grande Tedesca**, the German Synagogue, was built in 1528 while its neighbour, the **Schola Canton**, possibly intended for Jews from Provence, dates from 1532. Adjoining it is the **Schola Italiana**, founded for Italians in 1575. Also on the square is a small museum of Jewish history, the **Museo Ebraico** *(closed Saturday; with multilingual guided tours of the synagogues every 30 minutes past the hour from 10.30am–5.30pm daily except Friday. To attend a Saturday morning religious service, tel: 041-715012)*. The hinges of the former Ghetto gates can be seen on **Sottoportego Ghetto Nuovo**, with the

overall effect often likened to a drawbridge leading to a mysterious world. Beyond the spacious square and bridge lies the **Ghetto Vecchio** (Old Ghetto), an overspill ghetto created in 1541, with two more synagogues. The **Schola Spagnola**, designed for Spanish and Portuguese Jews, was built in 1538 but gained a Baroque facade attributed to Longhena. The hall is graced with an oval *matroneum*, or women's gallery, reminiscent of the grand circles of Venetian theatres.

The nearby **Schola Levantina**, linked to Sephardic Jews from the Middle East, dates from the 1530s. It is an architectural variant on the Scuola Spagnola since it, too, was renovated by Longhena. Inside, the highlight is the *tevà* or wooden canopied altar. Outside is a low-key everyday atmosphere, totally unlike the impressions of Théophile Gautier, the 19th-century poet. He was not alone in showing his distaste and unconscious anti-Semitism: "Curious figures, furtive and silent, slipped by close to the high walls with a fearful air... the alleyways got narrower and narrower, the houses rose like towers of Babel, hovels stacked one on top of another to reach for a little air and light above the darkness and filth through which crept misshapen beings." Today's visitors are more likely to be detained by the Jewish bakery or the kosher restaurant; Woody Allen was not alone in finding the kosher souvenirs distinctly kitsch.

Palazzo Labia and the railway station

From the Ghetto, head for the railway station via **Ponte delle Guglie**, the charming bridge over the **Canale di Cannaregio**. an area lined with waterside stalls. On the far side of the bridge lies the **Palazzo Labia** ⓲, a splendidly restored palace, with the ballroom ceilings frescoed by Tiepolo. As the cluster of aerials would suggest, this is now the headquarters of RAI, the state broadcasting network. The former owners, the noble Labia family, were renowned for their extravagance: once, after a rumbustuous banquet, the gold plates and cutlery were hurled theatrically into the canal as the host cried out: *"Le abbia o non le abbia sarò sempre Labia!"* ("Whether I have them or not, I'll always be a Labia"). The occasion for this extravagant pun had been planned in advance, with precautionary nets placed in the water to catch the precious heirlooms so they could be salvaged once the party was over. Next-door, on **Campo San Geremia**, is the 18th-century church of the same name.

From here, you can explore **Lista di Spagna**, a lively shopping street lined with jewellers and boutiques. Tiny streets branch off the wide boulevard and end in pretty courtyards and restaurants. Just beside the station looms the bold church of the **Scalzi** ⓳, the only ancient building to survive the redevelopment of this area. Ironically, this lavish church was built for the barefoot (*scalzi*) order of Carmelites. Although designed by Longhena, the great Baroque architect, the bold ornamentation of the church is distinctly Rococo.

The street bustle reaches fever pitch at the **Ferrovia Santa Lucia** ⓴. In conjunction with the causeway, this railway station opened Venice up to the world, for good and ill. Venice is an extraordinarily safe city but the rare criminal incidents that do occur tend to happen around here. Join the stream of visitors crossing the square *en route* to the *vaporetti*. ❏

Map, page 232

"I am a Jew... Hath not a Jew eyes? Hath not a Jew hands, organs, dimensions, senses, affections, passions? Fed with the same food, hurt with the same weapons?"

— SHYLOCK, THE MERCHANT OF VENICE

BELOW: typical *tabaccaio*, city news-stand.

Tintoretto (1518–94)
was nicknamed after
his father's trade
as a dyer.

BELOW: "The Fall of
Man" in San Rocco.

THE TINTORETTO TRAIL

Tracking down the works of Venice's most prolific painter
will take you all over the city, from Cannaregio to San Polo,
to Dorsoduro and, of course, to the Doge's Palace itself

U nlike Titian, who moved in select social circles in courtly Italy, Tintoretto restricted his whole life and works to the world of Venice. Tintoretto's prolific output in his native city can be appreciated on an engrossing day's stroll that takes in many of his masterpieces. The walk dips into several different districts but allows for breaks in bars and restaurants. Since *vaporetti* rides are included, take a good map and don't try this walk before getting your bearings. (Consider purchasing a one-day *vaporetto* pass; *see Travel Tips page 305*). To shorten the walk, start at San Cassiano. Bear in mind that churches are closed for at least three hours in the middle of the day.

Begin by taking the 52 *vaporetto* from San Zaccaria on Riva degli Schiavoni to the Madonna dell'Orto stop in Cannaregio (make sure it's the right direction). This was the artist's parish, where he lived and worked, assisted by two sons and a daughter. Despite being made official painter to the Doge in 1574, Tintoretto lived a precarious existence, often painting for the costs of the materials alone; he died penniless. However his humble background gave him a sympathy for the lives of the poor, a theme which, combined with religious fervour, distinguishes him from many of his contemporaries.

His parish church was **Madonna dell'Orto ❶** (*see page 233*), the most

Map,
page 232

assured Gothic church in Venice. This is very much a shrine to the artist, who is buried in a small chapel to the right of the chancel. The church contains a clutch of early works, with the *Presentation of the Virgin* showing Tintoretto's typical theatricality and grandiosity.

Cross the Rio Madonna dell'Orto canal to reach Fondamenta dei Mori on Rio della Sensa. At number 3399 is Tintoretto's house, a relatively humble affair, where he lived from 1574 until his death in 1594. From here, return to the Madonna dell'Orto *vaporetto* stop and take the 52 ferry one stop to **Fondamenta Nuove ⑥** (*see page 235*). Here is the **Gesuiti ⑦** (*see page 236*), a Baroque church containing Tintoretto's *Assumption of the Virgin*, influenced by Veronese's luminous colours. Ignoring the indifferent cafés on the Fondamenta Nuove, walk to Campo Santa Sofia on the Grand Canal, the square next to the Ca' d'Oro *vaporetto* stop. Pause in the pleasant café on the Campo and take the Santa Sofia *traghetto* across the Canal. (The *traghetto* is a gondola acting as a cheap ferry service from one side of the Grand Canal to the other).

Once in the San Polo district on the other side, cross Rio degli Beccarie to the church of **San Cassiano** *(8am–noon, 4.30–6.30pm)*. Inside are several works by Tintoretto, including a theatrical *Resurrection,* and a *Crucifixion.*

Around the Rialto

From here, it is a short walk to a lively lunch in a Rialto Market *bacaro*, a traditional rough and ready wine bar. (All bars are hard to find in the den of the Rialto so you might need to get a market trader to point you in the right direction.) If early, try the rumbustuous **Do Mori**, *(9am–1pm, 5–8pm, closed Wednesday)*, Calle de Do Mori, tucked just off Ruga Vecchia di San Giovanni. Since the bar

Numbered sights on this and the previous page refer to places already mentioned in the Cannaregio chapter and shown on the Cannaregio map (page 232).

BELOW: "The Slaughter of the Innocents", also at San Rocco.

**Map,
page 214**

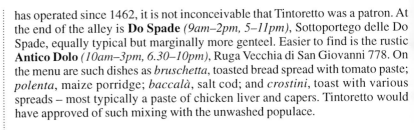

TIP

Baccalà mantecato,
dried salted cod, is
made into a paste with
parsley, garlic and
olive oil. Also sample
*sèpe nère (seppie alla
veneziana)*, cuttlefish
served with polenta, or
in a sauce for risotto or
pasta.

BELOW: Tintoretto's
grave, in Madonna
dell'Orto.
RIGHT: "The Theft of
St Mark's Body", in
the Accademia.

has operated since 1462, it is not inconceivable that Tintoretto was a patron. At the end of the alley is **Do Spade** *(9am–2pm, 5–11pm)*, Sottoportego delle Do Spade, equally typical but marginally more genteel. Easier to find is the rustic **Antico Dolo** *(10am–3pm, 6.30–10pm)*, Ruga Vecchia di San Giovanni 778. On the menu are such dishes as *bruschetta*, toasted bread spread with tomato paste; *polenta*, maize porridge; *baccalà*, salt cod; and *crostini*, toast with various spreads – most typically a paste of chicken liver and capers. Tintoretto would have approved of such mixing with the unwashed populace.

Around San Polo

From the Rialto district, it is a straightforward stroll to **San Polo ㉒** *(see page 226)*, after San Marco, the largest square in Venice. The church of San Polo *(8am–noon, 3.30–6.30pm)* contains several accomplished Tintoretto works, including an *Assumption* and *Last Supper*. Do not worry if the church happens to be closed; San Polo is just a stepping stone on the way to the main shrine to Tintoretto. Follow Calle Corner and Rio Terra to Campo dei Frari and Campo San Rocco to the **Scuola Grande di San Rocco ⑲** *(see page 223)*. Dwarfed by the Frari church, this confraternity represents Tintoretto's crowning glory. Magnificent Mannerist paintings adorn every surface: the works are larger than life, full of chiaroscuro effects and floating, plunging figures in dramatic poses.

Before leaving the appealing San Polo quarter, pause for an ice-cream at one of the ice-cream parlours that lie behind the **Frari** church **⑱** *(see page 222)*: **Millevoglie**, in Salizzada di San Rocco, is one of the city's best. From here, follow signs to the San Tomà *vaporetto* stop on the Grand Canal and take ferry 82 or 1 two stops to Accademia (in the San Marco direction). Leave the crowds by strolling towards the charming canal of Rio di San Trovaso and the church of the same name. **San Trovaso ⑧** *(see page 254)* is an inviting church containing several paintings by Tintoretto and his followers.

Depending on the time of day, stop for a drink in an engaging wine bar before or after visiting the church. **Cantine del Vino** is set on Fondamenta Nani, virtually facing the church, just by Ponte di Trovaso, the bridge over the canal. Given that this is the university quarter, the neighbourhood bar may well be full of students and academics. You might find it hard to tear yourself away from the delightful Dorsoduro quarter, even for another Tintoretto. To reach a romantic restaurant or simply to return to the San Marco area, walk along the Rio di San Trovaso to the **Zattere ❸** *(see page 251)*. Overlooking the Giudecca, the Zattere abounds in scenic, if undistinguished, bars and restaurants. From here, a number 82 *vaporetto* zigzags back to San Zaccaria, close to San Marco.

On another day, dedicated Tintoretto lovers can return to the **Accademia** *(see page 259)* to appreciate the chiaroscuro effects of the *Life of St Mark* cycle. But the **Doge's Palace** *(see page 144)* is the place to view the artist's splendid works for the Venetian State.

In particular, the Sala del Senato contains grandiose works by Tintoretto and his followers. The Sala del Maggior Consiglio, where the Great Council met, is decorated by his vast *Paradise*, one of the largest single canvases ever painted. ❏

DORSODURO

The smartest area of Venice, and a haven for expatriates, stretches from La Salute, the church facing St Mark's, to the Accademia, the city's most illustrious art gallery

Map, page 250

Dorsoduro simply means "hard back" so called because the district occupies the largest area of firm land in Venice. This is the chicest *sestiere*, and the grandest section is defined by the Punta della Dogana, the Gesuati and the Accademia. This most fashionable residential district has long been favoured by foreign residents, particularly the American and British communities. Dorsoduro remains a haven for wealthy expatriates of all nationalities. The southern flank, essentially on the left bank, contains poorer areas towards the west.

Yet historically, Dorsoduro was a mixed district, with the nobles and *nouveaux-riches* ensconced in splendid Grand Canal palaces, the impoverished nobility living close to Campo San Barnaba, and sailors and fishermen confined to the scenically shabby west. Today, socially and geographically, there is considerable overlap: Campo Santa Margherita, the hub of Dorsoduro, is a cheerful district of shopkeepers, students and self-consciously cultured people.

The closeness of the university quarter, based on Ca' Foscari, ensures that the bars are full and service friendly. The parishes of San Trovaso and San Barnaba offer a similar mixture of youthful high spirits and discreet privilege. In chic Dorsoduro, foreign bohemianism meets Venetian conservatism, resulting in discreet good taste spiced with a touch of the cosmopolitan.

PRECEDING PAGES: Punta della Dogana by night.
LEFT: Palazzo Bembo, heart of the university quarter.
BELOW: pensive gondolier.

La Salute

Dorsoduro is the most charming quarter for idle wandering, with wisteria-clad walls, secret gardens and distinctive domestic architecture. Apart from the Accademia gallery and Salute church, the district is surprisingly free from visitors. The southern spur of the Zattere makes the most beguiling Venetian promenade, bracing in winter and refreshing in summer. These quaysides offer panoramic views from the glittering sea customs post and the stately Salute church.

This landmark basilica is rivalled by several major churches and confraternities. San Sebastiano and the Carmini can compete with entrancing interiors decorated by Veronese and Tiepolo. Culturally, Dorsoduro is surpassed only by San Marco: the district is home to numerous galleries, of which the Accademia reigns supreme as the treasury of Venetian painting. Many of the finest waterside palaces also lie along Dorsoduro's spine. However, Dorsoduro is essentially understated, with peace and quiet prized more than glittering sights.

One such secluded spot is the fishermen's church of San Nicolò on the outer rim of the city. Another quaint corner is the *squero*, the gondola docks, where boats wait to be planed or repainted. No wonder that Dorsoduro's more precious residents feel that simply to step outside the *sestiere* produces a lowering of the spirits.

Eastern Dorsoduro is dominated by the Baroque

TIP

Particularly for children:
La Salute *traghetto*
(gondola ferry) makes an
enjoyable and
inexpensive jaunt across
the Grand Canal to Santa
Maria del Giglio.

basilica of **La Salute** ❶ *(8.30am–noon, 3–6pm)*, a Venetian landmark guarding the entrance to the Grand Canal. Officially dedicated to Santa Maria della Salute (Our Lady of Good Health), the church was created as a thanksgiving for delivery from the 1630 plague. Longhena, the great Baroque architect, wished it to be "strange, worthy and beautiful" and succeeded magnificently. Henry James's celebrated conceit springs to mind: "like some great lady on the threshold of her salon. She is more ample and serene… with her domes and scrolls, her scalloped buttresses and statues forming a pompous crown, and her wide steps disposed on the ground like the train of a robe".

However, Longhena's triumphal and grandiose church is also indebted to Palladio's Redentore. Although Longhena learnt from his Classical forebear's choice of theatrical settings and magnificent use of space, lavish sculptural decoration was his own Baroque contribution. Begun in 1631, the church took 50 years to complete and is the focal point of a colourful festival, celebrated every November, when even cynical gondoliers bring their oars to be blessed by a priest on the basilica steps (*see page 96*).

La Salute marks the end of Venetian Mannerism and heralds an era of bold Baroque statements. Devised before Rome's Bernini and Borromini masterpieces, it became one of the few Italian churches to challenge the supremacy of Roman Baroque. The interior boasts a spectacular central plan, with its revolutionary octagonal space surmounted by a huge dome. The octagonal structure alludes to the symbolic eight-pointed Marian star while the theatrically raised high altar evokes the Virgin's rescue of Venice.

The major works of art include Tintoretto's *Wedding at Cana*, paintings by Titian in the sacristy, and a small Byzantine *Madonna*, overawed by all this

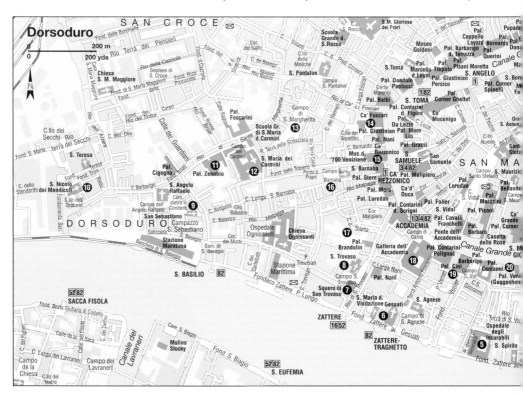

Baroque splendour. While eminently praiseworthy, the interior is rather solemn and cold, clad in Istrian stone. The exterior is more joyous, with the majestic dome dominating the Venetian skyline. At the bottom of a dramatic flight of steps, a *traghetto* links La Salute with Santa Maria del Giglio on the far bank while the *vaporetto* sweeps visitors over to San Marco or down the Grand Canal.

The Zattere

Alternatively, stroll around the point, the **Punta della Dogana** (the Customs Point), the start of a popular Venetian walk. Occupying the triangular tip of Dorsoduro is the **Dogana di Mare ❷**. This was the sea customs post, as opposed to the land-based customs post (Dogana della Terrà, on the Riva del Vin on the Rialto). Here ships and cargoes were inspected before being allowed to drop anchor in front of the Doge's Palace. Still used as a customs house, this is the only Republican civic building to have maintained its original function. Although the present sea customs post dates from the 1670, it occupies the site of an earlier customs house and medieval defensive works.

Facing St Mark's Basin, a porticoed corner tower is crowned by a rich composition: bronze atlases bear a golden globe with a weather-vane featuring the figure of Fortune glinting in the sun.

The **Zattere ❸** stretches all the way round Dorsoduro's southern shore, with its quaysides flanked by cafés and churches, boathouses and warehouses. This promenade was created in 1516 and named after the cargoes of wood that were unloaded on these quaysides (*zattere* means "floating rafts"). This a refreshing *fondamente* and the Venetians' favourite walking place; the residents prefer windswept sea views to neat parks, which are usually deserted. This promenade

Map, page 250

One of the most delightful walks in Venice stretches from La Salute to the Zattere quays, rounding the Customs Point. Depending on the number of pauses, the walk lasts from half an hour to half a day and could easily encompass visits to the Gesuati church and the Guggenheim.

BELOW: Santa Maria della Salute.

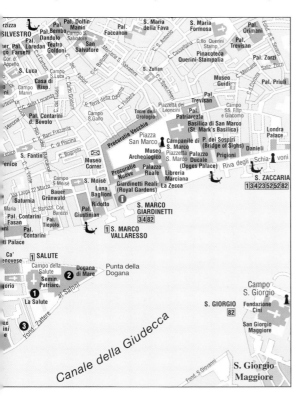

*"Sgropin", lemon
sorbet, is made with
vodka and Prosecco
and traditionally
served at the end of a
fish course.*

was also popular with the poet Ezra Pound (*see page 289*). The Zattere is far
more appealing than its northern counterpart, the quaysides of the Fondamente
Nuove. In all seasons, strolling along the Zattere represents a local ritual. At the
first sign of spring sunshine, Venetian sun-worshippers flock to the landing
stages and decks that line the shore. Summer *passeggiate* are also *de rigueur*,
partly to combat the heat and city claustrophobia, partly to parade the latest pastel fashions and sip drinks in stylish cafés. Just around the point is the first of
the open-air cafés beside the waterfront. Linea d'Ombra, set by the bridge of
Rio della Salute, is a romantic spot for cocktails and people-watching.

Gesuati and the Squero di San Trovaso

Facing the island of the Giudecca are the **Magazzini del Sale ④**, the former
salt warehouses, where the city's sole raw material was stored. The low, regular
Neo-Classical frontage conceals a 15th-century structure. The interior, an occasional boathouse, also doubles as an exhibition space during the Biennale art
festival. Just before Rio delle Torresele lies **Ospedale degli Incurabili ⑤**, an
austere former hospice for syphilitics (and later orphans), a medieval building
redesigned by Sansovino in the 16th century. In its time, it has also been a music
conservatoire, a barracks, and a rehabilitation centre; it is now a children's home.

Further along the Zattere stands the grandiose church of the **Gesuati ⑥**
(*8am–noon, 3–7pm*), a supreme example of 18th-century Venetian architecture,
not to be confused with the Gesuiti in Cannaregio (*see page 236*). The facade,
with its lofty Corinthian columns and Palladian motifs, was designed by Massari,
an early Rococo architect. The church is often seen as a counterpoint to Palladio's Redentore over the water (*see page 271*). The Gesuati, dedicated to Santa

BELOW: View of La
Salute, with Il
Redentore beyond.

Maria del Rosario, dates from 1726 and was commissioned by the Dominicans. The theatrical yet graceful interior boasts Tiepolo masterpieces (1739), visible in their original setting. The master of the Rococo adorned the vaulted ceiling with a heavenly vision, the air stirred by the beat of angels' wings. The central panel celebrates the *Institution of the Rosary* showing the Madonna offering the rosary to St Dominic; the side panels illustrate the *Life of St Dominic*. Easier to see, in the first chapel on the right, is Tiepolo's exuberant altarpiece of the *Madonna*, accompanied by three venerated Dominican saints. Only a Tintoretto *Crucifixion* disturbs the Dominican orthodoxy and Rococo mood.

Next-door is **Santa Maria della Visitazione** *(8am–noon, 3–7pm)*, a Renaissance oratory attributed to the Coducci school. On the facade is a lion's mouth letter box for secret denunciations. Access to the oratory, with its 16th-century Umbrian coffered ceiling and cloisters, is through the gateway of a charitable institute. The **Zattere boarding stage** lies on this stretch of quays, with ferries to the Giudecca and San Marco. Towards the San Trovaso end of the Zattere are open-air cafés and *pizzerie*, perched on waterfront rafts. Even if the views are finer than the food, few can complain.

Nico (Dorsoduro 922, *open 7am–10pm, closed Thursday*) is by common consent the best city *gelateria*. The Venetian ice-cream speciality here is *gianduiotto*, an indulgent blend of honey, hazelnuts, chocolate and whipped cream.

From here, turn down **Rio di San Trovaso** to explore a privileged domestic district dotted with university buildings. Set on the corner of Rio Trovaso and Rio Ognissanti is the **Squero di San Trovaso ➐**, a picturesque gondola repair yard best viewed from Fondamenta Nani on Rio di San Trovaso. Gondolas are overhauled at one of three *squeri*, the traditional boatyards and workshops. This

Map, page 250

Welcome to the inviting parish of San Trovaso.

BELOW LEFT: Gesuati church. **BELOW:** globe and weather-vane figure of Fortune on the Customs House.

In the local inns try *fegato alla Veneziana*, tender calf's liver flavoured with parsley, onion, and olive oil or *bigoli*, dark skeins of wholewheat spaghetti, often served with an anchovy and onion sauce.

BELOW: traditional waterside wine bar.

is the oldest surviving boatyard in Venice, dating from the 17th century. Naturally, the *squeri* are always set on the waterfront, with the yard sloping down to the canal. Beside the boatyard is a wooden galleried construction, a geranium-clad outhouse with living quarters above. The resemblance to an alpine chalet is not accidental: many of the early boat-builders came from the Dolomites. Nowadays, the main concern is the maintenance of the 400 or gondolas still in use. In summer, the upturned boats are traditionally scraped of weeds and retarred but weeds are less of a problem since the council banned phosphate-rich detergents.

A shortage of skilled craftsmen and the labour-intensive nature of the work means that there is a waiting list for new gondolas: only a handful are made a year, mostly destined for millionaires' pleasure lakes. Today, this asymmetric half-ton craft costs up to US$80,000 to make. Yet Nedis Tramontin, the master craftsman at San Trovaso, recalls the 1920s, "and seeing my father's team make seven gondolas in 21 days flat for 700 lire each".

Further along **Fondamenta Nani** lies a cluster of university buildings, including the sculpted Palazzo Nani Mocenigo, currently being restored. The scenic Rio di San Trovaso links the Grand Canal and the Giudecca Canal, with the Cantine del Vino, an old-fashioned wine bar, overlooking the Ponte di San Trovaso. Towards the Grand Canal end of the *rio* are several wisteria-clad palaces and a small bridge leading across the canal to the church of **San Trovaso** ❽ *(8–11am, 3–5pm, closed Sunday)*. Originally medieval, the church was remodelled at the end of the 16th century in Palladian style. Curiously, there are two matching facades, one facing the canal, the other facing a raised stone *campo*. Tradition has it that two entrances were required to keep the warring clans of the Castellani and Nicoletti apart. The square and well-head conceal a rainwater cistern (*see*

page 60). Despite its setting, the church is disappointing, with a somewhat gloomy interior redeemed by several paintings by Tintoretto and his son.

Map, page 250

San Sebastiano and San Nicolò dei Mendicoli

From here, the charming Calle della Toletta leads to Campo San Barnaba and the Grand Canal palaces beyond. Alternatively, follow the Zattere westwards to Rio di San Sebastiano and the start of a scruffy but appealing district. **San Sebastiano** ❾ *(3.30–5.30pm, closed Sunday)* is an early 16th-century church, a Classical canvas for Veronese's opulent masterpieces, painted in 1555–65. The church is often praised as a perfect marriage of the arts, with architecture, painting and sculpture in complete accord with one another. Veronese's works are enhanced by lavishly carved ceilings and a galleried choir, which adds to the sense of spaciousness. This resplendent cycle of paintings shows Veronese in all his glory, exalting grace, harmony and serenity while indulging in occasional whimsy and caprice.

"The buildings people the sky; the pedestrian is master of the ground."

— LE CORBUSIER

Veronese's *trompe l'oeil* interior is an architectural flight of fancy created by frescoed loggias, columns and statues. Radiant blocks of pure colour adorn every surface, from the nave ceiling to the organ panels. The individual subjects are secondary to the overall effect, a broad spectrum of religious, historical and mythological motifs. However, the paintings in the choir illustrate the martyrdom of St Sebastian while the sacristy ceiling is devoted to the Virgin and the Evangelists, and the nave ceiling to Esther. For 18th-century connoisseurs, Veronese's paintings were the noblest, the most sought after and most pleasing; today they strike a particular chord with the French.

Behind the painter's parish church lies a traditional working-class district

BELOW: gondola yard and tide markers.

The Armenians formed a prominent community in Venice, with the merchant class settled in the city centre (see page 190) and the religious community still based on the island of San Lazzaro (page 293).

once populated by fishermen, now home to factory workers and officials from the maritime station. On the next square west is the 18th-century church of **Angelo Raffaele** *(8.30am–noon, 4–6pm)* which stands on ancient foundations. The adjoining canal leads to the most remote waterside church in western Dorsoduro, **San Nicolò dei Mendicoli**  *(10am–noon, 4–6pm)*. Set in a dilapidated district, this former fishermen's and artisans' church is surprisingly sumptuous. San Nicolò presents a squat Romanesque belltower and a bare brick facade lit by mullioned windows; a rare Gothic portico graces the west facade.

The church is one of the oldest in Venice, founded in the 7th century but remodelled between the 12th and 14th centuries. It was sensitively restored by Venice in Peril in the 1970s. The endearing interior is one of the best-loved in the city, with a single nave ending in a Romanesque apse. Other parts of the original structure include Byzantine cornices. The nave is graced by Romanesque columns, Gothic capitals and beamed ceilings. The interior is embellished with Renaissance panelling, gilded statues and school of Veronese paintings.

Palazzo Zenobio and Santa Maria dei Carmini

From here, Rio di San Nicolò winds back to civilisation. Following the eastern bank of the canal, which changes its name to Rio Santa Margherita, brings you to the quayside of Fondamenta Briati. Overlooking the *rio* on the other side is **Palazzo Zenobio** , a rare example of Roman Baroque in Venice. Although originally Gothic, the palace was remodelled in the late 17th century and given a long, monotonous facade. At the back is a Neoclassical library and Italianate gardens. The interior is sophisticated, with a T-shaped *portego* or grand hall. The *pièce de résistance* is the sumptuous, frescoed ballroom, with a minstrels'

BELOW: San Nicolò dei Mendicoli.
BELOW RIGHT: The Carmini.

gallery, gold and white stuccos and *trompe l'oeil* effects. The mirrors, chandeliers and door handles are all 17th-century. The palace has been an Armenian College since 1850 but the ballroom is often open to visitors.

On the same western bank is the church of **Santa Maria dei Carmini** ⓬ *(3–5pm, closed Sunday)*. The Baroque belltower is surmounted by a statue of the Virgin bearing the scapular (these two small white strips of cloth form the distinguishing badge of the Carmelites). The church is often described as a display of Renaissance works in a Gothic setting but the truth is more complex. The solemn nave has 17th-century arcades and a number of ponderous Baroque paintings in honour of the Carmelite order. Renaissance panelling covers a number of Gothic features, with the choir lofts decorated with 16th-century works. The finest Renaissance painting is a Cima da Conegliano *Nativity* in the second altar on the right. The Gothic cloisters now form part of an art institute.

On the same square is **I Carmini** *(9am–12.30pm, 3.30–6pm, closed Sunday)*, the home of the Scuola Grande dei Carmini and headquarters of the Carmelite confraternity. The uninspired facade, built by Longhena, conceals a lavishly frescoed 18th-century interior. The ground floor comprises a frescoed great hall and sacristy. A monumental twin staircase, complete with barrel-vaulted ceilings encrusted with stuccoes, leads to a splendid showcase to Tiepolo.

On the left is the Sala dell'Albergo, which housed pilgrims, and the Sala dell'Archivio, where the confraternity archives were stored. The decoration of the Salone, or assembly room, on the right was entrusted to Tiepolo. Since the wealthy order prospered during the Counter Reformation, with the cult of Mary acting as a counterweight to Protestantism, the Carmelites could afford to summon the services of the greatest Rococo painter. Tiepolo repaid their confidence

Map, page 250

"The only way to care for Venice as she deserves is to give her a chance to touch you often – to linger and remain and return."

– HENRY JAMES

BELOW: interior of Santa Maria dei Carmini.

with a series of sensuous masterpieces, a floating world of pale skies and illusionistic effects. In the centre of the ceiling is a visionary work, *Simon Stock receiving the scapular from the Virgin* (1774). Tradition has it that, while living in Cambridge, Stock had a vision of the Virgin bestowing the Carmelites with their sacred badge, the scapular. As the order was re-established during the 13th century, Stock became one of the first Englishmen to join, leading the Carmelites during the time of their realignment to the Mendicant Friars. The corners of the ceiling are graced by four voluptuous Virtues, a radiant allegorical work.

Statuesque pose.

Campo Santa Margherita

Just beyond lies **Campo Santa Margherita ⓭**, the liveliest square in the district, and the archetypal Venetian meeting place. At one end of the sprawling square is a free-standing building, the Scuola dei Varotari, formerly the tanners guild. Just above several fish stalls lies an ancient stone sign prescribing the minimum size of fish permitted (eel must be over 25 cm long and sardines at least 7 cm). Neighbourhood shops are set amidst homely yet scruffy palaces. A slice of Venetian life can be seen browsing in the antiquarian print shop, discount bookshop or alternative pharmacy. The locals refill dubious containers at the rustic wine shop (number 2897) while students prefer the friendly bars, including the fashionable café with the minimalist name of Caffè.

One side of the square is bordered by dignified palaces with overhanging roofs, a style rare in Venice, because of the fear of fire and a desire to let light into dark alleys. One house has a distinctive Gothic doorway, adorned with a noble crest, while the adjoining facade boasts Veneto-Byzantine windows. At the end of the square is the truncated *campanile* of Santa Margherita, with the church interior now a lecture hall. From here, the splendours of the Grand Canal beckon. Milling students may lead one to **Ca' Foscari ⓮**, the magnificent university palace (*see page 173*). Just south is **Ca' Rezzonico ⓯** (*10am–4pm, closed Friday, see page 171*), the museum of 18th-century art, and one of the finest city galleries.

BELOW: shady spot near Ca' Foscari.

Alternatively, follow Rio Terrà across the canal to **Campo San Barnaba ⓰**. Bordering the scenic square is Rio San Barnaba, signalled by a colourful barge laden with fruit and vegetables. The square is reached by **Ponte dei Pugni**, the main bridge between San Barnaba and Santa Margherita. This was the scene of factional fisticuffs between rival clans until such brawls were banned in 1705. When not at church in San Trovaso the Castellani and Nicolotti, from Castello and San Nicolò respectively, staged their ritual battles here. Their footprints, embedded in the stonework, are reminders of the bloodshed that left many dead.

Yet the square also has decidedly aristocratic associations since this was the parish of the *barnabotti*, the impoverished nobility, who gambled or begged in order to survive. Tradition has it that the presence of open sewers kept house prices artificially low. The sewers now lie below water level but ironically the square has become the home of the local Communist Party. Yet politics and an austere 18th-century church do little to dampen the spirits of this bustling square, with its boisterous cafés and picturesque market stalls.

From here, Sottoportego Casin dei Nobili, once a refuge for ruined nobles, crosses Rio Malpaga to the quaysides of Fondamenta Calle della Toletta and **Calle della Toletta ⑰**. This charming, winding alley passes several bars and a good bookshop before returning to the delightful Rio di San Trovaso. On the far side of the canal, Campiello Gambara leads to the **Accademia bridge**, a fine place from which to watch the water traffic. The distinctive wooden bridge, built in 1932 and restored in the 1980s, replaced a cast iron bridge dating from the time of the Austrian occupation. Controversial plans to replace the bridge with a transparent modernist structure were defeated by Venetian conservatism.

The Accademia

The bridge is busy during the day, with visitors flocking to the **Accademia ⑱** *(daily 9am–7pm, Sunday 9am–2pm)* and students attending the adjoining art school. As the world's finest collection of Venetian art, the Accademia is the city's most popular gallery. The American art critic Bernard Berenson (1865–1959) judged Venetian painting the most appealing Italian school: "Their colouring not only gives direct pleasure to the eye but acts like music upon the moods." Venetian art is characterised by vibrant colour, luminosity and a supreme decorative sense; it is often tinged with a poetic sensibility. The collection is housed in La Carità, a complex of church, convent, cloisters and charitable confraternity.

The church was deconsecrated in Napoleonic times and became a repository of work created during the Venetian Republic, including paintings saved from suppressed monasteries. However, the core collection was assembled by Venetian artists themselves in the 18th century. Since the gallery is lit by natural light, choose a bright day. On wet days or in high summer, long queues often form

Map, page 250

The Accademia is not an obvious choice for young children but the Venetians' concern for everyday life means that historical scenes are enlivened by animals, boats, lavish costumes and quirky details, which they may enjoy.

BELOW: inviting Campo Santa Margherita.

TIP

To visit the artists'
work in situ, see the
Tintoretto Trail
(page 242); the Bellini
route (page 70) and
the Tiepolo Trail
(page 170).

outside the Accademia's Neo-Classical facade, so return at lunch-time or retreat to the adjoining Le Belle Arti bar until the crowds disperse.

Although multi-lingual descriptive cards are available in most rooms, the collection is confusing and only chronological until Room XI, with chronology resuming from Room XIV to XVIII. The final section, from Room XIX to the end, returns to the Renaissance, with the finest ceremonial paintings. If time is short, focus on the first 11 rooms and the last five. The highlights include 15th-century works by Carpaccio and the Bellini brothers, 16th-century paintings by Giorgione, Titian, Tintoretto and Veronese, and 17th and 18th-century works by Tiepolo, Guardi and Canaletto. The Republic set great store by the institution of the state painter, with artists of the calibre of Bellini, Titian and Tintoretto expected to capture Venetian glory through official festivities. In Venetian painting, much effort is dedicated to charting the ceremonial, with the protocol of receiving prelates, foreign ambassadors and other dignitaries.

The first room occupies the Gothic former chapterhouse of the Scuola Grande, decorated with a gilded panelled ceiling. **Room I** is dedicated to **Byzantine and Gothic artists**, noted for their symmetrical but static decorative works on a gold background. Paolo Veneziano is credited with introducing the taste for panel painting to Venice. His *Coronation of the Virgin* (1325) is symbolic rather than realistic, bathed in radiant colours. Lorenzo Veneziano (active 1356–72) combines Gothic and Byzantine elements in his luminous panel paintings, which show an interest in the softness of line and the fall of drapery. The paintings of Antonio Vivarini (*c*1419–*c*76) seen here and in the final room, represent a subtle break with Gothic style, thanks to their rapt stillness of mood.

Rooms II to **IV** display expressive **early Renaissance altarpieces** by Gio-

BELOW: Gentile Bellini's "Procession in San Marco", in the Accademia.

vanni Bellini, noted for their poetic atmosphere and harmonious composition. **Room V** contains the most celebrated works in the collection, Giorgione's *Tempest* (c1507), a moody and enigmatic canvas, and his *Portrait of an Old Woman*, a meditation on time. **Rooms VI** to **X** feature other **Venetian Renaissance and Mannerist masters**, from Titian to Veronese and Tintoretto. Titian's poignant *Pietà*, intended for his own tomb, is lit by a diffuse light and infused with an anguished questioning about the meaning of life; the troubled *Nicodemus* is seen as Titian's last self portrait. In the *ex-voto*, Titian also portrays his son, Orazio, who died of the plague in 1576. Titian probably also died of the same cause but his fame ensured that he was buried in the Frari (*see page 222*).

Veronese's *Feast in the House of Levi* (1573) covers an entire wall in **Room X** but was painted for the church of Santi Giovanni e Paolo. Intended as a *Last Supper*, the subject was a pretext for the depiction of a profane feast. The seemingly sacrilegious work invoked the Inquisition's wrath, with its portrayal of "buffoons, drunkards, Germans, dwarfs and similar indecencies". Veronese sidestepped the issue by renaming his work in more secular vein. Also here is Tintoretto's *Miracle of the Slave*, the work that made his reputation.

Paintings by Veronese and Tintoretto are also on display in **Room XI**, as are fragments of **Tiepolo ceilings** from destroyed or damaged churches, including the Scalzi. Amongst other mythological subjects is his *Rape of Europa*, a triumph of pulsating light and shade very unlike the pastel frescoes with which he is generally associated. This capricious work features a cherubic *putto* on a cloud trying to extinguish the lightening with a jet of urine. Bernard Berenson was unforgiving of such frivolity: "Tiepolo lived among people whose very hearts had been vitiated by its measureless haughtiness". **Rooms XII** to **XVII** display

Map, page 250

Typical funnel-shaped Venetian chimneys, known as "fumaioli", are depicted in Carpaccio's painting below.

BELOW: Carpaccio's "Miracle of the True Cross".

Map, page 250

"Longhi, Canaletto and Guardi lack the quality of force, without which there can be no important style."

– BERNARD BERENSON

BELOW: Giorgione's enigmatic "The Tempest".
RIGHT: Carpaccio's "Arrival of the English Ambassadors".

18th-century landscapes and genre paintings beloved by Grand Tour visitors. Guardi's caprices hang alongside Longhi's studies of patrician homes and a rare Canaletto perspective painting, which uses a pastiche Venetian background. Rosalba Carriera's informal pastels show that the vanity of Venetians was amply served by portraiture.

Room XX and **XXI** are a showcase for the pomp and pageantry of the Venetian Republic, seen in vibrant **ceremonial paintings**. Carpaccio and Bellini were prime exponents of the narrative cycles known as *istorie*, a Venetian Renaissance phenomenon. Ironically, Gentile Bellini, Giovanni's less talented brother, received greater recognition in his day and created the most reproduced view of Venice, *The Procession in Piazza San Marco* (1496). This is a grand affair of prelates and senators parading outside the Basilica. Lovely though it is, the effect is airless, its iconographical fidelity frozen into pageantry.

Also in **Room XX** is Carpaccio's *Miracle of the Relic of the True Cross* (1496), a glorious picture painted for the Scuola di San Giovanni Evangelista. While notionally depicting the healing of a madman, Carpaccio's scene is more celebratory than religious, with dignitaries and cosmopolitan merchants milling below a loggia, spectators flanking the Rialto Bridge, turbaned Turks, a cooper rinsing out a wine barrel, a mason at work, and a jaunty parade of gondolas. Carpaccio is noted for a love of detail, narrative talent and sensitive use of colour.

Room XXI displays his most famous work, *The Life of St Ursula* cycle, painted for the confraternity of the same name. This nine-part cycle traces the life of a pious Breton princess who consented to marry an Englishman on condition that he converted to Christianity and undertook a pilgrimage to Rome with her, accompanied by 10,000 virgins. On their return journey, they were massacred by Huns at Cologne. The last room, the **Sala dell'Albergo**, retains its Gothic ceiling and panelling. Titian's *Presentation of the Virgin*, painted for this very room, makes a fitting finale.

Between the Accademia and La Salute, the Grand Canal is lined with the finest palaces and museums. The charming **Campo San Vio** is home to St George's Anglican Church, which serves the English-speaking community in Venice. Here, too, is **Palazzo Cini** ⑲ *(tel: 041-521 0755 for opening times, summer only)*, the former residence of Count Vittorio Cini (1884–1977), a noted industrialist. The Count created the fine Cini Foundation at San Giorgio *(see page 269)* but lived here, filling his palace with period furniture, silver, ceramics and illuminated manuscripts. However, the highlights are the Tuscan Renaissance masterpieces by such artists as Piero della Francesca, Fra Filippo Lippi and Botticelli.

From here, Calle della Chiesa leads to the **Guggenheim** ⑳, the superb collection of modern art *(11am–6pm, closed Tuesday; see page 168)*. Virtually next door is the beguiling **Ca' Dario** ㉑ *(see page 176)*. Calle del Bastion leads back to **La Salute**, allowing one a last lingering look at the Baroque church before taking the *traghetto* across to the right bank or a *vaporetto* along the Grand Canal. Like Henry James, you may find it hard to leave the Salute steps, "with all the sweet bribery of association and recollection". ❏

ISLANDS OF THE LAGOON

*Visit San Giorgio and Giudecca for the churches,
Torcello for astonishing mosaics, Murano for glass, Burano for
lace, and the Lido for its seaside airs*

Map,
see each
island

The lagoon is a floating world between the smoking oil refineries on the mainland and the fish slithering in the reeds. At times, the fumes intermingle with the cedar-perfumed air of the islands and the songs of cicadas. The desolation of the lagoon waters is relieved by sightings of wild ducks, mute swans or the fragile-looking black-winged stilt. Despite their proximity, the lagoon islands are startlingly different, embracing marshland, orchards, vineyards and even beaches. These low-lying islands have a chequered past as monasteries or munitions dumps, mental asylums or market gardens, leper colonies or crumbling fortifications. However, the strangest places tend to be the "minor" or outlying islands. By comparison with these diverse but dying communities, the main islands survive on their location and separate identities. Certain islands are the preserve of fishermen, lace-makers and glass-makers while others are home to silk-workers, boat-builders or urban sophisticates.

Visitors with little time available to spend in Venice would do well to make the islands of San Giorgio and Torcello their priorities. San Giorgio, facing San Marco, is the closest to the city, and the only major island untouched by commerce. The belltower offers the most romantic view of Venice. Torcello, the remotest of the islands, offers a stirring impression of the earliest Venetian settlement. The mood is set by the surreal isolation of the site, the air of stagnation, the sluggish canal, the scattered buildings, the solitary red-brick belltower.

PRECEDING PAGES:
island with channel
and tide markers.
LEFT: after the ball.
BELOW: colourful
Burano waterfront.

Out of season, Torcello is the place for bathing in what the writer Jan Morris calls "an ecstasy of melancholia". By contrast, Burano is a splash of colour in a bleak lagoon, dispelling any mournfulness with its parade of colourful fishermen's cottages. However, visitors tempted by gaudy Venetian glass or soft-shelled crabs will choose its neighbour, Murano. Giudecca, just off Dorsoduro, is celebrated for its Palladian church but is a complex and raffish island in its own right. The Lido cannot compete historically but its beaches and graceful Art Nouveau architecture offer a semblance of escape from the summer heat.

San Giorgio Maggiore

The island of **San Giorgio Maggiore** was once known as *isola dei cipressi* because of the cypress-framed vistas. Seen from afar, the majestic monastery appears suspended in the inner lagoon, with its cool Palladian church matched by a belltower modelled on St Mark's. Together with the Baroque beacon of La Salute, these two great symbols guard the inner harbour of Venice. San Giorgio is a hallowed spot, with its famous Benedictine monastery. Despite the island's proximity to San Marco, the absence of bars and commercial distractions means that San Giorgio has retained its secluded air.

The monastery boldly looks out over St Mark's Basin instead of following the standard model of an inward-looking institution enclosed by cloisters. The medieval monastery was remodelled in the late 15th and early 16th centuries but owes its classical grace to Palladio. Although the Napoleonic suppression of the monasteries in 1806 was accompanied by French plundering of San Giorgio, the monks refused to leave. The harbour was developed at the same time, with part of the monastery used to store munitions during World War II. Today, the Benedictines remain the sole island residents, enhancing the mood of spiritual seclusion.

San Giorgio Maggiore ❶ *(10am–noon, 2.30–5pm)* is undoubtedly the finest monastic church in the lagoon. Only the churlish aesthete Ruskin found it "barbarous" and "childish in conception". Endowed by Doges and favoured by humanist scholars, the monastery became a famous centre for learning.

Although most visitors restrict their visit to the church and belltower, to appreciate the size and diversity of the monastic site, you need to tour the Cini Foundation (see below). In 1565 Palladio was commissioned to rebuild the church, his finest Venetian legacy, rivalled only by Il Redentore. Here Palladio shows his mastery of the classical idiom, using the basic geometric volumes of cube, pyramid and sphere. Based on Alberti's precepts, this is a Christian church founded on classical principles and mathematical proportions.

The facade is composed of two overlapping temple fronts, with a central portico. The cool church is a model of perspective with a domed interior bathed in white light. The overall sense of order is more impressive than the component parts: the vaulted ceiling, elegant choir and choir stalls, the striking marble floor and two minor works by the hand of Tintoretto.

BELOW RIGHT: view from Campanile di San Giorgio.

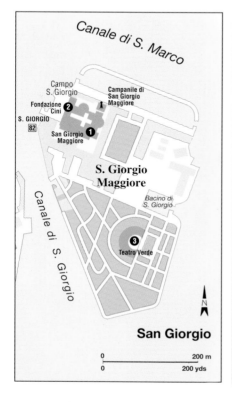

A lift whisks visitors to the top of the **belltower** for fabulous views over the city, whatever the weather. The angel on top of the tower fell off during a violent storm in 1993 but has been restored, with the original now displayed inside the church and a bronze copy on the roof. If the lift attendant is not too busy, he may be persuaded to unlock the Sala del Conclave, where the conclave met to elect Pope Pius VII in 1800, while Rome was occupied by French troops. Although it is now used as a private music room by the monks, members of the public can occasionally attend classical concerts here, as well as performances of Gregorian chant in the church.

The **Fondazione Cini ❷** occupies much of the great Benedictine complex. (Some sections can be viewed during exhibitions but for a fuller tour, call the foundation in advance, tel: 041-528 9900). Count Vittorio Cini (1884–1977) bequeathed his home to the city and created the foundation as a memorial to his son who died in a flying accident. The centre funds restoration projects and conventions as well as staging major exhibitions. The Baroque architect Longhena designed the monastery's ceremonial double staircase and library, built on the site of Michelozzi's Renaissance library.

Other highlights are the huge Renaissance dormitory and the cross-vaulted Palladian refectory. More impressive still are the Renaissance Cloister of the Laurels *(Chiostro degli Allori)* and the Palladian Cloister of the Cypresses *(Chiostro dei Cipressi)*. Palladio also designed the ceremonial guest quarters overlooking the lagoon. The sumptuous setting is more reminiscent of a palace courtyard than of a cloistered retreat. The Palladian cloisters lead to the monastic gardens and the **Teatro Verde ❸**, the open-air theatre; this pastoral setting provides an atmospheric stage set for occasional summer concerts.

Map, page 268

TIP

Even if you have only a day in Venice, the view from the top of San Giorgio is an unmissable experience.

BELOW: intimate, cloistered San Giorgio.

Cool, Palladian interior of the Redentore.

Giudecca

Giudecca is the most contradictory of Venetian islands, home to the city's most luxurious hotel and to one of its most deprived districts. At first sight, this depressed island of decaying tenements and blind alleys is deeply unappealing. Yet it was once celebrated for palatial villas, exotic gardens and risqué clubs. It probably began as a place of exile for punished nobles but became a veritable pleasure garden. From Renaissance times onwards, the island was the place for nobles to indulge in the decadent *dolce far niente* (sweet idleness) typical of a Venetian summer. The Giudecca was also noted for its convents, including one notorious for Casanova's amorous exploits. Industrialisation put an end to the patrician idyll: from the 19th century until the 1950s, the island became Venice's industrial inner suburb. The horizon was dotted with flour mills, fabric and clock factories, a brewery and boatyards. Decline set in with the growth of the industrial zone on the mainland, which left the Giudecca an urban wasteland.

Although considered the most *popolare*, or working-class, area of Venice, the island is currently undergoing a resurgence, with the restoration of several landmark buildings. While parts of the Giudecca remain resolutely shabby, abandoned lofts are being bought by artists, giving the district a bohemian air. While many warehouses are roofless or boarded up, the famous Fortuny silk factory continues to survive. On the waterfront facing the city, several functional buildings have been put to new uses, including a granary which has been converted into a youth hostel and a brewery turned into flats.

For those interested in industrial architecture, the section from Campo di San Cosmo to Rio Ponte Lungo runs through the area's old manufacturing district. However, apart from the great Palladian church and the quayside facing the city, the Giudecca is still immune to tourism.

Although it is tricky to walk across the island, tiny pastoral pockets survive. Dirk Bogarde, while filming *Death in Venice*, luxuriated in solitude on the Giudecca, with the Lagoon lapping beside him, "the wheeling swifts, swooping like commas high above the dome of the Redentore, and the distant bells of the city drifting across the Lagoon, all mixed with the bumble of pollen-heavy bees nudging into the white and pink discs of hollyhocks."

ABOVE: Giudecca's busy waterfront.

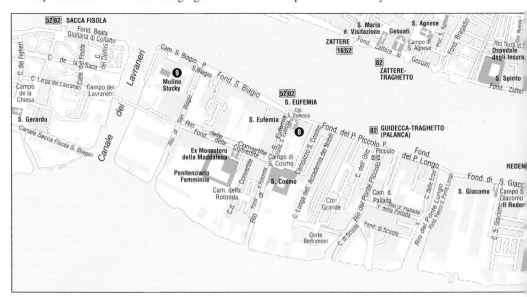

Il Redentore ❹ *(8am–noon, 3–7pm)* is a Venetian landmark, visible from every side of St Mark's Basin, and the main reason for visiting the island. The church of the Redeemer was built in thanksgiving for the end of the 1576 plague. Designed as a votive temple, the church is still the scene of Venice's most beguiling summer festival (*see page 95*). Architectural purists feel that this Palladian masterpiece, inspired by the Pantheon in Rome, surpasses even San Giorgio (*see page 268*). Certainly, the facade is more subtle, resting on a rusticated pediment, with a sweeping flight of steps echoing the style of a gracious Palladian country villa.

From here, the eye is inevitably led to the lantern surmounted by the figure of Christ the Redeemer. However, compared with the lovely view of the floodlit facade, seen from the quaysides of the Zattere, across the water, the interior can feel disappointing. Nonetheless, the church is designed according to rigorous classical principles, with its mastery of geometrical forms and effortless grandeur. Palladio was also influenced by contemporary Roman architecture, with the choir echoing Bramante's central plan for St Peter's. Certainly, this restrained and graceful church is the Venetian building most faithful to Palladian principles.

From the church, Ramo della Croce leads to the exotic **Garden of Eden** ❺, named after the Englishman who created it. Facing the garden is the former English Hospital, which cared for impecunious British expatriates during Edwardian times. Retracing one's steps leads back to the waterfront and another Palladian gem. **Le Zitelle** ❻, situated to the east of Il Redentore, is a church

Standing guard over Palladio's legacy.

and convent attributed to Palladio. It bears the Palladian hallmarks of stylistic unity, coherent classicism and an inspired sense of proportion. In keeping with Venetian tradition, the complex was originally designed as a convent but became a noted musical conservatoire. Recently restored, the complex has now taken on the role of a convention centre, making access difficult. Although Le Zitelle has a landing stage, with frequent services back to central Venice, many visitors prefer to be tempted by the luxurious Hotel Cipriani bar, which lies just beyond the convent.

The **Hotel Cipriani** ❼, set on the eastern spit of the island, enjoys sweeping

Map, page 270

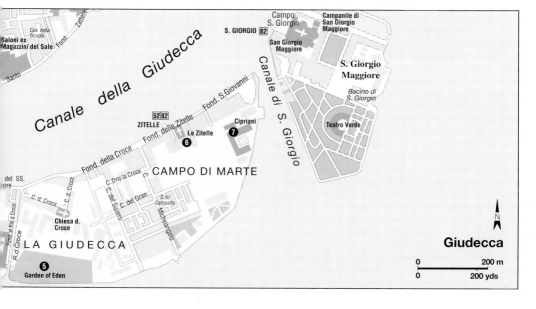

Giudecca

0   200 m
0   200 yds

TIP

In Harry's Dolci, try the *carpaccio*, the wafer-thin raw beef dressed with olive oil, rocket and Parmesan. (For a full description of the restaurant, see page 325.)

views over the lagoon, especially from the summer terrace. Now one of the world's most exclusive hotels, the Cipriani originally belonged to the founders of Harry's Bar (*see page 157*). Today it is favoured by international stars and celebrities such as Robert de Niro, Gérard Depardieu and Sophia Loren. Cipriani's liveried motor boats regularly ferry guests across from San Marco to this oasis of peace. The hotel incorporates a Gothic palace and boasts gardens of azaleas, rhododendrons and oleanders framing the wide expanse of the swimming pool. Less affluent visitors must content themselves with refreshments taken in **Harry's Dolci**, a popular offshoot of Harry's Bar, located on Fondamenta San Biagio.

Fans of industrial architecture can walk back along the waterfront past distinctive factories to the island's oldest church. **Sant'Eufemia** ❽ *(9am–noon, 6–7pm, Sunday 7am–noon)* faces the great Gesuati church across the water on Dorsoduro (*see page 252*). While dating back to the 9th century, Sant'Eufemia has been marred by remodelling. The bizarre mixture of styles includes a 16th-century portico, Veneto-Byzantine capitals, Rococo stuccowork and 18th-century paintings.

Unfortunately, the church is also overshadowed by a neighbouring mill, and by the decaying industrial wasteland behind. Next door, on the western edge of the island, lies **Mulino Stucky** ❾, a Neo-Gothic industrial relic. The novelist L.P. Hartley looked "almost with affection on the great bulk of Stucky's flour mill, battlemented, pinnacled, turreted, machicolated, a monument to the taste of 1870, that might have been built out of a child's box of bricks." Giovanni Stucky, the overbearing Swiss owner, was murdered by one of his workers in 1910. After decades of neglect, this fortress-like former grain silo, pasta factory and flour

BELOW: dining out on Murano.

mill is being converted into a convention centre. Giudecca residents hope that this grandiose monument to the Victorian age may yet come to symbolise an economic regeneration.

Map,
page 273

Murano

"The most curmudgeonly of the Venetian communities, where it always feels like early closing day," denounced writer Jan Morris. Yet Murano is proud of its past as a celebrated glass-making centre and a summer resort for the nobility. In the 18th century, the island was noted for its villas, gambling clubs and literary salons. However, the closure of many churches and the rapaciousness of the glass factories has somewhat blunted its appeal. On a sunny day, Murano can pass for a smaller version of Venice but it can be bleak in winter, with scruffiness and commercialism outweighing picturesque charm. Nonetheless, Murano makes a pleasant enough stopping-off point on the way to austere Torcello. Most visitors are enticed by the glass-making, although an impressive Byzantine church and a cluster of bars add to Murano's appeal.

Navigational channels are marked by "bricole", sturdy poles roped together, while "paline" are individual poles, often striped, for tethering private craft.

Murano glass is an acquired taste, which many lifelong Venice fans fail to acquire. While few visitors would turn down an antique Murano mirror or an 18th-century chandelier, modern Murano glass is another matter. It errs on the side of virtuosity and garishness rather than refinement and elegance. However, the skill of the Murano glass-blowers makes an impressive display.

Resist the touts on Riva degli Schiavoni, offering free boat trips to Murano. Freedom is costly, with victims marooned in one glass factory and subjected to heavy selling techniques. Instead, travel independently and select the showrooms you wish to see at leisure.

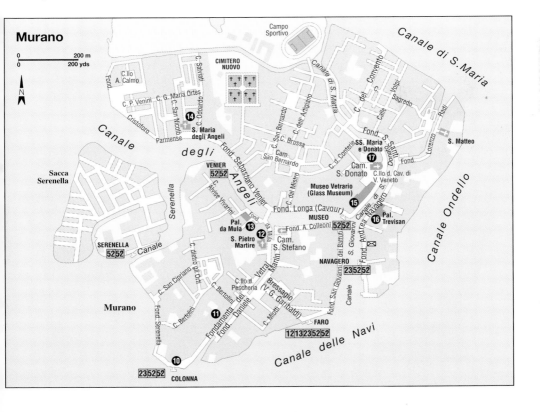

Visitors who only want a brief visit to Murano should stay on board until **Museo**, the third stop, close to the glass museum. However, serious shoppers will choose **Colonna** ⑩, the best stop for exploring the myriad glass factories.

The quayside opens onto **Fondamenta dei Vetrai** ⑪, the heart of the glass-making district, with the 16th-century Palazzo Contarini on the left. The show-rooms along the quayside offer opportunities to admire the glass-blowers' skills. Barovier e Tosso (Fondamenta Vetrai 28) are one of the better firms for collectors' items but kitsch creations abound in Murano, from peacock-shaped glasses to gondola vases. Towards the end of the quayside, a bridge crosses the canal to the left bank and the church of **San Pietro Martire** ⑫ *(8am–noon, 3–7pm)*. This Gothic church boasts a Renaissance portal and a subtle altarpiece by Bellini, *The Madonna, Doge Barbarigo and Saints* (1488). This "holy conversation" between the Doge and the Virgin, the temporal and spiritual powers, is a harmonious work: the drapery of the Madonna's blue cloak is deliberately blurred, with the rich colours creating a soft atmosphere.

Further down the quayside, just before Ponte Vivarini, stands the **Palazzo da Mula** ⑬, a glassworks set in a Gothic palace and Byzantine walled garden. From here, there is a picturesque view looking west along Canale degli Angeli to the abandoned church of **Santa Maria degli Angeli** ⑭.

From Palazzo da Mula, cross the main bridge over Canale Grande and turn to the right, following the quaysides of Fondamenta Cavour to the **Museo Vetrario** ⑮ *(10am–5pm, closed Wednesday)*, the Glass Museum. This occupies the imposing Palazzo Giustinian, a Gothic palace remodelled in the style of the 17th-century. It was originally the seat of the Bishop of Torcello, which was transferred here after the earlier settlement was abandoned. Although the

TIP

See *Insight On ... Murano Glass,* page 284, with additional shopping advice on page 332.

BELOW: window-shopping for Murano glass.

palace retains a few original frescoes, it is now essentially a showcase for Murano glass, from platters and beakers to crystal chalices and the finest chandeliers. Non-Venetian pieces include a Roman mosaic bowl, matched by fragments of mosaics from the island church of Santi Maria e Donato. As well as Renaissance enamelled glassware, there are Art Nouveau *objets d'art* and 19th-century pieces with satirical scenes mocking the Austrian rulers. The museum's finest piece is the glittering blue Coppa Barovier, a Gothic wedding chalice, adorned with allegorical love scenes.

Murano's finest church

On the right bank, facing the museum, lies the classical **Palazzo Trevisan** ⑯, with its interior frescoed by Veronese. On the left bank, just north of the glass museum is a beguiling church reflected in the water. **Santi Maria e Donato** ⑰ *(9am–noon, 4–6pm)* is the finest church on Murano, despite a misguided 19th-century restoration. The church was founded in the 7th century but remodelled in Veneto-Byzantine style. The most characteristic sections are the 12th-century apses, decorated with blind arches and loggias leaning over the canal. As in Santa Fosca, on Torcello, the brick and terracotta apses are studded with zigzag friezes and dog-tooth mouldings. The plain facade is currently scaffolded.

The charm of the interior has survived much tampering, with its Gothic ship's keel ceiling, Greek marble columns and Veneto-Byzantine capitals. The apse is dominated by a luminous Byzantine-style mosaic of the *Madonna and Child*, rivalled by a charming altarpiece by Paolo Veneziano (*c*1310). However, the highlight is the patterned mosaic floor, depicting interlaced foliage and allegorical animals, which was fully restored in the 1970s. The pattern includes

Map, page 273

Palaces generally had water and land gates, with the grandest displaying the owner's coat of arms.

BELOW: Burano, Venice's Greek island.

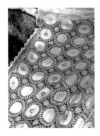

*Burano lace –
beware of imitations.*

BELOW: Santi Maria
e Donato, Murano.

fragments of ancient glass mosaics, recalling the finest Murano craftsmanship. When leaving Murano from the **Museo** boat stop, look out for the jaunty lighthouse (*faro*) located on the east of the island.

Burano

This most vibrant of Venetian islands makes a cheery stop en route to Torcello, its polar opposite. Hemingway mocked the islanders for having nothing better to do than make boats and babies. However, Burano is better known as the home of fishermen and lace-sellers. Weary visitors may be relieved to find that there are few cultural sights but atmosphere aplenty. Burano is one of the friendliest islands, partly the product of its self-sufficiency: a history of modest prosperity has made it less dependent on tourism than many other islands. To help preserve its character, the community regularly rejects applications for hotels.

Burano feels like an authentic old fishing village, with nets hung out to dry and boxes of crabs blocking the doorways. Burano romantics even portray lacemaking as an aesthetic extension of the net-mending tradition. After several glasses of wine, visitors can easily imagine themselves transported to a Greek island, aided by visions of bobbing boats in the dappled sunlight.

From the ferry stop, follow the flow to **Via Galuppi** ⑱, the main street, lined with fishermen's cottages. Tradition has it that the houses were painted different colours to enable fishermen to recognise their homes from out at sea. When not ruining their eyesight poring over lace, the fishermen's wives painted the family homes in bold colours, often adding geometrical motifs over the doorways. By the same token, when ashore, the fishermen spent their time mending nets or boat-building. Burano remains the best place for boat-building, with craftsmen

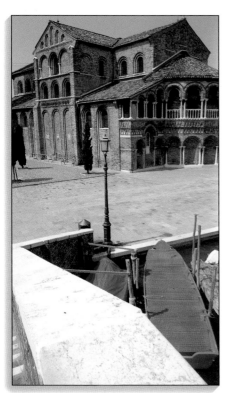

building by eye, not by design. The street is lined with lace shops and traditional *trattorie*, the place for the best crab and squid dishes. After a visit to the lace school, visitors learn to distinguish between Taiwanese products and genuine Burano lace, as light as tulle.

Piazza Galuppi, the colourful town square is home to the **Scuola dei Merletti** ⑲ *(10am–4pm, closed Monday)*, the lace school and museum, housed in a Gothic palace. Given the difficulties of preserving lace, most samples on display tend to be from the 19th century, including a fine wedding train. Lace was made in Venetian convents since medieval times but the *punto in aria* method, using a needle and thread, only emerged in the 16th century. The art fell into decline with the Industrial Revolution but was saved from extinction on Burano by the creation of a lace-making school in 1872. By the turn of the century, the local industry sustained 5,000 people, but factory-made lace also fell out of fashion. Ironically, the islanders now import Taiwanese lace to boost their scant sales of hand-made lace. Genuine hand-made Burano-point lace is ridiculously expensive: but then, it takes 10 women up to three years to make a single tablecloth, with each woman specialising in a different stitch.

From here, the leaning tower of **San Martino** ⑳ *(8am–noon, 3–6pm)* looms into view. The 16th-century church is best-known for its paintings, especially a Tiepolo *Crucifixion*. A short walk leads to **Fondamenta della Giudecca** ㉑, and a chance to stroll along the colourful quaysides. The more adventurous should consider a short boat trip to an atmospheric Franciscan retreat: Burano is the only sensible embarkation point for the lush island of **San Francesco del Deserto** *(see page 289)*. From the quays close to the church there is an idiosyncratic family-run shuttle service in a *sandolo*, a traditional rowing boat. Alter-

Map,
page 276

TIP

In island restaurants try *brodo di pesce* (fish soup), Adriatic fish or *granseola*, lagoon crab with its meat dressed in oil and lemon, and served in its shell.

BELOW: Burano, a parade of pastels.

natively, on your way back to the ferry, consider crossing the footbridge to **Maz-zorbo** ㉒, a former island for exiles. The verdant island is unremarkable but there are evocative views towards Venice. (Ferry services usually stop at Maz-zorbo as well as Burano but check the times.)

Torcello

The long boat trip to Torcello helps one appreciate the remoteness of this evocative island, the earliest centre of Venetian civilisation . It is strange to think that Venice arose from these solemn marshes, a 7th-century settlement uprooted from its mainland home of Altinum. As an autonomous island and trading post, Torcello flourished, with 10,000 inhabitants in the 10th century. Decline set in with the rise of Venice, hastened by the silting up of this corner of the lagoon, which turned Torcello into a malarial swamp after the 14th century. Now only about 50 people live here permanently.

The novelist George Sand captured the pastoral mood of her visit in the 1830s: "Torcello is a reclaimed wilderness. Through copses of water willow and hibiscus bushes run saltwater streams where petrel and teal delight to stalk." But where Sand celebrated life, other commentators have seen the haunting spirit of a ghost town. Ruskin mused on the poignant scene, "this waste of wild sea moor, of a lurid ashen grey… the melancholy clearness of space in the warm sunset, oppressive, reaching to the horizon of its level gloom."

From the jetty, a canal towpath leads through the lush countryside to the Byzantine complex. **Locanda Cipriani** ㉓, a deceptively modest rural inn, lies just beyond the bridge. Film stars and royals have feasted on the self-consciously simple seafood dishes. Hemingway, who stayed here while working on his

"More like a storm refuge than a great church"

— JOHN RUSKIN

BELOW: symbolic statuary on the Cathedral walls.

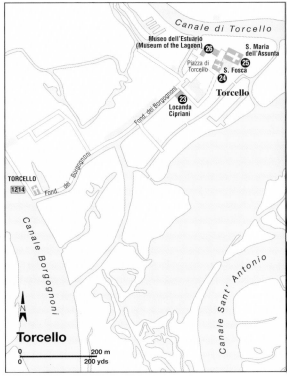

Torcello

0 _____ 200 m
0 _____ 200 yds

Venetian novel, has one of his characters give a simplified view of the creation of Venice: "Torcello boys were all great boatman. So they took the stones off all their houses on barges… and they built Venice." Certainly, as the city declined, building materials were often recycled first on Murano and Burano, and then in Venice itself.

At the end of the path stands the austerely lovely basilica of **Santa Fosca** ㉔ *(10am–12.30pm, 2–5pm)*. Built by Greeks, it was designed as a *martyrium*, housing the relics of a martyr. The church is a coherent masterpiece, a harmonious structure combining Romanesque with Byzantine elements. The basilica was built in the 11th century, at the same time as San Donato in Murano, and boasts the same blind arcading and geometrical motifs. The outer walls are girded by an octagonal portico resting on stilted arches, with sculpted columns. The portico balances the thrust of the dome and vaults, and also heightens the sense of interior space. The central plan, a Greek cross inscribed within an octagon, is emblematic of Byzantine architecture, with the pentagonal apses echoing Oriental forms. The Byzantine interior is barrel-vaulted but the planned dome was never built.

Santa Fosca is linked by a portico to **Santa Maria dell'Assunta** ㉕ *(10am–12.30pm, 2–5pm)*, a model of an early Christian church. To Ruskin, the stark exterior was reminiscent of a storm refuge. The cathedral is the oldest monument in the lagoon, founded in 639 AD as an episcopal seat. The basilica was modelled on those in Ravenna but modified in the 9th and early 11th centuries to create a superb Veneto-Byzantine building. The church was first restored in 1008, with the raising of the floor and creation of a crypt: the lovely mosaic floor dates from this period. The dignified interior is punctuated by slender

Map, page 278

For a description of Veneto-Byzantine architecture, see page 60, and for mosaics see page 71.

BELOW: Santa Fosca with the cathedral beyond.

*Preening peacocks
on the iconostasis
(rood screen).*

ABOVE: detail from
the Weighing of
Souls mosaic in the
Cathedral.

Greek marble columns, bearing Byzantine capitals. Among the treasures included here are the original 7th-century altar, the pulpit, the ceremonial throne, and a Roman sarcophagus containing the relics of St Heliodorus, the first Bishop of Altinum. The iconostasis is painted with Byzantine panels and supported by marble peacocks drinking from the fountain of life.

The solemnity of the architecture is counterpointed by the richness of the **mosaics**. These date from the 7th century, with some in the apse from the 9th century. A masterpiece of Byzantine design adorns the central apse: a slender, mysterious *Madonna* bathed in a cloth of gold. The frieze of the *Twelve Apostles* close by dates from the 12th century. Henry James admired these "grimly mystical mosaics", with the Apostles "ranged against their dead gold backgrounds as stiffly as grenadiers presenting arms". The 13th-century *Last Judgement* counterbalances the apse mosaics and is the most compelling narrative sequence. One should read it from top to bottom, with the *Crucifixion* leading to the *Descent into Limbo*, the *Day of Judgement* and, at the bottom, the *Weighing of Souls*. Although sections of the work have been over-restored, it is still engrossing, with angels, devils and disembodied corpses competing for attention.

In front of the church lie the vestiges of the 7th-century **baptistry**, built on a circular plan like the Roman baths. Also on the piazza is **Attila's throne**, a Roman potentate's marble seat. Nearby stands the Torcello museum, the **Museo dell' Estuario** ㉖ *(10am–12.30pm, 2–5.30pm, closed Sunday and Monday).* While not outstanding, the museum is a quiet complement to the site, spread over two buildings, the former town hall and city archives. Exhibits include mosaics from Ravenna and fragments from Torcello's *Last Judgement*, lost during a clumsy restoration in 1853. Compared with the largely intact and original buildings, these are the broken shards of a lost civilisation.

Like Ruskin, most writers strike an elegiac note when faced with the collapse of this early Venetian settlement: "The lament of many human voices mixed with the fretting of the waves on the ridges of the sand." However, if you are fortunate, and the crowds are in abeyance, you may share George Sand's enchantment with Torcello: "The air was balmy and only the song of cicadas disturbed the religious hush of the morning." If the ferry fails to come, or if you

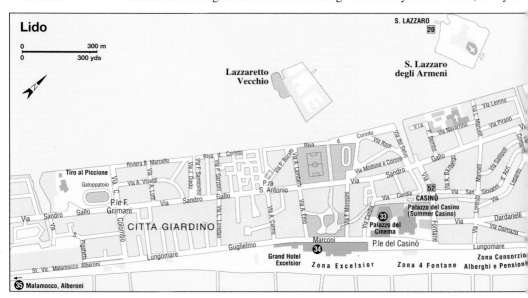

are overcome by the exquisite aromas from the Locanda Cipriani, retire to lunch at its gentrified rustic rival, the **Osteria Ponte del Diavolo**.

The Lido

This long strip of land, sandwiched between the city of Venice and the waters of the Adriatic, belongs neither to Venice nor the mainland. This reflects the Lido's prime function, to protect Venice from the engulfing tides. In spirit, it is a place apart, not quite a traditional summer resort nor a residential suburb. After the time warp of historic Venice, the sight of cars, large villas and department stores can be disconcerting. Yet the island cannot be dismissed as soulless. There is a touch of unreality about the Lido, as there is about Venice itself, hence its role as a superior film set. In this faded fantasy, Neo-Gothic piles vie with Art Nouveau villas and a mock-Moorish castle.

In the Romantic era, Byron and Shelley raced on horseback along the empty sands, but the advent of sea-bathing in the 1840s brought the fashionable elite and the world in its wake. The English and Germans were the chief culprits, but by the 1880s the Venetians had also succumbed to the spell of sun, sand and sea. The island became the world's first lido, spawning a rash of brash or glitzy imitators across the globe. Ruskin railed against the crowds of uncouth smokers who filled "his" steamers: the populace "smokes and spits up and down the piazzetta all day, and gets itself dragged by a screaming kettle to the Lido next morning to sea-bathe itself into capacity for more tobacco." The once-windswept dunes gave way to mass tourism in the 1920s, with D.H. Lawrence decrying the beach as "a strand with an endless heap of seals come up for mating."

However, the Lido is also Thomas Mann's Venice, a place of decadence and spiritual dislocation. Curiously, this does not dispel its staid reputation as a bourgeois retreat. The Lido has long been a bulwark of conservatism, residential rather than industrial, conventional yet cosmopolitan.

Since the Lido cannot compete with the historical riches of the rest of Venice, it generally remains the preserve of residents and visitors staying on the island. Although most day-trippers stray no further than the beaches, the summer casino and the smart hotels, the Lido offers more subtle pleasures for those willing to

Map, page 281

TIP

On Torcello, try *castraure*, tiny spring artichoke hearts cooked in *olio e aglio* (olive oil and garlic) or fried. Also sample *risi e bisi*, rice and peas, a cross between a risotto and a soup (*bisi* is dialect for peas).

ABOVE: the Jewish Cemetery on the Lido.

Map,
page 281

*"Has anyone
remarked that the
seat in such a bark,
the armchair
lacquered in coffin-
black, is the softest,
most luxurious, most
relaxing seat in the
world?"*

— THOMAS MANN

BELOW: final
farewell to Burano.

look, from *belle époque* architecture to a delightful cycle ride along the sea walls to Malamocco.

The ferries from San Marco deposit visitors amongst the traffic at the edge of the shopping district. Close to the jetties stands the 16th-century church of **Santa Maria Elisabetta ㉗**, with the main shopping street beyond. **Gran Viale di Santa Maria Elisabetta ㉘** cuts across the island from the Lagoon shore to the Adriatic. An air of gracious living permeates the broad promenade, embracing the graceful Art Nouveau **Villa Montplaisir** at No 14. At the far end of the Viale lies the **Lungomare**, the seafront promenade and the focus of the summer evening *passeggiata* (promenade). Beyond are the best Adriatic beaches, private pockets of sand bedecked with colourful cabins.

The Lido is home to several of the city's most elegant hotels, including the **Grand Hotel des Bains ㉙** (Via Lungomare Marconi 17). Thomas Mann's stay in this ecletic Edwardian palace helped inspire *Death in Venice*. Even Mann's beach spelt foreboding: "Evening too was rarely lovely, balsamic with the breath of flowers and shrubs from the nearby park."

Beaches and the summer casino

Following the seafront north leads to the public beach and airstrip. **Nuovo Cimitero Israelitico ㉚**, the Jewish cemetery, lies on Via Cipro, the street cutting across the island. The cemetery dates back to 1386 and reflects the special status of Jews in Venice (*see page 114*). Via Cipro leads to the lagoon shore and **San Nicolò ㉛**, a church and Benedictine monastery. It was here that the Doge prayed after the Marriage of the Sea ceremony on Ascension Day (*see page 94*). From here, there is a clear view of the **Fortezza di Sant'Andrea** on the island

of Le Vignole, the impressive bastion that defended the lagoon (*see page 291*). If beaches appeal, bear in mind that most are private and charge a fee, unlike the **Spiaggia Comunale ㉜**, the scruffy public beach in the east of the island. The reports of pollution in the Adriatic do not deter the crowds. At the grander end of the seafront stands the **Palazzo del Cinema ㉝**, typical of the functionalist buildings of the Fascist era, and the focus of the Venice Film Festival. Next door looms the **Palazzo del Casino**, the summer casino, as functional as the winter casino is beautiful.

On Lungomare Marconi, along the seafront, towards the Gran Viale, stands the **Hotel Excelsior ㉞**. This exuberant turn-of-the-century hotel was inspired by exotic Moorish models and Veneto-Byzantine traditions.

A cycle ride or leisurely walk lead south past the grand hotels and manicured beaches, following the sea walls into oblivion. The route passes **Malamocco ㉟**, the site of the first capital of the Lagoon before it was engulfed by a tidal wave. Although there are no traces of the 8th-century capital, this fishing village offers several seafood restaurants and a belltower echoing the *campanile* of San Marco. The spit eventually peters out in the sand dunes of **Alberoni**, with the windswept views beloved by Goethe now only visible across golf courses. Beyond is the island of **Pellestrina**, a narrow strip of land bounded by the *murazzi*, the great sea walls (*see page 54*). ❑

Film festival

Venice is a star on the international film circuit, although trailing behind Cannes in terms of prestige. The festival takes place over a fortnight in late August or early September. The Lido then recovers a little of its turn-of-the-century lustre. Stars can be spotted sipping Bellinis on the terrace of the Excelsior Hotel or parading along the seafront. It was on this grand terrace that the first film festival opened in 1932. Thus Venice claims to be the world's oldest international film festival, predating Cannes by 14 years. Founded as a showcase for Fascist Italy, the festival's success belies its unpromising origins.

Early film festivals were backed by powerful hoteliers, with Spencer Tracy nominated for his role in *Dr Jekyll and Mr Hyde* in the first festival. In 1937 the Palazzo del Cinema was built, still the heart of the festival. The event celebrated such vintage performances as Greta Garbo in *Anna Karenina* (1935) and Laurence Olivier's *Hamlet* (1948). Although early directors of the calibre of John Ford and Auguste Renoir brought glamour to the Lido, the festival has a checkered past, frequently beset by bureaucracy and political wrangling. The glory days coincided with New Wave cinema in the 1960s, a fame which was sealed by movies from Godard, Pasolini, Tarkovsky and Visconti.

Since the 1980s, there have been constant charges of jury bias, reflected in comments made by Spike Lee, the black American director, and other prominent film-makers. Certainly, controversial directors have not always fared well in Venice. Yet the 1990s marked a revival in the festival's fortunes, both in terms of audience appreciation and in film quality. The Golden Lion (Leon d'Oro) award may now mean a little more.

The prestige of the festival is emphasised by Gillo Pontecorvo, the long-standing director, who successfully exploits his Hollywood connections. In recent years, the festival has managed to woo back Jack Nicholson, Mel Gibson and Kevin Costner, with Venice being favourably compared with Cannes as a destination. However, a new director in 1998 gave a change in direction for the festival, and Venice has begun to turn its back on American blockbusters in an attempt to return to its more radical roots. European films are now favoured, a policy the Venetians hope will give a boost to the ailing Italian film industry, which has been in the doldrums since the death of Fellini. A radical change would displease Count Volpi di Misurata, the son of the festival founder: from his villa on the Giudecca, Volpi still hosts the best première parties in Venice, with privileged movie stars invited to stay.

Whatever the failings of the films, the city always shines. For two weeks the Lido is awash with film executives and stars scurrying from the Moorish Hotel Excelsior to the Stalinist Palazzo del Cinema where the films are shown. At night, motor boats ferry sleek stars to glamorous Harry's Bar or the Cipriani. Screenings are held at the Astra or Palazzo del Cinema on the Lido, with tickets available to the public on the day of the performance. To coincide with the festival, films are sometimes also shown on Campo Santa Margherita, in the city centre. ❏

RIGHT: sheltering from the limelight.

THE GLASSWORKS OF MURANO

The refinement of Venetian glass developed on the island of Murano made it a byword for superb chalices, chandeliers, mirrors and objets d'art

The shimmering objects in the Murano Museum (Museo Vetrario) bear witness to the skill and artistry of the Venetian glass-blowers. Some vessels seem spun in the finest lace while others are covered with a skein of white threads. Murano was the centre of the European glass industry from the 13th to 18th centuries, when Bohemian crystal came to dominate the market. The Venetian glass industry flourished after the Sack of Constantinople in 1204. Venetian booty included precious Islamic and Byzantine glassware – and captive Syrian or Saracen craftsmen who created the local glass industry. In 1291, the Venetian government moved the glass furnaces to Murano, in an attempt to control the burgeoning industry, a pillar of the Venetian economy.

PRECIOUS TRADE SECRETS

The making of mirrors was for long a Venetian monopoly. In the 14th century, Muzio da Murano created a reflecting surface by coating a glass sheet with a solution of tin and mercury. Venetian blown-glass mirrors, graced by shimmering glass frames, were the envy of Renaissance Europe. Such was the significance of the Venetian monopoly that glass-makers guarded the secrets of their craft and left Murano on pain of death. In return, the glass-makers formed a powerful and privileged guild, with members even allowed to marry into the nobility. Yet neither threats nor rewards could prevent a few glass-makers from fleeing abroad to open their own factories, often with dire consequences. Several who escaped to the court of Louis XIV of France were poisoned after giving up their secrets. Although Murano's fate was sealed by the Industrial Revolution, a post-war revival keeps 100 glassworks in business.

▽ **MUSEUM PIECE**
This ornamental glass bucket is on display in the Museo Vetrario, the recently remodelled Glass Museum.

▽ **MURANO VASE**
Affluent shoppers can reject the gaudier glass souvenirs in favour of hand-crafted designer objects.

▷ **GEM DESIGN**
This beautiful 15th-century bottle is of chalcedony glass, which imitates gemstones.

△ **MARRIAGE CUP**
This celebrated Barovier marriage cup (c. 1460–70) is decorated with allegorical scenes and portraits of the bride and groom.

△ **REPUTABLE NAMES**
Choice buys, like this unusual vase, are best made from one of the reputable names, such as Barovier or Salviati.

◁ **GLASS PENGUIN**
This bizarre designer objet d'art comes from the Murano showrooms: for a wide choice, visit the island workshops on the Fonda-menta dei Vetrai.

△ **ANTIQUE GOBLET**
This Barovier goblet from 1878 comes fom the Salviati workshops, which operate from a Grand Canal palace.

THE CRAFT OF GLASS-MAKING

The Venetians revived the art of enamelled glass, a technique that had been lost since antiquity. Yet this is just one of the sophisticated techniques introduced by Murano glassmakers. By using the best Oriental raw materials, craftsmen also created a delicate, light-weight glass. The purity and clarity of this cristalline glass was the origin of the term *cristallo* or crystal. Bright colours were obtained by the addition of metal oxides. Glittering aventurine glass was created by setting tiny particles of copper into molten glass. However, the most sophisticated creation of the glass-makers' art is the "netted" or filigree *reticelli* glassware.

Most furnaces on Murano welcome spectators. In general, the filigree effect is created by a process of twisting, turning and blowing, moulding the glass into a vivid animal, vase or goblet. Lightness of touch is everything. Initially, a blob of molten paste is placed on the red-hot end of a hollow tube and then shaped. To make a spherical form, such as a goblet, the glassblower may shape the blob on a wooden mould before blowing down the tube to pierce the resultant ball. This ball is then reblown and rotated to attain its rough shape, with steel pincers used to draw the glass out to a point. Further reheating and reblowing occur until the final shape is achieved.

THE MINOR ISLANDS

*The smaller islands of the lagoon show a different face of
Venice: among the delightful backwaters are a famous cemetery,
isolated monasteries, and a rural way of life*

Map,
page 132

Adrift between the industrial and the rural world, the lesser-known islands of the Venetian lagoon are abandoned to bird song, howling dogs and the prayers of monks. Apart from the religious communities who cherish their isolation, the minor islands are searching for a new identity. In the past, they served specific functions, with the city defences bolstered by the islands close to the Lido, the monastic islands clustered around San Marco, and outlying islands used as hospitals or munitions stores.

Remoteness rendered the islands suitable for such esoteric uses as quarantine centres and lunatic asylums, hermitages and monastic retreats – even cemeteries, leper colonies and dog sanctuaries. Many of these survive, although some have been transformed into market gardens and vineyards.

Nonetheless, about 20 of the 34 lagoon islands are virtually abandoned, although there are plans to sell them to reclusive millionaires, cultural associations and leisure clubs. In 1995, the Italian State, daunted by the future upkeep of the islands, decided to auction some of the minor treasures. As a result, a local engineer became the proud possessor of a mound of mud bearing one apple tree: "Now I have a place to go fishing, watch birds and sunbathe," he cried.

The State decided to lease out the larger islands on condition that their forts, monasteries and hospitals were restored. By the late 1990s, the fate of Poveglia, Lazzaretto Vecchio and San Clemente still hung in the balance. San Servolo, however, is a success story – it was converted into an international university in 1997.

Pastoral preserve

Yet thanks to the shifting tides and the shallowness of the lagoon, the islands preserve a pastoral way of life, one that is rarely visible to visitors who stay close to the shore. At low tide, the shrimp fishermen leave their boats and seem to walk across water; families picnicking on remote sandbanks appear from nowhere and then disappear again with the tide. With the blur of mainland pollution merging into a heat haze, you may catch sight of the vivid plumage of a migratory bird or two, or spot a solitary reed-cutter tramping over the mudflats. In the *valli* fisheries, locks are checked and the fish directed into different ponds while, to the east of Torcello, the salt pans continue to be worked. Children play happily in the vineyards of Le Vignole while their uncles tend to their market gardens on neighbouring Sant'Erasmo, and the sun-worshippers simply stretch out on the sand bars of Pellestrina.

Island-hopping is not always an easy task: the local fishermen have grown tired of rescuing stranded tourists. Even so, with many islands not served by ferry, occasional journeys in private rowing boats are

LEFT: a fading rural paradise.
BELOW: the unchanging lagoon.

inevitable (*see page 306*). Bargaining with fishermen may be the only alternative to an exorbitant motor launch, but the reward is a view of Venice beyond the confines of St Mark's. The holy grail for any visitor to this area is a plate of risotto steeped in black cuttlefish sauce – ideally cooked by a lapsed monk in an isolated tavern deep in the lagoon.

San Michele and its cemetery

San Michele, site of the city cemetery, is known affectionately as 'the island of the dead'. From afar, its silhouette is often appropriately swathed in mist, floating as ethereally as a city in the afterlife. As the island closest to Venice, it is served by ferries from the Fondamente Nuove. The quayside and adjoining alleys are devoted to the business of death: monumental masons vie with funeral florists, both doing their briskest business in winter. From the shore, one's eye is drawn to the contrast between the solemn cypress trees, black against the sky, and the high rose-coloured brick walls.

Coducci's innovative Renaissance church.

Just by the landing-stage lies **San Michele in Isola**, a cool, austere Renaissance church by Coducci. As the first church faced in blanched white Istrian stone, San Michele set a building trend throughout the Veneto. Beside the church is a domed Gothic chapel and cloisters leading to the cemetery.

This was where Napoleon decreed the dead should be despatched, away from the crowded city graves. The adjacent island of **San Cristoforo** was co-opted shortly afterwards, with additional land periodically reclaimed. The Austrians used the former monastery as a political prison but the island is now tended by Franciscans. Although there are sections for foreigners here, the Jews bury their dead in a separate cemetery on the Lido (*see page 282*). Famous foreigners are

BELOW: San Michele, the "island of the dead."

allowed to rest in peace but more modest souls are evicted after ten years. The rambling cemetery is lined with gardens stacked with simple memorials or domed family mausoleums awaiting further members. Here lie the tombs of several Dogal families, obscure diplomats, and the victims of malaria or the plague. The grounds are studded with grotesque statuary encompassing the grandiose and monumental, the cute and the kitsch.

In the eastern corner is the Protestant *(Evangelisti)* section, containing the grave of American poet Ezra Pound (1885–1972). Untended and overgrown, this is also the last resting place of obscure Swiss, German and British seamen. In the *Greci* or Orthodox section lie the tombs of composer Igor Stravinsky (1882–1971) and ballet impresario Diaghilev (1872–1929) along with the tombs of long-forgotten Russian and Greek aristocrats.

Although the writer Jan Morris is enchanted by the cemetery's "seductive desolation", nurse Livio Nardo has a sunnier relationship with San Michele and says of it: "It's the most cheerful cemetery in the world, as cemeteries go. You've got good company there – Stravinsky and Ezra Pound. We get tourists committing suicide in Venice just so they can be buried there."

The friary on San Francesco del Deserto

Another fascinating island is **San Francesco del Deserto** *(9–11am, 3–5pm)*, a Franciscan retreat. Since there are no ferry services to the island, visitors will need to hire a *sandolo*, a Venetian rowing boat, from **Burano**, the closest inhabited island *(see page 276)*. (You will probably need to bargain with the canny fisherman who runs this unofficial shuttle service.) Legend has it that St Francis visited the island on his return from the Holy Land, symbolised by a tree that

Map,
page 132

For more on illustrious deaths in Venice, see page 116.

BELOW: speeding away from the ghosts in the lagoon.

When shopping for
fruit and vegetables in
Venice itself, request
produce that is
"*nostrano*" ("our
own"), meaning grown
on Sant' Erasmo.

supposedly sprouted from the saint's staff. A Franciscan community was certainly established here by the 13th century. In the course of its history, it has been abandoned twice, after an outbreak of malaria and military occupation. A friar takes visitors round the original cloisters and modest 15th-century church. A restoration in 1962 revealed some of the original floor and foundations.

The monastery exudes an air of self-sufficiency, from the serene friars to the well-tended vegetable gardens. A contemplative mood is induced by the lofty cypresses and emblematic Franciscan paintings. Ten friars live on the island, and there are visiting novices.

Lazzaretto Nuovo and Sant'Erasmo

Just south is **Lazzaretto Nuovo**, a former quarantine island for contagious diseases. (To reach it, hire a rowing boat in **Sant'Erasmo** or shout to a boatman across the water channel.) Now largely abandoned, the island began as a *lazzaretto* or isolation centre for plague victims. After the epidemics had passed, the site was abandoned but later converted into a military site. Amidst the overgrown vegetation lies a ruined gunpowder warehouse and the recently unearthed foundations of a 6th-century church. There are plans for the island to become a sports and recreation centre.

Facing Lazzaretto is **Sant'Erasmo**, the market garden in the heart of the lagoon. Reached by line 13 from Fondamente Nuove (*see page 235*), the island is home to just 800 people, most of them poor farmers. It is best-known for its spring *radicchio*, asparagus and artichokes, delivered to the Rialto market by boat. Although the island has a church and farmhouse restaurant, the locals grumble that, without a doctor or school, the future outlook is bleak.

BELOW: paddling
towards Chioggia.

Le Vignole and its fortress

Le Vignole lies just south of Sant'Erasmo but can be viewed from the northern end of the Lido. Its sole claim to fame is that it served as the main plank in the Venetian defensive system. The fort (*see page 306*), designed by Sanmicheli in 1543, guarded the lagoon, with chains stretching right across from it to a matching fortress on the Lido. The entrance was thus completely sealed off and reinforced by lines of cannons resting on rafts.

Although rather dilapidated, the structure of the fort is still clear, forming an arched bastion with apertures at water level for more cannon. Although not easy to reach, the island is popular with Venetians, thanks to its patchwork of vineyards and small-holdings. In summer months, the adults congregate in a makeshift café while their children dive off their parents' boats.

The Southern Lagoon

Santa Maria della Grazie, immediately south of the Giudecca , began as a resting place for pilgrims on the way to the Holy Land. The island then became a monastic site and military base but its latest incarnation is as a hospital for infectious diseases. (The island is served by line 10 from San Zaccaria, as is its neighbour, **San Clemente.**)

This island has endured an even more complex history as a pilgrims hostel, hermitage, munitions depot, and a haven for the Doge and his entourage. In the 19th century it became a lunatic asylum, and later mutated into a less rigorous psychiatric hospital, which it remained until 1992. Nostalgic former residents return to visit occasionally but, like many islands in the lagoon, its fate hangs in the balance.

Map, page 132

Venetian delicacies are often seasonal, from "risi e bisi", a rice and pea spring soup, to "fiori di zucchini", courgette flowers stuffed with fish mousse. Autumn is heralded by "funghi porcini", the finest mushrooms.

BELOW: freedom from culture vultures.

The living lagoon

The lagoon is often dismissed as a desolate marsh but it is also a patchwork of sand banks, salt pans and mud flats, with sections cultivated as fish farms, market gardens and vineyards. Parts are noxious marshes, leaving the stench of stagnation in one's nostrils; parts are dreamy, winding creeks, with reed-cutters at work. In Palude dei Setti Morti, west of Pellestrina, fishermen still build *casoni*, huts on stilts. At low tide, the mud flats (*barene*) off Burano are dotted with fishermen seemingly walking on water.

Sea water enters the lagoon through three main entrances: these breaks or "ports" in the sand bars (*lidi*) are at Chioggia, Malamocco and Porto di Lido. Thanks to the tides, the water channels are cleansed of debris and sediment. While the "dead" lagoon is only fully covered at high tide, the other half is the "living" lagoon, with sea water coursing through this navigable section. The lagoon marshes are criss-crossed with canals and

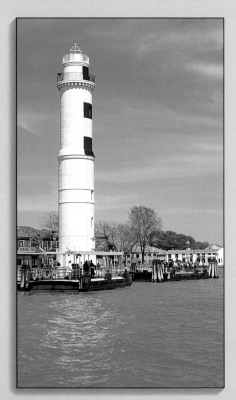

sand banks, with an outlying area of diked lakes mostly set aside for fisheries. The salinity of the lagoon varies, with water cleaner yet muddier near river deltas, brackish near the middle and sandiest yet saltiest near the lagoon entrances. Many sections of the lagoon are unnavigable because of the mud flats and sand banks; but skilled boatmen can weave through the shifting channels and sandbars, guided by the *bricole*, the distinctive navigational markers.

Venetian watermen and engineers have long struggled to protect the lagoon from encroachment by the sea. In response to high tides and floods, early palisades were built along the coast to divert the course of rivers.

Silting has been a problem since the 13th century: flooding rivers, extreme tides and the action of wind and waves threatened to build up the submerged banks of sand and silt in the Adriatic and move them across the *porti* (lagoon entrances). In response, the city built breakwaters and two lighthouses on the Lido, the main lagoon entrance. Even so, doommongers predict that the noxious mainland factories spell ecological disaster (*see page 55*). Certainly, the reduction of oxygenated water has had a detrimental effect on plant and marine life. The speed and depth of the tides have also been affected by land reclamation, whilst constant scouring of the water channels to enable navigation by large boats has eroded the natural build-up of silt – the gloomier prophets predict that the sandbanks will disappear altogether by 2050.

However, on a positive note, much lagoon life survives, from kingfishers, cormorants and coots to grey herons and little egrets. As for fish, bream, sea bass and eels feed in lagoon. There is a bold proposal to turn the Venetian Lagoon into a marine park stretching from the Lido to Chioggia.

More modest initiatives are already underway, with attempts to capture the imagination of the future protectors of this unique ecosystem. Local clubs offer nature rambles on the lesser-known lagoon islands, visiting fish farms, isolated spits and marshes; the mud flats provide safe footholds for accompanied or experienced ramblers. ❑

LEFT: the Murano lighthouse, a welcoming beacon in the lagoon.

San Servolo and its university

Between the Giudecca and the Lido lies **San Servolo**, served by line 20 from San Zaccaria. San Servolo rose to prominence as a Benedictine monastery in the 8th century, then became a Benedictine nunnery until 1615. After welcoming refugee nuns from Crete, a former Venetian colony, San Servolo started operating as a hospital. In 1725, it became an asylum for Venetian "maniacs of noble family" of whom there were many. The asylum was built within the monastic shell, with the church remodelled and new wards created. Byron often passed the island on his marathon swims from the Lido to the Grand Canal. His friend Shelley referred to the asylum as "a windowless, deformed and dreary pile… which calls the maniacs, each one from his cell, to vespers". The French poet Théophile Gautier, who visited in 1850, also found it deeply dispiriting: "It had been no great task to adapt their use from monks to madmen".

However, in recent years the complex has housed a prestigious craft centre. In 1997, after a lengthy period of restoration, it has re-opened as Venice International University, with English the medium of instruction, and close links with the participating universities of North Carolina, Munich and Barcelona. The complex has managed to preserve its 18th-century pharmacy and library as well as the cloisters and its lush grounds.

Map, page 132

A local islander.

San Lazzaro and its monastery

San Lazzaro degli Armeni *(3.20–5pm)*, an island off the **Lido**, is one of the most intriguing monasteries in the lagoon, distinguished by its onion-shaped cupola. (This Armenian enclave is served by line 10 or 20 from San Zaccaria, with tours coinciding with the ferry times.) The Armenians, along with the Greeks and Jews, form the oldest foreign community in Venice. The Armenians settled in Venice from the 13th century onwards and always remained on good terms with the Republic. The island was a leper colony until 1717 when the Armenians were granted asylum from Turkish persecution. The leader, Mechitar the Consoler, had been driven from the monastery he had established in the Morea (the Peloponnese).

BELOW: turning one's back on a monastic future.

Today, the island is a scholarly centre for Armenian culture, supported by the 8-million strong Armenian diaspora. The setting is idyllic, with the church and cloisters surrounded by orchards, gardens and strolling peacocks. The remodelled Romanesque church is decorated with starry mosaics, the air laden with incense. The 18th-century refectory is where the monks and seminarians eat in silence while the Scriptures are intoned in Classical Armenian.

The picture gallery and public rooms contain fine Venetian and Armenian paintings, including a Tiepolo. The museum displays a bizarre collection of exhibits, from Phoenician artefacts to an Egyptian mummy. The library boasts priceless books and illuminated manuscripts, while the typesetting hall displays an ancient printing press capable of reproducing 36 languages.

Although the printing centre closed in 1993, the Armenian press is still administered from this nerve centre. One room is dedicated to Byron, because of his enthusiasm for Armenian culture and his contribution

Map,
page 132

*Farewell to La
Serenissima.*

BELOW: Pellestrina
campanile and
harbour.

to an Armenian-English dictionary in 1816. The poet was motivated by the linguistic challenge: "my mind wanted something craggy to break upon". Browning, Longfellow and Proust were equally impressed by this serene monastery.

Declining fortunes

Lazzaretto Vecchio, another island off the Lido, is at present a home for stray dogs but is mooted to become a sports complex. The island can be seen from the summer casino boat which passes close by. In its time, the island has housed a pilgrims' hostel, plague hospital and military site. The outbreak of the first plague in the 14th century led to the creation of an isolation centre. In 1423 this became Europe's first permanent quarantine hospital for plague victims.

Poveglia, a distinctive hump-back island, hugs the southern shore of the Lido. The island was once a powerful centre but decline set in after the devastation of the Genoese war in 1380. Poveglia's chequered past includes a spell as a noble summer residence, a barracks and munitions depot and, until the 1960s, a hospice and retirement home. Despite its virtual abandonment, the island is now coveted as a potential secluded holiday resort or marina.

Pellestrina, which protects Venice from the open sea, makes a relaxing summer excursion. (It is best reached from the Lido, with bus 11 to Alberoni connecting with the ferry for a five-minute boat ride to Pellestrina). This narrow strip of land forms a natural barrier enforced by the Murazzi, the great sea walls. The island is a haunt of sunbathing Venetians or solitary walkers, with a quaint fishing village, gossipy bars and brightly coloured cottages. As part of the dike which preserves Venice for generations to come, Pellestrina makes a fitting end to an exploration of the lagoon. ❑

Venice in winter

People in hats and coats, "pigeons flying away from deserted squares as the walkers approach, the peculiar luminescence of winter sunlight, dozing cats; an unseen piano playing, the peremptory parp! of the boat horns". British journalist Frank Barrett perfectly evokes the spirit of Venice out of season. Lovers of Venice have long had a secret pleasure: visiting the Lagoon in winter. Only then does the romantic city regain its legendary composure. Venice in winter may no longer be a closely guarded secret but it remains special. Out of season, the sleepy city has an everyday air, with Venetians left to their own devices.

The monochromatic Venetian winters provide a canvas for one's moods. The city lends itself more readily to shades of melancholy but it is a subtle palette allowing for all shades of self-absorption, poetic solitude and serenity. When a damp miasma settles on the city, there are always galleries bursting with the colour and light that define Venetian painting. The city of brick and stone is also a fertile ground for the imagination: it is only too easy to conjure a decadent Doge from the mist. Day-dreaming is a natural Venetian state of mind, particularly in winter when everyone can embark on private voyages of discovery.

Yet winter is also a palpably physical season in Venice. It threatens tarpaulined gondolas, battened down against predicted rains, and duck-boards stacked in readiness for high tides. Winter means heavy fog, visitors standing dejectedly in soggy shoes, forlornly shuttered restaurants, the wash splashing against clammy stone foundations.

Fortunately, a host of indoor pleasures can take the chill off the coldest day. Winter also means a city immured in fur coats and snug bars, a simmering seafood risotto or comforting fish soup in a Rialto inn. Winter is the time for Venetians to reclaim their favourite bars. For visitors, the season is conducive to intimate visits to St Mark's and an appreciation of the glittering mosaics without the crowds. Winter also promises a romantic interlude by the fireside of the Danieli Hotel

or a glass of sparkling Prosecco at the Londra Palace. Outside, the gondoliers' nightly serenade rings out over the canals.

La Serenissima can be unfriendly between November and April, with memories of Mediterranean summers blotted out by pale, wintry light. The city can seem somewhat cold and unwelcoming, a damp and clammy place with permanently grey skies, teeming rain and choppy canals. Winter is also the season of flood sirens and wet feet.

Although the dreaded high water means duck-boards and disruption, the Venetians take the floods in their stride: shops with barricaded entrances still stay open; in a bar, Venetians stand knee-deep in water to enjoy an *espresso* and a brioche. The monochrome seascape is interspersed with days of streaming sun. Memories of rain-drenched *campi* and *calli* are banished and the mood lightens.

A bracing walk around the Zattere dispels any gloom, with a cluster of cafés along the quayside and the sunlight glinting off the golden globe of a weather vane on the Customs Point. ❑

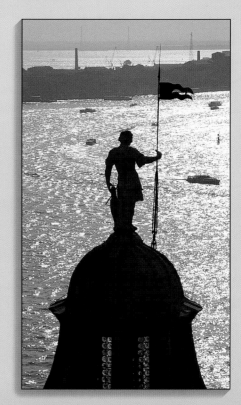

RIGHT: The glinting campanile of San Giorgio.

INSIGHT GUIDES
TRAVEL TIPS

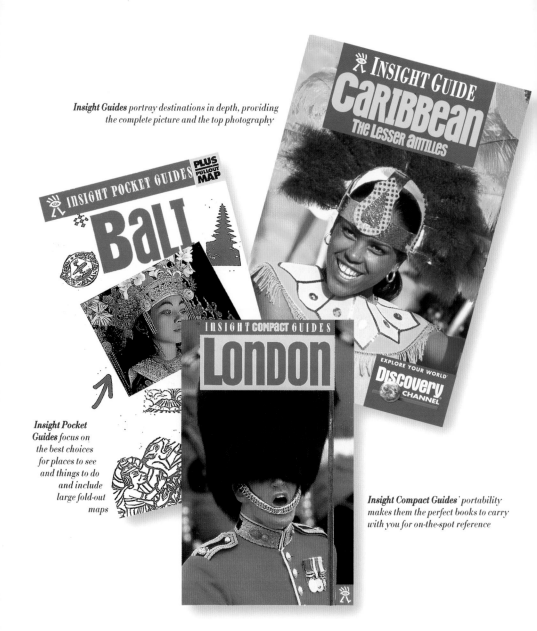

Insight Guides *portray destinations in depth, providing the complete picture and the top photography*

Insight Pocket Guides *focus on the best choices for places to see and things to do and include large fold-out maps*

Insight Compact Guides*' portability makes them the perfect books to carry with you for on-the-spot reference*

Three types of guide for all types of travel

INSIGHT GUIDES Different people need different kinds of information. Some want *background information* to help them prepare for the trip. Others seek *personal recommendations* from someone who knows the destination well. And others look for *compactly presented data* for on-the-spot reference. With three carefully designed series, Insight Guides offer readers the perfect choice. Insight Guides will turn your visit into an experience.

The world's largest collection of visual travel guides

CONTENTS

Getting Acquainted

The Place

Area: The city is built on 118 islands which lie 2 miles (4 kms) off the mainland.
Population: Around 320,000.
Language: Italian (and Venetian dialect).
Religion: Roman Catholic.
Time Zone: Central European Time (GMT plus one hour).
Currency: Italian lira.
Weights and Measures: Metric.
Electricity: 220 volts. You will need an adaptor to operate British three-pin appliances and a transformer to use 100–120 volt appliances.
International Dialling Code: To call Venice from the UK, dial 00 39 41 plus the number you require. If calling Venice from within Italy, dial 041 plus the number. If you are calling from within Venice, there is no need to use any code.

Geography

The Venetian lagoon covers an area of more than 500 square kilometres (193 square miles), which is roughly divided between the "dead" and the "living" – biologically speaking.

Venice itself comprises 118 islands, 45 kilometres (28 miles) of canals and 400 bridges.

Population

Of the 320,000 inhabitants of Venice (including the mainland communities), fewer than 80,000 live in historic Venice, about 45,000 have homes on the islands and the remainder inhabit the mainland.

The numbers in historic Venice have fallen by more than 50 percent since 1945. This is because the cost of accommodation and the demands of living in Venice are provoking an exodus to the mainland. This has also resulted in the population of central Venice, which has an average age of 45 years, being considerably older than the European average.

Government

Venice is the capital of the Veneto, the wealthy region in north-eastern Italy which has one of the highest per capita incomes in Italy.

In administrative terms, Venice and the mainland communities come under the same local government. Despite a referendum in which the city decided to retain its links with the mainland communities, the relationship makes for uneasy bedfellows: historic Venice and modern Mestre have very different needs.

As in the United States, the city mayor wields considerable power. In the early 1990s, Gianni de Michelis, the colourful Mayor of Venice and Italian foreign minister, was imprisoned for corruption. His place was taken by a "clean", forward-looking administration run by Massimo Cacciari. However, factional in-fighting between the two communities of mainland Venice and historic Venice means that the city is likely to experience continuing turmoil.

Climate

The Venetian climate is notoriously capricious, with a spectrum of different weather possible in one day, particularly in spring and winter. January can be bitterly **cold**, wet and windy, then suddenly illuminated by warm sunshine.

Humidity affects the hottest and coldest days. Venice in the height of summer can be oppressively muggy but there is always the Lido to escape to. The weather is **hottest** in August, with an average of 24°C/75°F.

The most **rain** generally falls in March to April and November to December but *acqua alta*, which occurs between the autumn and spring, is the condition Venetians loathe: exceptionally high tides, which flood the low-lying areas of the city, including San Marco. Although it rarely **snows** in Venice, the city is exposed to frequent fogs and two harsh **winds**: the *bora* blows from the Steppes in winter and is associated with low atmospheric pressure, while the *scirocco* brings hot weather from the Middle East. That said, Venice experiences sunny days and limpid light over the lagoon in all seasons.

The **loveliest months** are probably May, June and September but it is a matter of taste: cliché though it is, each season has its fans, even the dark depths of winter, swathed in **romantic mists**. In spring, the city can be highly dramatic, viewed from the top of San Giorgio, with the wind buffeting the tower and the boats on the lagoon. (*See Venice in Winter, page 295*). The average temperatures are: **January** 3.8°C (38.8°F); **April** 12.6°C (54.6°F); **July** 23.6°C (74.4°F); and **October** 15.1°C (59.1°F).

Public Holidays

Banks and most shops are closed on the following public holidays:
- **New Year's Day** (*Capodanno*) 1 January
- **Epiphany** (*Befania*) 6 January
- **Easter Monday** (*Lunedi di Pasqua*) varies
- **Liberation Day** (*Anniversario della Liberazione*) 25 April
- **May Day** (*Festa del Lavoro*) 1 May
- **August holiday** (*Ferragosto*) 15 August
- **All Saints** (*Ognissanti*) 1 November
- **Immaculate Conception** (*Immacolata Concezione*) 8 December
- **Christmas Day** (*Natale*) 25 December
- **Boxing Day** (*Santo Stefano*) 26 December

Economy

In terms of the economy, there is a big gulf between the mainland and historic Venice. While the mainland communities of Mestre and the port of Marghera are essentially industrial, dealing with shipping, petro-chemicals, metal-working and food processing, the economy of "central" or historic Venice is heavily dependent on tourism. This includes such sectors as independent, package and conference tourism and catering as well as more traditional activities: glass-making, lace-making, mask-making, restoration and antique dealing. The city is currently experiencing something of a crafts revival, which is the result of a city initiative to stem the tide of young families moving to the mainland. Tourism and the craft industry are supplemented by the declining sectors of fishing, boat-building and market-gardening.

Planning the Trip

What to Wear

Clothes for the capricious Venetian climate can be tricky (*see Climate opposite*). If visiting between October and April, it is worth bringing a raincoat, scarf, umbrella and warm outdoor clothes for the chilly evenings, windy ferry trips and frequent fogs. The secret to an enjoyable Venetian stay is to wear layers of clothes that can be added or removed as the weather changes during the course of a day.

Comfortable walking shoes are the first requirement for any trip to Venice, however. And, if you are unfortunate enough to experience *acqua alta*, the seasonal flooding, then you will need to buy Wellington boots in Venice. Although wet, it is, in fact, a strange and exciting experience.

Take some beachwear if visiting Venice in summer. Shorts are acceptable for visiting the Lido beaches or smaller islands, but less so for the city itself. To avoid offence, dress decently in churches, with women covering up arms and shoulders, and neither sex wearing shorts. Smart casual wear is accepted in all but the grandest hotels and restaurants, but most Venetians dress smartly when dining out. Certainly, visitors will feel more comfortable (and may be treated better) if dressed fairly elegantly for chic clubs, hotels and city *ristoranti*.

Entry Regulations

For visits up to three months, visas are not required by visitors from EU countries, the US, Canada, Australia or New Zealand. A valid passport (or in the case of those from EU member countries, a valid identification card) is sufficient. Nationals of most other countries require a visa. This must be obtained in advance from an Italian Embassy. (For a list of Consulates in Venice *see Consulates, page 304.*)

Money Matters

Bear in mind that, given its unique location and circumstances, Venice is the most expensive city in Italy.

The unit of currency in Italy is the lira. There are 1,000, 2,000, 5,000, 10,000, 50,000 and 100,000 lire bills and 100, 200 and 500 lire coins. The exchange rate floats against other currencies, but at the time of writing, was around 2,800 lire to the pound sterling and 1,600 to the US$.

Travellers' cheques are the safest way to carry money, and American Express and Thomas Cook are the best known in Italy. But these are not always economical, since banks charge a commission for cashing them, while shops and restaurants give less favourable exchange rates. Many hotels do not accept travellers' cheques but the larger stores probably will. Major credit cards are accepted by most large shops and restaurants in Venice but are generally less common in Italy than in North America or Northern Europe.

Eurocheques can be cashed in certain banks but are not generally popular with traders. Cash is often preferred, but should not be carried in large quantities.

Banks are open from 8.30am–1.30pm, Monday–Friday. Some are also open in the afternoon from 2.30–3.30pm or from 3.30–4.30pm. You will need to have your passport or identification card with you when changing money. Remember that changing money is a slow operation in Italy: there is only half-hearted computerisation and separate queues exist for changing money and receiving money. Regular customers will tend to be served before you, so allow plenty of time and, ideally, visit in the morning. You may sometimes be asked to leave handbags, cameras and metal objects such as keys in a secure locker at the entrance. This is intended to prevent robberies: for a tourist laden with luggage it can be inconvenient since the lockers are usually small.

Not all banks will provide cash against a credit card and a few of the smaller banks may refuse to cash travellers' cheques in certain currencies. Generally speaking, the larger banks (those with a national or international network) will best handle tourist transactions. Venice now has a number of automatic cash dispensers, which can be operated with certain cashpoint cards. Some also have instructions in foreign languages. (Ask your home bank for a list of cash dispensers that accept your cards in Venice.)

Banks may close early the day before a public holiday. Note that if a holiday falls on a Tuesday or a Thursday, then many offices may also close on the preceding Monday or the following Friday. This is known as a "*ponte*"– bridging the gap.

Getting There

Visitors from abroad are most likely to arrive by air. Other modes of travel offer benefits, but all require time.

By air
The main airport for Venice is **Marco Polo** on the edge of the lagoon, 13 km (8 miles) from the city centre. However, some charter companies confusingly also refer to **Treviso** airport as "Venice airport". This is, in fact, 30 km (19 miles) to the north of Venice and far less convenient, so check which airport your travel agent is really offering you. You may wish to choose a flight-plus-hotel package to Venice which can often be cheaper and easier than travelling independently (*see Package Tours opposite*). Bear in mind, too, that in summer hotels you book independently may insist on half-board, which adds to the holiday price.

Alitalia is the main agent for flights to Venice. Information can be obtained from your local Alitalia office or travel agency.

Domestically, there are direct flights from Naples, Rome and Palermo to Venice. In addition, international flights operate between Venice and London, Amsterdam, Brussels, Paris, Nice, Barcelona, Madrid, Cologne, Frankfurt, Munich, Vienna, Zurich and Lugano. From Ireland, Aer Lingus (01-844 4747) and Alitalia (01-677 5171) connect Dublin and Venice.

There are direct scheduled and charter flights from several UK airports, with Apex British Airways (0181-897 4000) or Alitalia (0171-602 7111) tickets providing good value. Skybus (0171-373 6055) and Italy Sky Shuttle (0181-748 4999) operate competitive charter flights to Venice.

Further Information

For information on buses, boats and water taxis from Venice Marco Polo airport to the city, *see Getting Around, page 304.*

From North America, there are flights to Venice, usually via London, Rome, Milan, Frankfurt or Amsterdam. In the United States, Alitalia, for instance, operates regular flights from New York, Boston, Miami, Chicago and Los Angeles to Milan and Rome, with onward connections to Venice. From Australia and New Zealand, flights are generally to Rome, with onward connections possible from there.

By car
Travelling to Venice by car from abroad is not cheap. Costs include petrol, motorway tolls, hotels en route and the car park fees in Venice. If you do decide to travel by car, you will require a current driving licence (with an Italian translation unless it is the standard EU licence) and valid insurance (green card).

Reputable Banks in Venice

American Express, Salizzada San Moisè (just west of St Mark's Square), tel: 1678-72000 (toll-free). This is open Monday–Friday, 9am–5.30pm, Saturday 9am–12.30pm.
Banca d'Italia, San Marco 4799, tel: 270 9111.
Banca Nazionale del Lavoro, Bacino Orseolo, tel: 667 511.
Monte dei Paschi di Siena, Santa Croce 574, tel: 520 400.
Foreign exchange offices give a less favourable rate of exchange than banks but are plentiful in Venice and convenient for times when banks are closed. These tend to be clustered around the San Marco, Rialto and station areas, but there is also one at both Marco Polo and Treviso airports, and in the Tronchetto and Piazzale Roma car parks.

Additional insurance cover, which can include a get-you-home service, is offered by a number of organisations including the British and American Automobile Associations. However, arriving by car is best avoided since it will have to be left in a car park outside Venice (see Getting Around, page 304).

By train

For those arriving in Venice from abroad, there are international services from London (changing in Paris), Moscow, Munich, Nice, Paris, Vienna, St Petersburg and Zurich. Train fares from these destinations are often about the same as flying. However, the advantages of travelling by train are the chance to see some of Europe's most beautiful landscapes and to make stops along the way.

There are several options available to train travellers. **InterRail** and **Eurail** cards allow passengers unlimited travel throughout Europe for a month, for a fixed price. Then there are return tickets to Venice, which are valid for two months and allow passengers to make as many stops as they wish en route. On the other hand, if you are travelling from the UK – and wish to reach Venice as fast as possible – consider paying extra to use the fast Eurostar service to Paris, then change.

Within Italy, there are direct services to Venice from Bologna, Genoa, Ferrara, Milan, Turin and Verona. If arriving in Venice from Rome, take the high-speed Pendolino service, for which a supplement is payable.

In Italy, there are also a number of special deals available: eg. the **chilometrico**, which allows one or more people to travel a specified number of kilometres at a special rate. Enquire at stations or travel agents for details of current offers.

The Orient Express

This is a wonderful way to reach Venice in style – certainly the most romantic. The service operates from March to November. From London, the train stops in Paris, Dusseldorf, Cologne, Frankfurt, Zurich, Innsbruck and Verona. If you wish – and if you can afford it – you can travel both ways on the Orient Express, but you must stay a minimum of five days in Venice. Sybarites can check into the luxurious Cipriani hotel (see page 312), owned by the same group as the Orient Express. Alternatively, buy a single either to or from Venice, and Alitalia will throw in a single ticket to allow you to complete your journey. For reservations, tel: 0171-805 5100.

Once at Venice's **Santa Lucia** station, call in at the tourist office in the entrance hall and then buy your vaporetto (ferry) ticket from the kiosk just outside the station, by the waterfront.

Train timetables change twice a year, so for up-to-date information from the UK, contact British Rail European Enquiries, Victoria Station, London SW1, tel: 0990-848 848, or the Italian tourist office. In Italy, stations and travel agents have details of train times and can make reservations.

If you are planning more than one rail journey, invest in the current Italian state railway handbook (published commercially and on sale in station kiosks for a few thousand lire). For travel within Italy or abroad, consider buying train tickets from most Italian travel agents, which saves you queuing – often for quite some time – at the railway station.

Package Tours

From the UK, Ireland, or the USA, this is usually the easiest and most economical way to visit Venice. It can be an advantage to travel with a company that has good local representation. Current brochures are generally available from your travel agent. The following are among the most reputable UK companies now specialising in travel to Venice.

Citalia,
8 Lansdowne Rd,
Croydon CR9 1LL.

Tel: 0181-686 5533. Citalia, an Italian specialist and one of the market leaders, provides one of the most complete services. In a sense, it is the official Italian agency, formed as a joint initiative between the Italian tourist board and the Italian State Railways.

At the top end of the scale, Citalia runs trips on the Orient Express (see above). The company also offers particularly good City Breaks, with the choice of staying in two to five star hotels. The prices of these flight-and-hotel packages are generally much lower than if you booked the trip independently. Moreover, since Venice is often fully booked, it makes sense to involve a travel agent in organising your trip. Flights leave from London and regional airports, using carriers such as Alitalia, BA and Sabena. Aternatively, Citalia will book clients on Eurostar. In addition, Citalia organises holidays for independent travellers, with personalised itineraries and multi-centre stays.

Venice is one of Citalia's major destinations, so the company has excellent arrangements with many of the best hotels in different price ranges, such as the Londra Palace, Luna Baglioni, Danieli and Cipriani (see Hotels, page 307). Visitors can choose to stay on the Lido or in the historic centre. Helpful English-speaking representatives are on hand in Venice.

Magic of Italy,
227 Shepherd's Bush Road,
London W6,
Tel: 0181-748 2661.
Magic of Italy provides civilised
package holidays, with a good
choice of accommodation and
the presence of an English-
speaking representative.
Italian Escapades,
227 Shepherd's Bush Road,
London W6,
Tel: 0181-748 7575.
This is a similar operation to
Magic of Italy, but it is designed
for more independent travellers.
They also arrange Fly-Drive and
individual holidays.

Many British package holiday
companies (Thomsons, Page &
Moy, Cadogan) run holidays to
Venice. Two-centre holidays are
increasingly popular, with a
chance to stay in two major
cities, such as Venice followed
by Rome. A wonderful alternative
to a standard package tour is to
rent an apartment in Venice (*see
page 314*).

Practical Tips

Business Hours

Shops are open from 9am–
12.30pm or 1pm and from 3pm
or 3.30pm–7.30pm. Most, apart
from those aimed at tourists,
are closed on Sunday.

Banks: *see page 300.*

Bars and restaurants are
legally obliged to close one day a
week: a notice on the door
indicates which day.

Office hours are normally
7.30am–12.30pm and 3.30pm–
6.30pm. Government offices are
usually only open to the public in
the mornings.

Churches tend to be open
from 7.30am–noon, and then
from 3.30pm or 4pm–6.30pm or
7pm.

Museums tend to close on
Mondays (opening times are
indicated in the colour section of
the book).

Tipping

In Italy, it is customary to tip
various people for their services,
so it is worth carrying around a
number of low denomination
notes. The following are general
guidelines. Most restaurants
impose a cover charge (*pane e
coperto*) of up to 10,000 lire. In
addition, there is often a 10
percent service charge
(*servizio*) added to the bill. If the
menu says that service is
included, then a small additional
tip is discretionary. If service is
not included, it is usual to leave
between 12 and 15 percent of
the bill. Gondoliers need not be
tipped but water taxis may
expect a small tip of around 5

percent . Tips to local guides
depend on their ability and the
length of the trip: 5,000–10,000
lire per person is normal. In
certain churches, there is
usually a custodian (or elderly
"helper") somewhere nearby
who will be pleased to open the
door. A tip of around 3,000 lire
per person and many "*grazie*"
are then appropriate.

Media

International publications, such
as British, American and
Northern European newspapers
and magazines, can be found in
Venice – generally one day after
publication. The main **Italian
papers** (*Corriere della Sera, La
Repubblica*) publish northern
editions, but the local dailies,
Nuova Venezia and, especially, *Il
Gazzettino* have a high
circulation in Venice. Both are
conservative, but *Il Gazzettino*
has a better reputation and also
carries plenty of local
information. Particularly useful
for the visitor are the sections
covering current transport
timetables, together with
entertainment listings and daily
information on duty chemists.
This is presented in a clear
fashion, so visitors with a
smattering of Italian should
understand it.

Radio and Television

There are dozens of private **radio**
stations, mostly
indistinguishable. The
commercial stations provide a
mix of pop and phone-ins. Flip
the dial to find one that suits
your pop tastes. Since many are
very local, you will need to re-
tune frequently. The national
radio stations (**RAI**) include
news, current affairs and
documentary-type programmes,
and, particularly on **RAI 3**, some
classical music. As far as
television is concerned, **Canale
5**, run by Berlusconi (the media

magnate), is resolutely commercial and populist, with numerous game shows and dubbed American films. There are some local news programmes on the national television channels, particularly RAI 3, and occasionally a travelogue or documentary makes it onto the local television stations. In general, though, local television is bad to appalling. It is worth watching, however, just so that you will appreciate the quality at home, wherever you live. The bigger hotels have satellite television, with channels in numerous languages, from English to German and Japanese.

Postal Services

Post offices are generally open Monday–Friday 8.30am–1.20pm. In Venice, the main post office is at Fondachi dei Tedeschi 929 (tel: 041-529 9111; open 8am–8pm), where you can also dial direct and pay afterwards. This is a wonderful old warehouse on the Grand Canal (*see page 175*).

Stamps (*francobolli*) are available from tobacconists (*tabacchi*), card shops and some bars. The postal service is not renowned for its speed. If you need to send an urgent letter, ask for it to be sent *espresso*. In a real emergency, send a telegram. This may be done from a post office, or in Telecom Italia. If you are staying in Venice for some time, it is possible to have mail sent to you at the main post office – letters should be marked *fermo posta* (poste restante).

Telephone

Telephone boxes take coins (100, 200 and 500 lire) but card phones are now much more common. Phonecards (*schede telefoniche*) may be bought at bars, newspaper kiosks and

tabacchi for 5,000 or 10,000 lire. To request one, say: "*Vorrei una scheda telefonica da cinquemila lire/diecimila lire*" (I'd like a phonecard for 5,000/10,000 lire). It is not uncommon to find telephone boxes out of order. More reliable are the public telephones in many bars and in Telecom Italia offices (the home of the telephone company) or in the larger post offices. Telephone directories are available in Telecom Italia offices. The main one is at Piazzale Roma (open 8am–9.30pm), where you can also make phone calls; the call is metered and you pay upon completion. You can also call from the central post office (*see above*). If making phone calls from a hotel, you will pay an additional charge of about 25 percent, so try to use public phones. Cheaper rates apply to calls made after 9pm and at weekends.

You can also make calls using a British BT chargecard or one of the cards issued by Sprint, MCI, AT&T and other North American long-distance telephone companies. (Calls made this way are billed to your home address.)

Dialling Codes

International dialling codes: 00, followed by:

Australia	61
Canada	1
France	33
Germany	49
Ireland	353
Italy	39
New Zealand	64
UK	44
USA & Canada	1

European directory enquiries 176
European operator assistance 15
Intercontinental operator assistance 170
Telegrams and cables 186

Tourist Offices

Italian ENIT (state tourist) offices abroad:
ENIT Canada, 1 Place Ville Marie, Suite 1914, Montreal, Quebec, H3B 2E3 (tel: 514-866 7667).
ENIT Ireland, 47 Merrion Square, Dublin 2 (tel: 01-766 397).
ENIT UK, 1 Princes Street, London W1R 8AY (tel: 0171-408 1254).
ENIT United States: 630 5th Avenue, New York, NY 10111 (tel: 212-245 4822); 500 N Michigan Avenue, Chicago, IL 60611 (tel: 312-644 0990); Suite 801, 360 Post Street, San Francisco CA 94108 (tel: 415-392 6206).

APT tourist offices in Venice: The most convenient tourist office is close to St Mark's: **San Marco**, Giardini ex Reali (tel: 041-522 6356; fax: 041-529 8730). The offices are in a pavilion on the waterfront, beyond the Royal Gardens and close to the San Marco Vallaresso *vaporetto* stop. However, while the office is handy for picking up leaflets on what's on in Venice, it is run by rather indifferent staff (for complaints call 167-355 920, toll-free). In summer, the office is supplemented by native speakers of foreign languages. The administrative office is at Castello 4421, on the Grand Canal (tel: 041-529 8711; fax: 041-523 0399). A handy, small but friendly office is at the **Santa Lucia train station** (tel: 041-529 8727; fax: 041-719 078). **The Lido** office on the Gran Viale (tel: 041-526 721; fax: 041-529 8720) has limited information on historic Venice but is generally helpful. There is also a small office at **Marco Polo airport** (tel: 041-541 5887), which mostly deals with accommodation and transport tickets. If you are between 14 and 26, buy a **Rolling Venice** card from here. This entitles you to discounts in restaurants and on ferries.

Consulates

Venice has around 35–40 consulates. However, many foreign nationals will need to contact their embassies in Rome.
UK, Palazzo Querini, Dorsoduro 1051, by the Accademia bridge, tel: 522 7207.
The nearest **United States** consulate is in Milan, Largo Donegani 1, tel: 02-290 351.
Australian, **Canadian** and **Irish** citizens will need to contact their embassies in Rome.

Health Precautions

Before travelling, ensure that you have a valid **health** and **personal insurance policy**. An Italian **pharmacist** is qualified to advise on minor health complaints. For the current list of night **pharmacists** (*farmacie*), consult your hotel, Venice newspapers (*see Media, page 302*) or *Un Ospite di Venezia/A Guest in Venice* (a free booklet available from major hotels). If you are seriously ill, telephone 113 or go to the **Pronto Soccorso** (casualty department) of the nearest hospital. In central Venice, this is likely to be the Ospedale Civile, Campo Santi Giovanni e Paolo (San Zanipolo), tel: 523 0000/520 5622 (set beside the church of Santi Giovanni e Paolo and also accessible by water taxi).

Tap water is safe to drink in most places but Venetians generally prefer to drink mineral water, and this will usually be offered in restaurants. In some places, especially in historic palaces, the water supply can become erratic and visitors should make every effort not to waste water.

It is worth taking **mosquito repellent** in the summer, when the creatures breed in the canals and lagoon. If bothered by mosquitoes in your room, buy a green, slow-burning mosquito repellent coil, which is cheap and effective, as are the small electrical devices which plug into a standard socket.

Emergencies

For certain difficulties, including lost passports, consult Consulates (*see above*). For illness, *see Health Precautions above*. In general, these are the most useful emergency telephone numbers:
112: Police (*Carabinieri*).
113: SOS; to contact any emergency service.
113: request "*Questura*" if you have a lost passport (you'll also have to visit your nearest consulate).
115: Fire brigade (*Vigili del Fuoco*).
116: Road assistance en route to Venice (*Soccorso Stradale*).
118: Medical emergencies.
167-864 064: missing credit cards (toll-free number).
041-785 238: Santa Lucia rail station lost property office.
041-780 310: Lost property on the *vaporetti* (ferries).
041-523 0000: Ambulance (in Venice).
041-260 9260: Marco Polo airport information office.

Getting Around

City Transport

In this section, you will find details of how to get around Venice once you arrive, whichever way you have decided to get there. One of the best ways to get around the city is by boat – once you have mastered a few key ferry routes, water transport is quite straightforward. If you would rather walk around, *see the introduction to Where to Stay, page 307*, which will help you get a grip on the complicated system of Venetian addresses.

Car Parks

Visitors arriving by car will need to leave it at one of several car parks at the entrance to the city. The multi-storey car park at **Piazzale Roma** is close to the centre and has good ferry services (see *over*) but is expensive. By contrast, the island of Tronchetto (built on reclaimed land) forms the **largest car park in Europe** and, although cheaper, is further away from the centre and less accessible by ferry (you may have to wait for half an hour or so for a ferry). Prices vary considerably at both car parks, depending on the car and the season but 30,000 lire per day is an absolute minimum. Queues can be long at the height of summer. Ferry line 82 links Tronchetto with central Venice (*see City Ferries opposite*).

The Airports

Many charters arrive at **Treviso airport**, 30 km (19 miles) from Venice and often include a bus link to the city centre. If this is not provided, take the number 6 bus from outside the terminal. Both scheduled and charter flights arrive in **Marco Polo Airport**, enquiries (tel: 041-260 6111), on the edge of the lagoon. You can buy your water travel pass from the *tabacchi* in the airport lounge (*see City Ferries below*). From here to the city centre, you have a choice of routes. If you choose to splash out on a **water taxi** (at more than 100,000 lire), this is a magical way to see Venice for the first time. Alternatively, there are **car taxis** (about 35,000 lire) to Piazzale Roma, the site of the Venice bus terminal. In addition, there are ATVO public bus services (5,000 lire) to Piazzale Roma, with tickets on sale in the airport lounge. (The journey takes about half an hour; ask for the timetable for the return journey to the airport.) From the waterside close to Piazzale Roma, you can catch a line 1 (*vaporetto*) ferry (*see details of route below*). You can also buy a **travel pass** from the transport office there.

Alternatively, if you are staying on the Lido or in central Venice, close to San Marco, then a **water bus** is the most appealing yet inexpensive way to reach the city from the airport. The water buses leave from outside the terminal (costing about 9,000– 20,000 depending on the destination). The most reliable is the newish private service, Alilaguna (tel: 041-523 5775/ 522 2303), with stylish boats connecting the airport with San Marco and the Lido. (Check times with the tourist office or ask for a timetable for the return journey.) The delightful journey takes about an hour.

The Train Station

Ferrovia Santa Lucia (Venice train station) has a tourist office, buffet, lost property office and 24-hour left luggage office. A variety of ferries leave from outside the terminal (*see City Ferries below*), where tickets are on sale. In theory, one large piece of baggage can travel free but additional baggage requires a ticket (costing the same as a passenger ticket). This only seems to be enforced in peak season but be it at your own risk.

City Ferries

These ferries or water buses are usually known as *vaporetti*.

For an overview of the ferry routes see the Transport Map inside the back cover of this book. When you arrive in Venice, it is worth buying a one-day, three-day or weekly **travel pass** which will allow you to travel on any city ferries during this period, including the islands (only the boats to the airport are excluded). The travel passes are relatively expensive (much more than the Venetians pay) but are cheaper and less fuss than buying individual trips, and also help subsidise city transport for Venetians, acting as a type of tax on tourism. A three-day pass currently costs 30,000 lire (about £15) while a weekly pass costs around 50–60,000 lire (about £25–35, depending on the exchange rate). If you are found without a ticket, a fine is payable on the spot (there are warning signs about this on the ferries in various languages). The pass can be bought in Piazzale Roma and at San Zaccaria, amongst other places. The times displayed are generally reliable but it doesn't hurt to check with a boatman. The **most confusing landing**

stages are at San Zaccaria (on Riva degli Schiavoni), San Marco and Fondamente Nuove because they are spread out along the quaysides, with different services running from different jetties.

Ferry **timetables** change twice a year but most of the numbers remain the same, with extra ferries and additional lines added in summer. If you are going to be in Venice for more than a few days, it is worth picking up the current transport map from the office at Piazzale Roma or collecting a copy of the invaluable booklet *Un Ospite a Venezia/A Guest in Venice* (in Italian and English) from grand hotels.

Not that ferries are clearly numbered. One of the easiest mistakes is to travel in the **wrong direction**, adding up to 40 minutes to your journey (especially if it's dark and you can't see any landmarks). Ferries are usually designated as being "*circolare a destra*" or "*circolare a sinistra*"; these do the same route in both directions. The easiest solution is to ask one of the boatmen as you board: "*Va bene per San Marco/Il Lido/Torcello?*" (Is this right for San Marco/the Lido/Torcello? etc.). Also be warned that ferries with barred numbers do not necessarily operate the same route as the unbarred ferry of the same number: it is often a truncated or restricted route.

The Islands

The quickest services to **Murano**, **Burano** and **Torcello** leave from Fondamente Nuove but for all routes always check ferry numbers and the direction. To find out how to reach the so-called "minor islands" see the Minor Islands chapter.

Line 1: this is one of the most useful and scenic lines and runs the length of the Grand Canal.

The ferry starts at Piazzale Roma and covers the Grand Canal and San Zaccaria before heading out to the Lido. Despite its name (*accelerato*), this is the slow service, stopping everywhere.

Line 82: this provides a faster service down the Grand Canal, calling in at only six stops before going westwards to Tronchetto (the car park island), then running eastwards along the Giudecca canal to San Giorgio and San Zaccaria. (In peak season, it continues to the Lido).

Line 52: this provides a long, scenic, circular tour skirting the periphery of Venice and also stops at Murano; in summer it also goes to the Lido. (You may need to change at Fondamente Nuove to do the whole route.) The 52 barred runs through the Arsenal.

Line 12: this hourly service stops at Murano, Burano and Torcello (usually in that order) and is best picked up at Fondamente Nuove. (You can pick it up at San Zaccaria or the Lido but this makes for a much longer journey.)

Line 14: this is a longer version of Line 12, stopping at Murano, Burano and Torcello but going via the Lido, Punta Sabbioni and Treporti. (You can pick it up at San Zaccaria or the Lido but this makes for a much longer journey.)

Water Taxis

Except during such events as the Film Festival and the Biennale, water taxis are readily available. There are taxi stands at Piazzale Roma; Santa Lucia railway station (Ferrovia); at the Rialto; San Marco; on the Lido; and at Marco Polo airport. This is a stylish but prohibitively expensive option for most visitors to Venice and hence best kept for emergencies. Even though there are official rates from the airport to the city

centre, and from the city centre to the main islands, it is tricky to get many water taxis to agree to them. Certainly, try and agree a price before setting out to your destination. The current official rate from the city centre to Burano or Torcello is 120,000 lire, for instance. However, if the taxi is dropping you off outside the city centre (eg. at Burano) and returning to the centre empty, you will probably also have to pay this fare or his hourly rate. In addition, there are numerous extra charges, including a call-out charge, a charge per person, a baggage charge, a nightly rate (and many more). Current official rates are listed in *Un Ospite a Venezia/A Guest in Venice*, a booklet available from grand hotels. To call a taxi, tel: 522 2303; 723 112 (general); 522 9750 (San Marco).

Gondolas

Nowadays, gondolas tend to be a quaint or romantic option rather than a mode of transport. Nevertheless, most people feel they have to do it once. The city has a number of gondola stands, indicated by the word "*stazio*" on a map. The biggest official stands are at Bacino Orseolo, just behind St Mark's; at Calle Vallaresso, west of St Mark's; and on the Molo, just in front of the Doge's Palace. However, many more stands are scattered throughout the city and will be readily visible. A good place for watching gondolas (to decide whether you would like the experience) is from the café overlooking the canal on Campo Santa Maria Formosa; there is a gondola stand beside it.

The official rate is around £30 (US$50) for 50 minutes for up to five people (but more after 8pm). You can negotiate for a shorter ride (about £20, US$30 for about 25 minutes). You should not pay more than the official

Gondola Ferries

For an utterly cheap gondola ride, pick up a gondola acting as a ferry. Known as *traghetti*, these boats ferry passengers across the banks of the Grand Canal at seven fixed points along the route (and cost under 1,000 lire per crossing). The gondola station by the Baroque church of La Salute is a good one to try. Custom has it that you stand rather than sit during the crossing.

rate unless entertainment is provided. In any case, you must agree on a price with the gondolier before starting. For the current official prices, pick up *Un Ospite a Venezia/A Guest in Venice* from one of the grand hotels.

Music or **singing** is always extra but first agree a price (not all gondoliers sing or play music but they can organise it quickly with a colleague). Although this service can be derided as hackneyed, it is often surprisingly good; some gondoliers are fine accordionists or tenors – even if the repertoire is rather limited, owes little to Pavarotti, and is sometimes more Neapolitan than Venetian.

Boat Trips

Some of the minor islands are hard to reach on public transport so always check ferries before setting off. However, in some cases, bargaining with fishermen is often the only alternative to an exorbitant motor launch, which should be saved for emergencies. Nowadays, it is virtually impossible for tourists to hire a boat independently in Venice. However, bargaining with a fisherman need not make a costly excursion, provided that the distances are relatively short.

Where to Stay

The first choice is between staying in an apartment or a hotel: each has its own appeal. The following covers hotels.

Seasons and Rates
In international terms, Venetian hotel rates are currently the third highest in the world, after Hong Kong and Moscow. Given the unique situation of the city, Venetian hotel rates are also between 10 and 30 percent higher than the Italian mainland. Many visitors would do well to book a package with a reputable Italian specialist. Demand exceeds supply during the main tourist season (April–September) so early bookings are essential. Venetian hoteliers often boast that there is no **off-season** in Venice. Certainly, city hotels are also likely to be heavily booked during the Venetian Carnival in February, while Christmas and New Year are becoming increasingly popular. Off-season, particularly in November, January and March, many of the hotels on the Lido close, leaving visitors with less choice. Certain grand hotels also close their doors in the winter. However, room rates in some hotels will also be lower during this period.

In **summer**, many hotels, especially those on the Lido, may insist on a half or full-board arrangement.

If choosing Venice for a **short break**, bear in mind that visitors who can travel during the week rather than at weekends may have more choice of accommodation. If Venice is officially full, visitors are sent to Mestre or Lido di Jesolo, the former a characterless overspill city and the latter a seaside resort some distance from Venice. Both options are best avoided unless budgets are tight or you have a young family who would appreciate the seaside.

Location
If you wish to eschew both grandeur and impersonality, then choose a smaller, moderately-priced hotel. Since these are incredibly popular, try to book three months in advance or book a particular hotel on a package with a reputable agent. In choosing a hotel, it is best to be clear about whether you wish to stay in historic (central) Venice or on the islands, essentially the Lido. For romance and atmosphere, central Venice is the obvious choice. Apart from the chance to stay in atmospheric palaces and feel part of the city, the advantages are that transport is slightly more straightforward and dining choices are greater. The drawbacks are that, outside the grand hotels, rooms tend to be smaller, even poky; nor can a canalside view, or any pleasant view, be guaranteed in these densely-packed palaces. In historic palaces or simpler hotels, there may be no lifts; likewise, in winter, more modest hotels can be slightly chilly.

Choosing a hotel on the islands essentially means the Lido, although there is an excellent deluxe hotel on the Giudecca and another small but selective hotel on Torcello. The Lido is a sound choice for a summer holiday for those with young families. The hotels on the Lido are often family-run and friendlier towards children. Even so, it is best to choose a hotel with its own private beach since public beaches are of poor quality. Choosing a half-board arrangement on the Lido can make sense since, unless you are planning to eat dinner in central Venice on a regular basis, the choice and variety of restaurants on the island is unremarkable. As a general rule, Venetian breakfasts are notoriously paltry or uninspired, even in some of the grander hotels. Staying on the Lido means at least a 20 minute boat journey into central Venice but the boats run until very late at night.

The official Italian rating system (one to five stars) can be misleading. Confusingly, many hotels offer different rates for different rooms. Breakfast is not always included in the room rate so check.

Addresses
Bear in mind that in Venice official addresses can be meaningless, with numbers in the thousands merely linked to the *sestiere* or district. (The street name is not included in official addresses, in theory to avoid confusion since the same name may exist in another district.) However, the effect of this can be confusing for visitors. When booking a hotel, unless planning to arrive by expensive water taxi (*see Getting Around, page 304*), always check which is the nearest *vaporetto* (boat) stop and how far it is from there on foot. If it is a small hotel, also enquire which is the nearest landmark, whether parish church, *campo* (square) or bridge.

Price categories
For convenience, the hotels listed below have been classified into the following categories: **Luxury, Expensive,**

Moderate and **Inexpensive**. At the top end of the scale, Venice boasts a clutch of starry hotels that can compete with any in the world. **Expensive** hotels offer international standards of service and facilities, with the exception of sports and leisure. (Outside the Lido, only one hotel, the Cipriani, has a pool; health clubs and gyms are virtually unheard of.) However, the grander city hotels usually have access to a private beach on the Lido. **Moderate** hotels are the most varied in their atmosphere, service and facilities, ranging from chic and sophisticated to old-fashioned and family-run.

Given that Gothic palaces are not easily transformed into pristine modern hotels, there will undoubtedly be some poky bedrooms in all but the grandest hotels. Often both exist in the same hotel, hence the element of surprise, and sometimes pleasure. Unfortunately, Venice is not a destination with many acceptable budget hotels (generally one and two-star). Those that exist tend to be a bit off the beaten track or booked well in advance, but there are exceptions. All the hotels listed below have been categorised according to one of two locations, "historic" central Venice and the islands.

The dialling code for Venice is 041 (from abroad 39-41).

Central Venice Hotels

LUXURY
Danieli,
Riva degli Schiavoni,
Castello 4196,
tel: 522 6480;
fax: 520 0208.
This world-famous hotel occupies the 14th-century Palazzo Dandolo overlooking St Mark's Basin and virtually next door to the Doge's Palace. This opulent hotel has drawn celebrities since 1822, from Dickens, Ruskin, Wagner, Proust

and George Sand to Fred Astaire, Sofia Loren and David Bowie. (The hotel is fully described from an historical point of view in the *Castello*, *Grand Canal* and *Ghosts* chapters.) The loveliest part of the Danieli is the lobby, built around a Gothic courtyard. Rooms are decorated in classic Venetian Fortuny fabrics and are furnished with genuine antiques, gilt mirrors and oriental rugs. Service is as impeccable as one would expect for a hotel in this class. However, if choosing to stay in the Danieli, avoid the comfortable but characterless modern extension next-door; stay in the historic wing (which is more expensive). The terrace restaurant offers superb views across to San Giorgio (*see Restaurants, page 316*). (To reach the hotel, take a private launch or *vaporetto* 1, 52 or 82 to San Zaccaria and you will see the hotel facing the landing stage.)
Gritti Palace,
Santa Maria del Giglio,
San Marco 2467,
tel: 794611;
fax: 520 0942.
This sumptuous hotel occupies a Gothic palace overlooking the Grand Canal. The Gritti rests on its laurels as one of the legendary Venetian hotels but is aesthetically more beguiling than the Danieli. (The hotel is fully described from an historical point of view in the *Grand Canal* and *San Marco* chapters.) Despite the cost, the romantic public rooms, the prestigious location and impeccable service make for a memorable stay. The Ducal suite is the place for a honeymoon. The Gritti also has apartments that can be rented for periods of over a week. The restaurant, Terrazza del Doge, is elegant and formal, with its terrace overlooking the Grand Canal. In winter, the dining room is also desirable, with its painted beams and elegant ambience.

However, Venetian critics consider that the quality of cuisine has declined of late, becoming too blandly international. Certainly, one can dine on smoked salmon, calamari and lamb cutlets, but there are Venetian specialities as well. However, it would be fair to say that the setting outshines the cuisine. Service is as impeccable as one would expect for a hotel in this class. There is access to a private beach on the Lido. (To reach the hotel, take *vaporetto* 1 or a private launch to the Santa Maria del Giglio landing stage, beside the Gritti.)

EXPENSIVE
Bauer Grunwald,
Campo San Moisè,
San Marco 1459,
tel: 520 7022;
fax: 520 7557.
Although essentially a modern and rather ugly hotel beside the Baroque San Moisè church, it is situated close to St Mark's and is comfortable, convenient and efficient. However, there is a medieval part off the main square; try to avoid one of the blander rooms overlooking Campo San Moisè. Compensations also include Grand Canal views. (To reach the hotel, take *vaporetto* line 1 to the San Marco Vallaresso stop and walk down Calle Vallaresso to Campo San Moisè. The hotel can also be reached by gondola.)
Europa e Regina,
Calle Larga XXII Marzo,
San Marco 2159,
tel: 520 0477;
fax: 523 1533.
This prestigious hotel is situated in a chic shopping district close to St Mark's. While lacking the history of some of its snootier rivals, this hotel provides exceptional value in its price range. In fact, its décor is equally grand, with splendid public rooms decorated in Venetian style. Some bedrooms offer Grand Canal views (but

check when booking). The restaurant, Terrazza Tiepolo (tel: 521 3785), overlooks the Grand Canal and is noted for its Venetian and international dishes, including grilled fish. The view is stunning, overlooking the church of La Salute and St Mark's Basin. While the service is punctilious, the cuisine has declined somewhat of late and prices remain high. (To reach the hotel, take *vaporetto* line 1 to the San Marco Vallaresso stop and walk down Calle Vallaresso for 30 metres; then turn left to reach Campo San Moisè; once in the square, cross over the bridge, turn left and then turn right into Corte Barozzi where the hotel is situated.)

Londra Palace,
Riva degli Schiavoni,
Castello 4171,
tel: 520 0533;
fax: 522 5032.

The Londra Palace is situated close to the Danieli (*see opposite*) but exudes a gracious yet homely ambience. The Londra Palace is renowned for its intimate tone, welcoming atmosphere, understanding staff, ideal location and fine cuisine. The Londra rightly boasts "a hundred windows overlooking the lagoon". Some guests are unable to tear themselves away from watching the waterside bustle from their balconies or windows. The staff are particularly welcoming for a grand hotel; indeed, the Londra Palace prides itself on its intimate atmosphere, a world apart from the impersonality and aloofness of more opulent rivals. The reception rooms are decorated in tasteful Biedermeier style. In general, the bedrooms are suitably warm and intimate, decorated in rich fabrics, with the "de luxe" rooms at the front, overlooking the lagoon. Although these are far more beguiling than the "superior" rooms at the back, the latter are particularly

peaceful, with views overlooking quiet courtyards and typical Venetian rooftops. A couple of rooms at the front boast coffered ceilings. The hotel completed a major renovation programme in 1997.

For a romantic break, select a "de luxe" room at the front with magical balconies overlooking the lagoon. All the rooms have a subtle lighting system, with impressive bathrooms and whirlpool baths. Breakfast is better than in many Venetian hotels while the bar makes a delightfully intimate spot for cocktails. Part of the terrace is covered over for winter dining but this is removed in summer. The Do Leoni restaurant (*see Restaurants, page 321*) is recommended. (This hotel is described in the *Castello* chapter; to reach it, take *vaporetto* 1, 52 or 82 to San Zaccaria: the hotel is in front.)

Luna Baglioni,
Calle Vallaresso,
San Marco 1243,
tel: 528 9840;
fax: 528 7160;
free number for bookings within Italy: 1678-21057.

The hotel itself, arguably the oldest in Venice, dates its origins back to a Knights Templar lodge called Locanda della Luna, which was in existence in 1118, for pilgrims travelling to the Crusades. Certainly it was operating as an inn in the 16th century. Although the grand public rooms are decorated in noble Venetian

style, with frescos, stucco-work and paintings, the hotel has lost its authentic Venetian character. Nonetheless, the Marco Polo salon boasts 18th-century frescos and the hotel is recommended for its setting, close to St Mark's, and its waterside views. A clever drainage system means that the hotel, unlike many of its neighbours, is protected from flooding during high tides (*acqua alta*). The bedrooms are suitably spacious and grand, some with whirlpool baths. The refined Canova restaurant has a fine reputation (*see Restaurants, page 319*). The hotel applies lower rates in January, February and March, apart from the Carnival period. (To reach the hotel, take the *vaporetto* 1 to San Marco Vallaresso and walk down Calle Vallaresso, the alley facing you; the hotel is halfway down on the right.)

Metropole,
Riva degli Schiavoni,
Castello 4149,
tel: 520 5044;
fax: 522 3679.

This former patrician residence is decorated in grand 19th-century style and has been romantically renovated, dotted with well-chosen antiques. The Metropole also enjoys fine views across courtyards and over the lagoon itself. The hotel is popular with both independent travellers and upmarket package groups. (To reach the hotel, take a gondola to the hotel's private jetty or catch *vaporetto* 1, 52 or 82 to San Zaccaria; turn right, walking along the quayside; cross two bridges and the hotel is on your left just before the third bridge.)

Monaco & Grand Canal,
Calle Vallaresso,
San Marco 1325,
tel: 520 0211;
fax: 520 0501.

Set in an 18th-century palace, this impressive hotel overlooks the Grand Canal towards the Baroque church of La Salute.

Central Venice (continued)

Thanks to enlightened management, the hotel has improved in recent years. The public rooms tend to be cosier and more stylish than many other grand hotels. The bedrooms are decorated in warm, well-chosen fabrics. (The ground floor rooms overlooking the Grand Canal are the ones to request.) The recommended restaurant on the terrace overlooks the Grand Canal and the dining room also has superb waterside views. The pleasant piano bar is open from 7pm–midnight. The hotel is popular with both independent travellers and upmarket package groups. (To reach the hotel, take the *vaporetto* 1 to San Marco Vallaresso and walk down Calle Vallaresso, the alley facing you.) The hotel is convenient for Harry's Bar in the same street (*see Restaurants, page 318*).

MODERATE

Accademia,
Villa Maravegie, Fondamenta Bollani, Dorsoduro 1058,
tel: 521 0188;
fax: 523 9152.
Situated at the Grand Canal end of Rio di San Trovaso, this romantic, wisteria-clad hotel has long been popular with foreigners, particularly the British. Originally a Gothic palace remodelled in the 17th century, this small but much sought-after hotel was once the Russian consulate. The welcome verges from offhand to indifferent and the interior is somewhat shabby, but this enhances its period charm, with some rooms furnished with antiques. With its roses and fruit trees, the garden provides a charming retreat from the city heat. If seeking peace and quiet, request a room overlooking the front or back garden rather than the noisy annexe or rooms over the busy canal. The district, Dorsoduro, is one of the most delightful.

Price Categories

Price categories (in lire) are based on single occupancy without breakfast:
Luxury = more than 500,000
Expensive = 350–500,000
Moderate = 200–350,000
Inexpensive = under 200,000

La Calcina,
Zattere ai Gesuati 780,
tel: 520 6466;
fax: 522 7045.
This russet-coloured hotel is situated along the charming quaysides of the Zattere in the Dorsoduro district. This inn is where John Ruskin, the aesthete and art critic, stayed in 1876. The hotel is aware of its heritage and has redecorated most of its rooms in genteel style, using muted colours and tasteful furniture. All the rooms are different, with the best ones on the corners: numbers 2, 22 and 32. At the moment, there is a considerable price differential between rooms. Unmodernised rooms without bathroom are much cheaper but these will be revamped in the future. Set by the bridge, this unpretentious but popular hotel enjoys appealing views over the Giudecca Canal. In summer, guests can enjoy the typical Venetian *altana*, or roof terrace, and take breakfast on a pier above the water.

La Fenice et des Artistes,
Campiello della Fenice,
San Marco 1936,
tel: 523 2333;
fax: 520 3721.
This well-known, yet highly individualistic hotel has long been welcoming discreet guests, including film stars and opera singers who like to keep a low profile (Pavarotti, a regular guest, is an exception). Ask to see the guest book if curious about recent arrivals. This low-key, yet sophisticated hotel is close to the site of La Fenice,

the famous opera house which is currently being rebuilt after a disastrous fire. The rooms are all different, decorated in charming, old-fashioned Venetian style; some are beamed but all possess period furniture and exude cosiness. The staff are proud of the hotel's refined yet welcoming atmosphere, with its small garden and intimate bar; little wonder that many celebrities choose to return incognito. In fine weather, breakfast is served in the garden. Small private apartments can also be booked on a long-term basis. Unlike many hotels, this one is open all year round. There are a number of good restaurants around the hotel, which is also only a few minutes' walk from San Marco.

Flora,
Calle Bergamaschi (off Larga XXII Marzo), San Marco;
tel: 520 5844;
fax: 522 8217.
This small but friendly hotel has long provided a welcome retreat for discerning visitors. While the idyllic atmosphere of the secluded garden feels far from the madding crowd, this family-run hotel is very close to St Mark's and is set in a quiet alley just off a prestigious shopping district. The courtyards are delightful, draped in foliage, and provide a charming setting for a quiet breakfast. Inside is a grand Liberty-style staircase. The more imposing rooms (numbers 45, 46 and 47) have distinctive *fin de siècle* furniture but some rooms, notably the singles, are slightly cramped and unwelcoming. (Lone travellers should book a double room.) Since the Flora is often full (and may be closed from November to January), book well in advance or through a well-known Italian-specialist agency.

Pausania,
San Barnaba, Dorsoduro 2824,
tel: 522 2083;
fax: 522 2989.
This characteristic three-star hotel is housed in a converted palace in the San Barnaba district of Dorsoduro, an area once reserved for the impoverished nobility but now popular with students. This genteel hotel has recently been restored but retains its charming but steep stone staircase in the courtyard, which leads to the upper bedrooms. On the canal, a colourful vegetable barge sells its wares from early in the morning. There are a number of small but lively young restaurants nearby. For its category, the hotel is slightly over-priced, despite the restoration.

Piccola Fenice,
Calle della Madonna,
San Marco 3614,
tel/fax: 520 4909.
This small hotel is linked to the Hotel Fenice et des Artistes (*see opposite*). In fact, the hotel is more akin to an apartment building, consisting of serviced apartments. Set in a 16th-century palace, it makes a pleasant change from staying in a hotel. The small apartments are surprisingly spacious and contain a kitchenette (with a fridge, toaster and coffee pot but no cooker). Bookings can be for a short or long stay but need to be made well in advance.

San Cassiano,
Calle della Rosa,
Santa Croce 2232,
tel: 524 1768;
fax: 721 0330.
This sought-after hotel is housed in a Gothic palace facing the wonderful Ca d'Oro art gallery on the Grand Canal. Special package deals are available through such recognised British tour operators as Magic of Italy. San Cassiano is charming and reasonably priced, with a welcoming staff. Features

include an elegant entrance and a breakfast room overhanging the Grand Canal. However, the bedrooms are distinctly variable in size and quality, with some full of character and others cramped and possessing negligible views. Since at least six bedrooms have superb views, make a point of requesting the proverbial room with a view on booking. The stairs are steep and there is no lift so the bedrooms on the ground floor are designed for frailer visitors. The hotel has its own jetty, permitting visitors to arrive by motor boat from the airport or to return by gondola after an evening's ride.

Santo Stefano,
Campo Santo Stefano,
San Marco 2957,
tel: 520 0166;
fax: 522 4460.
Situated in an historic palace, this small hotel is a welcome recent addition to the Venetian scene. This tall, thin building was once an ancient watchtower (and former convent). The hotel is set on one of the city's most spacious and stylish squares (close to the Accademia and on a campo lined with fashionable bars). The young management are friendly and efficient. The bedrooms are small but tastefully furnished in muted colours and lit by Murano glass chandeliers. In fine weather, breakfast is served in a tiny courtyard beside an ancient well-head. (Breakfast is also better than in many Venetian hotels.) A babysitting service is available on request.

Seguso,
Zattere ai Gesuati,
Dorsoduro 779,
tel: 528 6858;
fax: 522 2340.
This two-star hotel occupies a 15th-century palace next door to La Calcina (*see opposite*). The Seguso is situated along the charming quaysides of the Zattere in the Dorsoduro district. The front rooms overlook the

Giudecca Canal while the side rooms have views over a smaller canal. Italians consider the place to exude a quaint atmosphere of "old England" but if so, it is faded charm with a Venetian twist, redolent of a turn-of-the-century *pensione*. The Seguso is dotted with charmingly second-rate antiques. In fine weather, breakfast is served on tables outside. Half-board is usually obligatory.

INEXPENSIVE

Agli Alboretti,
Rio Terro Sant'Agnese,
Dorsoduro 884,
tel: 523 0058;
fax: 521 0158.
This seemingly tiny building actually houses 25 rooms. Situated close to the Accademia, this reasonably priced two-star hotel is a good choice for budget travellers. It is particularly popular with American and British guests. The wood-panelled reception leads to slightly small bedrooms (avoid room 19). Unlike most small hotels, it has its own perfectly acceptable restaurant and a small but charming courtyard and garden at the back for breakfast or a rest after a day's sightseeing. The gastronomic restaurant (open 7–11pm, evenings only) employs a creative touch: as well as serving such dishes as Venetian shellfish or avocado and shrimps, it offers veal with cherries and saffron risotto. In summer, diners can eat under a pergola in the garden. While the hotel is modestly priced, the restaurant has more pretensions and is moderately priced.

Albergo Al Piave,
Ruga Giuffa, Castello 4838/40,
tel: 528 5174;
fax: 523 8512.
This functional but acceptable one-star hotel is tucked into an everyday shopping street in Castello district, close to Campo Santa Maria Formosa and under

Central Venice (continued)

ten minutes walk from St Mark's Square. The hotel also operates a simple dining room for guests and breakfast is usually included in the price. (The hotel has a bar service, air conditioning and central heating.) The staff speak basic English and French. The Piave is ideal for budget travellers who wish to experience a slice of domestic Venice: in the morning and early evening the narrow street is full of Venetian shoppers choosing bread, pasta and vegetables.

Antica Locanda Montin,
Fondamenta di Borgo,
Dorsoduro 1147,
tel: 522 7151;
fax: 520 0255.

This tiny inn is set on the banks of Rio delle Eremite, a canal in Dorsoduro, between San Barnaba and San Trovaso. These extremely inexpensive rooms are attached to the well-known restaurant Montin, whose premises are below (*see Restaurants, page 323*). Despite lacking private bathrooms, these seven unpretentious rooms are delightfully appealing and in a charming location but need to be booked several months in advance.

Antico Capon,
Campo Margherita,
Dorsoduro 3004 B,
tel/fax: 528 5292.

These modestly priced rooms are on Campo Margherita, one of the liveliest and most appealing squares in Dorsoduro. Since the seven rooms are pleasant but undistinguished, the location is everything. A welcoming *trattoria* is also linked to the hotel (*see Restaurants, page 323*).

La Residenza,
Campo Bandiera e Moro,
Castello 3608,
tel: 528 5315;
fax: 523 8859.

Tucked into a quiet square in the Castello district, the hotel occupies a Gothic palace overlooking a church. In particular, there is a splendid *salone* on the aristocratic *piano nobile* which is decorated with paintings and stuccowork; bedrooms are far simpler. The atmosphere, privacy and tranquility offset a slightly frosty reception. (The management speaks Italian and French.) This low-key domestic quarter is eminently suitable for those who wish to escape the crowds and explore the charming churches and bars in the Castello district, towards the Arsenal. The interior is delightfully authentic but the delicate fabrics mean that young children may not be welcome. (The hotel may well close for a time in winter.)

Hotels on the Islands

LUXURY
Hotel Cipriani,
Giudecca 10, Venezia 30133,
tel: 041-520 7744;
fax: 520 3930.

(Also booked through the Orient Express Hotels in the UK: 0181-568 8366.) This is considered the most luxurious hotel in Venice. It is certainly the quietest, set in pleasant gardens on the island of Giudecca, just five minutes away from San Marco in the hotel's complimentary 24-hour motor launch. The hotel was founded in 1958 by the Harry's Bar management, but is now in American hands. (Privileged guests can reach the hotel on the Orient Express — *see Getting There, page 301*). The majority of guests are affluent Americans and Japanese, drawn to the lovely location, excellent service and the air of exclusivity. The Cipriani also offers the only hotel tennis courts and swimming pool in Venice itself, with the wide expanse of the pool framed by a garden of azaleas, rhododendrons and oleanders. The hotel interior spells international luxury, with its piano bar, fine paintings, stuccowork and private corners. Bedrooms are decorated with Fortuny fabrics and have whirlpool baths. Beware of celebrities: the Cipriani is the haunt of such famous faces as Robert de Niro, Jack Nicholson, Elizabeth Taylor, Sofia Loren, Gerard Depardieu, Joan Collins and Roman Polanski.

Palazzo Vendramin
(same address and number as the Cipriani above) is the hotel's palatial annexe, a Gothic affair linked to the main Cipriani hotel by a charming courtyard and flower-bedecked loggia. The hotel has been expanded recently, with the creation of many private suites and self-contained serviced apartments, including one with its own swimming pool. Some have private terraces or superb views, including number 76 (favoured by the late Princess Diana, among other celebrities). All the apartments provide butler service and private kitchens, with afternoon tea and cocktails a feature of this luxurious experience. (To reach both the Cipriani and Palazzo Vendramin, take *vaporetto* 1 to San Marco Vallaresso and then look out for the complimentary and clearly recognisable Cipriani motor launch which takes guests across to the Giudecca.)

Excelsior Palace,
Lungomare Marconi 41, Lido di Venezia 30126,
tel: 526 0201;
fax: 526 7276.

This bizarre looking turn-of-the-century Lido hotel looks vaguely Moorish or Byzantine, with Gothic flourishes. It is ideally situated for the summer casino, the beach and the Venice Film Festival. The beach boasts cabins that resemble Moorish tents. Out of season, the hotel can seem marooned and distinctly miserable, rather a white elephant. The interior is sumptuous, if distinctly over the top but at least half the bedrooms have sea views. There is a private motor launch as well as a private beach.

EXPENSIVE
Hotel des Bains,
Via Lungomare Marconi 17,
Lido di Venezia 30100,
tel: 526 5921;
fax: 5206 0113.
This cool yet atmospheric hotel has been popular since its creation at the turn of the century, with the stately reception rooms displaying an Art Deco elegance. This Lido hotel was immortalised by the novelist Thomas Mann, whose stay here in 1911 helped inspire *Death in Venice*. (The film was also partly shot here.) The swimming pool and tennis courts are surrounded by pleasant grounds. The hotel also has a private beach and can arrange various watersports. There are several restaurants, including a terraced one, a second on the beach and another by the pool. It is ideally situated for the summer casino, the beach and the Venice Film Festival (*see Restaurants, page 325*).

Quattro Fontane,
Via Quattro Fontane 16,
Lido di Venezia,
tel: 526 0227;
fax: 526 0726.
This small, gabled four-star hotel lies in secluded gardens, making it one of the most charming hotels on the Lido. This is the place for visitors who are looking for comfort and pleasant surroundings without the formality of the larger luxury hotels. The mood is enhanced by bedrooms and reception rooms decorated with antiques. The rambling, vaguely alpine hotel is most appealing in summer, with its courtyard for summer dining and drinks, tennis courts and proximity to the sea. (The *vaporetto* stops by the Casino pier from midday until early in

Price Categories

Price categories (in lire) are based on single occupancy without breakfast:
Luxury = more than 500,000
Expensive = 350–500,000
Moderate = 200–350,000
Inexpensive = under 200,000

the morning and takes visitors directly to San Marco.)

MODERATE
Locanda Cipriani,
Piazza Santa Fosca 29,
Isola di Torcello;
tel: 730150/735433.
This four-bedroomed inn is set on the lovely but fairly remote island of Torcello. It makes a delightfully rural spot for a low-key Venetian holiday, only slightly marred by the daily stream of visitors to the island. The inn is run by Bonificio Brass, nephew of Arrigo Cipriani, the current owner of Harry's Bar and son of Tinto Brass, the well-known Italian film director. As such, cuisine as well as privacy are the rationale behind choosing the Locanda. (Although the inn is reasonably priced, the cuisine is more costly but you may be expected to take half-board in any case, which makes the package expensive.) However, with its idyllic setting and cuisine, the Cipriani is a memorable experience. Like Harry's Bar, to which it is still linked, this is a Venetian gastronomic institution and trains chefs for prestigious postings. The inn closes for a while in winter.

La Meridiana,
Via Lepanto 45, Lido di Venezia,
tel: 526 0343;
fax: 526 9240.
Surrounded by pleasant grounds, this soberly decorated 1930s villa makes a quiet retreat for a holiday on the Lido. It even has access to a private beach. (The hotel is generally

closed in winter, from November to February.)

Villa Ada (Biasutti),
Via Dandolo 24, Lido di Venezia,
tel: 526 0120;
fax: 526 1259.
This welcoming three-star Liberty villa is set in a pleasant garden in a residential area between the Adriatic and the lagoon. It is managed by the pricier Biasutti villa complex, a group of three villas (tel: 526 0120; fax 526 1259) in the same street. These well-positioned villas, linked by terraces and gardens, have a restaurant in the grounds as well as access to a private beach. (The hotel is closed for part of the winter, usually in December and January – check in advance.)

Villa Pannonia,
Via Doge Michiel 48,
Lido di Venezia,
tel: 526 0162;
fax: 526 5277.
This Art Nouveau hotel is set five minutes away (on foot) from the Santa Elisabetta landing stages. The family-run three-star hotel is particularly suitable for families. (For British-based visitors it can be booked on a package through Citalia.) The Pannonia is a welcoming place, with a small bar, knowledgeable receptionist and inquisitive cat. The dining room is particularly pleasant, overlooking peaceful gardens. Breakfasts are grim, even by Venetian standards and dining service is variable. Half or full-board is encouraged during the summer season but discuss this on booking. (It probably makes a sensible choice, certainly for those with young families.) The rooms are comfortable and reasonably furnished but those nearest the staircase can be noisy. The hotel has access to a private beach and organises trips to the Murano glass factories.

The Islands (continued)
INEXPENSIVE

Apart from the Lido, most islands have few – or no – hotels. However, there are usually rooms to rent in Murano and Burano, with Burano the more appealing choice. (There are often a few simple rooms to rent over a couple of *trattorie* in the main street.) For a list of current accommodation available, contact the Venice tourist office (*see page 303*).

Al Soffiador,
Viale Bressagio 10,
Isola di Murano;
tel: 739 430.

This simple *pensione* is located on Murano, an island with a regular and reliable boat service to central Venice. It also has a pleasant fish restaurant.

Locanda-Ristorante Raspo da Ua, Piazza Galuppi 560,
Isola di Burano;
tel: 730 095

Set on the colourful island of Burano, this cosy inn makes a change from more historic Venetian hotels. The six-bedroomed property is housed in a charming, former patrician, residence and is modestly priced. (Closed mid-November–December.)

Price Categories

Price categories (in lire) are based on single occupancy without breakfast:
Luxury = more than 500,000
Expensive = 350–500,000
Moderate = 200–350,000
Inexpensive = under 200,000

Budget

Archie's House,
Rio Terrà San Leonardo,
Cannaregio 1814b;
tel: 720884.

Set in lively, working-class Cannaregio, this rough-and-ready place is part budget hotel, part hostel, aimed at students. Facilities are basic; the atmosphere is noisy and somewhat chaotic.

Istituto Ciliota,
Calle delle Muneghe 5,
San Marco 2976;
tel: 520 4888

This popular mixed hostel is pretty central, close to Campo Sant Stefano. The atmosphere is good but prices are relatively high for a hostel. (Open mid-June–mid-September.)

Ostello Venezia,
Fondamenta delle Zitelle 86,
Giudecca,

tel: 523 8211;
fax: 523 5689.

The city's official youth hostel enjoys splendid views across the Giudecca Canal, but is very popular and often booked months in advance (book in April for the summer). The disadvantages are that the hostel applies fairly strict rules, including an 11pm curfew.

Apartments

Staying in an apartment is an increasingly popular option in Venice. For jaded travellers, it offers a subtly different way of seeing the city, from the inside. You can, as the Venetians say, *andare per le fodere*, slip between the linings of the city, and, after creeping into the crevices of your private palace, can declare yourself a Venetian by adoption, at least for the duration of your stay.

Venetian hotel breakfasts are notoriously meagre, while meals are rarely worthy of the glistening fish and fruit from the Rialto markets. In one of the world's most visited cities, hotel service can be perfunctory or brusque. But the experience is not simply about negatives but

Venice on the Cheap

Venice is not an ideal city for real budget travellers (especially students) but it can be done out of season, or in season if you don't mind some discomfort. Even for budget travellers, it is best to avoid mainland Mestre in favour of somewhere cheap, if very basic, in Venice itself.

It is illegal to camp in historic Venice and there is little point coming to Venice and camping in remote Chioggia or grim Mestre on the mainland. There is a camp site on the edge of the lagoon but prices for the pitch and ferries into central

Venice make this an uneconomical option. Real budget hotels are concentrated around the Lista di Spagna, in eastern Cannaregio, close to the railway station, but most of these are noisy and few have any character. More atmospheric are the small hotels situated in the quieter parts of Dorsoduro and Castello districts but these fill up fast. Alternatively, for students who can face a bit of regimentation, there are the hostels run by various religious orders. This is usually in cheap, single-sex dormitory

accommodation, with curfews often imposed. For advance bookings of all budget accommodation, contact the Venetian tourist office for a complete list: (APT, Venice tourist office: tel 041-522 6356; fax: 041-529 8730).

Since the budget accommodation situation literally changes overnight, for a room at short notice, also contact the APT for a list of vacancies (this is updated daily). In peak periods, local schools are also converted into temporary hostel accommodation.

about the liberating feeling of independence and the chance to live like a Venetian, however spurious that may seem. But this is the life of the leisured Venetian classes: there is always a maid. Your apartment may be full of antiques, from Murano mirrors, chandeliers and wooden chests to chaise-longues, oriental rugs and painted bed-heads. Even beds can be hard to leave if it is a canopied four-poster affair framed by Fortuny silk hangings and frescoed ceilings.

Visitors come to feel part of Venice, to belong to their small neighbourhood in a surprisingly short space of time, even in the course of a day. All it takes is a stroll to the local *alimentari* (grocery shop), rarely more than a few streets away. By stocking up on such provisions as olive oil and lagoon artichokes, you convey the impression of living in Venice rather than simply staying in Venice. The daily pleasures lie in the simplest of tasks. After buying your morning bread or wine from the same place more than once, you may be greeted in a warmer way by the shopkeeper. Again the seductive illusion: you are a treasured resident not a common tourist. As you become more adventurous, forays to the local markets, particularly the Rialto fish and vegetable markets, will tempt you to cook Venetian concoctions at home, back in your Venetian bolthole. By now, this feels like a genuine home, even if it is a palace with Gothic windows and a medieval kitchen.

The pleasures are deeply domestic. It is delightful to drink coffee on the terrace overlooking a private Venetian garden, possibly overrun by wispy wisteria or lean Venetian cats. After tramping the streets looking at glittering galleries and Baroque churches, it is wonderful to come home to a spacious apartment and fling

the shutters wide open to the last of the sunshine. Grand *palazzetti* may have private jetties, from which one can watch the world go by. Even in the humblest attic, there is usually a beguiling view over the Venetian rooftops, a corner of a church tower or a secluded garden. With a private terrace or balcony, even a storm can be a magical experience. Many palaces have canal views, allowing you to watch the water traffic to your heart's content. The soothing experience is more sybaritic than a gondola ride, since one can sip a glass of Prosecco at the same time. For the deeply industrious, there are always bookshelves lined with tomes on the city treasures.

Gracious apartment living provides a retreat from the hurly-

Price Categories

Prices (equivalent to a Moderate or Luxury hotel) reflect the size and luxury of the apartment, rather than the number of sharers (usually from 2–10).

burly of the crowded city; it frees you from the stuffiness, tedium and regimentation of superior hotels; in an odd kind of way, it even frees you from your duller self. After several days spent in idle contemplation of the view through Gothic windows, the changing light on canals and courtyards works its soothing spell: the old skin is sloughed off and a sleepier, more contented creature emerges. Plans to visit museums and galleries are deferred in favour of padding around the palace jetty, breakfast on a sun-drenched terrace, or simply listening to the church bells. From the privacy of your palace, even the strains of Chopin played by an unmusical neighbour can seem more beguiling than a visit to Vivaldi's

church around the corner. Vivaldi's Venice, Marco Polo's Venice, even Casanova's Venice, will all have to wait for another visit. This is the proof that you have swallowed the fatal potion of apartment living.

Venetian Apartments are the sole Venice apartment specialists: 38 Palmerston Road, London SW14 7PZ, UK; tel: (44) (0)181-878 1130; fax: 0181-878 0982. While based in the UK, they have representatives in Venice but reservations need to be made through the London office. If you wish, the company will handle all the travel arrangements, from flights to onward travel. Apartments can house from two to 11 people and, given the exorbitant rates of Venetian hotels, make a good alternative. For practical purposes, there is always a maid or apartment owner in Venice to contact over matters from keys to crises (in addition to a representative in Venice). The maid is usually there to meet you and can also be there to clean the apartment if wished. While most apartments lie in historic, central Venice, there are alternatives on the islands of the Giudecca and the Lido. In terms of budget and atmosphere, you can choose between a bolthole with beamed attic rooms and views over the russet rooftops, or a sumptuous Grand Canal palace complete with frescoed ceilings, silk hangings and canopied beds. Such delights are not confined to the grander palaces: at the other end of the scale are small but equally individualistic apartments.

Where to Eat

What to Drink

The Veneto is a good wine-growing area and superior DOC Veneto wines can be found in all Venetian bars. The big names are **Bardolino** and **Valpolicella**, light, fruity reds, as well as **Soave**, the best-known but sometimes bland white wine. **Bianco di Custoza** is a richer version of Soave. Most restaurants stock a fair range of Italian regional wines, with the grander hotels also serving French wines. (Non-European, so-called New World wines are rare.) Venetians drink much more white wine, partly through habit, partly because it better accompanies seafood, and partly because it is considered more refreshing. Venice is also noted for its cocktails, especially the **Bellini**, that was created in Harry's Bar (*see page 157*). The cocktail hour between 7pm and 8pm is a Venetian ritual: the locals can often be seen sipping wine or classic Italian cocktails at neighbourhood bars, chic cafés or *bacari* (wine bars). Sparkling **Prosecco**, from Conegliano, close to Treviso, makes a good choice of *aperitivo* or refreshing drink at any time of day. Prosecco can be dry (*secco*), medium-sweet (*amabile*), semi-sparkling (*frizzante*) and sparkling (*spumante*). The Veneto also produces a number of post-prandial *digestivi*, including **grappa**.

Where to Drink

Almost without exception, the grand hotels or piano bars provide a stylish setting for sipping *aperitivi* before dinner. However, the Venetian bar culture is far broader than **piano bars** and **sophisticated hotels**. There are a number of historic cafés close to San Marco where coffee has been sipped for centuries (*see Café Society, page 88*). In addition, there are numerous **delightful neighbourhood bars**. However, visitors should also try the *bacari*, traditional basic and **boisterous Venetian bars**, which are mainly concentrated in the San Polo and Santa Croce districts, close to the Rialto. Most *bacari* also serve food, essentially Venetian snacks. To sample a wide range of wines, visit an *enoteca* (**specialist wine shop and bar**) such as Al Volto (Calle Cavalli di San Marco, San Marco 4081). However, one can request *un ombra* (literally a "shadow") from any neighbourhood bar. This is a tiny (and usually inexpensive) glass of local Veneto wine, usually white, and downed in one go. In areas of Cannaregio, Dorsoduro and San Polo you will also see **wine shops** (*vinai*), where draught wine can be bought to take away. (If you are interested, have a container to hand and look out for the tell-tale *vino sfuso* sign in bars as well.)

What to Eat

Venetian cuisine is essentially fish-based, and embraces **risotto** cooked in black cuttlefish sauce, **soft-shelled crabs** from Murano as well as **Adriatic fish** such as mullet, sea bass and mackerel. For a description of Venetian cuisine and typical dishes, *see Cuisine, page 85*. For a comprehensive list of Italian dishes (with translations) *see Language, page 334*. However, visitors are not restricted to Venetian dishes: **Tuscan cuisine** is well represented in Venice while most menus feature **classical Italian dishes**, although often with a Venetian twist. Moreover, in the grander hotels and restaurants, or in those more obviously catering for tourists, a number of **international dishes** will be on the menu. For visitors who want to sample the taste of everyday Venice, then *cichetti* (**bar snacks**) represent the Venetian equivalent of Spanish *tapas* and are highly recommended. To eat *cichetti e l'ombra*, "**a snack in the shade**", is a Venetian tradition. These

Directions and Reservations

In Venice, official addresses can be meaningless, with numbers in the thousands merely linked to the *sestiere* or district but giving no indication of the street name. The street name is not given in official addresses, in theory to avoid confusion since the same name may exist elsewhere; in practice, it creates more confusion. When booking a new place, it is best to ask which is the nearest *campo*, church, bridge or significant monument. To be helpful, we have included landmarks within the addresses of restaurants and bars.

Reservations are usually required for the grander or better restaurants. These tend to be fairly dressy affairs, reflecting the elegant settings. The opposite is true of the *bacari*, the traditional wine bars, where you can dress as a market trader if you feel like it. In the case of inns (*osterie*) and middle-range restaurants, their popularity means that it is also sensible to reserve but you can also try just turning up if you happen to be in the area.

snacks can make a good choice for a light lunch or supper, best tried in a traditional bar (*bacaro*) or inn (*osteria*). In recent years, a number of ethnic bars and restaurants have opened in Venice so **Chinese** and **Syrian** cuisine are just two of the options.

Where to Eat

In style, Venetian restaurants seem to opt for cool, 18th-century elegance or the exposed beams and copper pots that spell rustic gentility. There are a number of restaurants that are more original, however, and many that are tucked under pergolas or spill onto delightful terraces and courtyards. The grander restaurants are generally known as *ristoranti* but may be known as *locande* or *osterie* (**inns**) if they stress the traditional nature of the cuisine or a rustic ambience. The *osterie* generally make excellent choices. In Venice, these tend to be genuine restaurants serving homely but surprisingly good cuisine in an intimate atmosphere. To confuse the issue, some of these inns have bars which act like traditional *bacari* so that one can opt for a quicker, cheaper snack at the bar or a full meal sitting down at a table. The *osterie* have been classed as restaurants in the categories below unless they are very basic or more like *bacari*, in which case they are classed as bars. Bear in mind that in Venice there is often a lot of overlap.

The **restaurants, inns, cafés, bars, cake shops** and **ice cream parlours** are all grouped together by district (*sestiere*). For the sake of simplicity, restaurants and inns (*osterie, locande*) are grouped together as one category within their relevant districts. Likewise, cafés, bars, *pasticcerie* (cake shops) and *gelaterie* (ice cream parlours) form a separate category. At the

end of each entry, a rough price listing is given. However, certain restaurants, especially inns, operate different prices within the same establishment, depending on whether one eats at the bar or at the table or, in certain cases, in one of two differently priced dining rooms.

San Marco

The district offers a wide choice of drinking and dining options. Given that San Marco is home to some of the city's most prestigious café s and restaurants, there is no shortage of sophisticated places for visiting at any time of day, from morning coffee to afternoon tea and cocktails. Many of the top hotels are nearby and have bars and restaurants celebrated in their own right (see Hotels). However, privacy should not be expected in most of these goldfish bowl settings and, in many cases, one pays a premium for dining close to St Mark's Square. Further away from the bustle, dining experiences tend to be more varied. Not that visitors should ignore the historic café s and celebrity restaurants close to St Mark's Square; the Venetians patronise them too.

CAFÉS, BARS & GELATERIE

Caffè Florian,
Procuratie Nuove,
Piazza San Marco 56,
tel: 528 5338
(closed on Wednesday in winter).
Protected by awnings but spilling out on to the piazza, this is considered the most Venetian and most prestigious of the grand café s, founded in 1720. If the weather is fine, sit under the awnings and enjoy the band while getting one's bearings on the famous square. However, in

winter or bad weather, the faded plush interior is the place for sipping Prosecco or cocktails. Florian also serves light lunches and dinners as well as afternoon tea. It sells variable souvenirs linked to over 250 years of the café's history. **E**

Caffè Lavena,
Piazza San Marco 133,
tel: 522 4070,
(open 9–1am, closed on Tuesday in winter).
This historic café ia close to Florian and Quadri, its more famous rivals. The café has been here since 1879 and is proud of its connection with Wagner, who came here (betwen 1879 and 1883) supposedly to avoid Verdi, a rival composer. Lavena is reputed to serve the best coffee in Venice and some of the finest ice cream. The bright interior makes for cheerful tearooms, with chandeliers and an 18th-century marble floor. **E**

Caffè Quadri,
Procuratie Vecchie,
Piazza San Marco 120,
tel: 528 9299/522 2105,
(closed on Monday in winter).
This historic café faces Caffè Florian across the square. Byron, Proust and Alexandre Dumas were all habitués in their day, although the café acquired a bad reputation as an unpatriotic haunt during the Austrian occupation. Quadri is decorated in Venetian colours, adorned with elegant stucco-work, red damask walls, Murano chandeliers and gilded mirrors. Along with Florian, this is the place for sipping Prosecco or cocktails while getting one's bearings on the famous square. Quadri also boasts a well-known, if rather obvious restaurant, with

San Marco (continued)
fine views over the square a
justification for the high prices
(*see Restaurants below*). **E**
Harry's Bar,
Calle Vallaresso,
San Marco 1323,
tel: 528 5777,
(closed on Monday).
 This legendary bar is fully
described on page 187. The
founder invented the Bellini
cocktail. (The bar is also a
restaurant – *see Restaurants
opposite*.) **E**
Paolin,
Campo Santo Stefano,
San Marco 2962.
This famous café, bar and
gelateria has a reputation as
one of the best in Venice, with a
mixed clientele, good
atmosphere and prompt service.
Certainly, the setting is
pleasant, with outside tables
overlooking the square.
However, the interior is rather
soulless, particularly since most
Venetians are now taking their
custom to other bars on the
square, given Paolin's high
prices and slightly offhand
manner. That said, the home-
made ices are worth sampling if
you happen to be in the area. **M**
Pasticceria Marchini,
Ponte San Maurizio,
San Marco 2769,
tel: 522 9109,
(closed on Tuesday).
This excellent *pasticceria* lies
just on Calle dello Spezier, off
Campo Santo Stefano, in the
direction of Campo San
Maurizio. As the most
prestigious *pasticceria* in Venice,
it serves award-winning and
sophisticated pastries, cakes
and sweets, including cream-
filled concoctions and fruit tarts.
More traditional offerings are
torta del Doge and *le baute
Veneziane* (sweets). This is
where well-heeled Venetians buy
their weekend treats. **M**
Rosa Salva,
Campo San Luca,
San Marco 4589,

tel: 522 5385,
(closed on Sunday).
Despite a slightly clinical
atmosphere, this is one of the
best places for a *cappuccino* in
the area, not to mention the
place for a good-quality ice
cream, pastry or snack.
Although tasty sandwiches are
available at midday, the
pasticceria is better-known for
its wide assortment of
traditional cakes. **I/M**

Al Volto,
Calle Cavalli di San Marco,
San Marco 4081,
tel: 522 8945,
(open 5pm–10pm, closed on
Sunday).
This *enoteca* (bar and wine-
tasting centre) is close to
Campo San Luca in the San
Marco district. Despite being the
oldest wine bar in Venice, Al
Volto attracts a young clientele.
The wine bar has accumulated a
superb array of wines, with
several thousand different
bottles on offer. This is the place
to drink a variety of *ombre*
("shadows"), small glasses of
wine traditionally drunk in one
go. Wine-tasting is accompanied
by the sampling of *cichetti*,
traditional Venetian snacks. **I**.
Vino Vino,
Calle del Café tier,
San Marco 2007a,
tel: 523 7027,
(closed on Tuesday).
Situated by Campo San Fantin,
close to La Fenice, this bar
attracts a fashionable young
clientele. This is a cramped but
cosy place for a quick snack,
lunch, and the chance to drink a
variety of *ombre* ("shadows"),
small glasses of wine
traditionally drunk in one go.

Wine-tasting is accompanied by
the sampling of *cichetti*,
traditional Venetian snacks
(served only until 9pm). **I**

RESTAURANTS
Antico Martini,
Campo San Fantin,
San Marco 1980,
tel: 522 4121,
(open until 1am, closed on
Tuesday, Wednesday and at
lunchtime between 1 December
and 20 March).
This classically correct
restaurant has been in existence
since 1720, when it was a
coffee house. The elegant
setting is matched by punctilious
service but exudes a slightly
oppressive atmosphere, the air
of too many expense account
lunches and celebrity wallets.
Nonetheless, it is a Venetian
institution, even if it has lost
some of its lustre with the
burning down of La Fenice opera
house. The menu is distinctly
Venetian, with all the classics,
from *granceole* (lagoon crab) and
fegato alla veneziana (chopped
liver on a bed of onions), to
risotto, *paste e fagioli, pennette
al pomodoro* and *carpaccio*. The
restaurant also prides itself on
its luxurious ingredients, spun
together with a creative twist to
produce, for instance, breast of
duck with black truffles. The
wine list is one of the best in
Venice. **E**
Caffè Quadri,
Procuratie Vecchie,
Piazza San Marco 120,
tel: 528 9299,
(closed on Monday out of
season only).
As well as the famous bar (*see
previous page*), this is the
setting for a fine restaurant, the
only proper one on the Piazza,
serving Venetian specialities as
well as creative twists on classic
Italian cuisine. The refined
atmosphere and punctilious
service are matched by
innovative cuisine. Fish may be
served in a Cabernet Sauvignon

sauce or unusual spices added to a classic dish. However, traditional Venetian dishes, such as a straightforward seafood grill, risottos or cuttlefish with polenta, are also available. Prices are predictably high but acceptable by Venetian standards, particularly given the setting and the improved standards at Quadri. **E**

Canova,
Hotel Luna Baglioni,
San Marco 1243,
tel: 520 9550,
(closed in August).
The hotel's main restaurant is a quiet yet elegant place despite its proximity to St Mark's. Unusually for Venice, the restaurant offers both smoking and non-smoking rooms. The cuisine embraces classic international dishes as well as staples of Venetian cuisine. The cooking is characterised by a light touch and very fresh ingredients; good home-made desserts and gracious service. Prices are predictably high but, despite the setting, are not quite justified by the current quality of the cuisine. The hotel itself, arguably the oldest in Venice, is also recommended (*see Hotels, page 309*). **E**

Da Ivo,
Ramo dei Fuseri,
San Marco 1809,
tel: 5285004,
(open until midnight, closed on Sunday.)
The interior strikes a romantic, self-consciously rustic note, belied by the high prices. This small yet luxurious restaurant is rated highly by Americans and focuses on Tuscan and Venetian dishes, including *bistecca alla fiorentina* (Florentine-style steak), *tartufi* (truffles) and *funghi porcini*, the finest mushrooms, in season. The Venetian menu features grilled fish and seafood. Some private dining rooms are available. Prices are high but acceptable by Venetian standards particularly

given the setting, although standards are considered to have fallen recently. **E**

Harry's Bar,
Calle Vallaresso,
San Marco 1323,
tel: 528 5777,
(closed on Monday).
This legendary bar is fully described on page 157. Despite its name, Harry's Bar serves an utterly fresh menu and is considered one of the most consistent restaurants in Venice. This is one of the few establishments close to San Marco to attract wealthy Venetians as well as visitors. Typical dishes play with such ingredients as risotto, seafood, lamb and veal, cooked simply yet superbly. The high prices reflect the exquisite ingredients and utterly professional service, led by the current Arrigo (Harry) Cipriani. Guests are asked to refrain from smoking cigars, wearing strong perfumes or using mobile phones. The restaurant is expensive but worth it, despite a 15,000 lire cover charge and a 15 percent service charge. Slight reductions if you settle the bill in lire. **E**

Trattoria da Fiore,
Calle delle Botteghe,
Campo Santo Stefano,
San Marco 3461,
tel: 523 5310,
(closed on Tuesday).
This simple Venetian *trattoria* is exceptionally good value, considering its location, in a little alley off chic Campo Santo Stefano. The inn is divided into two sections: a *bacaro* (traditional bar) in which one can drink wine or order a wide range of dishes, from snacks to a full meal, eaten at the bar, (this is particularly popular with young Venetians, both students and professionals); and the adjoining dining room serves a wider range of dishes at higher but still modest prices. The rustic atmosphere is cosy and

welcoming, with a good cold buffet on display. The menu focuses on Venetian dishes, but these are all accessible choices. The voluble cook, Marcello, does the restaurant proud (and even manages to find time to socialise with diners from time to time). **M/I**

San Polo & Santa Croce

While this district has a few stylish restaurants, it is also an ideal place for sampling the Venetian *bacari*, traditional wine bars or boisterous inns, especially rough and ready ones. Some are mentioned within the San Polo chapter and most serve typical *cichetti*, Venetian snacks such as meatballs, salami, cheeses, cuttlefish and polenta, *baccalà mantecato* (cod paste on toast) and *crostini*. If you just want a typical Venetian snack or light supper, see the *bacari* (traditional bars) listed in *Cafés, Bars & Gelaterie* below.

CAFÉS, BARS & GELATERIE

The Rialto is the ideal place to indulge in a Venetian bar crawl, (*giro di ombre*), mixing with anyone from visitors, students and elderly shop-keepers to the great unwashed populace. The bars recommended in this district are mainly *bacari*, rough and ready wine bars, suitable for a lively lunch or an early evening pub crawl in the Rialto Market district (many close after 8 or 9pm). These are at the opposite end of the scale to the cocktail and piano bars in the grand hotels, but are equally part of the Venetian social scene. Most *bacari* are hard to find in the den of the Rialto, so you might need to get a market trader to point you in the right direction.

San Polo & Santa Croce (cont'd)
Aliani, Ruga Rialto
Ruga Vecchia di San Giovanni,
San Polo 654;
tel: 522 4913.
This is one of the finest
delicatessens in Venice, the
place to buy delicious ham or
cheese for a picnic. Those
renting an apartment in Venice
can use the shop as a wonderful
source of fresh pasta, not to
mention cold meats, olive oil,
vegetables, fruits and jams.
Antico Dolo,
Ruga Vecchia di San Giovanni
778,
tel: 522 6546,
(10am–3pm, 6.30–10pm,
closed Sunday).
Easier to find than most bars in
the Rialto district, this rustic
osteria (inn) began as the haunt
of the boatmen who plied the
Rialto, delivering fresh produce
to the markets. The bar offers
such dishes as *bruschetta*,
polenta, radicchio, *baccalà
mantecato* (cod paste on toast)
and *crostini*. **I**
Do Mori,
Calle de Do Mori,
429 San Polo,
tel: 522 5401,
(open 9am–1pm, 5–8pm; closed
Sunday and Wednesday
afternoon).
This basic but authentic bar is
tucked just off Ruga Vecchia di
San Giovanni. Hung with knick-
knacks, this popular and
atmospheric inn serves a range
of Venetian *tapas*, including
cuttlefish and polenta, as well as
tramezzini, tiny sandwiches
stuffed with aubergines, crab or
shrimps. The wine, served by the
glass and drunk standing up, is
also good. **I**
Da Pinto,
Campo delle Beccarie (or
Pescheria),
San Polo 367,
tel: 522 4599,
(open 7.30am–2.30pm, 6–
8.30pm, closed Monday).
This long-established bar is one
of many rough and ready places

on the Rialto for lunch, a snack
or just a drink. A window
overlooks Campo della
Pescheria, allowing market
traders to have an *ombretta*
(glass of wine) without coming in.
This is the place for *cicchetti*,
snacks such as salami,
polpettine (meat balls) and
cheese or *baccala mantecato*
(cod paste on toast). **I**

Price Guide

For two with wine (in lire)
● **E** (expensive) over 200,000
● **M** (moderate) 100–200,000
● **I** (inexpensive) 50–100,000
Menu Decoder: *page 335*

Do Spade,
Sottoportego delle do Spade,
San Polo 860,
tel: 521 0574,
(open 9am–2pm, 5–11pm;
closed Sunday).
Do Spade claims to have been in
existence since 1475 and lies
close to Do Mori (*see above*).
This basic bar provides a sound
selection of Venetian snacks,
especially sausages and hams,
as well as fish, spicy sandwiches
and mozzarella snacks. Some of
these *ciccheti* are more original
than those found in other bars.
Snacks are eaten at the bar or
on simple refectory tables. **I**
Millevoglie,
Salizzada di San Rocco,
(close to the Frari and Scuola
Grande di San Rocco).
To find this popular ice cream
parlour from San Toma *vaporetto*
stop, follow the signs to the
Frari; it is behind the church. **I**

RESTAURANTS

Alla Rivetta,
Campiello dei Meloni,
San Polo 1479,
tel: 523 1481,
(closed on Monday).
This restaurant, lying between
Campo San Polo and
Sant'Aponal, is an exception to
the rough and ready inns in the

district. As a fully fledged
restaurant, Alla Rivetta serves
sound cuisine at prices to
match. This is a reputable
canalside *trattoria* and bar
serving good Venetian fare. **M**
Antica Bessetta,
Salizzada di Ca' Giusto 1395,
tel: 721 687,
(closed Tuesday and
Wednesday, as well as in July
and August).
Off the beaten track, just north
of San Giacomo dell'Orio, this is
a deceptively rustic Venetian
trattoria where standards (and
prices) are suitably high. It is
considered a temple of Venetian
home cooking. Despite (or
because of) its simplicity, this is
a foodies paradise, regularly
raved about by food critics and
even chefs. The menu is limited
but chosen according to season.
The *antipasti* are all Venetian
classics, usually followed by *risi
e bisi* (rice and peas), *granceole*
(lagoon crab), seafood risotto or
the whatever is the day's catch.
Fish are simply grilled or baked.
The well-chosen wines are
mostly from the Veneto and
Friuli. **M/E**
Da Fiore,
Calle del Scaleter,
San Polo 2202a,
tel: 721 308,
(closed on Sunday and Monday.)
A stylish and simple restaurant
praised by both locals and
foreigners, Da Fiore lies off
Campo San Polo. Many
Venetians find it an accurate
reflection of the subtlety of
Venetian cuisine, from grilled
calamari and *granceola* (lagoon
crab) to fried Adriatic fish and
risotto *al nero di seppia* (rice
with cuttlefish). The cooking
style aims for balance and
relative lightness. Desserts are
good, including sorbets,
chocolate tarts and mature
cheeses. Prices are generally
high but the consensus seems
to be that the cuisine currently
merits it. **M**

Ai Poste Vecie,
Rialto Pescheria, San Polo,
tel: 721 822.
(closed on Tuesday and from
15th July–15th August).
Set beside the fish market, this
is a Venetian institution, a 16th-
century dining room with
fireplace and wood-panelled
walls hung with Venetian knick-
knacks. Decorated in gentrified
rustic style, this noted fish
restaurant serves traditional
dishes as seafood grills, *baccalà
mantecato* (cod paste on toast)
and *sarde in saor*. According to
critics, however, the restaurant's
reputation has declined of late,
but the prices have failed to
reflect this. **M/E**

Castello

Given that Castello is home to
some of the city's most
prestigious hotels, there is no
shortage of sophisticated
places for visiting at the
cocktail hour. However, off the
Riva degi Schiavoni, dining
experiences tend to be more
varied. In fact, the district
offers a wide choice of
drinking and dining options,
many of which indulge in
traditional Venetian home
cooking. Between Campo
Santi Filippo e Giacomo and
Campo San Provolo are
several simple, but authentic,
restaurants amongst the stale
tourist fare. Likewise, in the
Arsenal district there are
several good, simple *trattorie*.

CAFÉS, BARS & GELATERIE

See the entries for the grand
hotels (*page 308*), which all
have romantic or impressive
bars. (These include the Danieli,
Londra Palace and Metropole.)

Rosa Salva,
Campo Santi Giovanni e Paolo,
Castello 6779,
tel 522 7949.
This well-established café has
occupied the ground floor of
Palazzo Bressana, a Gothic
palace, since the 18th century.
The bar doubles as a *gelateria*
for home-made ices (made with
fruit, chocolate and yoghurt),
and a *pasticceria* for pastries
and cakes. Specialities include
fruity aperitifs, chocolate ice
cream and zaleto pastries made
with yellow maize flour. **M**

RESTAURANTS

Antica Sacrestia,
Calle Sacrestia, Campo Santi
Filippo e Giacomo,
Castello 4442,
tel/fax: 523 0749,
(closed Monday).
Set in an alley off Campo Santi
Filippo e Giacomo, this old-
fashioned restaurant and
pizzeria has considerable charm.
Much of this is due to its history
as a converted sacristy.
Specialities include Adriatic fish
and Venetian dishes. Apart from
pizzas, the restaurant offers a
choice of well-priced menus, with
one based on fish, another
Venetian and a third vegetarian.
You can watch the chef making
pizzas using a traditional wood-
fired oven. The service is quite
efficient and prices reasonable.
The only snag is the welcome:
even if visitors speak Italian,
there seems to be a warmer
welcome for Venetians than for
foreigners, then the service is
slower service and there is a
reluctance to describe dishes in
much detail. **M**

Corte Sconta,
Calle del Pestrin, Castello 3886,
tel: 522 6546/522 7024,
(closed on Sunday and Monday,
and in part of July and August).
This excellent restaurant lies
east of the church of San
Giovanni in Bragora. This began
as an authentic *osteria* (inn) but

has become a fashionable
temple of Venetian gastronomy.
It looks much the same, a
romantic spot tucked into a
hidden courtyard, slightly off the
beaten track. The atmosphere is
relaxed and welcoming but the
menu is only written outside the
restaurant so make a mental
note of prices if this is of
concern to you. Fish is the
essence of a changing menu,
with seasonal produce also to
the fore. The *menu degustazione*
provides a sampling of the finest
Venetian dishes that would cost
much more elsewhere. Some
Venetians complain that the
portions are too small. **M/E**

Do Leoni,
Hotel Londra Palace,
Riva degli Schiavoni,
Castello 4171,
tel: 520 0533,
(open until midnight; closed on
Tuesday evening out of season).
Do Leoni is a member of a group
of loosely linked restaurants well
known for high standards of
cuisine at relatively reasonable
prices. The adjoining hotel bar
makes a charmingly intimate
spot for an aperitif. The
restaurant itself enjoys
wonderful views over the lagoon.
(In winter, part of the restaurant
is covered by a roof, which is
removed in summer.) Venetians,
in a standard criticism of the
established hotel restaurants,
complain that these days the
food is more bland and
adulterated to appeal to
international tastes. However,
Do Leoni seeks to steer a
sensible course in this
gastronomic minefield, pleasing
different palates with different
dishes. For those who wish to
sample Venetian fare, there are
specific menus offering fish of
every description, from
traditional *sarde in saor* to fish
soup and seafood grills. For so-
called international palates,
there is prawn cocktail, Parma
ham and melon as well as
classic Italian staples, including

Castello (continued)

pasta and grilled meats. In the evening, there is live music on a regular basis. Service is attentive yet discreet, with the waiters generally able to advise guests in English, French or Italian. **E**

Hostaria da Franz,
Fondamenta di Sant'Iseppo (Fondamenta San Giuseppe), Castello 754,
tel: 522 0861,
(closed on Tuesday).
This canalside *trattoria* was opened in 1842 by an Austrian soldier who fell in love with a Venetian girl. Off the beaten track, the building, which used to be a *corderia* (rope factory), was damaged in a fire which spread rapidly when the restaurant's fine collection of *grappa* exploded in the heat. Da Franz serves typical Venetian seafood dishes with a twist, such as risotto, gnocchi with prawns and spinach, marinated prawns, grilled fish, *paste e fagioli* and fish with polenta. **M/E**

La Nuova Perla,
Ponte Veneta Marina,
Castello 1645,
tel: 520 6764,
(closed Monday).
Set along the waterfront to the east of Riva degli Schiavoni, this restaurant is close to the Naval Museum and the beginning of Via Garibaldi. The food is pleasant but unexceptional, with pizzas as well as standard Venetian and Italian fare. The restaurant also doubles as a snack bar and ice cream parlour. Its location, with a terrace overlooking the waterfront, makes most of its appeal. Although slightly overpriced for what it is, prices are not outrageous and the pizzas are particularly good. **M**

Pizzeria San Giacomo,
Rimpeto della Sacrestia,
Campo Santi Filippo e Giacomo, Castello 4499,
tel: 521 1431,
(open noon–2.30pm and 7–

10pm, closed on Wednesday). This popular and inexpensive pizzeria lies just north of Campo Santi Filippo e Giacomo, a square due north of the prisons on Riva degli Schiavoni. It has a lively young atmosphere and is set on two floors and service is prompt and friendly. **I**

Price Guide

For two with wine (in lire)
● **E** expensive) over 200,000
● **M** (moderate) 100–200,000
● **I** (inexpensive) 50–100,000
Menu Decoder: *page 335*

Da Remigio,
Salizzada dei Greci,
Castello 3416,
tel: 523 0089,
(closed Monday evening and all Tuesday).
This erstwhile simple *trattoria* has long been a favourite with locals. Although it remains fairly genuine, it is increasingly popular, with its prices reflecting the fact. The menu includes typical Venetian dishes such as grilled fish and *fegato alla Veneziana* (liver Venetian style), with gnocchi a house speciality. Service can be a touch slow but the welcome is genuine enough, particularly to habitués. **M**

Alla Rivetta,
Ponte San Provolo,
Castello 4625,
tel: 528 7302,
(closed on Monday).
Set on the bridge across Rio del Vin, between Campo Santi Filippo e Giacomo and Campo San Provolo, this is a simple eaterie popular with Venetians and foreigners alike. Despite being close to San Marco, the brisk and breezy atmosphere makes it less touristy than many places; it is also reasonably priced. Fish and seafood are the specialities, including grills and *seppie in nero*, cuttlefish spaghetti; also on offer are polenta, plates of roast vegetables and standard

Venetian fare. Trade is brisk in this unpretentious inn (which shouldn't be confused with the more sophisticated restaurant with the same name in San Polo). **I/M**

Terrazza,
Hotel Danieli,
Riva degli Schiavoni,
Castello 4196,
tel: 522 6480.
The view alone is worth an entrance fee: from the lofty hotel terrace one looks out on St Mark's Basin. The cuisine focuses on Mediterranean dishes. The *antipasti*, chosen from the buffet, are generally admirable, as are the giant prawns in parsley, the fish soup and the seafood. The hotel is also one of the most historic in Venice. The prices are as high as one would expect for dining in one of the city's top hotel restaurants but a careful selection of wines can make the event less exorbitant. **E**

Al Vecio Canton,
Calle della Corona,
Castello 4738/a,
tel: 528 5176.
This is one of the best *pizzerie* in Venice, with a wood-fired oven and an old-fashioned, family atmosphere. Although only a stone's throw from Campo San Provolo and a few minutes from Riva degli Schiavoni and Campo Santa Maria Formosa, the restaurant is tucked away in an obscure alley. From Campo San Provolo, cross the Rio di San Provolo and walk north along Calle Rotta (this eventually becomes Ruga Giuffa), turning left along Calle della Corona, you will see the pizzeria on the corner in front of you. The restaurant (with a downstairs bar) is set on two floors in a wood-panelled setting. The inexpensive menu includes a reasonable range of dishes as well as pizzas. Service is helpful and friendly, with views best from the upper floor. **I**

Dorsoduro

Dorsoduro has a wide range of bars and restaurants, many of which have delightful gardens. On the whole, these are not the greatest restaurants in Venice but the setting and atmosphere provides a lot of charm. Even so, there are a sprinkling of authentic *trattorie* providing genuine Venetian cuisine. These tend to be quickly booked as Dorsoduro is such a popular area, especially in summer. Dorsoduro also has the greatest concentration of appealing open-air bars and reputable *gelaterie* (ice cream parlours), with Nico Gelati probably the best in Venice.

CAFÉS, BARS & GELATERIE

Il Caffè,
Campo Santa Margherita,
Dorsoduro 2963,
(closed Sunday).
The red awnings of this stylish café make it clearly distinguishable on the bustling square. Set on one of the most inviting Venetian *campi*, the terrace is a popular place for cocktails. **I**

Cantine del Vino,
Fondamenta Nani,
Dorsoduro 922.
Set on Rio di San Trovaso, this old-fashioned, canalside wine bar is popular with locals from all walks of life. It is a good place for eating *cichetti*, typical bar snacks. To savour the atmosphere, consider popping in at Venetian cocktail hour, from 7pm–8pm. **I**

Causin,
Campo Santa Margherita,
Dorsoduro 2996,
(closed Sunday).
This is a good ice cream parlour (with seats on the campo itself) but Nico Gelati (on the Zattere) is better. **M**

Gelateria Squero,
Fondamenta Nani, is next-door to Cantine del Vino (*see above*). This is an acceptable ice cream parlour but several on the Zattere nearby are better. **I**

Linea d'Ombra,
Punta della Dogana 19 (on the bridge of Rio della Salute),
tel: 520 4720/528 5259,
(open from 8am–2am; closed Wednesday and Sunday evening).
This well-sited piano bar and pricey restaurant makes a trendy spot for cocktails, live music and people-watching. The restaurant serves good quality versions of Venetian classics, such as *sarde in saor*. With its views across to the Giudecca, it also makes a romantic waterside spot for idling into the early hours, especially in summer, when the terrace comes into its own. **M/E**

Nico Gelati,
Zattere, Dorsoduro 922,
tel: 522 5293,
(open 7am–10pm; closed Thursday and in late December and January).
This *gelateria* on the charming Zattere quayside is reputed to be the best in Venice, with delicious speciality ice creams. The best-known is the *gianduiotto* (praline ice cream drenched in whipped cream). Ask for it to be *da passeggio* (to take away). **M**

RESTAURANTS

Ristorante El Chef,
Campo San Barnaba,
Dorsoduro 2765,
tel: 528 8422.
This is one of the many Venetian restaurants which one chooses for the setting rather than the cuisine. Lurking behind sturdy stone walls, the restaurant conceals a curious, covered garden with a friendly, rustic atmosphere. The restaurant is run by an established chef and his jokey son. The food is pleasant, particularly the fish

soup, seafood risotto, seafood grills, meatballs, polenta and the typical chopped Venetian liver on a bed of onions (*fegato alla Veneziana*). **I/M**

Taverna San Trovaso,
Fondamenta Priuli,
Dorsoduro 1016,
tel: 520 3703,
(closed on Monday).
This lively *trattoria* and pizzeria makes a good choice for those looking for an inexpensive place to eat by the canalside. It is set on two floors and is usually popular with students from the university further along the quayside. The *trattoria* fare is fine if rather predictable while the pizzas are more than acceptable. **I/M**

Trattoria Pizzeria Antico Capon,
Campo Santa Margherita,
Dorsoduro,
tel/fax: 528 5252.
This lively and inexpensive *trattoria* and pizzeria is opposite Il Caffè. It is at its most appealing on a spring or summer evening, when one can eat outdoors and enjoy looking at the lovely square. The menu is prime Italian fare with a few Venetian specialities. It is also a simple hotel. **I/M**

Montin,
Fondamenta di Borgo (or Fondamenta delle Eremite),
Dorsoduro 1147,
tel: 522 7151,
(closed Tuesday evening and Wednesday).
This is a well-established garden restaurant with an associated inn (*see Antica Locanda Montin in Hotels, page 312*). Montin began as a rustic *trattoria* favoured by artists and musicians, including Ernest Hemingway, Ezra Pound and Peggy Guggenheim. However, this artistic haunt has long been discovered by latter-day visitors, leading to the expected change in prices and atmosphere. Even if the rustic ambience now feels rather false, the enchanting garden provides compensations.

Dorsoduro (continued)

Although the food is variable and no longer first division, it is pleasant enough although over-priced. Set in the Campo San Barnaba quarter of Dorsoduro, Montin is particularly popular in summer so booking is essential. The dining room is cosy and welcoming should the weather change. The restaurant also incorporates an art gallery. **M**

Cannaregio

In general, this tends to be a relatively cheap district for restaurants, although many are just bars, inns or a *tavola calda* operation. Strada Nuova offers tempting *bacari*, typical bars and food shops displaying juicy hams and home-made pasta. The side streets close to the Campo Santi Apostoli end of Strada Nuova also conceal plenty of traditional bars, as do some of the seemingly bleak quaysides in Cannaregio.

In the Ghetto (*see page 240*), hungry visitors may like to try the genuinely kosher restaurant or sample unleavened bread in the Jewish bakery in Calle del Forno.

CAFÉS, BARS & GELATERIE

Barada,
Fondamenta Ormesini,
Cannaregio 2754,
(evenings only, 6pm–2am, closed on Sunday).
The ambience of this Syrian bar is enhanced by the cuisine: couscous, falafel, houmous and *foul* (beans) are staples, as is middle-eastern coffee and mint tea (the restaurant needs to be booked, but bar snacks are available). **I**
Al Promessi Sposi,
Calle dell'Oca,
Cannaregio 4367,
tel: 522 8609,

(open 10am–3pm, 5–11pm, closed on Wednesday.) This bar and restaurant serves a good selection of *ciccheti*, Venetian tapas, as well as clams and pasta and *pasticcio di crespelle al pesce* (stuffed pancakes). **I**.

RESTAURANTS

Bentigodi,
Calleselle, Cannaregio 1423,
tel: 716 269,
(open 10am–3pm, 6–11pm, closed Sunday).
This is a homely inn, lined with wooden tables, serving a good selection of *ciccheti*, Venetian *tapas*, including chickpea soup, aubergine snacks, gnocchi and anchovies. **I**
Al Paradiso Perduto,
Fondamenta della Misericordia, Cannaregio 2540,
tel: 720 581,
(open 7pm–1am, closed Wednesday).
This trendy, vaguely bohemian inn is only open in the evening, but is a variant on the Venetian *bacaro*, with a clubby atmosphere and refectory tables. However, unlike a traditional inn, there is usually live music and poetry on Wednesday and Saturday (when prices are higher). The arty crowd enjoys dining on home-made *bigoli* (wholemeal spaghetti, often in anchovy sauce) as well as other filling pasta. **M**
Alla Vedova,
Ramo Ca' d'Oro,
Cannaregio 3912,
tel: 528 5324,
(open 11.30am–3pm and 6–11pm, closed Thursday).
This welcoming *osteria* (inn) is very popular with Venetians, with students clustered around the bar to sample such *tapas* as *baccala*, fried vegetables (including peppers and courgettes) and seafood. You can also eat sitting down at a table. **M**

Island Restaurants

The following include a selection of the best restaurants on the islands of Burano, Mazzorbo, the Giudecca, the Lido and Torcello. *Also see Hotels, page 312*. It is best to book before setting out to the islands, certainly in the case of the grander restaurants. All the islands can be reached from central Venice by boat but you should check the times of the last ferries back (*see page 305*).

Burano

Al Pescatori,
Via Baldassare Galuppi 371, Burano,
tel: 041-730 650,
(closed on Wednesday).
This welcoming fish restaurant is situated on Burano's main street. In fine weather diners can eat outside. The specialities feature both fish and game, depending on the season. Typical dishes include fish, seafood risotto and *tagliolini* with cuttlefish (*seppie*). The wine list is more extensive than usually found in Venetian restaurants. **M**
Da Romano,
Piazza Galuppi 221,
Burano,
tel: 041-730 030,
(closed on Tuesday).
This old-established, traditional restaurant is the best-known on Burano and considered the best. A pretty interior is lit by glass lamps and decorated with paintings in every style, donated by artists passing through and inspired by the island. The atmosphere is reminiscent of a dance-hall of the 1920s. Try the seafood grills or *riso nero*, a risotto with black squid sauce. In the evenings, one can eat in the open air on the terrace and watch the Burano locals enjoying their evening *passeggiata* on the

island. (At weekends it is best to make a booking.) **M**

Antica Trattoria alla Maddalena,
Mazzorbo;
tel: 041-730 151.
This endearing inn lies over a bridge from Burano, technically on another island, in the verdant space of Mazzorbo, close to the *vaporetto* jetty. (The Burano ferry also stops at Mazzorbo on its way to or from Venice but check the times before settling down to dinner.) The charm of this simple inn is both the location and the lagoon cuisine. A limited menu focuses on lagoon specialities such as wild duck, usually served with polenta or pasta (generally *fettucine*). **I**

The Giudecca

Do Mori,
Fondamenta San Giacomo,
Giudecca 558,
tel: 041-522 5452,
(closed on Sunday).
Formed by a breakaway group from Harry's Bar, this is the place for those who cannot afford the elevated prices of Harry's Dolci and the Cipriani (*below*). The food is still good, essentially Venetian home cooking, with a preponderance of fish dishes, pasta, tasty *antipasti* and soothing desserts. **M**

Harry's Dolci,
Fondamenta San Biagio,
Giudecca 773,
tel: 041-522 4844/520 8337,
(closed Tuesday).
For *la gente per bene* (the Venetian middle classes), there is the Sunday morning ritual of crossing over from central Venice after Mass to waterside Harry's Dolci for brunch or lunch. A relatively economical version of Harry's Bar in the San Marco district, it was originally just a tearoom selling pastries and sweets, but now serves a similar menu to Harry's Bar. (Tasty and delicate patisseries

are still served outside main meal times.) Try the American brunch, the very good Venetian risotto, curried chicken or *baccalà mantecato*, and don't forget to have a Bellini in the American bar. **E/M**

Hotel Cipriani,
Giudecca 10,
30133 Venezia,
tel: 041-520 7744;
fax: 520 3930
(closed from early November–mid-March).
This is considered one of the finest city restaurants and is set in the most luxurious city hotel (*see Hotels, page 312*). The elegant restaurant spills out onto a glorious summer terrace. The dishes include *carpaccio*, clams with asparagus, scampi and *calamari*, and veal with artichokes; desserts are fresh and subtle, including sorbets and home-made pastries. The setting is exquisite, the service discreet and the prices high. **E**

Price Guide

For two with wine (in lire)
● **E** (expensive) over 200,000
● **M** (moderate) 100–200,000
● **I** (inexpensive) 50–100,000
Menu Decoder: *page 335*

The Lido

Liberty Restaurant,
Hotel des Bains,
Via Lungomare Marconi 17,
30100 Venezia Lido,
tel: 041-526 5921.
The grand restaurant is decorated in Art Nouveau style and reflects the atmosphere of the opulent hotel. The cuisine, which offers Venetian and Italian specialities, is perfectly pleasant but the setting is more impressive than the food. There is an additional beach restaurant as well as buffets and snacks around the pool. **E**

Taverna,
Hotel Excelsior,

Lungomare Marconi 41,
30126 Venezia Lido,
tel: 041-526 0201.
The hotel's Taverna Summertime restaurant spreads under a pleasing terrace overlooking the beach. Specialities include a buffet with classic Italian *antipasti* as well as grilled fish and cold cuts. **E**

Torcello

Locanda Cipriani,
Piazza Santa Fosca 29,
Isola di Torcello,
tel: 041-730 150;
fax: 041-735 433,
(open noon–3pm, 7–9pm, closed Tuesday except between May and September; also closed completely in January).
This small inn is set on the lovely, but remote, island of Torcello. It makes a delightfully rural spot for lunch or dinner. The inn is run by Bonificio Brass, nephew of Arrigo Cipriani, the current owner of Harry's Bar and son of Tinto Brass, the well-known Italian film director. Like Harry's Bar, to which it is linked, this is a Venetian gastronomic institution and trains chefs for prestigious postings. Try the seafood salad, the grilled fish, the fillet steak or the *risotto alla torcellana*. **E**

Osteria al Ponte del Diavolo,
Via Chiesa 10,
Isola di Torcello,
tel: 041-730401;
fax: 041-730250.
(open for lunch every day except Thursday; open for dinner only upon reservation).
This friendly inn stands beside the so-called Devil's Bridge, close to the Locanda Cipriani. The atmosphere is warm and welcoming, and the service highly efficient. The food is somewhat over-priced but the setting is engaging. Specialities include fish dishes and the wonderful home-made pasta, including one cooked with spring vegetables. **M**

Culture

Attractions & Sights

The locations and opening times of most sights are featured within the Places chapters. These include museums, churches, belltowers, palaces, galleries and historic monuments. If you wish to be doubly sure, request an up-to-date list of *Museums, Churches and Exhibitions* from the tourist office. These are handy leaflets to carry around with you. Also pick up a copy of the invaluable free booklet *Un Ospite a Venezia/A Guest in Venice* (in Italian and English) from one of the grand hotels. This bi-monthly magazine is a mine of information on all Venetian sights and services. Bear in mind that there will always be unexpectedly closed sections of galleries and churches in Venice: ongoing restoration is a feature of the city.

Guided tours

Standard guided tours are offered by American Express (tel: 041-520 0844) or World Vision Travel (041-523 0933) amongst others. Most of the big agencies around St Mark's Square and off Calle Vallaresso offer city tours and visits to the islands. The latter can consist of a hard sell in a glass factory so check the itinerary carefully (and read the Murano chapter in the colour section of the book). There are usually a couple of unusual thematic tours (conducted in English, French or Italian), such as *Sherlock Holmes' Venice* or *Wagner's Venice*. The tour of the Jewish Ghetto is also worth doing.

If you speak Italian, a number of unusual walking tours are open to you; walks change according to the season. These might include *Casanova's Venice* or a thematic exploration of a specific quarter. The Venice tourist offices should be able to tell you what's on (or check in the local paper). The *Secret Itinerary* (*itinerari segreti*) around the Doge's Palace is recommended to anyone with a smattering of Italian. Few could fail to be enthralled by this exploration of the "shadow-palace", with its maze of alleys, secret passageways, torture chambers, prisons and air of murk and mystery.

Cinemas & Theatres

To find out what's on, consult the tourist office and the local newspapers. Best of all, pick up a copy of the invaluable free booklet *Un Ospite a Venezia/A Guest in Venice* (in Italian and English) from one of the grand hotels.

Tickets for most events can either be booked at the tourist offices or through one of the many travel and tourist agencies around San Marco. The latter are infinitely more helpful, reflecting the usual Italian dichotomy between the state and private sectors.

As far as films are concerned, the usual American and international releases are shown but are usually dubbed into Italian. Key cinemas include: **Accademia** (in Dorsoduro); **Centrale** (in the Frezzaria, close to San Marco); and the **Rossini** (close to San Luca).

The **Teatro Goldoni** (Calle Goldoni, San Marco 4650b; tel: 5205 422) is a venue for plays, usually performing works by Goldoni, the Venetian dramatist (in Italian only, as is the case in general). **Del Ridotto** (Calle Vallaresso; tel: 522 2939) stages modern works, by Harold Pinter, for instance.

Venice Film Festival

An exception to the Italian language rule is the glitzy Venice Film Festival, held in late August and early September, when films are shown in their original versions. Venice is the oldest film festival in the world and second only to Cannes. Today the festival concentrates on art house movies rather than blockbusters. Nightlife is certainly more cosmopolitan during the Film Festival, and centred on the Palazzo del Cinema and the Astra on the Lido (*see Film Festival, page 283*).

Concerts & Opera

Venice is a deeply musical city (*see page 77*). Many of the sounds of the city are free: visitors wandering the canals will often hear music students laboriously practising their Chopin or Schubert. Vivaldi and Monteverdi lived in Venice and Vivaldi's concerts are commonplace. Music can usually be listened to in lovely settings, especially in churches and the *scuole*, the charitable confraternities (*see Scuole box, page 220*).

To check details such as the opening times of casinos, exhibitions, concerts and shows, see *Un Ospite a Venezia/A Guest in Venice*, available free from the grand hotels. A number of bars also stage performances of live music.

La Pietà (Riva degli Schiavoni), the lovely Rococo church linked to Vivaldi, is a splendid setting for concerts of Vivaldi and Baroque music.

Teatro Goldoni (tel: 520 5422) is a venue for classical concerts, occasional jazz and plays.

Classical concerts are often held in the lovely Gothic church of I Frari as well as in the splendidly decorated confraternity houses (Scuola Grande di San Rocco, Scuola Grande di San Giovanni Evangelisti and the Ospedaletto). Many of the best concerts are conducted by the Accademia di San Rocco, a musical ensemble which stages Baroque and other recitals in traditional Venetian settings.

Fondazione Querini-Stampalia (Castello 4778; tel: 271 1411) is a small gallery providing an intimate yet sumptuous setting for evening and lunchtime recitals. (You can visit the gallery before or after a concert.)

Since **La Fenice** opera house burnt down in 1996, the opera company has moved into the temporary **Palafenice** (tel: 521 0161) by Tronchetto car park. The rebuilt opera house on Campo San Fantin should re-open by the millennium. The homeless opera house orchestra and choirs are either playing in Venetian palaces or churches, or touring.

Nightlife

Where to Go

Venice's harshest critics claim that the city has no nightlife. Certainly, Venetian nightlife is distinctly tame, with few nightclubs, discos or alternative bars. Given that the average age of Venetians is 45, most people usually opt for a meal out or cosy drinks in a bar. What entertainment there is tends to be low-key, focused on piano bars, the historic cafés around San Marco and chic hotel bars. For visitors, the alternatives include gondola rides or strolls along the Zattere to buy delicious ice cream. Alternatively, you can do as the Venetians do and visit the traditional bars known as *bacari*. The best *bacari* are covered in the Eating Out section, *see page 317*, but since many close early, late-night bars are listed below.

During Carnival, nightlife includes outside balls and a great deal of people-watching and strolling from café to café *(see Carnival chapter, page 101)*. In winter (October–March), visitors should try to visit the gorgeous Winter Casino in Palazzo Vendramin-Calergi (tel: 529 7111) on the Grand Canal. Smart casual clothes are acceptable (as long as jackets are worn).

The Summer Casino, set in the Fascistic-looking Palazzo del Casino on the Lido, is also a focus for summer nightlife. Certainly, the livelier nightlife scene switches to the Lido in summer and focuses on the seafront and the grand hotels. For brasher and younger

nightlife, especially discos, young Venetians dance the night away with tourists in the clubs on the Lido di Jesolo on the Adriatic coast. (You will need to go there by car, taking a road with a high accident rate.) Given the ageing Venetian population, the historic centre of Venice has no recommended discos, only a few stuffy and rather old-fashioned nightclubs.

Late Night Bars

Antico Martini
Campo San Fantin 1983.
This old-fashioned nightclub has an elegant, middle-aged clientele, piano bar and a rather staid atmosphere.

Fiddler's Elbow
Cannaregio 3847, close to Strada Nuova,
tel: 523 9930.
This is a themed Irish pub.

Linea d'Ombra
Punta della Dogana, Zattere 12.
A piano bar, restaurant with jazz at weekends in a chic waterside location. (*See Cafés, Bars and Gelaterie, page 323.*)

Ai Musicanti
Ponte della Canonica 4309,
tel: 520 8922,
(open nightly).
A rumbustious venue where a wide range of music, from folk to French and Italian chansons, opera and classical music, is performed.

Paolin
Campo Santo Stefano.
This café and good gelateria is one of the few open very late (until midnight in summer).

Il Paradiso Perduto
Fondamenta della Misericordia Cannaregio 2450,
tel: 720 581.
This is a bustling restaurant with live music.

Do Leoni
Hotel Londra Palace,
Riva degli Schiavoni.
This welcoming restaurant offers live guitar music to accompany dinner (*see page 322*).

Children

What to Do

At first sight, Venice, with its great art and architecture, may seem unsuitable for children, but this is not necessarily so.

Minor daily activities can be very entertaining: watching glass-making displays on Murano; visiting mask shops; feeding the pigeons; and jumping on and off boats. **Crossing the Grand Canal** on the *traghetto* (gondola-ferry) is an inexpensive and amusing activity, especially if children are encouraged to stand up, as the natives do. **Climbing towers** is another engaging activity: the best are probably San Giorgio (on the island of the same name) and the Campanile di San Marco on St Mark's Square.

The city offers a number of fun outdoor activities and **sports**, from tennis to riding and sailing. The **beaches** on the Lido are obviously ideal for family holidays, although it is worth choosing a hotel with a private beach. (The public beach at the northern end of the Lido is more crowded than the one at the southern end.) In fine weather, take a boat to the islands, with Burano probably the most fun for children. To avoid the tourist rush, arrive before 11am (before then and after 5pm, the island belongs to the *Buranelli*, as the inhabitants are called).

Venice offers a few charming **walks**, especially the one along the Zattere quaysides in Dorsoduro. Apart from waterside views, there are numerous cafés

and *gelaterie* where you can eat pasta or ices while sitting on jetties over the water. (Nico Gelati is the best: try the rich *giandiuotto* ice cream.)

Although Venetian children occasionally play in the Giardini Pubblici, the city's main park in eastern Castello, most prefer their local *campi*, the small parish squares. **Games** are sometimes set up on Campo San Polo and Campo Santa Margherita. Squares such as Santa Margherita and Campo Santa Maria Formosa are child-friendly, with appealing pigeons and well-heads, cafés and gondolas. Campo San Polo is the square where one is most likely to encounter young Venetian children en masse.

As far as **art** is concerned, the Scuola Grande di San Giorgio degli Schiavoni is a lovely choice, even for young children: Carpaccio's engrossing scenes are rather like fairy tales peopled by dragons, knights, princesses and lions. The "secret tour" of the Doge's Palace is also worth a try, if you speak a smattering of Italian: it covers prisons, secret passages and torture chambers.

The **Aquarium** (open 9am–7pm; closed on winter Tuesdays), on Calle degli Albanesi, west of St Mark's Square, displays lagoon fish as well as those from the Adriatic, Mediterranean and the Tropics.

Older children will enjoy the **Naval Musem** (Museo Navale), with its boats and guns.

As far as food is concerned, many **restaurants** offer children's portions while Venice has very good ice cream parlours and neighbourhood pastry shops.

The city **festivals** are of considerable appeal to children. Fireworks accompany many of the special events and during Carnival children can dress up and parade around.

Festivals

Calendar of Events

For a description of the main festivities, *see Regattas and Water Festivals, page 93* and *Carnival, page 101*.

Public holidays are listed on *page 229*.

For a complete list of annual festivals and events, request the *Special Events* brochure from the Venice tourist office and pick up a copy of *Un Ospite a Venezia/A Guest in Venice* from one of the grand hotels.

The following list details the major Venetian festivals.

February: *Carnevale* (Carnival) opens the festive season.

25 April: *Festa di San Marco* is an annual celebration of the city saint, with a ceremonial Mass in the Basilica and the romantic presentation of a *bocolo* (rosebud) to women. On the same day, a rowing competition known as the *Vogalonga* is held.

March: Start of the chamber music season.

Mid-April to early May: Vela Venezia is a popular boat show and jaunty yachting regatta.

May: *Festa della Sensa* (Ascension Day) is a re-enactment of the Marriage of Venice with the Sea; this is followed by a regatta and *La Vogalonga*, a marathon rowing race, a week later.

June (odd years only): Biennale modern art show.

July (third weekend): *Festa del Redentore* (Festival of the Redeemer). This bridge of boats across the Giudecca canal is in thanksgiving for the city's survival from the plague; an exceptional fireworks display takes place over the water.

Early July: Murano Regatta (on the island of Murano).

August: Venice Regatta.

Late August: Venice Film Festival.

September (first Sunday): *Regatta Storica* (Historic Regatta) is the finest regatta in Venice. It includes a procession up the Grand Canal led by all manner of craft containing Venetians in traditional costumes; this is followed by gondola races.

September: Burano Regatta (on the island of Burano).

November: *Festa della Madonna della Salute* is a procession across the Grand Canal on floating pontoons to La Salute church; it is in thanksgiving for the city's survival from the plague.

November: Opening of the Venice opera season.

December: Christmas concerts in San Marco and La Pietà.

Festival Extras

Nightlife is certainly glitzier and more cosmopolitan during the two major city events: the Biennale, held in odd-numbered years; and the Venice Film Festival, held in late August and early September.

Sport

Spectator Sports

Venice is not a destination for spectator sports with the exception of the numerous regattas, which are part sporting events, part festivities (*see Regattas and Water Festivals, page 93*). For a list of current regattas, water festivals and the odd football match on the island of Sant'Elena, pick up *Un Ospite a Venezia/A Guest in Venice*, a useful brochure available free from the grand hotels.

Participant Sports

Despite the water, Venice is not a great place for swimmers. Only one hotel, the luxurious Cipriani, has a private pool in central Venice. However, many hotels on the Lido have private pools, making them suitable for families with young children. Cycling, riding, sailing, tennis and golf are also possible on the Lido, as are short trips in private planes.

Beaches

The Lido is the Venetian summer resort, with the east of the island fringed with sandy beaches. The private hotel beaches are vastly superior to the public beaches in terms of cleanliness, privacy and facilities. (*See Where to Stay, page 307*, for a list of hotels on the Lido that have access to a private beach.) Of the public beaches, the one at the northern end is more crowded than the one at the southern end. Holidaymakers regularly swim in the Adriatic, but the

more fastidious may prefer to stick to the hotel pool.

Nature Excursions

Different local organisations offer nature rambles on the lesser-known lagoon islands. These tours, which visit market gardens, fishing ponds, sand bars, salt pans and mud flats, are aimed at increasing the ecological awareness of visitors and Venetians alike. On a visit to a fish farm in the lagoon, you might see bream, sea bass and eels (which feed in the lagoon in spring). Other tours visit wildlife, including mute swans, kingfishers, cormorants, coots, grey herons and egrets. The Lido tourist office (Gran Viale, Lido (tel: 041-526 721; fax: 041-529 8720) is by far the best-informed about such tours.

The most typical tours are to Torcello, Burano, and Sant'Erasmo's orchards and market gardens. The Archeoclub d'Italia also organises trips to ancient fortifications on the lagoon.

Shopping

What to Buy

In order to enjoy the excitement of finding something truly old and Venetian, you need curiosity, conviction and a comfortable income. The Venetian maze is full of hidden treasures. The markets, particularly the Rialto, are a shopper's paradise, even if the prices act as a deterrent.

Shopaholics would do well to focus on arts and crafts, especially luxury fabrics, glassware and masks. Certainly, the most popular Venetian souvenirs are **marbled paper**, **Murano glass** and **carnival masks** of every description.

Apart from the odd pullover or shirt, avoid buying clothes – unless you have no other shopping opportunities in Italy (designer clothes can be bought elsewhere, usually at lower prices). However, chic **leather goods** and **hand-crafted jewellery** also compete for space with kitsch souvenirs such as glass gondolas. In larger stores and on costly purchases, visitors from non-European countries can reclaim their 19 percent sales tax by filling in a form.

Rialto Markets

Wandering through the labyrinthine alleys of the Rialto fish and vegetable markets is an intoxicating experience, especially in the morning. For visitors staying in an apartment, a trip to the Rialto provides a wonderful selection of foodstuffs. If choosing

vegetables, listen for the word "*nostrano*" (our own) applying to produce grown on the market garden island of Sant'Erasmo. The *Erberia* is the colourful fruit and vegetable market overlooking the Grand Canal, while the *Pescheria,* the fish market, is set in an arcaded Neo-Gothic hall by the quayside.

Even for those not intent on buying foodstuffs, the Rialto remains an enticing experience, with a variety of goods on offer at some of the lowest prices in Venice (still higher than most other Italian cities, but worth it if something catches your eye, particularly Venetian crafts).

The Rialto remains a hive of commercial activity, with everything on sale between the Rialto Bridge and the Mercerie in the San Marco district. Ignore the tourist tat in favour of **angora sweaters**, **supple shoes**, **crafts** and foodstuffs galore, including **pasta**, **cheese** and **salami** shops. A better variety of crafts are found in the side streets behind San Zaccaria (*see Castello chapter, page 185*) or in the *Mercerie* (*see below*).

The shopping alleys are also lively in the early evening when locals stroll down Calle della Rughetta in search of fine foodstuffs (Aliani, at San Polo 655, is a superb delicatessen and cheese shop). Ruga Vecchia di San Giovanni is home to good food shops (which keep normal shop hours) and close to typical bars.

The Mercerie

A shopping spree in the city centre reveals several different facets of consumerist Venice: first, the *Mercerie*, the classic shopping quarter sandwiched between Piazza San Marco and the Rialto; second, the down-to-earth shops between Campo San Salvatore and Santo Stefano; and finally the elegant establishments in Calle Larga XXII Marzo, west of San Marco. You will find the dark, narrow alleys of the *Mercerie* – which simply means haberdashery (a place where fabrics of every description were sold) – behind the Torre dell'Orologio, the clocktower on Piazza San Marco.

Shopping Spree

Mercerie dell'Orologia is now home to souvenir shops and jewellers, including Buccellati (San Marco 214; tel: 522 6540), a famous Italian group. Some shops sell what purports to be Murano glassware but it is best to buy on Murano itself or in a well-known store.

Branches of the better firms and fashion designers are in evidence in the San Marco district. Turning into Merceria San Zulian reveals an array of goods, from cotton shirts to the princely offerings at **Gucci** (San Marco 729; tel: 522 3838) and **Cartier** (San Marco 606; tel: 522 2071). A watchmaker, also in the luxury class, is **Gioielleria**, nearby.

While strolling through the Mercerie, glance at the upper storeys and note the contrast between the decorative chic of the shop fronts and the faded façades above.

Behind the church of San Zulian, a detour towards Campo Santa Maria Formosa passes Salizzada San Lio, with a supermarket on the corner, a rare sight in the city. Back at San Zulian, bear north in the direction of the Rialto.

In the Merceria San Salvatore, which goes past the church of the same name, there are expensive boutiques with elegant leatherware. Exclusive jewellery is sold by **Salvad'ori** (San Marco 5022; tel: 523 0609), noted for wordplay as well as gems ("oro" means gold). Things are just as chic at **Rosa Salva**, a smart *pasticceria* stocked with fine pastries and cakes. On Campo San Salvatore (or Salvador) is **La Perla**, the top Italian lingerie store (San Marco 4828; tel: 522 6459).

Leave the Merceria by turning left into Calle dell'Ovo and walking west towards **Campo Santo Stefano**. En route, you pass Campo Manin, Campo Sant'Angelo and numerous family-run *alimentari*, grocers selling hams and spicy salami, and cafés tempting one with aromas of fresh *espresso*. On the way back to San Marco from Campo Santo Stefano, cross Campo San Maurizio to see **the shop selling Fortuny fabrics** on the small square (*see Luxury Fabrics, page 332*) and to pause at **Marchini**, the city's most celebrated *pasticceria* (Ponte San Maurizio; tel: 522 9109).

For the Venetians, the Mercerie has long been displaced by the district around the **Via Largo XXII Marzo** as the smartest shopping address in town. This wide, ritzy street is lined with antique shops, antiquarian bookshops, fashion boutiques (including **Ferrè** and **Versace**) and jewellers, all interspersed with banks. The gap between Calle Larga XXII Marzo and San Marco is closed by Salizzada San Moisè. In the vicinity of the Bauer-Grunwald hotel are luxury shops: clothes from **Valentino**, leatherware from **Fendi**, luggage from **Louis Vuitton** and shoes from **Magli**. The **Missoni** boutique, selling quality designer knitwear, is tucked away in the Calle Vallaresso (San Marco 1312; tel: 520 5733) as is **Dolce e Gabbana** (San Marco 1314, tel: 520 5733) and **Camiceria San Marco** (San Marco 1340; tel: 522 1432), which sells made-to-measure shirts and pyjamas.

Salizzada San Moisè leads back to Piazza San Marco via the Napoleonic Wing. The arcades of "the finest drawing-room in Europe" offer Murano glass, gold and jewellery as well as hand-worked lace, with showrooms in the arcades of the Procuratie Nuove. If you hanker after ersatz designer bags and belts, fake Louis Vuitton or Chanel, the **African traders** will catch your attention around Calle Larga XXII Marzo or on bustling Riva degli Schiavoni, close to St Mark's.

Off the Beaten Track

Shopping in Venice is not only the elegance of Piazza San Marco, Salizzada San Moisè and Calle Larga XXII Marzo, or the curious little corners of the Mercerie. It is rewarding to leave the main streets and wander off the beaten track. The inquisitive will find small art galleries and antiquarian bookshops stuffed with *objets d'art*, precious prints and books. However, only buy antiques if you know what you are buying.

Food

This is mostly covered in the Rialto Markets section (*see opposite*), the best place for cheeses, hams and bottled delicatessen goods. Venice also has a good selection of *pasticcerie*, with the **Rosa Salva** group, **Marchini** and **Harry's Dolci** the best of the upmarket *pasticcerie* and tearooms (*see page 316* for a full list of addresses). In addition, there are a number of neighbourhood *pasticcerie* of varying quality. Most stock the dry Venetian biscuits that sustained sailors on long sea voyages. The best of these neighbourhood areas is **Spagnol** (set on the arcaded bridge of Ponte della Madonnetta, San Polo 1463; tel: 520 3627). This bustling bakery sells a wide range of speciality breads (including olive and rosemary breads and *schiacciata*), pizza slices and traditional Venetian biscuits (made with egg or stuffed with raisins, fruit or chocolate). Try the *dolci del doge*, *buranello* and the curiously named *xaeto*. The bakery was a favourite of the late President Mitterrand.

Luxury Fabrics & Lace

Venice is well-known for its Fortuny fabrics – essentially silks and velvets – either relatively plain or gloriously patterned. These can be bought at **Fortuny Tessuto Artistici** (Giudecca 805, 30123 Venezia, tel: 041-522 4078) or in its elegant retail outlet on Campo San Maurizio, in central Venice. **Venetia Studium** (Calle Larga XXII Marzo, San Marco 2403/04; tel: 522 7353) produces exclusive fabrics, including Fortuny designs, from scarves to cushion covers to lamps, and delicately patterned fabrics and soft furnishings. Although the silks are produced elsewhere, notably in Como, they are designed and painted in Venice. **Frette** (Calle Larga XXII Marzo, San Marco 2070/a; tel: 522 4914) is the place for fine linens and exquisite sheets, cushions and bathrobes. **Jesurum** (Merceria del Capitello, San Marco 4857; tel: 520 6177) also sells princely household linen, including embroidered sheets. **Arras** (Campiello Squellini 3234; tel: 522 6460) sells lovely handwoven fabrics.

Venice is well-known for its Burano lace, made on the island of the same name. However, much of what is on sale is fake, mass-produced in the Far East. To spot the genuine article, visit the **lace museum** on Burano. After that, if you can afford the stratospheric prices, buy on Burano.

Marbled Paper

In the district of San Maurizio and Santa Maria del Giglio are shops selling marbled paper. Called *legatoria* or "book-binding", this ancient craft gives paper a decorative marbled veneer. A special mixture is spread on impregnated paper while wavy patterns, resembling peacock's feathers, are formed with a comb.

Marbled paper used to be popular for binding books and pamphlets and as a background for documents, thus providing protection against forgery.

Today, it is used to make a wide choice of photo albums, writing cases, greeting cards and notebooks.

If you are interested in buying some, try **Paoli Olbi** (Calle della Mandola 3653) for marbled paper cards, notebooks, diaries and boxes; and **Alberto Valese-**
Ebru (Santo Stefano 3471; Salizzada San Samuele 3135; and Calle della Fenice 1920), which sells delicate hand-tooled paper gifts.

Murano Glass

Refrain from buying Murano glass until you have visited the Murano glass museum (*see page 274*) and watched the glass being made at a local factory. Also, resist the hard-sell before you know what you like. **Barovier e Tosso** (Fondamente Vetrai 28 30141 Murano, tel: 041-739 049) is one of the most respected glass-makers (and is in simpler, better taste than many others). **Salviati**, at Fondamenta Radi 16, Murano, with a big palace on the Grand Canal and in Murano, is one of the best-known for plates, lampstands and general artistic glassware.

Masks

Before buying a mask, always check what it is made of and persuade the seller to tell you how it fits into the Venetian tradition: it may simply be a "*fantasia*" (fantasy mask) or a character from the *commedia dell'arte* (see *Carnival, page 101*, for the history of carnival masks).

Some of the most appealing smaller mask shops lie in the Castello district, in the quiet canal-lined streets behind San Zaccaria. One such is: **Ca' del Sol** (Fondamenta del Osmarin, Castello 4964; tel: 528 5549), run by an eccentric and creative character. Nearby is **Trilly** (Fondamenta del'Osmarin, Castello 4974; tel: 521 2579), close to the Greek church. The shop sells hand-made dolls as well as masks made of papier maché, ceramics, and unusual fabrics; these range from tasteful to
hideous. For women, the *civetta* is a flirtatious, catlike mask while the *colombina* is more ladylike. **Il Cignoca** (Calle Rimpeto la Sacrestia, Castello 4361; tel: 454 846) is another mask shop with a variety of hand-crafted products made in papier-mâché, ceramics or leather. **Laboratoria Artigiano Maschere** (Barbarie delle Tole, Castello 6657; tel: 522 3110) is also recommended.

However, masks can be bought all over Venice: **Mondonovo**, makers of inventive "fantasy" masks, are on Rio Terro Canal, off Campo Santa Margherita, Dorsoduro 3063; tel: 287 344. As well as papier-mâché fantasy creations, there are classic *commedia dell'arte* masks. In addition, look out for miniature china masks for the collector's cabinet, some portraying classical gods.

Language

First Steps

The language of Italy is Italian, supplemented by regional dialects. In large cities and tourist centres you will find many people who speak English, French or German. In fact, due to the massive emigration over the last 100 years, you may encounter fluent speakers of foreign languages: do not be surprised if you are addressed in a New York, Melbourne, London, Brussels or Bavarian accent: the speaker may have spent time working abroad.

It is well worth buying a good phrase book or dictionary, but the following will help you get started. Since this glossary is aimed at non-linguists, we have opted for the simplest options rather than the most elegant Italian.

Communication

Yes *Si*
No *No*
Thank you *Grazie*
Many thanks *Mille grazie/tante grazie/molte grazie*
You're welcome *Prego*
Alright/That's fine *Va bene*
Please *Per favore* or *per cortesia*
Excuse me (to get attention) *Scusi* (singular), *Scusate* (plural)
Excuse me (in a crowd) *Permesso*
Excuse me (to attract attention from, eg. a waiter) *Senta!*
Excuse me (sorry) *Mi scusi*
Could you help me? (formal) *Potrebbe aiutarmi?*

Certainly *Ma, certo*
Can I help you? (formal) *Posso aiutarla?*
Can you show me...? *Può indicarmi...?*
Can you help me? *Può aiutarmi, per cortesia?*
I need.... *Ho bisogno di....*
Wait a minute! *Aspetta!*
I'm lost *Mi sono perso*
I'm sorry *Mi dispiace*
I don't know *Non lo so*
I don't understand *Non capisco*
Do you speak English/French *Parla Inglese/Francese?*
Could you speak more slowly *Può parlare piu lentamente, per favore?*
Could you repeat that please? *Può ripetere, per piacere?*
Slowly/quietly *Piano*
Here/there *qui/la*
Yesterday/today/tomorrow *ieri/oggi/domani*
Now/early/late *adesso/ presto/tardi*
What *Quale/come?*
When/why/where *quando/ perchè/dove?*
Where is the lavatory? *Dov'è il bagno?*

Greetings

Hello (Good day) *Buon giorno*
Good afternoon/evening *Buona sera*
Good night *Buona notte*
Goodbye *Arrivederci*
Hello/Hi/Goodbye (familiar) *Ciao*

Mr/Mrs/Miss *Signor/ Signora/Signorina*
Pleased to meet you (formal) *Piacere di conoscerla*
I am English/American/ *Sono inglese/americano/*
Irish/Scottish/ *irlandese/scozzese/*
Canadian/Australian *canadese/australiano*
Do you speak English? *Parla inglese?*
I'm here on holiday *Sono qui in vacanze*
Is it your first trip to Milan/Rome? *E il Suo primo viaggio a Milano/Roma?*
Do you like it here? (formal) *Si trova bene qui?*
How are you (formal/informal)? *Come sta (come stai)?*
Fine, thanks *Bene, grazie*
See you later *A piu tardi*
See you soon *A presto*
Take care *Sta bene*
Do you like Italy/Florence/ Rome/Venice/my city? *Le piace Italia/Firenze/ Roma/Venezia/la mia città?*
I like it a lot (is the correct answer) *Mi piace moltissimo*
It's wonderful (an alternative answer: both responses can equally be applied to food, beaches, the view) *E meravigliosa/favolosa*

Telephone calls

The area code *il prefisso telefonico*
I'd like to make a reverse charges call *Vorrei fare una telefonata a carico del destinatorio*
May I use your telephone, please? *Posso usare il telefono?*
Hello (on the telephone) *Pronto*
My name's *Mi chiamo/Sono*
Could I speak to...? *Posso parlare con...?*
Sorry, he/she isn't in *Mi dispiace, è fuori*
Can he call you back? *Può richiamarLa?*
I'll try again later *Riproverò piu tardi*
Can I leave a message? *Posso lasciare un messagio?*
Please tell him I called *Gli dica, per favore, che ho telefonato*
Hold on *Un attimo, per favore*
A local call *una telefonata locale*
Can you speak up please? *Può parlare piu forte, per favore?*

In the Hotel

Do you have any vacant rooms? *Avete camere libere?*
I have a reservation *Ho fatto una prenotazione*
I'd like... *Vorrei*
a single/double room (with a double bed) *una camera singola/doppia (con letto matrimoniale)*

Pronunciation Tips

Italians claim that pronunciation is straightforward: you pronounce it as it is written. This is approximately true but there are a couple of important rules for English speakers to bear in mind: **c** before **e** or **i** is pronounced ch, eg. *ciao, mi dispiace, la coincidenza.* **Ch** before **i** or **e** is pronounced as **k**, eg. *la chiesa.* Likewise, **sci** or **sce** are pronounced as in sheep or shed respectively. **Gn** in Italian is rather like the sound in onion while **gl** is softened to resemble the sound in bullion.

Nouns are either masculine (**il**, plural **i**) or feminine (**la**, plural **le**). Plurals of nouns are most often formed by changing an **o** to an **i** and an **a** to an **e**, eg. *il panino: i panini; la chiesa: le chiese.*

Words are stressed on the penultimate syllable unless an accent indicates otherwise.

Like many languages, Italian has formal and informal words for "you". In the singular, "**Tu**" is informal while "**Lei**" is more polite. Confusingly, in some parts of Italy or in some circumstances, you will also here "**Voi**" used as a singular polite form. (In general, "Voi" is reserved for you plural, however.) For visitors, it is simplest to use the formal form unless invited to do otherwise.

There is, of course, rather more to the language than that, but you can get a surprisingly long way in making friends by mastering a few basic phrases.

a room with twin beds *una camera a due letti*
a room with a bath/shower *una camera con bagno/doccia*
for one night *per una notte*
for two nights *per due notti*
How much is it? *Quanto costa?*
On the first floor *Al primo piano*
Is breakfast included? *E compresa la prima colazione?*
Is everything included? *E tutto compreso?*
half/full board *mezza pensione/ pensione completa*
It's expensive *E caro*
Do you have a room with a balcony/view of the sea? *C'è una camera con balcone/con una vista del mare?*
With a bath/shower *con doccia/con bagno*
A room overlooking the park/the street/the back *una camera con vista sul parco/che da sulla strada/sul retro*
Is it a quiet room? *E una stanza tranquilla?*
The room is too hot/cold/noisy/small *La camera è troppo calda/ fredda/rumorosa/ piccola*
We have one with a double bed *Ne abbiamo una matrimoniale.*
Could you show me another room please? *Potrebbe mostrarmi un altra camera?*
Can I see the room? *Posso vedere la camera?*
What time does the hotel close? *A che ora chiude l'albergo?*
I'll take it *La prendo*
big/small *grande/piccola*
What time is breakfast? *A che ora è la prima colazione?*
Please give me a call at... *Mi può chiamare alle...*
Come in? *Avanti!*
Can I have the bill, please? *Posso avere il conto, per favore.*
Can you call me a taxi please? *Può chiamarmi un taxi, per favore?*
dining room *la sala da pranzo*
key *la chiave*

lift *l'ascensore*
towel *un asciugamano*
toilet paper *la carta igienica*
pull/push *tirare/spingere*

Bar Notices

Prezzo in terrazza/a tavola **Terrace/table price (often double what you pay standing at the bar)**
Si paga alla cassa **Pay at the cash desk**
Si prende lo scontrino alla cassa **Pay at the cash desk,** *then take* **the receipt** (*lo scontrino*) *to the bar to be served; this is common procedure*
Signori/Uomini **Gentlemen (lavatories).**
Signore/Donne **Ladies (lavatories).**

At a Bar

I'd like...... *Vorrei.....*
coffee *un caffè espresso*
(small, strong and black) *un cappuccino*
(with hot, frothy milk) *un caffelatte*
(like café au lait in France) *un caffè lungo*
(weak, served in tall glass) *un corretto*
(with alcohol, probably brandy) tea *un tè*
lemon tea *un tè al limone*
herbal tea *una tisana*
hot chocolate *una cioccolata calda*
(bottled) orange/lemon juice *un succo d'arancia/di limone*
orange squash *l'aranciata*
fresh orange/lemon juice *una spremuta di arancia/di limone*
(mineral) water *acqua (minerale)*
fizzy/still mineral water *acqua minerale gasata/naturale*
a glass of mineral water *un bicchiere di acqua minerale*
with/without ice *con/senza ghiaccio*
red/white wine *vino rosso/ bianco*

(draught) beer *una birra (alla spina)*
a gin and tonic *un gin tonic*
a bitter (Vermouth etc) *un amaro*
milk *latte*
(half) a litre *un (mezzo) litro*
bottle *una bottiglia*
ice-cream *un gelato*
cone *un cono*
pastry/brioche *una pasta*
sandwich *un tramezzino*
roll *un panino*
Anything else? *Desidera qualcos'altro?*
Cheers *Salute*
Let me pay *Offro io*
That's very kind of you *Grazie, molto gentile*

In a Restaurant

I'd like to book a table *Vorrei riservare una tavola*
Have you got a table for ... *Avete una tavola per ...*
I have a reservation *Ho fatto una prenotazione*
lunch/supper *il pranzo/la cena*
we do not want a full meal *Non desideriamo un pasto completo*
Could we have another table? *Potremmo spostarci?*
I'm a vegetarian *Sono vegetariono/a*
Is there a vegetarian dish? *C'è un piatto vegetariano?*
May we have the menu? *Ci dia la carta?*
wine list *la lista dei vini*
What would you like? *Che cosa prende?*
What would you recommend? *Che cosa ci raccomanda?*
What would you like as a main course/dessert? *Che cosa prende di secondo/di dolce?*
What would you like to drink? *Che cosa desidera da bere?*
a carafe of red/white wine *una caraffa di vino rosso/bianco*
fixed price menu *il menu a prezzo fisso*
the dish of the day *il piatto del giorno*
home-made *fatto in casa*
VAT (sales tax) *TVA*

cover charge *il coperto/pane e coperto*
the bill, please *il conto per favore*
Is service included? *Il servizio è incluso?*
Where is the lavatory? *Dovè il bagno?*
Keep the change *Va bene così*
I've enjoyed the meal *Mi è piaciuto molto*

Menu Decoder

Antipasti – Starters
antipasto misto mixed hors d'oeuvres; cold cuts, cheeses, roast vegetables (ask for details)
buffet freddo cold buffet
caponata aubergine, olives, tomatoes
insalata caprese tomato and mozzarella salad
insalata di mare seafood salad
insalata mista/verde mixed/ green salad
melanzane alla parmegiana fried or baked aubergine with parmesan and tomato
mortadella/salame similar to salami
pancetta bacon
proscuitto ham
peperonata grilled peppers drenched in olive oil

Primi – First Courses
Typical first courses include soup, *risotto*, *gnocchi* or myriad pastas in a wide range of sauces.

gli asparagi asparagus (in season)
il brodetto fish soup
il brodo broth
crespolini savoury pancakes
gnocchi potato and dough dumplings
la minestra soup
il minestrone thick vegetable soup
pasta e fagioli pasta and bean soup
il proscuitto (cotto/crudo) (cooked/cured) ham
i suppli rice croquettes
i tartufi truffles (fresh in season,

otherwise bottled or vacuum-packed)
la zuppa soup

Pasta

cannelloni stuffed tubes of pasta
farfalle bow or butterfly-shaped pasta
penne pasta quills, smaller than *rigatoni*
ravioli and *tortellini* different types of stuffed pasta
tagliatelle similar to *fettucine*

Typical pasta sauces include:
aglio e olio garlic and olive oil
arrabiata spicy tomato
burro e salvia butter and sage
matriciana ham and tomato
panna cream
pesto with basil and pine nuts
ragù meat sauce

Secondi – Main Courses
Typical main courses are fish, seafood or meat-based, with accompaniments (*contorni*), including vegetables, that vary greatly from region to region.

La Carne – Meat
allo spiedo on the spit
arrosto roast meat
al ferro grilled without oil
al forno baked
al girarrosto spit-roasted
alla griglia grilled
involtini skewered veal, ham, etc
stagionato hung, well-aged
ben cotto well-done (steak, etc)
al puntino medium (steak, etc)
al sangue rare (steak, etc)
l'agnello lamb
il bresaolo dried salted beef
la bistecca steak
il capriolo/cervo venison
il cinghiale wild boar
il controfiletto sirloin steak
le cotolette cutlets
il maiale pork
il fagiano pheasant
il fegato liver
il fileto fillet
il lepre hare
il manzo beef
l'ossobuco shin of veal

la porchetta roast suckling pig
il pollo chicken
polpette meatballs
polpettone meat loaf
la salsiccia sausage
saltimbocca (alla Romana) veal escalopes with ham
le scaloppine escalopes
il stufato braised, stewed
il sugo sauce
la trippa tripe
il vitello veal

Eating Out

For local specialities, *see page 85*. Restaurant listings begin on page 317.

Frutti di Mare Seafood
Beware the word *'surgelati'* meaning frozen rather than fresh.

affumicato smoked
alle brace charcoal grilled
al ferro grilled without oil
alla griglia grilled
fritto fried
ripieno stuffed
al vapore steamed
acciughe anchovies
l'anguilla eel
l'aragosto lobster
il baccalà dried salted cod
i bianchetti whitebait
il branzino sea bass
i calamari squid
i calamaretti baby squid
la carpa carp
il carpaccio wafer-thin beef
i crostacei shellfish
le cozze mussels
il fritto misto mixed fried fish
i gamberi prawns
i gamberetti shrimps
il granchio crab
il merluzzo cod
molecche soft-shelled crabs
le ostriche oysters
il pesce fish
il pescespada swordfish
il polipo octopus
il risotto di mare seafood risotto
le sarde sardines
la sogliola sole
le seppie cuttlefish

la triglia **red mullet**
la trota **trout**
il tonno **tuna**
le vongole **clams**

I Legumi/La Verdura – Vegetables

a scelta **of your choice**
gli asparagi **asparagus**
la bietola **(similar to spinach)**
il carciofo **artichoke**
le carote **carrots**
i carciofini **artichoke hearts**
il cavolo **cabbage**
la cicoria **chicory**
la cipolla **onion**
i contorni **side dishes**
i funghi **mushrooms**
i fagioli **beans**
i fagiolini **French beans**
fave **broad beans**
il finocchio **fennel**
l'indivia **endive/chicory**
l'insalata mista **mixed salad**
l'insalata verde **green salad**
la melanzana **aubergine**
le patate **potatoes**
le patatine fritte **chips/French fries**
i peperoni **peppers**
i piselli **peas**
i pomodori **tomatoes**
le primizie **spring vegetables**
il radicchio **red, slightly bitter lettuce**
ripieno **stuffed**
rughetta **rocket**
i ravanelli **radishes**
spinaci **spinach**
la verdura **green vegetables**
la zucca **pumpkin/squash**
zucchini **courgettes**

La Frutta – Fruit

le albicocche **apricots**
le arance **oranges**
le banane **bananas**
il cocomero **watermelon**
le ciliege **cherries**
i fichi **figs**
le fragole **strawberries**
frutti di bosco **fruits of the forest**
i lamponi **raspberries**
la mela **apple**
la pesca **peach**
la pera **pear**
le uve **grapes**

I Dolci – Desserts

Al carrello **desserts from the trolley**
la cassata **Sicilian ice cream with candied peel**
il dolce **dessert/sweet**
le fritelle **fritters**
un gelato (di lampone/limone) **(raspberry/lemon) ice cream**
una granita **water ice**
una macedonia di frutta **fruit salad**
un semifreddo **semi-frozen dessert (many types)**
il tartufo (nero) **(chocolate) ice cream dessert**
il tiramisu **cold, creamy rum and coffee dessert**
la torta **cake/tart**
zabaglione **sweet dessert made with eggs and Marsala**
zuccotto **ice-cream liqueur**
la zuppa inglese **trifle**

Basic Foods

aceto **vinegar**
aglio **garlic**
burro **butter**
formaggio **cheese**
focaccia **oven-baked snack**
frittata **omelette**
grana **parmesan cheese**
grissini **bread sticks**
olio **oil**
marmellata **jam**
pane **bread**
pane integrale **wholemeal bread**
parmigiano **parmesan cheese**
pepe **pepper**
riso **rice**
sale **salt**
senape **mustard**
uova **eggs**
yogurt **yoghurt**
zucchero **sugar**

Sightseeing

Abbazia (Badia) **Abbey**
Basilica **Church**
Belvedere **Viewpoint**
Biblioteca **Library**
Castello **Castle**
Centro Storico **Old town/historic centre**
Chiesa **Church**
Duomo/Cattedrale **Cathedral**
Fiume **River**
Giardino **Garden**
Lago **Lake**
Mercato **Market**
Monastero **Monastery**
Monumenti **Monuments**
Museo **Museum**
Parco **Park**
Pinacoteca **Art gallery**

Numbers

1	*Uno*	13	*Tredici*	70	*Settanta*
2	*Due*	14	*Quattordici*	80	*Ottanta*
3	*Tre*	15	*Quindici*	90	*Novanta*
4	*Quattro*	16	*Sedici*	100	*Cento*
5	*Cinque*	17	*Diciasette*	200	*Duecento*
6	*Sei*	18	*Diciotto*	500	*Cinquecento*
7	*Sette*	19	*Dicianove*	1,000	*Mille*
8	*Otto*	20	*Venti*	2,000	*Duemila*
9	*Nove*	30	*Trenta*	5,000	*Cinquemila*
10	*Dieci*	40	*Quaranta*	50,000	*Cinquantamila*
11	*Undici*	50	*Cinquanta*	Million	*Un Milione*
12	*Dodici*	60	*Sessanta*		

Visiting a Sight

Can one visit? *Si può visitare?*
Is it possible to see the church? *E possibile visitare la chiesa?*
Entrance/Exit *Entrata/Uscita*
Where can I find the custodian/sacristan/key? *Dove posso trovare il custode/il sacristano/la chiave?*
We have come a long way just to see X *Siamo venuti proprio per visitare X*
It is really a pity it is closed *E veramente peccato che sia chiuso.*
(The last two should be tried if entry seems a problem!).

Ponte **Bridge**
Ruderi **Ruins**
Scavi **Excavations/ archaeological site**
Spiaggia **Beach**
Tempio **Temple**
Torre **Tower**
Ufficio turistico **Tourist office**
il custode **Custodian**
il sacristano **Sacristan**
Suonare il campanello **Ring the bell**
aperto/a **Open**
chiuso/a **Closed**
chiuso per la festa **Closed for the festival**
chiuso per ferie **Closed for the holidays**
chiuso per restauro **Closed for restoration**

At the Shops

What time do you open/close? *A che ora apre/chiude?*
Closed for the holidays (typical sign) *Chiuso per ferie*
Pull/push (sign on doors) *Tirare/Spingere*
Entrance/Exit *Entrata/Uscita*
Can I help you? (formal) *Posso aiutarLa?*
What would you like? *Che cosa desidera?*
I'm just looking *Sto soltanto guardando*

How much does it cost? *Quantè, per favore?*
How much is this? *Quanto viene?*
Do you take credit cards *Accettate carte di credito?*
I'd like... *Vorrei...*
This one/that one *questo/quello*
I'd like that one, please *Vorrei quello lì per cortesia*
Have you got...? *Avete...?*
We haven't got (any).. *Non (ne) abbiamo.*
Can I try it on? *Posso provare?*
The size (for clothes) *La taglia*
What size do you take? *Qualè Sua taglia?*
The size (for shoes) *Il numero*
Is there/do you have X? *C'è (un/una)...?*
Yes, of course. *Si, certo*
No, we don't (there isn't) *No, non c'è*
That's too expensive *E troppo caro*
Please write it down for me *Me lo scriva, per favore*
Cheap *Economico/A buon prezzo*
Don't you have anything cheaper? *Ha niente che costa di meno?*
It's too small/big *E troppo piccolo/grande*
Brown/blue/black *marrone/ blu/nero*
green/red/white/yellow *verde/rosso/bianco/giallo*
pink/grey/gold/silver *rosa/grigio/oro/argento*
No thank you, I don't like it *Grazie, ma non è di mio gusto*
I (don't) like it *(Non) mi piace*
I'll take it/I'll leave it *Lo prendo/lo lascio*
It's a rip-off (impolite) *Sono prezzi da strozzini*
This is faulty. Can I have a replacement/refund? *C'è un difetto. Me lo potrebbe cambiare/rimborsare?*
Anything else? *Altro?*
The cash desk is over there *Si accomodi alla cassa*
Give me some of those *Mi dia alcuni di quelli lì*
(half) a kilo *un (mezzo) kilo*

100 grams *un etto*
200 grams *due etti*
More/less *piu/meno*
With/without *con/senza*
A little *un pochino*
That's enough/no more *Basta cosi*

Types of Shops

Antique dealer *l'antiquario*
Bakery/cake shop *la panetteria/pasticceria*
Bank *la banca*
Bookshop *la libreria*
Boutique/clothes shop *il negozio di moda*
Bureau de change *il cambio*
Butcher's *la macelleria*
Chemist's *la farmacia*
Delicatessen *la salumeria*
Department store *il grande magazzino*
Dry Cleaner's *la tintoria*
Fishmonger's *la pescheria*
Food shop *l'alimentari*
Florist *il fioraio*
Grocer's *l'alimentari*
Greengrocer's *l'ortolano/il fruttivendolo*
Hairdresser's (women) *il parucchiere*
Ice cream parlour *la gelateria*
Jeweller's *Il gioielliere*
Leather shop *la pelletteria*
Market *il mercato*
Newsstand *l'edicola*
Post office *l'ufficio postale*
Shoe shop *il negozio di scarpe*
Stationer's *la cartoleria*
Supermarket *il supermercato*
Tobacconist *il tabaccaio* (also usually sells travel tickets, stamps, phone cards)
Travel agency *l'agenzia di viaggi* (also usually books domestic and international train tickets).

Travelling

Transport
airport *l'aeroporto*
aeroplane *l'aereo*
arrivals/departures *arrivi/ partenze*
boarding card *un biglietto di bordo*
boat *la barca*
bus *l'autobus/il pullman*

bus station *l'autostazione*
coach *il pullman*
couchette *la cucetta*
connection *la coincidenza*
ferry *il traghetto*
ferry terminal *la stazione marittima*
first/second class *la prima/ seconda classe*
flight *il volo*
hydrofoil *l'aliscafo*
left luggage (office) *il deposito bagagli*
motorway *l'autostrada*
No smoking *vietato fumare*
platform *il binario*
port *il porto*
porter *il facchino*
railway station *Ferrovia (la stazione ferroviaria)*
return ticket *un biglietto di andata e ritorno*
single ticket *un biglietto di andata sola*
sleeping car *la carrozza letti/il vagone letto*
smokers/non-smokers *fumatori/non-fumatori*
station *la stazione*
stop *la fermata*
taxi *il taxi*
ticket office *la biglietteria*
train *il treno*
WC *gabinetto*

At the Station
(trains, buses & ferries)
Can you help me please? *Mi può aiutare, per favore?*
Where can I buy tickets? *Dove posso fare i biglietti?*
At the ticket office/at the counter *alla biglietteria/allo sportello*
What time does the train leave? *A che ora parte il treno?*
What time does the train arrive? *A che ora arriva (il treno)?*
Can I book a seat? *Posso prenotare un posto?*
Are there any seats available? *Ci sono ancora posti liberi?*
Is this seat free/taken? *E libero/occupato questo posto?*
I'm afraid this is my seat *E il mio posto, mi dispiace*

You'll have to pay a supplement *Deve pagare un supplemento*
Do I have to change? *Devo cambiare?*
Where does it stop? *Dove si ferma?*
You need to change in Rome *Bisogna cambiare a Roma.*
Which platform does the train leave from? *Da quale binario parte il treno?*
The train leaves from platform one *Il treno parte dal binario uno*
When is the next train/bus/ ferry for Naples? *Quando parte il prossimo treno/ pullman/traghetto per Napoli?*
How long does the crossing take? *Quanto dura la traversata?*
What time does the bus leave for Siena? *Quando parte l'autobus per Siena?*
How long will it take to get there? *Quanto tempo ci vuole per arrivare?*
Will we arrive on time? *Arriveremo puntuali?*
Next stop please *La prossima fermata per favore*
Is this the right stop? *E la fermata giusta?*
The train is latem *Il treno è in ritardo*
Can you tell me where to get off? *Mi può dire dove devo scendere?*

Directions
right/left *a destra/a sinistra*
first left/second right *la prima a sinistra/la seconda a destra*
Turn to the right/left *Gira a destra/sinistra*
Go straight on *Va sempre diritto*
go straight on until the traffic lights *Va sempre diritto fino al semaforo*
Is it far away/nearby? *E lontano/vicino?*
It's 5 minutes' walk *Cinque minuti a piedi*
It's 10 minutes by car *Dieci minuti con la macchina*
You can't miss it *Non può non vederlo*
opposite/next to *di fronte/accanto a*
up/down *su/giu*
traffic lights *il semaforo*
junction *l'incrocio, il bivio*
building *il palazzo (it can just as easily be a modern block of flats as a Gothic palace)*
Where is ....? *Dov'è ....?*
Where are ....? *Dove sono ....?*
Where is the nearest bank/petrol station/bus stop/hotel/garage? *Dov'è la banca/il benzinaio/la fermata di autobus/l'albergo/l'officina più vicino?*
How do I get there? *Come si può andare? (or: Come faccio per arrivare a...?)*

At the Airport

Where's the office of BA/Alitalia? *Dov'è l'ufficio dell'Alitalia/ della British Airways?*
I'd like to book a flight to Venice *Vorrei prenotare un volo per Venezia.*
When is the next flight to ..? *Quando parte il prossimo aereo per...?*
Are there any seats available? *Ci sono ancora posti liberi?*
Have you got any hand luggage? *Ha bagagli a mano?*
I'll take this hand luggage with me *Questo lo tengo come bagaglio a mano*
My suitcase has got lost *La mia valigia è andata persa*
My suitcase has been damaged *La mia valigia è rovinata*
The flight has been delayed *Il volo è rimandato*
The flight has been cancelled *Il volo è stato cancellato*
I can put you on the waiting list *Posso metterLa sulla lista d'attesa*

How long does it take to get to...? *Quanto tempo ci vuole per andare a...?*

Can you show me where I am on the map? *Può indicarmi sulla cartina dove mi trovo.*

You're on the wrong road *Lei è sulla strada sbagliata.*

On the Road

Where can I rent a car? *Dove posso noleggiare una macchina?*

Is comprehensive insurance included? *E completamente assicurata?*

Is it insured for another driver? *E assicurata per un altro guidatore?*

By what time must I return it? *A che ora devo consegnarla?*

Underground car park *garage sotterraneo*

Driving licence *la patente (di guida)*

Registration number *la targa*

Petrol *la benzina*

Petrol station/garage *la stazione servizio*

Oil *l'olio*

Fill it up please *Faccia il pieno, per favore*

Lead free/unleaded diesel *senza piombo/benzina verde diesel*

My car won't start *La mia macchina non s'accende*

My car has broken down *La macchina è guasta*

I've had an accident *Ho avuto un incidente*

How long will it take to repair? *Quanto tempo ci vorrà per la riparazione?*

The engine is overheating *Il motore si scalda*

Can you check the..? *Può controllare..?*

There's something wrong (with/in the)... *C'è un difetto (nel/nella/nei/nelle)...*

-l'acceloratore **accelerator**

-le candele **spark plugs**

-la cinghia del ventilatore **the fanbelt**

-i freni **the brakes**

-la gomma (le gomme) **tyre (tyres)**

-i luci **headlights**

-il motore **engine**

-il parabrezza **windscreen**

-la scattola del cambio **gear box**

-lo scarico/scappamento **exhaust**

Road Signs

Accendere le luci in galleria **Lights on in tunnel**

Alt **Stop**

Autostrada **Motorway**

Attenzione **Caution**

Avanti **Go/walk**

Caduta massi **Falling rocks**

Casello **Toll gate**

Dare la precedenza **Give Way**

Deviazione **Deviation**

Divieto di campeggio **No camping allowed**

Divieto di sosta/Sosta vietata **No parking**

Divieto di passaggio/Senso Vietato **No entry**

Dogana **Customs**

Entrata **Entrance**

Galleria **Tunnel**

Guasto **Out of order (eg, phone box)**

Incrocio **Crossroads**

Limite di velocito **Speed limit**

Non toccare **Don't touch**

Passaggio a livello **Railway crossing**

Parcheggio **Parking**

Pedaggio **Toll road**

Pericolo **Danger**

Pericolo di incendio **Danger of fire**

Pronto Soccorso **First Aid**

Rallentare **Slow down**

Rimozione forzata **Parked cars will be towed away**

Semaforo **Traffic lights**

Senso unico **One way street**

Sentiero **Footpath**

Solo Uscita **No Entry**

Sosta Vietato **No Parking**

Strada interrotta **Road blocked**

Strada chiusa **Road closed**

Strada senza uscita/Vicolo cieco **Dead end**

Tangenziale **Ring road/bypass**

Tenersi in corsa **Keep in lane**

Traffico di transito **Through traffic**

Uscita **Exit**

Uscita (autocarri) **Exit for lorries**

Vietato il sorpasso **No overtaking**

Vietato il transito **No transit**

Health

Is there a chemist's nearby? *C'è una farmacia qui vicino?*

Which chemist is open at night? *Quale farmacia fa il turno di notte?*

I feel ill *Sto male/Mi sento male*

Where does it hurt? *Dove Le fa male?*

It hurts here *Ho dolore qui*

I suffer from... *Soffro di...*

I have a headache *Ho mal di testa*

I have a sore throat *Ho mal di gola*

I have a stomach ache *Ho mal di pancia*

Have you got something for air sickness? *Ha/Avete qualcosa contro il mal d'aria?*

Emergencies

Help! *Aiuto!*

Stop! *Fermate!*

I've had an accident *Ho avuto un incidente*

Watch out *Attenzione*

Call a doctor *Per favore, chiama un medico*

Call an ambulance *Chiama un'ambulanza*

Call the police *Chiama la Polizia/i Carabinieri*

Call the fire brigade *Chiama i pompieri*

Where is the telephone? *Dov'è il telefono?*

Where is the nearest hospital *Dov'è l'ospedale piu vicino?*

I would like to report a theft *Voglio denunciare un furto*

Thank you very much foryour help *Grazie dell'aiuto*

Have you got something for sea sickness? *Ha/Avete qualcosa contro il mal di mare?*
It's nothing serious *Non è niente di male*
Do I need a prescription? *Ci vuole la ricetta?*
antiseptic cream *la crema antisettica*
sunburn cream *la crema antisolare*
sticking plaster *il cerotto*
tissues *i fazzoletti di carta*
toothpaste *il dentifricio*
upset stomach pills *le pillole anti-coliche*
insect repellent *l'insettifugo*
mosquitoes *le zanzare*
wasps *le vespe*
sunburn *scottato del sole*

Times and Dates

Morning/afternoon/evening *la mattina, il pomeriggio, la sera*
Yesterday/today/tomorrow *ieri/oggi/domani*
The day after tomorrow *dopodomani*
Now/early/late *adesso/presto/in ritardo*
A minute *un minuto*
An hour *un'ora*
Half an hour *un mezz'ora*
A day *un giorno*
A week *una settimana*
Monday *Lunedi*
Tuesday *Martedi*
Wednesday *Mercoledi*
Thursday *Giovedi*
Friday *Venerdi*
Saturday *Sabato*
Sunday *Domenica*
First *il primo/la prima*
Second *il secondo/la seconda*
Third *il terzo/la terza*

Further Reading

Literature & Biography

Lord Byron, *Childe Harold's Pilgrimage*, a classic poem.
Giacomo Casanova, *Memoirs* (translated into many languages).
Michael Dibdin, *Dead Lagoon*, a subtle detective story.
Ernest Hemingway, *Across the River and into the Trees* (1952), poorly written but quite entertaining nonetheless.
Patricia Highsmith, *Those Who Walk Away*.
Henry James, *The Wings of the Dove* (1902) and *The Aspern Papers* (1888), evocative accounts from one of the greatest observers of Venice; the former was made into a film in 1997.
Erica Jong, *Serenissima* (1987).
Thomas Mann, *Death in Venice* (1912), a haunting novella.
Ian McEwan, *The Comfort of Strangers* (1981), a fey, insubstantial tale that still manages to stay on the mind.
A. Palazzeschi, *The Doge*.
Marcel Proust, *Albertine Disparue* (1925), translated as 'The Fugitive' or 'The Sweet Cheat Gone'.
William Riviere, *A Venetian Theory of Heaven* (1992), atmospheric scene-setting but ultimately predictable.
Frederick Rolfe (alias Baron Corvo), *The Desire and Pursuit of the Whole* (published posthumously in 1934).
George Sand, *Lettre d'un Voyageur* (1971).
William Shakespeare, *The Merchant of Venice* and *Othello*.
Muriel Spark, *Territorial Rights* (1979), not one of her best but it makes an engaging holiday read.

Jeanette Winterson, *The Passion* (1987), one of the most bizarre books ever written about Venice; her best.

History, Art, Architecture

Bettin, *Nascita di una Città* (1978), a history.
Roberta Curiel and B Dov Couperman, *The Ghetto of Venice*, a history of the Jewish community in Venice.
Umberto Franzoi, *Palaces and Churches along the Grand Canal*, well-illustrated palace-by-palace guide; readily available in Venice in various languages.
JR Hale (Ed.), *Renaissance Venice* (1973).
Christopher Hibbert, *Venice, A Biography of a City* (1988).
Emily Lane (Ed.), *Venetian 17th-Century Painting* (1979).
Frederick C Lane, *Venice, A Maritime Republic*, dry but one of the core historical accounts.
Peter Lauritzen, *Venice. A Thousand Years of Culture and Civilisation* (1981) and *Venetian Palaces* (1979).
Michael Levey, *Painting in 18th-Century Venice* (1959).
John Julius Norwich, *A History of Venice* (1988), *The Rise to Empire* (1980), *The Greatness and Fall* (1981), engaged and engaging historian of Venice.
Marco Polo, *The Travels of Marco Polo* (1958), appears in various other languages.
Brian Pullen, *Crisis and Change in the Venetian Economy* (1968), an academic account of shipping and trade.
The Genius of Venice 1500–1600 (Royal Academy of Arts, Catalogue of the great Renaissance exhibition in 1983).
John Ruskin, *The Stones of Venice* (1851–53), influential volume on Venetian art history, published in various languages.
R. Shaw-Kennedy, *Art and Architecture in Venice* and *The Venice in Peril Guide* (1972).
John Steer, *A Concise History of*

Venetian Painting (1970), a brisk trot through the art treasures.
Francesco Valcanover, *Carpaccio* (1989), widely available in Venice in various languages.
Sabina Vienello, *The Churches of Venice* (1993), widely available in Venice in various languages.

NB: In Venice, the best art monographs are published by Electra and Scala publishers in various languages.

Travel Memoirs

Toby Cole (Ed), *Venice, A Portable Reader* (revised 1995), literary extracts by celebrated visitors.
Charles Dickens, *Pictures from Italy* (1846).
Théophile Gautier, *Voyage en Italie* (1930).
JW von Goethe, *Italian Journeys* (1786–88).
Hugh Honour, *The Companion Guide to Venice* (1970).
William Dean Howells, *Venetian Life* (1866) and *Italian Journeys* (1867). The author was the American Consul in Venice between 1861 and 1865.
Henry James, *Italian Hours*, includes an evocative portrait of Venice in the 1860s and 1870s.
Jonathan Keates, *Italian Journeys* (1991), a sharp yet persuasive travel memoir with sections on Venice.
JG Links, *Venice for Pleasure* (1966), a quirky classic.
Ian Littlewood, *Venice: A Literary Companion* (1991), informed, literary presentation of lesser-known Venice.
Giulio Lorenzetti, *Venice and its Lagoon* (1980): legendary cultural compendium of the city.
Mary McCarthy, *Venice*

Observed (1961, revised 1982), cool, acerbic look at Venice from an intelligent observer.
Jan Morris, *Venice* (revised 1993). Purple prose meets anecdotal account; engrossing yet whimsical.
Mrs Oliphant, *The Makers of Venice* (1898): quirky personal account of Venetian Doges, travellers and painters.
John Pemble, *Venice Rediscovered* (1995), thoughtful and sustained critical account of Venice as a cultural icon.
George Sand, *Letter of a Traveller*.
Stendhal, *Voyages en Italie* (1973).
Mark Twain, *A Tramp Abroad* (1880).
Gore Vidal, *Vidal in Venice* (1985).

Other Insight Guides

Italy is comprehensively covered by three types of Insight Guide, designed to meet the needs of every traveller.

The 190-title **Insight Guides** series, featuring the same high standard of photography and in-depth coverage as the present volume, includes a general guide to *Italy* and individual guides to *Rome, Tuscany, Florence, Umbria, The Bay of Naples, Sardinia, Sicily* and *South Tyrol (Italian Alps)*.

The 110-title **Insight Pocket Guides** series offers the authors' personal recommen-dations for how to make the most of a short visit and includes a full-size fold-out map. Titles include *Venice, Rome, Milan, Tuscany, Florence, Sardinia* and *Sicily*.

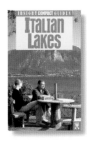

Complementing the above books is the 97-title **Insight Compact Guide** series, whose portability and exhaustive cross-referencing make them ideal guides for consulting on the spot. Titles include *Venice, Rome, Italian Lakes, Italian Riviera, Milan, Tuscany,* and *Florence*.

ART & PHOTO CREDITS

INSIGHT GUIDE
Venice

Cartographic Editor **Zoë Goodwin**
Production **Mohammed Dar**
Design Consultant **Klaus Geisler**
Picture Research **Hilary Genin**

Index

Palazzo Ducale (The Doge's Palace)

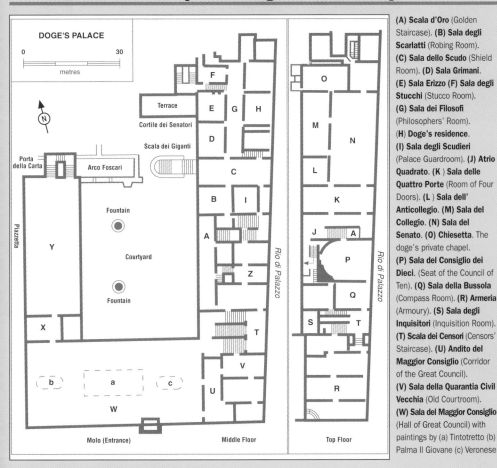

DOGE'S PALACE

0   30

metres

Terrace

Cortile dei Senatori

Scala dei Giganti

Porta della Carta

Arco Foscari

Fountain

Courtyard

Fountain

Piazzetta

Molo (Entrance)

Middle Floor

Rio di Palazzo

Rio di Palazzo

Top Floor

(A) Scala d'Oro (Golden Staircase). **(B) Sala degli Scarlatti** (Robing Room). **(C) Sala dello Scudo** (Shield Room). **(D) Sala Grimani**. **(E) Sala Erizzo (F) Sala degli Stucchi** (Stucco Room). **(G) Sala dei Filosofi** (Philosophers' Room). **(H) Doge's residence**. **(I) Sala degli Scudieri** (Palace Guardroom). **(J) Atrio Quadrato. (K) Sala delle Quattro Porte** (Room of Four Doors). **(L) Sala dell' Anticollegio. (M) Sala del Collegio. (N) Sala del Senato. (O) Chiesetta**. The doge's private chapel. **(P) Sala del Consiglio dei Dieci**. (Seat of the Council of Ten). **(Q) Sala della Bussola** (Compass Room). **(R) Armeria** (Armoury). **(S) Sala degli Inquisitori** (Inquisition Room). **(T) Scala dei Censori** (Censors' Staircase). **(U) Andito del Maggior Consiglio** (Corridor of the Great Council). **(V) Sala della Quarantia Civil Vecchia** (Old Courtroom). **(W) Sala del Maggior Consiglio** (Hall of Great Council) with paintings by (a) Tintoretto (b) Palma Il Giovane (c) Veronese

Basilica di San Marco (St Mark's)

Narthex: The 13th-century mosaics of the domes and arches are on Old Testament themes: **(A)** *Creation and the Fall of Man*, **(B)**)the *Story of Noah and the Flood*, **(C)** the *Tower of Babel*, **(D)** the *Story of Abraham*, **(E)** the *Story of Joseph*, **[F]** *Joseph is Sold to Potiphar*, **(G)** *Joseph Rules Egypt*, **(H)** the *Story of Moses*.
Paintings: (J) *The Passion* (13th-century).**(K)** *Scenes from the Life of Christ*, based on sketches by Jacopo Tintoretto (16th century). **(L)** *The Passion, the Agony in the Garden, Deeds of the Apostles* (13th-century). **(M)** *Christ and the Apostles; the Deeds of the Apostles* (13th to 16th-century).**(N)** *Christ Pantocrator*, based on sketches by Tintoretto (16th-century). **(O)** *Scenes from the Life of Christ* (12th–13th-century).**(P)** *Deeds of John the Evangelist*;; the *four Fathers of the Church* in the pendentives (late 12th-century). **(Q)** *St Nicola, St Clemente, St Biagio, St Leonardo* (13th-century).
The domes: The main **Dome of the Ascension [I]** shows Christ being carried by four angels, and Mary by two; the 12 Apostles frame the picture. The dome above the **altar [II]** shows the Religion of Christ as foretold by the Prophets. The **Dome of the Pentecost [III]** depicts the Triumph of Faith **I** Above the centre portal, *the Saviour between the Virgin and St Mark* (13th-century, restored); in the arch, *Scenes from the Apocalypse* (16th-century and modern); also a *Last Judgement* based on sketches by Jacopo Tintoretto (16th-century).

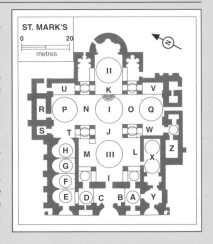

ST. MARK'S

0   20

metres

The Insight Approach

The book you are holding is part of the world's largest range of guidebooks. Its purpose is to help you have the most valuable travel experience possible, and we try to achieve this by providing not only information about countries, regions and cities but also genuine insight into their history, culture, institutions and people.

Since the first Insight Guide – to Bali – was published in 1970, the series has been dedicated to the proposition that, with insight into a country's people and culture, visitors can both enhance their own experience and be accepted more easily by their hosts. Now, in a world where ethnic hostilities and nationalist conflicts are all too common, such attempts to increase understanding between peoples are more important than ever.

Insight Guides:
Essentials for understanding

Because a nation's past holds the key to its present, each Insight Guide kicks off with lively history chapters. These are followed by magazine-style essays on culture and daily life. This essential background information gives readers the necessary context for using the main Places section, with its comprehensive run-down on things worth seeing and doing.

Finally, a listings section contains all the information you'll need on travel, hotels, restaurants and opening times.

As far as possible, we rely on local writers and specialists to ensure that information is authoritative. The pictures, for which Insight Guides have become so celebrated, are just as important. Our photojournalistic approach aims not only to illustrate a destination but also to communicate visually and directly to readers life as it is lived by the locals. The series has grown to almost 200 titles.

Compact Guides:
The "great little guides"

As invaluable as such background information is, it isn't always fun to carry an Insight Guide through a crowded souk or up a church tower. Could we, readers asked, distil the key reference material into a slim volume for on-the-spot use?

Our response was to design Compact Guides as an entirely new series, with original text carefully cross-referenced to detailed maps and more than 200 photographs. In essence, they're miniature encyclopedias, concise and comprehensive, displaying reliable and up-to-date information in an accessible way. There are almost 100 titles.

Pocket Guides:
A local host in book form

However wide-ranging the information in a book, human beings still value the personal touch. Our editors are often asked the same questions. Where do *you* go to eat? What do *you* think is the best beach? What would *you* recommend if I have only three days? We invited our local correspondents to act as "substitute hosts" by revealing their preferred walks and trips, listing the restaurants they go to and structuring a visit into a series of timed itineraries.

The result: our Pocket Guides, complete with full-size fold-out maps. These 100-plus titles help readers plan a trip precisely, particularly if their time is short.

Exploring with Insight:
A valuable travel experience

In conjunction with co-publishers all over the world, we print in up to 10 languages, from German to Chinese, from Danish to Russian. But our aim remains simple: to enhance your travel experience by combining our expertise in guidebook publishing with the on-the-spot knowledge of our correspondents.

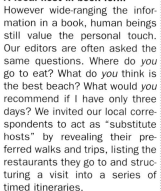

66 I was first drawn to the
Insight Guides by the
excellent "Nepal" volume.
I can think of no book
which so effectively
captures the essence of
a country. Out of these
pages leaped the Nepal
I know – the captivating
charm of a people and
their culture. I've since
discovered and enjoyed
the entire Insight Guide
series. Each volume deals
with a country in the
same sensitive depth,
which is nowhere more
evident than in the
superb photography. 99

Sir Edmund Hillary

The World of Insight Guides

400 books in three complementary series cover every major destination in every continent.